Martin Neisen and Stefan Röth

Basel IV

Martin Neisen and Stefan Röth

Basel IV

The Next Generation of Risk Weighted Assets

2nd edition

WILEY

WILEY-VCH Verlag GmbH & Co. KGaA

2nd edition

All books published by **Wiley-VCH** are carefully produced. Nevertheless, authors, editors, and publisher do not warrant the information contained in these books, including this book, to be free of errors. Readers are advised to keep in mind that statements, data, illustrations, procedural details or other items may inadvertently be inaccurate.

© 2018 Wiley-VCH Verlag & Co. KGaA, Boschstr. 12, 69469 Weinheim, Germany

All rights reserved (including those of translation into other languages). No part of this book may be reproduced in any form – by photoprinting, microfilm, or any other means – nor transmitted or translated into a machine language without written permission from the publishers. Registered names, trademarks, etc. used in this book, even when not specifically marked as such, are not to be considered unprotected by law.

Library of Congress Card No.:

applied for
A catalogue record for this book is available from the British Library.

Bibliographic information published by the Deutsche Nationalbibliothek

The Deutsche Nationalbibliothek lists this publication in the Deutsche Nationalbibliografie; detailed bibliographic data are available on the Internet at
<http://dnb.d-nb.de> abrufbar.

Layout: pp030 – Produktionsbüro Heike Praetor, Berlin, Germany
Cover design: Christian Kalkert Buchkunst & Illustration, Birken-Honigsessen
Cover photo: © Esin Deniz – stock.adobe.com
Satz: SPi, Chennai
Print ISBN: 978-3-527-50962-1
ePub ISBN: 978-3-527-82140-2

MIX
Paper from responsible sources
FSC
www.fsc.org   FSC® C013604

Contents

Foreword

Unimpressed by John M. Keynes' motto "I would rather be roughly right than precisely wrong", the Basel Committee on Banking Supervision is putting in motion the most comprehensive reform package in its entire supervisory history under the term "Basel IV". The banking and financial market is a highly interconnected and dynamic system in which the strong connections make it almost impossible to assess the risks of the system under certain conditions. Moreover, supervision keeps pace with the financial sector's increasing complexity by penning more and progressively detailed rules for determining the minimum capital requirement for a bank's risk positions.

Currently, every European bank must observe approximately 40,000 legally binding requirements of the European Union. In the field of banking supervision, four thousand and one different rules have been set down on 34,019 pages. With a reading speed of 50 words per minute and one hour reading time per working day, you would need around 32 years to read all the pages! And because the rules are constantly changing, they can never be fully read and understood. Today it is almost impossible to find any banking supervisor or bank practitioner who is able to explain exactly the supervisory rules and their consequences. The scope and complexity of the rules are just too great.

Behind this book is a highly qualified, expert team committed to a necessary reduction of regulatory complexity by providing this important companion volume to the reams of legislation. Broad knowledge is an especially crucial characteristic for dealing with complex systems. The authors come from pertinent sectors and have many years of consulting experience. The team of authors is led by Martin Neisen and Stefan Röth, two publishers whose experience and reputation are a guarantee of quality.

This book presents the innovations of the Basel IV package in a concise, understandable and practice-oriented way. It is committed to an optimised view by focusing on all relevant aspects. It is an outstanding work which, thanks to its clear structure and intellectual rigour, allows the reader to "see the wood for the trees".

I strongly recommended this volume to all scientific readers concerned with the development of banking supervision and risk management, as well as for practitioners interested in these issues. I hope this book will be openly received and widely distributed, and that the reader will find much of interest within these pages.

Professor Dr Hermann Schulte-Mattler – Dortmund, February 2016

Preface

Two years have passed since the publication of our book's first edition. These two years have seen an unprecedented dynamic in the area of banking regulation. Nearly all of the topics covered in the first edition are ripe for an update.

On the one hand, the Basel Committee on Banking Supervision published its final standards on those topics after the date of the editorial deadline of the first edition. Of note among these topics are the approaches for credit risk, CR SA and IRB, but also the methods for calculating capital requirements for operational risk and Credit Valuation Adjustments (CVA). And, of course, the capital floors responsible for the intensive debate that took until end of 2017 before a compromise was reached.

On the other hand, national rule-makers – and especially the European Union – have begun their work to transpose those rules already finalised by the Basel Committee before December 2017 into applicable law and regulations. At the time of the editorial deadline, this process is still ongoing and we have to rely on current drafts instead of finalised law. However, it is clear already that, for example, the EU will implement the Basel Committee's proposals – adding some elements of proportionality where adequate – that may inform other jurisdictions choice as well, when it comes to devising rules for smaller, less complex institutions.

Both changes are reflected in the following pages. We hope, this will make this book worthwhile even for readers of the first edition.

Our thanks to the individual authors for their contributions and to Professor Dr Schulte-Mattler for the Foreword.

Martin Neisen and Stefan Röth – Frankfurt, 30 March 2018

1 Revision of the Standardised Approach for Credit Risk

Luis Filipe Barbosa, Nikolaos Kalogiannis, Friedemann Loch and Sebastian L. Sohn

1.1 Introduction

As the original Basel I rules for credit risk – being the most relevant risk type for banks – were lacking an appropriate degree of risk sensitivity, they were considered to no longer adequately meet supervisory requirements. Therefore, aiming at greater economic differentiation of the credit risk, with a better recognition of exposures characteristics and a more appropriate reflection of risk-mitigation techniques, the Basel Committee developed two different approaches for the quantification of credit risk which represented the core elements of Basel II. The so-called "Standardised Approach" (standardised approach for credit risk, hereinafter also referred to as "SA") available to all banks and also – subject to supervisory approval – an "Internal Ratings-based Approach" (hereinafter referred to as "IRB Approach"), in which for the first time banks were permitted to use internal methods to determine risk parameters (e.g. probability of default) that could be used to quantify the capital requirements of credit risk for regulatory purposes. Figure 1.1 illustrates both approaches available to quantify the capital requirements for credit risk.

Under the SA, external ratings are used as a basis for the determination of risk weights and the quantification of capital requirements for certain exposure classes. The mapping of external ratings to risk weights, as well as the extent of eligible credit risk mitigation instruments and calculation of the risk mitigation effect, are entirely specified by the regulator. In contrast, the IRB Approach offers various options for internal estimation of risk parameters (see also Chapter 2 on the IRB Approach).

The quantification of risk-weighted assets (RWAs) and capital requirements under the SA is based on a set of components displayed in Figure 1.2.

It should also be highlighted that, under the standardised approach, exposures have to be risk-weighted net of specific provisions (including partial write-offs).

Once the Basel II rules on the standardised approach were finalised and implemented in the various national legislations it soon became apparent that the intended improvements in risk sensitivity within the standardised approach of Basel II were primarily achieved for claims on central governments – and depending on the national implementation also for banks. In many jurisdictions external ratings were only available to a small number of predominantly large corporates. The vast majority of corporates did not have any external ratings and had to be classified as "unrated" which resulted in the same risk weight as under Basel I.

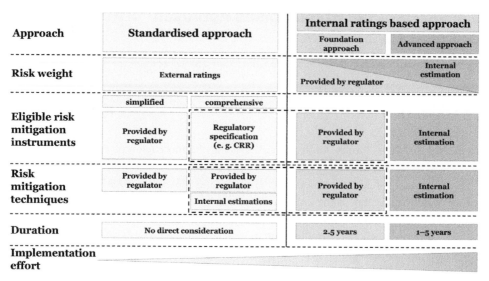

Figure 1.1: Approaches for credit risk quantification

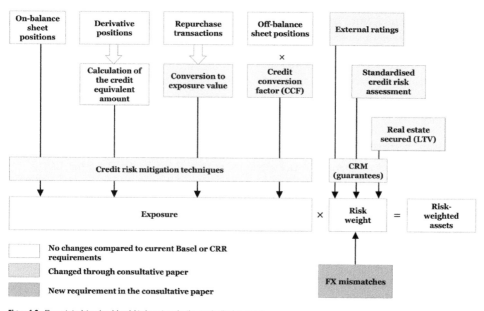

Figure 1.2: Elements to determine risk-weighted assets under the standardised approach

Over time – and especially within the financial market crisis starting in 2007 – the insufficient risk sensitivity of the standardised approach and the use of external ratings for supervisory purposes were increasingly criticised.

Within the Basel III framework the Basel Committee changed the structure and definition of regulatory capital and introduced new regulation on liquidity and leverage, but did not modify any elements of the standardised approach for credit risk.

As a response to the ongoing criticism on the standardised approach, the Basel Committee published an initial consultative paper on a revised standardised approach in December 2014, followed by a second consultative paper in December 2015. The approaches consulted in these papers were aimed at achieving a higher risk sensitivity without further increasing the complexity of the standardised approach. Another intention was to increase the comparability of capital requirements between banks by reducing differences in capital requirements between the standardised approaches and the IRB Approaches. In addition it is intended to limit national discretions in the application of the standardised approach. Moreover, the Basel Committee plans to reduce differences regarding the definition of exposure classes under the standardised approach and the IRB Approach. An additional aspect of the revision of the standardised approach is to decrease the mechanical dependence on external ratings. While the first consultative paper contained extremely wide-ranging modifications in this respect by removing the use of external ratings completely, the second consultative paper still allows the use of external ratings, the same holding true in the new Basel regulation. The use of external ratings is, however, complemented by additional requirements requesting the institution to conduct an independent credit risk assessment ("due diligence").

In contrast to the current requirements, the revised standardised approach needs also to be implemented by all IRB banks in the future, as the capital requirements under the standardised approach will serve as a floor for the capital requirements under the IRB Approach (see Chapter 9). Presently, IRB banks have the option of determining the capital floor based on the Basel I provisions ("Basel I Floor").

Securitisation exposures are addressed in the securitisation standard (Chapter 4). Credit equivalent amounts of OTC derivatives, exchange traded derivatives and long-settlement transactions that expose a bank to counterparty credit risk are to be calculated under the counterparty credit risk standards (Chapter 3). Equity investments in funds and exposures to central counterparties must be treated according to their own specific frameworks (Chapter 5).

Hereinafter the revisions based on the final Basel regulation are summarised and compared to the proposed changes of the first and second consultative papers as well as to the current requirements of the CRR.

1.2 General aspects

The Basel Committee's revision of the standardised approach for credit risk comprises all exposure classes, except for claims on sovereigns, central banks and public sector entities (PSEs) – in the latter case, only minor editorial changes have been made to remove reference to current options for banks. They are not included as the Basel Committee is considering these exposures as part of a broader and holistic review of sovereign-related risks.

While the first consultative paper replaced the use of external ratings by other risk drivers, the second consultative paper as well as the final Basel regulation still allows for the use of external ratings. However, in some countries (the USA for instance), the use of external ratings for regulatory purposes is not admitted. For these jurisdictions, and also for all exposures to unrated counterparties, a newly developed Standardised Credit Risk Assessment Approach (SCRA) will be available.

In order to avoid mechanistic reliance on external ratings, the due diligence requirements already included in the first consultative paper were further specified. Even in cases where ratings are used, due diligence is needed to assess the risk of exposures for risk management purposes and whether the risk weight applied is appropriate and prudent. This is to ensure that banks have an adequate understanding, both at origination and on a regular basis (at least, annually), of the risk profile and characteristics of their counterparties. Should the due diligence analysis reveal a higher risk compared to the risk weight based on external ratings, the higher risk weight has to be applied. However, if the due diligence analysis should reveal a very low risk compared to the external rating, it cannot result in a more favourable risk weight then determined by external ratings.

The exact extent and content of due diligence requirements is yet to be specified; the consultative paper only refers to the presently existing Pillar II-requirements of Basel II. Under Pillar II, banks are required to have methodologies that enable them to assess the credit risk involved in exposures to individual borrowers or counterparties. In this context, the importance of internal ratings as a tool to monitor credit risk on a borrower level is explicitly emphasised.

Banks need to ensure that they have an adequate understanding of the risk profile of the borrower at origination and thereafter on a regular basis (at least annually). They must take reasonable and adequate steps to assess the operating and financial performance levels and trends through internal credit analysis and/or other analytics outsourced to a third party, as appropriate for each counterparty. Banks need to be able to access information about their counterparties on a regular basis so that they can complete the due diligence analyses.

It is also necessary that banks can demonstrate to the supervisory authority that their internal policies, processes, systems and controls ensure an appropriate assignment of risk weights to counterparties.

Currently, it is expected that the majority of SA institutions in many countries will be largely compliant with the due diligence requirements due to their existing practice of applying rating procedures for bank-internal processes, even in their capacity as SA institution. It remains to be seen, however, how these requirements will be implemented at the European level.

1.2.1 Exposures to sovereigns

Exposures to sovereigns represent a very important asset class to many banks. In particular, during the financial market crisis, it became evident that the risk weighting of 0% for certain jurisdictions could not, ultimately, be fully justified. However the Basel Committee did not succeed in finding a compromise solution for a modification of the risk weighting for sovereign exposures. Consequently the treatment of sovereign exposures has been carved out from the Basel IV paper for both the standardised approach and the IRB Approach.

Separate from the work on Basel IV the Basel Committee has established a high-level Task Force on sovereign exposure to review the current treatment of sovereign exposures and develop recommendations on potential policy options. This review was completed in December 2017 and the Basel Committee has published the results of this review in a separate discussion paper.[1]

While this paper contains ideas on the possible treatment of sovereign risk the Basel Committee has pointed out that presently it has not reached a consensus to make any changes to the treatment of sovereign exposures, and has therefore decided not to consult on the ideas presented in this discussion paper.

Therefore, the treatment of sovereign risk remains unchanged from the current / the Basel II treatment which is described below:

The applicable risk weight to a sovereign exposure can either be derived by using the external rating of an external credit assessment institution (ECAI) or by using the risk score of an external credit agency (ECA). A very good external rating or ECA risk score results in a risk weight of 0%, unrated exposures receive a risk weight of 100%. The following tables in Figure 1.3 illustrate the applicable risk weighting based on the ECAI or the ECA score.

Risk weights for sovereigns and central banks						
External Rating (ECAI)	AAA to AA−	A+ to A−	BBB+ to BBB−	BB+ to B−	Below B−	Unrated
Risk weight	0%	20%	50%	100%	150%	100%

Risk weights for sovereigns and central banks					
ECA risk score	0 to 1	2	3	4 to 6	7
Base risk weight	0%	20%	50%	100%	150%

Figure 1.3: Risk weights for sovereign and central bank exposures

---

1 BCBS 425 The regulatory treatment of sovereign exposures (discussion paper), published 7 December 2017.

1.2.2 Exposures to public sector entities

The treatment of exposures to public sector entities remains largely the same. However, as the Basel II treatment of public sector entities had made references to the available options for the risk weighting for banks – which do not exist any more under Basel IV – some editorial changes were necessary.

The Basel Committee also allows for two options to derive the risk weight for public sector entities: either based on the external rating of the sovereign where the PSE is domiciled, or based on the individual external rating of the PSE directly.

Unlike the treatment for corporates or banks both options are based on the use of external ratings. There is no explicit reference to a different treatment in jurisdictions that do not allow the use of external ratings.

As with the current Basel II regulations, the risk weights are derived by using the tables as shown in Figure 1.4.

1.2.3 Exposures to multilateral development banks

The treatment of multilateral development banks has not changed significantly with respect to the current treatment. However, as the current treatment is partially similar to the risk weighting for banks, some changes had to be applied.

Unchanged from current treatment, the Basel Committee defines a multilateral development bank as an institution created by a group of countries, and which provides financing and professional advice for economic and social development projects. If certain quality criteria are being met, a risk weight of 0% can be applied. These qualitative requirements have not changed in substance and can be summarised as follows:

- very high-quality long-term issuer ratings;
- shareholder structure comprising a significant proportion of sovereigns with high quality external ratings;

Risk weights for public sector entities based on the external rating of the sovereign						
Rating	AAA to AA–	A+ to A–	BBB+ to BBB–	BB+ to B–	Below B–	Unrated
Base risk weight	20%	50%	100%	100%	150%	100%

Risk weights for public sector entities based on the external rating of the PSE						
Rating	AAA to AA–	A+ to A–	BBB+ to BBB–	BB+ to B–	Below B–	Unrated
Base risk weight	20%	50%	50%	100%	150%	100%

Figure 1.4: Risk weights for public sector entities

Risk weights for exposures to corporates under Basel IV based on external ratings						
Rating	AAA to AA−	A+ to A−	BBB+ to BBB−	BB+ to B−	Below B−	Unrated
Base risk weight	20%	30%	50%	100%	150%	50%

Figure 1.5: Risk weights for multilateral development banks (MDB)

- strong shareholder support;
- adequate level of capital and liquidity; and
- strict statutory lending requirements and conservative financial policies.

In jurisdictions that allow the use of external ratings, it is possible to derive the risk weight for all other multilateral development banks using the table shown in Figure 1.5.

1.2.4 Exposures to banks

Overall requirements

In this context, a bank exposure can be defined as a claim (including loans and senior debt instruments, unless considered as subordinated debt) on any financial institution that is licensed to take deposits from the public and is subject to appropriate prudential standards and level of supervision. Subordinated bank debt and equities are addressed in section 1.2.7.

Two approaches are available for calculating capital requirements of bank exposures: (i) the External Credit Risk Assessment Approach (ECRA); and (ii) the Standardised Credit Risk Assessment Approach (SCRA). These should be used hierarchically, according to the existence of the possibility, in the jurisdiction in which the bank is incorporated, of using external ratings for regulatory purposes. Additionally, SCRA should also be used for exposures regarding unrated banks, even when these are incorporated in jurisdictions that allow the use of external ratings.

Short-term claims between banks with an original maturity of less than three months, as well as on- or off-balance sheet exposures to banks that arrive from the movement of goods across national borders with an original maturity of six months or less, receive a reduced risk weight under most grades of both approaches, in an effort to avoid affecting negatively the liquidity of interbank markets.

In what concerns institutional protection schemes that allow for a 0% risk weight to exposures within these schemes, a preferential regime may be applied, with lower risk weights, subject to national supervisory option or discretion. This must not be applied to exposures giving rise to CET1, AT1 or T2 items.

1. External Credit Risk Assessment Approach (ECRA)

The ECRA shall be applied, provided that an external rating for the counter-party/exposure is available and that their use is allowed in the respective jurisdiction. Under this approach, each claim is assigned a so-called "base risk weight" based on the external rating. The resulting risk weights range from 20% to 150%. The referred ratings must not incorporate assumptions of implicit government support – in line with the objective of breaking the link between banks and their sovereigns – unless the rating refers to a public bank owned by its government. Banks based in jurisdictions that allow the use of external ratings for regulatory purposes can only apply SCRA for their unrated bank exposures.

For short-term exposures, or for those arising from the movement of goods across national borders with an original maturity of six months or less, reduced risk weights in 3 of the 5 buckets are in place.

As a second step, banks have to perform due diligence analysis to ensure that the external rating appropriately and conservatively reflects the credit risk of the exposure. As stated, if the due diligence reveals a higher risk than implied by the external rating, the risk weight shall be increased by at least one grade. If the outcome of the due diligence analysis is more favourable, the risk weight remains unchanged.

Figure 1.6 illustrates the risk weights to be used for banks based on applicable external ratings under the ECRA.

The consultative paper does not entail any changes in relation to the use of issuer and issues assessments. With the exception of the due diligence element, the proposed rules as well as the mapping of external ratings into risk weights is comparable with the current standardised approach. However, differences arise if no external rating exists for the counterparty or the exposure. Under current CRR regulation these claims receive a risk weight derived from the external rating of the borrowing bank's country of incorporation, leading to a risk weight of 20% for banks in Germany. The revised SA however will require the use of the Standard Credit Risk Assessment Approach (SCRA).

2. Standardised Credit Risk Assessment Approach (SCRA)

The SCRA is applied if no external rating is available or if the use of such external rating is not allowed in the respective jurisdiction. Under this approach the exposures are

Rating	AAA to AA−	A+ to A−	BBB+ to BBB−	BB+ to B−	Below B−
Base risk weight	20%	30%	50%	100%	150%
Risk weight for short-term exposures	20%			50%	150%

Figure 1.6: Risk weights for banks based on applicable external ratings (ECRA)

categorised into three grades (A, B, C). For each grade, the Basel Committee has specified criteria for the allocation. Main elements of these criteria are the extent to which the counterparty fulfils its financial obligations and the degree to which it complies with regulatory requirements.

- If a borrower exceeds the minimum regulatory requirements (e.g. leverage, capital ratios) and meets his financial commitments accordingly, he can be classified within Grade A, leading to a risk weight of 40%. Additionally, this risk weight can be reduced to 30% if the debtor bank meets or exceeds a CET1 ratio of 14% and a Tier 1 leverage ratio of 5% and meets criteria imposed to Grade A exposures.
- If one or more buffer requirements are not met, and the borrower is subject to substantial credit risk, a risk weight of 75% under Grade B has to be used. More concretely, Grade B refers to exposures to banks, where the counterparty bank is subject to substantial credit risk, such as repayment capacities that are dependent on stable or favourable economic or business conditions.
- Not meeting the requirements applicable to Grade B by not meeting the regulatory requirements, leads to a risk weight of 150% under Grade C. This grade refers to higher credit risk exposures to banks, where the counterparty bank has material default risks and limited margins of safety. In this context, for these counterparties, adverse business, financial, or economic conditions are very likely to lead (or have led) to an inability to meet their financial commitments. This Grade is also to be applied if the external auditor has expressed an adverse audit opinion.
- Exposures with an original maturity of three months or less, as well as exposures arising from the movement of goods across national borders with an original maturity of six months or less, receive reduced risk weight of 20%, 50% or 150%. Defaulted exposures receive a risk weight of 150%.

Also, under the SCRA, the bank has to perform the same due diligence assessment as under the ECRA and classify the exposure as Grade A, B or C, based on the result of the due diligence. If the due diligence reveals a higher level of risk, the bank has to assign the position to a more conservative grade than that which is applicable by simply using the minimum criteria. As under the ECRA, a due diligence can never result in a risk weight lower than that determined by the minimum criteria for each grade.

The Basel Committee specifies that the requirements referring to regulatory ratios include buffers, but are limited to publicly disclosed information, thus bank-specific supervisory-imposed requirements, such as Pillar 2 instruments (P2R or P2G) are not included. Moreover, when such information is nonexistent, or not publicly disclosed, such exposures must be classified as Grade B or lower.

Furthermore, under SCRA, to capture transfer, convertibility or currency risk, a risk-weight floor is applicable, based on sovereign risk of the country where the relevant counterparty is incorporated. This floor is applicable when the exposure is not expressed in the local currency of the debtor bank and must not be applied to short-term (i.e. with a maturity of less than 1 year), self-liquidating, trade-related contingent items that arise from the movement of goods.

Figure 1.7 Risk weights for banks based on the internal standardised risk assessment (SCRA)

Comparison of the new framework to the specifications of the first and second consultative papers and the current provisions

Exposures of banks with an external rating receive a risk weight ranging between 20% and 150. On the other hand, banks without external ratings may receive risk weighted between 30% (conditional on several criteria including the robustness of capital and leverage ratios) and 150%.

As the treatment for banks without external rating (thus under SCRA) will regularly result in a change in risk weights from the previous 20% to Grade A, the Basel Committee has lowered the base risk weight from 50% to 40% between the second consultation and its final form. Additionally, the risk weight of Grade B has been reduced from 100% to 75%. Alongside this, the base risk weight for Grade A may further be reduced to 30% if the debtor bank meets or exceeds a CET1 ratio of 14% and a Tier 1 leverage ratio of 5% and meets criteria imposed on Grade A exposures.

The first consultative paper aimed to remove completely the use of external ratings and proposed a derivation of risk weights based on the CET 1 ratio and the asset quality based on the Net Non-Performing-Asset-Ratio (Net-NPA-Ratio) of banks. In some circumstances, the risk weight was set at 300%. It became evident that this approach would represent a significant increase in the resulting risk weights without necessarily leading to increased risk sensitivity. Within the second consultative paper this approach was removed and the use of external ratings re-introduced. Quantitative impact studies showed that the capital requirements under the first consultative paper

Grade	Grade A	Grade B	Grade C
Base risk weight	40% / 30%*	75%	150%
Risk weight for short-term exposures	20%	50%	150%

* CET > 14% and LR >5%

Figure 1.7: shows the SCRA risk weights for banks.

would have been significantly higher than under current CRR requirements and also under the second consultative paper.

The current applicable standardised approach according to the CRR is based on external rating of the counterparty/issuance, the risk weight of the country of residence and the maturity of the exposure and represents a combination of the currently available two options under Basel II.

Furthermore, although the second consultative document included a reference to a sovereign risk-weight floor in order to reflect the macroeconomic profile of exposures, the final document does not incorporate such provision or better saying it only considers a floor when exposures are not expressed in the local currency of the debtor bank – i.e. it aims to capture transfer and convertibility risk, based on the country where the relevant counterparty is incorporated, resulting in lower risk weights for such exposures.

Short-term exposures against banks with an original maturity of less than three months are subject to a more favourable risk weight, under most grades of both approaches. If no rating is assigned, a general risk weight of 20% is applied. In practice, a risk weight of 20% is often applied as external ratings are frequently not available for short-term exposures. In the final version of the reform, in addition to short-term exposures, exposures to banks that arise from the movement of goods across national borders with an original maturity of six months or less may also be subject to the mentioned favourable regime.

With respect to the treatment of institutional protection schemes that allow for a 0% risk weight to exposures within these schemes and the preferential treatment of covered bonds, existing rules under CRR can now also be applied under the final document. In the case of institutional protection schemes, this preferential regime is subject to national supervisory option or discretion, and cannot be applied to exposures giving rise to CET1, AT1 or T2 items.

In situations where no external ratings are available, significant differences are evident. In countries where only a very small number of banks are externally rated, the resulting risk weight under SCRA will be at least 30% while these exposures currently receive a risk weight of 20%. This represents a significant increase in terms of risk weights.

Finally, the final version of the document introduces further detail on the requirements for the classification of bank exposures under the SCRA. In particular, the Basel Committee specifies that the requirements that regard supervisory-imposed ratios do include buffers but are limited to publicly disclosed information, thus not including bank-specific requirements, such as Pillar 2 instruments (P2R or P2G).

1.2.5 Exposures to corporates

Overall requirements

Comparable to exposures to banks two approaches are available for exposures to corporates.

Provided that the use of external ratings is allowed in the respective jurisdiction, these ratings can be used to derive base risk weights ranging from 20% to 150%. The mapping process between external ratings and risk weights has a slight extension with respect to Basel II. While under Basel II regulation the risk weight buckets range between 20%, 50%, 100% and 150%, Basel IV introduces an additional risk weight of 75% for exposures rated between BBB+ and BBB–. The corresponding risk weight under Basel II for these ratings is 100%.

Similarly to the treatment of exposures to banks, performance of due diligence analysis is necessary both at origination and on a periodic basis (at least annually). This analysis aims at ensuring that external ratings appropriately reflect the creditworthiness of the bank's counterparties. Since the operational impact of case-by-case periodic due diligence is expected to be significant, especially for smaller banks, the Basel Committee applies the proportionality principle. Therefore, the sophistication level of the assessment should be appropriate to the size and complexity of each bank's activities. In assessing the operating and financial performance of their counterparties, banks should perform adequate internal credit analysis and/or outsource this assessment to third parties.

Depending on the outcome of this analysis, an increase of risk weights may be required. It is noted that due diligence must not result in a lower risk weight – compared to external ratings approach – in any circumstances. Therefore, solely in case the due diligence analysis results in a higher rating, then a risk weight of at least one bucket higher must be assigned.

Since due diligence will form an integral part of risk weight assignment, a framework for governing due diligence, including internal policies, processes, systems and controls, is imperative.

Unrated exposures are subject to a risk weight of 100%, unless they refer to exposures to corporate small and medium sized entities (SMEs).

In jurisdictions that do not allow the use of external ratings, the following concept applies: A risk weight of 65% is assigned to all corporates that have – among other criteria – an adequate capacity to meet their financial commitments in a timely manner irrespective of the economic cycle and business conditions and can therefore be classified as "investment grade". All other corporate exposures receive a risk weight of 100% unless they refer to exposures to corporate SMEs.

The risk weights to be assigned to corporates are presented in detail in Figure 1.8.

Risk weights for exposures to corporates under Basel II					
Rating	AAA to AA−	A+ to A−	BBB+ to BB−	Below BB−	Unrated
Base risk weight	20%	50%	100%	150%	100%

Risk weights for exposures to corporates under Basel IV based on external ratings						
Rating	AAA to AA−	A+ to A−	BBB+ to BBB−	BB+ to BB−	Below BB−	Unrated
Base risk weight	20%	50%	75%	100%	150%	100%

Risk weights for exposures to corporates under Basel IV – no application of external ratings			
Classification	General treatment	SME	Investment Grade
Base risk weight	100%	85%	65% *(jurisdictions not allowing the use of external ratings)*

Figure 1.8: Risk weights for corporates based on external ratings

Regardless of the permission to use external ratings, unrated corporate SMEs, with (group) sales of up to EUR 50 million for the most recent financial year, are assigned a risk weight of 85%, which represents a more favourable treatment than under the previous Basel II framework.

This preferential risk weight can be applied to all corporate exposures that fall under the IRB definition of SMEs given that they do not meet the criteria allowing them to be classified as "retail SMEs". Claims to SMEs of up to EUR 1 million can be categorised as "retail SMEs" according to supervisory requirements and are allocated a risk weight of 75%. In contrast to the SME-scaling factor in Art. 501 of the CRR there is no total volume connected to the preferential treatment of SMEs. Figure 1.9 illustrates the determination of preferential risk weights for SMEs.

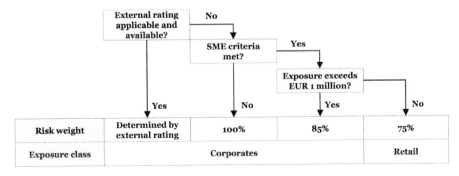

Figure 1.9: Determination of preferential risk weights for SMEs

Comparison of the new framework to the specifications of the first and second consultative papers and the current provisions

Under current CRR rules, exposures to corporates with an available external rating receive a risk weight between 20% and 150%. Unrated exposures are assigned a risk weight of 100%. If the risk weight of the country of incorporation has a higher risk weight than the corporation itself, the risk weight of the country has to be used.

The process of deriving risk weights from externally rated clients/exposures does not differ from the current CRR rules, only the additional due diligence requirements represent a new element that may lead to increased risk weights.

The new Basel regulation introduces a more favourable treatment of unrated corporate SMEs in terms of capital requirements regardless of the volume of the exposure, which is presented as an additional factor in the CRR. The introduction of a separate risk weight of 85% for SMEs represents a significant modification of the currently existing Basel rules. On a European level, however, Art. 501 CRR already contains a special factor to reduce the risk weight of exposures to SMEs ("SME factor"). A simple multiplier 0.7619 is used (for SA and IRB exposures) to requirements for SME. However, this factor is limited to a total exposure of EUR 1.5 million, whereas the SME treatment in the new Basel framework does not have an exposure limit. The draft document of the amendment of the CRR (so called "CRR II") however is proposing to modify the application of the factor as follows: Exposures up to EUR 1.5 million will receive the currently applicable factor of 0.7619 and any exceeding amount will receive a factor of 0.85. This procedure will combine "the best of the two worlds".

1.2.6 Specialised lending

In the specialised lending business, special purpose entities, created specifically for this investment and with little material assets, typically serve as borrowing entities and the primary source of repayment is the return on the investment. Furthermore, the lender is contractually entitled to a substantial degree of control over the assets and the income generated by the financed assets. For the identification of specialised lending exposures, the Basel Committee requires banks to apply this definition based on both the legal form and/or the economic substance of the financing.

The current credit risk standardised approach under Basel II does not comprise a separate exposure class for specialised lending. Specialised lending exposures are generally treated as regular corporate loans and receive a risk weight of 100% unless they have an external rating.

In order to increase risk sensitivity and to align the standardised approach with the IRB Approach, the five sub-classes of specialised lending of the IRB Approach are also included in the standardised approach: while the first consultative paper included these five sub-classes in the specialised lending exposure class, the second consultative paper as well as the final document considers specialised lending only in terms of

- project finances (e.g. factories, infrastructure, environmental technology),
- object finances (e.g. acquisition of vessels and aircraft), and
- commodities finances (e.g. crude oil and metal).

Specialised financing in connection with real estate investments is not recognised as specialised lending (unlike under the IRB) but as a separate form of real estate collateralised loans within the real estate exposure class.[2]

Although the Basel II definition of specialised lending provides the classification criteria cited above, various blurred lines can be observed in practice, especially with respect to the consideration of both economic and legal conditions of an exposure: loans in relation to hospitals, sport and multi-purpose halls, for instance, may be treated as project finance or real estate-secured exposure, depending on further criteria. Financing of car fleets can occur in the form as object finance as well as unsecured corporate exposures. National supervisors used to provide further guidance in relation with IRB specialised lending exposures and other reporting requirements.[3]

As for exposures to corporates, specialised lending exposures with external issue-specific ratings receive a risk weight between 20% and 150% using the same look-up table that would apply to corporate exposures in general.[4]

If no external issue-specific rating is available or allowed for regulatory purposes, a general risk weight of 100% is to be applied for object and commodities finances.

For specialised lending in the form of project finances the risk weight depends on the project phase. A risk weight of 130% is to be applied during the "pre-operational phase" and 100% for the "operational phase". Project finance exposures, which fulfil strict "high quality" criteria receive a more favourable risk weight of 80%.

Figure 1.10 contains the risk weights for specialised lending.

As specialised lending is not usually subject to external ratings it can be expected that the average risk weights for specialised lending will be between 100% and 130% (the second consultative paper proposed risk weights from 100% to 150%). In addition there is the possibility of assigning an 80% risk weight to "high quality" project finance exposures if strict criteria are met. However, this preferential treatment is expected to

---

2   For further details, see sub-categories "land acquisition, development and construction (ADC)" and "exposures where the repayment is materially depending on cash-flows generated by the financed property" in section "Exposures secured by real estate/Real estate exposure class".

3   In the European Union, the criteria are outlined in art. 147(8) CRR, with further guidance provided by the European Banking Authority (EBA) in the form of a final draft Regulatory Technical Standards (EBA/RTS/2016/02) as well as in several clarification in the context of the The Single Rulebook.

4   While an issuer rating usually classifies the credit risk of an entity's senior-ranked debt, an issue-specific rating relates to specific debt tranches or stand-alone financing like specialised lending. To determine the risk weight of specialised lending exposures in jurisdictions that allow the use of external ratings, only issue-specific ratings are applicable.

	Issue-specific rating available and applicable				
Rating	AAA to AA–	A+ to A–	BBB+ to BBB–	BB+ to BB–	Below BB–
Risk weight for object, project and commodities finance	20%	50%	75%	100%	150%

	Issue-specific rating not available or not allowed		
Risk weight for object and commodities finance	100%		
Risk weight for project finance	130% (pre-operational)	100% (operational)	
Risk weight for "high quality" project finance		80% (operational) *certain criteria must be met*	

Figure 1.10: Risk weights for specialised lending

affect new project finance exposures rather than existing ones since, presumably, only a few existing contracts might fulfil all the criteria.

Under the current Basel II regulation, object, project, and commodities finance exposures are generally treated as regular corporate exposures and receive a risk weight of 100%. Thus, RWA increases are limited to pre-operational project finance exposures while "high quality" project finance is subject to a more favourable treatment.

1.2.7 Subordinated debt instruments, equity and other capital instruments

Equity exposures, which are not deducted from regulatory capital, receive a risk weight of 250% after a 5-year phase-in period starting at 100% and with yearly increases of 30 percentage points.[5] Speculative unlisted equity investments are to be risk weighted by 400%, also subject to a 5-year phase-in arrangement starting at 100% and increasing by 60 percentage points each year. Certain equity holdings subsidised and regulated by the government can be eligible for a preferential 100% risk weight at national discretion.

Subordinated debt and capital instruments other than those subject to the Basel Committee's equity definition and those not subject to a capital deduction are risk weighed with 150%. This treatment also includes other TLAC liabilities as long as they are not subject to a regulatory capital deduction.[6]

For the risk weighing of subordinated debt instruments, equity and other capital instruments external ratings are not taken into account.

Figure 1.11 summarises the risk weights applicable to these instruments.

The final provisions for this exposure class basically follow the spirit of the second consultative paper and offer considerable relief compared to those of the first consultative

---

5   The document comprises a comprehensive definition of equity instruments for regulatory purposes, which focuses in particular on the economic characteristics of an instrument (e.g. repayability, rank of a claim, or conversion into generic equity instruments).
6   Presently it is not clear to which extent this concept is also applied to positions qualifying as "Minimum Requirements for Eligible Liabilities / MREL" which is the European equivalent of TLAC.

Subordinated debt instruments, equity and other capital instruments	
Equities which are not subject to capital deduction	250%
Speculative unlisted equity investments	400%
Certain equity holdings, subsidised and regulated by the government	Preferential treatment subject to national discretion: 100%
Subordinated debt, and capital instruments not subject to other capital deduction or equity treatment	150% *for these exposures, ratings are generally not applicable for regulatory purposes*

Figure 1.11: Subordinated debt instruments, equity and other capital instruments

paper which proposed risk weights of 300% for publicly traded equity exposures and of 400% in all other cases, as long as they were not deducted or assigned a risk weight of 250% pursuant to the Basel III framework.

However, a different picture emerges in comparison to the current Basel requirements. Currently, equity exposures and subordinated debt securities receive a risk weight of 100% (unless deducted from capital or risk weighted with 250%). Only in situations where the exposure is to be classified as "higher risk category" does a risk weight of 150% apply.[7]

Apart from the exceptions listed above, capital requirements will be subject to a considerable increase. Yet this increase is not as severe as the one discussed in the first consultative paper.

1.2.8 Retail exposures

The current Basel framework established four criteria that need to be met in order to classify an exposure as regulatory retail:

1. exposure refers to an individual person or persons or to a small business,

2. exposure takes the form of revolving credit, and lines of credit, personal term loans and leases and small business facilities and commitments,

3. there is appropriate level of diversification,

4. maximum value of EUR 1 million for the aggregated individual exposure.

In cases where an exposure meets all of the above criteria, a risk weight of 75% is assigned.

These rules will be implemented on EU level with no major amendments. The main difference is that under the current EU legislation, Art. 123 of CRR defines the term "small business" as "SME".

---

7   In the EU Capital requirement regulation, the corresponding exposure class is called "exposures with particularly high risk".

Under the revised standardised approach, the Basel framework has been aligned with the CRR defining the term "small business" as "SME". In addition the Basel Committee sets a quantitative "granularity" criterion to ensure "appropriate level of diversification" of the regulatory retail portfolio. Based on this criterion aggregated exposure to one counterparty in order to be eligible for treatment as a retail exposure must not exceed a maximum of 0.2% of the total retail portfolio. This quantitative criterion has already been introduced in Basel II, but only as an option for the supervisor to assess diversification of the portfolio.

The other two eligibility criteria for classifying exposures as retail remain unchanged.

Similar to current regulation, claims included in the regulatory retail portfolio are assigned a risk weight of 75% which is preserved from Basel II and CRR. However, in contrast to Basel II, a risk weight of 100% is applied to any exposure which does not meet all of the eligibility criteria unless they are exposures to SMEs which are classified as corporate SMEs and are risk weighted accordingly.

As under current Basel and EU regulation, defaulted loans and exposures secured by residential real estate are excluded from the regulatory retail exposure class.

A major change to the current regulation, constitutes the introduction of a new category of obligors, namely "transactors", which is treated in a favourable manner. Under Basel Committee's definition, transactors are retail obligors that are connected with facilities used to facilitate transactions and not as a source of credit. Typical examples of such facilities are: a) credit cards and charge cards where the transactor has repaid the balance in full each month according to the repayment plan for the past 12 months and; b) overdraft accounts with no drawdowns over the same time horizon. Under the new standardised approach, a 45% risk weight is assigned to this category of exposures.

1.2.9 Exposures secured by real estate/Real estate exposure class

Introduction

The concept for the recognition of real estate collateral shows significant changes to the current existing Basel requirements.

While the existing concept of differentiation between residential and commercial real estate exposures remains in force under the revised SA-CR, a new subcategory "land acquisition, development and construction" (ADC) has been introduced. In addition to that, exposures, where the repayment of the loan materially depends on the cash flows generated by the property (in previous consultative documents referred to as "income producing real estate" / IPRE exposures), generally receive higher risk weights – also differentiated by residential and commercial real estate – than loans, where the repayment does not materially depend on the cash flows generated by the financed object. In some cases, those assigned risk weights might even exceed the risk weights of unsecured exposures.

The real estate exposure class, in particular, has been subject to intense controversies and discussions in the course of the Basel IV finalisation, driven by its strategic and economic importance for the banking industry in most countries as well as the various national provisions specifics in mortgage-related regulations and practices among the member jurisdictions.

As a result, the final compromise includes several amendments to the previously proposed treatment (first and second consultative paper), as well as several methodological options subject to national discretions, and calls for further (national) guidance. While both consultative papers focused solely on a Loan-to-Value-based (LTV) risk weight determination, the final standard allows jurisdictions for some forms of real estate financing to elect a "loan splitting approach" alternatively which leads to an incorporation of different risk weights for the secured and unsecured part of an exposure, respectively, and is *inter alia* currently in use in some European jurisdictions.

Overall requirements

As in the Basel II framework, the revised standardised approach limits the application of this exposure class to jurisdictions where credit losses stemming from real estate-secured exposures are sustainably low. Therefore, national supervisors are expected to adjust the prescribed risk weights upwards, if appropriate, hence reflecting results from the observation defaults and losses or other indicators (e.g. reflecting market price stability).

To be eligible as real estate exposures, loans have to meet the following six operational requirements:

1) Finished property:

The property has to be fully completed to qualify as a real estate collateral, with an exception for forest and agricultural land.

However, subject to national discretion, loans to individuals can still be classified as residential real estate if the unfinished property is a residential one-to-four family housing unit that will be the primary residence of the borrower and is not subject to a rather conservative treatment as land acquisition, development and construction (ADC).

Another exemption might be granted if the Sovereign or PSE as borrower has the legal powers and ability to ensure that the property under construction will be finished.

2) Legal enforceability:

The claim is legally enforceable in all relevant jurisdictions. Collateral agreements and legal conditions must enable the bank to realise the value of the property within a reasonable time frame.

3) Claims over the property:

Types of claims that entitle banks to classify loans as real estate exposures include the following constellations:

- The bank needs to have a first lien on the property or the first as well as any subordinated liens.
- In jurisdictions where junior liens entitle creditors to a legally enforceable claim and qualify as effective credit risk mitigants, junior liens – as well as a combination of liens senior and junior, respectively, to a third party's intermediate liens – can be recognised as eligible claims.

In order to recognise junior liens over a property as appropriate claims, the national legal environment for liens must fulfil the following preconditions:

- Each holder of a lien shall be entitled to initiate the sale of a property independently from other holders of a lien and
- the sale of a real estate collateral is either carried out by public auction, or holders of senior liens are obliged to take reasonable steps to obtain a fair market value or the best price possible as they carry out the sale in order to also serve junior lien holders' financial interests.

In addition to these conditions and to the existing Basel II framework, the Basel Committee incorporates an exception to take the characteristics of certain jurisdictions and house financing markets into account where loans usually are guaranteed by a highly rated 'monoline' guarantor, rather than secured by a mortgage claim, while the bank is entitled to take a mortgage on the property in the event of the guarantor's default.

In general, such loans are treated as guaranteed exposures. However, they may be classified as residential real estate exposures under certain conditions:

- The borrower does not have the right to grant any mortgage liens to a third party without consent of the bank,
- the guarantor is either a bank, or a financial institution subject to similar capital requirements, or an insurer,
- guarantees are backed by a regularly calibrated and supervised fully-funded mutual guarantee fund or equivalent protection for insurers, and
- the bank has contractually and legally the right to take a mortgage on the property if the guarantor defaults.

4) Ability of the borrower to repay the loan:

This requirement focuses on a bank's assessment of the borrower's creditworthiness as well as on the national supervision of such policies: banks shall define one or several metrics including respective thresholds as part of their underwriting policies. The Basel Committee expects national supervisors to provide further guidance, though it lists the loan's debt service coverage ratio and, for repayments depending on cash flows generated by the property, the property's occupancy rate as examples.

5) Prudent value of property:

The property needs to be prudently valued and its value must not depend materially on the borrower's performance.

The value needs to be appraised based on prudently conservative valuation criteria and has to be independent from the bank's mortgage acquisition and loan decision process. While expected price increases are not to be incorporated, a potential excess of the current market price over to the sustainable value of the property shall be prudently reflected in the valuation.

If a market value is available, the value of the property cannot be higher than that market value. If the loan is used to finance a property purchase, the collateral value is not supposed to exceed the purchase price.

The value determined at the time of origination shall remain constant. However, subject to national supervisors' discretion, banks can be required to revise property values downward. In this case, subsequent upward adjustments, if appropriate, are capped at the value at origination.

In any case, idiosyncratic events that lead to a decrease of the property value, have to be reflected in the collateral value.

A bank could as well recognise modifications of a property with an unequivocally positive impact on its value.

6) Required documentation:

The Standard requires a proper documentation of the granting and monitoring of the loan, including details on the property valuation and the borrower's creditworthiness assessment.

Calculation of the loan-to-value ratio (LTV)

The LTV is the key indicator for the determination of risk weights for residential and commercial real estate exposures, with the exception of an optional loan splitting approach at national discretion for certain real estate exposures.

The loan-to-value ratio is a fraction with the loan amount as numerator and the collateral value as denominator.

The loan amount for senior lien loans is defined as the sum of the outstanding loan amount and any undrawn committed amount, gross of any provisions, risk mitigants, and credit conversion factors. However, balances of pledged deposit accounts with the lending bank can be deducted from the loan amount under specific conditions (*inter alia* balance sheet netting and sole purpose of mortgage loan redemption).

Hereby, loans secured by the same property are to be grouped to a single exposure as long as they are in subsequential ranks without intermediate third party liens.

In jurisdictions, where junior lien loans are considered exposures secured by real estate, the loan amount must include all equally or senior ranked third party liens for LTV calculation purposes. This holds as well for the incorporation of third party liens without sufficient information on their rank.

For the calculation of the collateral value as denominator, the aforementioned conditions for the prudent valuation of the property apply.

The LTV calculation must not consider any guarantees or financial collaterals which also might include certain mortgage insurances. However, these credit risk mitigants can be considered in the course of the exposure determination following the provisions for credit risk mitigation techniques.

Finally, the actual risk weight of an exposure is based on the LTV ratio and the property type and regularly ranges from 20% up to 110%, if not overridden by counterparty-related considerations as detailed below.

For junior lien loans whose LTV exceeds the upper boundary of the lowest LTV bucket (i.e. 50% for residential and 60% for commercial real estate exposures), a multiplier of 1.25 is to be applied to the base risk weight as in the look-up table (capped at the respective risk weight for exposures not fulfilling this exposure class's criteria).

Residential real estate exposure class

The residential real estate exposure class covers exposures secured by residential property which is defined as an immovable property that can be used for residential purposes in line with all applicable laws and regulations.

The treatment of loans in this exposure class is further differentiated by the expected source of funds for the repayment of the loan:

- exposures where the repayment does not materially depend on the cash flows generated by the property,
- exposures where the repayment materially depends on the cash flow generated by the property (in previous documents referred to as "Income producing real estate" exposures).

The Basel Committee suggests that this material dependency is recognised if more than 50% of the borrower's income (as considered in the bank's debt service coverage assessment)[8] is generated by the residential property, without any restriction to specific counterparty types. However, national supervisors can provide banks with further details on how to incorporate the material dependency criterion.

---

8   However, it is not stated whether changes to the shares of income sources – e.g., a rental income share of 60% at inception of a loan changes to 40% after a few years due to salary increases, or a rental income share exceeds the 50% threshold after the borrower's retirement – over the lifetime of the loan may lead to its reclassification.

Additionally there are qualitative criteria which might lead to a treatment of an exposure where the repayment materially depends on the cash flow generated by the property as an exposure where the repayment does not materially depend on the cash flow generated by the property regardless whether the quantitative criterion is met:

- the property which secures the exposure is the borrower's primary residence,
- the collateral is an income producing residential housing unit and the borrower has mortgaged less than a certain number of properties (threshold to be detailed by national supervisors),
- the borrower of the real estate exposure is an association or cooperative regulated under national law which aims to grant members a primary residence in the respective property, and
- the borrower of the real estate exposure is a public housing company or a non-profit association which serves social purposes in terms of providing tenants long-term housing.

In general, residential real estate exposures where the repayment does not materially depend on cash flows generated by the property receive lower risk weights, since the Basel Committee considers losses less probable in cases where the source of debt service coverage is not the collateral which secures the exposure.

Residential real estate exposures where the repayment does not materially depend on cash flows generated by the property

For these exposures, jurisdictions are entitled to choose the applicable approach, either a LTV-based risk weight determination or a loan splitting calculation, with different risk weights for both the secured and the unsecured part of a residential real estate loan.

Figure 1.12 compares illustratively the technical application of both approaches which are further detailed in this section.

1) LTV-based approach

The LTV-based approach requires banks to calculate the exposures LTV, following the aforementioned calculation steps, and determine the risk weight based on the exposure's LTV bucket.

Therefore, the Basel Committee provides a look-up table with 5 different LTV buckets: Exposures with a LTV that does not exceed 50% receive a risk weight of 20%, while a LTV of more than 100% – i.e. the loan amount exceeds the property value – leads to an applicable risk weight of 70%.

Exposures secured by junior liens that can be treated as real estate exposures in accordance with the aforementioned overall requirements, receive the base risk weight multiplied by 1.25 for all LTV buckets except for the lowest LTV bucket (with LTV $\leq$ 50%). However, the resulting risk weight is capped at the risk weight applicable for exposures that do not fulfil the overall requirements for real estate exposures. Thus, respective

Example

Real estate financing loan to an individual, secured by a senior lien on the financed residential property (used as residence by the borrower)

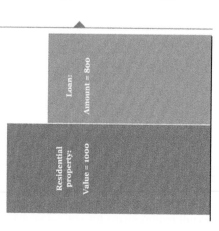

Residential property:
Value = 1000

Loan:
Amount = 800

Figure 1.12: LTV vs Loan Splitting approach

Jurisdictions applying the LTV approach

1 LTV calculation

LTV formula (simplified)

$$LTV = \frac{Loan\ amount\ (incl.\ off-balance\ and\ senior\ liens)}{Property\ value}$$

LTV formula applied to this example

$$LTV = \frac{800}{1000} = 80\ \%$$

2 Risk weights (look-up table)

According to the look-up table, a risk weight of 30% is applicable:

		Residential real estate		
LTV range	...	60% < LTV ≤ 80%	80% < LTV ≤ 90%	...
Risk weight	...	30%	40%	...

3 RWA calculation

$$RWA = 800 \times 30\% = 240$$

In case of a loan amount of 810:
$$RWA = 810 \times 40\% = 324$$

Jurisdictions applying the Loan Splitting approach

1 Loan splitting

Determination of secured and unsecured partial exposures

$$Exposure_{Res.RealEstate} = MAX(55\% \times property\ val. - senior\ liens;\ 0)$$

$$Exposure_{Counterparty,RW} = Exposure - Exposure_{Res.RealEstate}$$

Application to this example

$$Exposure_{Res.RealEstate} = MAX(55\% \times 1000;\ 0) = 550$$

$$Exposure_{Counterparty,RW} = 800 - 550 = 250$$

2 Prescribed risk weights

According to the look-up table, a risk weight of 20% is applicable for the secured part and 75% for the unsecured part of the loan

Residential real estate – Loan splitting approach		
	Secured part	Unsecured part Individuals
LTV Range		...
Risk weight	20%	75% ...

3 RWA calculation

$$RWA = 550 \times 20\% + 250 \times 75\% = 297.5$$

In case of a loan amount of 810:
$$RWA = 550 \times 20\% + 260 \times 75\% = 305$$

Residential real estate – LTV-based approach							If requirements for Real Estate exposure treatment are not met:
Repayment is _not materially dependent_ on cash flows generated by the property							
LTV Range	LTV ≤ 50%	50% < LTV ≤ 60%	60% < LTV ≤ 80%	80% < LTV ≤ 90%	90% < LTV ≤ 100%	LTV > 100%	
Base Risk weight (senior lien)	20%	25%	30%	40%	50%	70%	Risk weight as for unsecured exposures
Effective risk weight for junior lien (if applicable)	20%	31.25%	37.5%	50%	62.5%	87.5%	

Figure 1.13: LTV approach for residential real estate

exposures receive a risk weight between 20% and 87.5%, depending on the LTV and the type of counterparty.

Figure 1.13 shows the applicable risk weights in detail.

Exposures that do not fulfil the overall requirements of the real estate exposure class are treated like unsecured exposures.

As stated above, provisions, credit conversion factors and credit risk mitigation techniques cannot be considered for the calculation of the LTV in the course of the risk weight determination. However, their effects are to be incorporated in the exposure value which is multiplied by the determined risk weight in order to calculate the risk weighted assets.

2) Loan splitting approach

Unlike the LTV calculation, the loan splitting approach focuses on a single instrument rather than all instruments secured by the residential property. For every instrument secured by the property, the actual secured and the unsecured part of the instrument have to be determined as follows: the secured part is defined as the maximum of 55% of the property value less the value of all claims more senior than the relevant instrument and 0. If there are any liens of the same seniority ("pari passu" ranking), the collateral value shall be assigned pro rata to the pari passu ranked creditors.

First, the secured and unsecured exposure values are calculated:

$$Exposure_{Res.RealEstate}$$
$$= MIN(MAX(55\% \times property\ val. -\ senior\ liens; 0), Exposure_{gesamt})$$

$$Exposure_{CounterpartyRW} = Exposure - Exposure_{Res.RealEstate}$$

Residential real estate – Loan splitting approach					Only applicable if requirements for real estate exposure treatment are met
Only applicable where the repayment is <u>not materially dependent</u> on cash flows generated by the property					
LTV range	**Secured part** (max. 55% of the property value less senior claims)	**Unsecured part**			
		Individuals	**SME**	**Other counterparties**	
Risk weight *(for senior lien, as well as junior lien if applicable)*	20%	75%	85%	Risk weight as for unsecured exposures	

Figure 1.14: Loan splitting approach for residential real estate

The resulting secured and unsecured exposures receive different risk weights, with 20% risk weight assigned to the secured part and a counterparty-specific risk weight for the unsecured part (Figure 1.14).[9]

The loan splitting approach does not explicitly differ between senior and junior lien claims, as long as the overall requirements for the consideration of junior liens are met and the assigned collateral value is within the prescribed limits.

The loan splitting approach is newly introduced in the revised CR-SA concept although it had not been considered in the Committee's previous consultative documents. However, it is currently in use in some European jurisdictions.[10]

Comparing both approaches, as illustrated in Figure 1.15 , the risk weight is the same for LTV < 50% under both approaches (20%) while the risk weights for higher LTV ratios increase similarly with small deviations resulting from the cascaded (LTV-based approach) versus the continuous risk weight curve. However, for LTV ratios higher than 90%, the loan splitting approach leads to significantly lower risk weights with an advantage of approximately 25 percentage points when a 100%-LTV ratio is exceeded, though the advantage decreases with increasing LTVs.

Residential real estate exposures where the repayment depends materially on cash flows generated by the property

If the repayment of the residential real estate loan materially depends on the cash flows generated from the collateral, as detailed above (in previous documents referred to as "Income Producing Real Estate" or IPRE) and the requirements for a treatment as residential real estate exposure are met, the LTV-levels and resulting risk weights differ from the previously introduced type of exposure and range from 30% to 105% and for junior lien claims (if applicable) from 30% to 131.25%.

---

9   Deviating from the prescribed risk weights as illustrated in Figure 1.14, regular unsecured exposures to SME fulfilling all retail criteria would receive a 75% risk weight while exposures to individuals who do not meet the retail criteria (e.g. exposure exceeds the retail threshold) would receive a risk weight of 100%. The supervisors will have to finally clarify whether the unsecured part of an exposure subject to the loan splitting approach receives the prescribed risk weights (in line with the written word of the document, as stated above) or the general risk weights for unsecured exposures to respective counterparties. This holds for the treatment of both residential and commercial real estate exposures under the loan splitting approach.

10   Art. 124 CRR

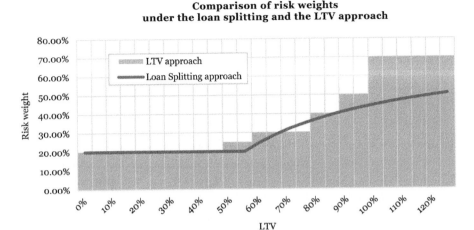

Figure 1.15: Risk weights of LTV vs loan splitting approach for residential real estate

If the overall requirements for real estate exposures are not fulfilled or only partially fulfilled, a risk weight of 150% has to be applied, leading to a risk weight which might be more conservative than for an uncollateralised loan to the same counterparty.

The applicable risk weights are summarised in Figure 1.16.

In general, the counterparty type of a borrower does not affect the possible treatment of a loan as a residential real estate exposure where the repayment depends materially on cash flows generated by the property. However, the abovementioned exemptions and qualitative criteria, *inter alia* for individuals and public housing companies, might apply, hence leading to more favourable risk weights.

Commercial real estate exposure class

The Basel Committee defines commercial real estate as any immovable property that is not a residential real estate in accordance with the respective Basel definition. As with

Residential real estate – LTV-based approach							If requirements for real estate exposure treatment are not met:
Repayment is materially dependent on cash flows generated by the property							
LTV Range	**LTV ≤ 50%**	**50% < LTV ≤ 60%**	**60% < LTV ≤ 80%**	**80% < LTV ≤ 90%**	**90% < LTV ≤ 100%**	**LTV > 100%**	
Base Risk weight (senior lien)	30%	35%	45%	60%	75%	105%	150%
Effective risk weight for junior lien *(if applicable)*	30%	43.75%	56.25%	62.5%	93.75%	131.25%	

Figure 1.16: LTV approach for residential real estate where repayment materially depends on cash flows generated by the property

the residential real estate exposure class, the treatment of exposures in the commercial real estate exposure class is differentiated in:

- exposures where the repayment does not materially depend on the cash flows generated by the property, and
- exposures where the repayment materially depends on the cash flow generated by the property (in previous documents referred to as "Income producing real estate" exposures).

The quantitative criterion to determine a material dependency on the property's cash returns is the same as for real estate exposures, while no qualitative exemption criteria are incorporated for commercial real estate exposures where the repayment depends on cash flows generated by the property. However, the revised CR-SA includes an option for national authorities to significantly ease the capital requirements of respective exposures which is further outlined in the respective subsection of this chapter.

Commercial real estate exposures where the repayment does not materially depend on the cash flows generated by the property

Loans secured by commercial real estate, where the repayment does not materially depend on the cash flows generated by the real estate and where the overall real estate exposure requirements are met, can be risk weighted using the LTV-based or the loan splitting approach which is to be specified by the national authorities.[11]

1) LTV-based approach

Under this approach, Commercial real estate exposures receive a risk weight of 60% if the LTV is less than 60% or the risk weight of the counterparty, provided the latter is lower. If the LTV exceeds 60%, the risk weight of the counterparty is applied.

For the risk weight of the counterparty, the Basel Committee prescribes 75% for Individuals (as with the retail exposure class, if respective criteria are met) and 85% for SME (which equals the general risk weight for non-retail SME exposures).

The details are illustrated in Figure 1.17.

Technically, this exposure class is not exempted from the additional capital surcharge (multiplier of 1.25) for junior lien claims, if applicable in accordance with the overall requirements, although it actually does not increase the risk weights due to the general exemption of the lowest LTV bucket and the cap at a risk weight for unsecured exposures (which equals the risk weight of the counterparty in this approach).

If the operational requirements for these loans are not fulfilled the exposure receives the risk weight of the counterparty.

---

11 For a detailed outline of both approaches, see section "Residential Real Estate exposure class" in the current chapter

Commercial real estate – LTV approach					If requirements for Real Estate exposure treatment are not met:
Repayment is *not materially dependent* on cash flows generated by the property					
LTV range	LTV ≤ 60%	LTV > 60%			
Risk weight (for senior lien, as well as junior lien if applicable)	MIN (60%, risk weight of counterparty)	**Risk weight of counterparty:**			Risk weight as for unsecured exposures
		Individuals	SME	Other	
		75%	85%	as unsecured exposures	

Figure 1.17: LTV approach for commercial real estate

2) Loan splitting approach

As for residential real estate exposures, the loan splitting approach leads to the splitting of loans in:

- a secured exposure with the lower risk weight of 60% or the counterparty-related risk weight for unsecured exposures, respectively, for a loan amount of up to 55% of the property value less claims with higher or equal (in this case with a pro rata consideration) rank, and
- an unsecured part which receives a risk weight based on the counterparty type.

The details are illustrated in Figure 1.18.

In a direct comparison of effective risk weights for commercial real estate exposures, the loan splitting approach leads, with the exception of a few constellations, to either identical – which holds for LTV ≤ 55% as well as for the whole exposures to counterparties with an individual risk weight lower than 60% – or lower risk weights than the LTV approach, as the following scenarios prove in detail.

For exposures to individuals, a risk weight of 75% is to assign to the unsecured part of a loan under the loan splitting approach, while the secured part (max. 55% of the property value) receives a risk weight of 60%. The LTV approach, in contrast, leads to a 75% risk weight for the full loan amount as soon as the LTV threshold of 60% is exceeded.

Thus, the resulting risk weights under both approaches are

- for LTVs ≤ 55% identical,
- for 55% < LTV ≤ 60% slightly better under the LTV approach, and

Commercial real estate – Loan splitting approach					Only applicable if requirements for real estate exposure treatment are met
Only applicable where the repayment is *not materially dependent* on cash flows generated by the property					
LTV range	Secured part (max. 55% of the property value less senior claims)	**Unsecured part**			
		Individuals	SME	Other Counterparties	
Risk weight (for senior lien, as well as junior lien if applicable)	MIN (60%, risk weight of counterparty)	75%	85%	Risk weight as for unsecured exposures	

Figure 1.18: Loan splitting approach for commercial real estate

- for LTV > 60% significantly lower (up to almost 14 percentage points) under the loan splitting approach (with a maximum the relative advantage decreases with increasing LTV).

The respective risk weight curves are shown in Figure 1.19.

The comparison of risk weights for commercial real estate exposures to unrated corporates (assuming a risk weight of 100%) leads to similar curve shapes, which are illustrated in Figure 1.20, as for exposures to individuals. However, the quantitative advantage of the loan splitting approach is even more material with a maximum advantage of more than 35 percentage points for LTV slightly above 60%.

Risk weights under the loan splitting and the LTV approach for commercial real estate exposures to individuals

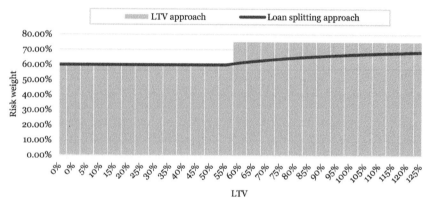

Figure 1.19: LTV vs loan splitting approach for commercial real estate exposures to individuals

Risk Weights under the Loan Splitting and the LTV approach for commercial real estate exposures to unrated corporates

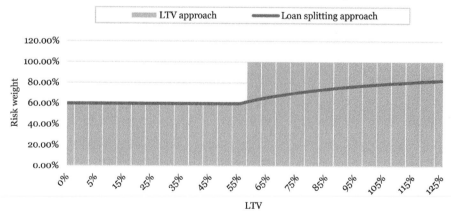

Figure 1.20: LTV vs loan splitting approach for commercial real estate exposures to unrated corporates

Commercial real estate exposures where the repayment materially depends on the cash flows generated by the property

If the repayment of the commercial real estate loan materially depends on the cash flows generated by the property, the following provisions apply (see Figure 1.21).

Unlike for residential real estate exposures, national authorities have the option to waive the assignment of more conservative risk weights to commercial real estate exposures where the repayment materially depends on the cash flows generated by the property. Instead they can opt for the standard commercial real estate exposure treatment.

For this option, certain conditions must be met in the respective jurisdiction at any year: losses from commercial real estate lending up to a LTV of 60% must not exceed 0.3% of the outstanding loans at any year, and overall losses among commercial real estate exposures must not exceed 0.5% of the outstanding loans.[12]

For those jurisdictions where these conditions are not met, as well as in jurisdictions not going for the preferential option, more conservative risk weights in accordance with the look-up table provided by the Basel Committee are applicable. Thereby, a risk weight of 70% is assigned to exposures with a LTV not exceeding 60%, while exposures with a LTV of up to 80% and more than 80% receive a risk weight of 90% and 110%, respectively.

Junior lien claims receive an effective capital requirement surcharge of 25% in the form of a risk weight multiplier, as introduced in the previous section.

If the overall real estate exposure requirements are not fulfilled, a risk weight of 150% is applied to these loans.

Land acquisition, development and construction (ADC)

The Basel Committee defines a specific treatment for loans to companies or SPVs with the purpose of financing land acquisition for development and construction purposes

Commercial real estate				If requirements for Real Estate exposure treatment are not met:
Repayment is materially dependent on cash flows generated by the property				
LTV range	**LTV ≤ 60%**	**60% < LTV ≤ 80%**	**LTV > 80%**	
Base risk weight (senior lien)	70%	90%	110%	150%
Effective risk weight for junior lien *(if applicable)*	70%	112.5%	137.5	

Figure 1.21: Commercial real estate where repayment materially depends on cash flows generated by the property

---

12 If at least one of these conditions is not met in one year, the preferential treatment of such exposures ceases for the respective year and the specific risk weights for commercial real estate exposures where the repayment materially depends on the cash flows generated by the property become applicable. Respective statistics have to be publicly disclosed.

or the development and construction of any residential or commercial property (with certain exemptions applicable, as set out in the residential real estate exposure section).

Loans granted for land acquisition development or construction purposes are assigned a risk weight of 150% in general.

However, ADC exposures for residential real estate building can qualify for a preferential risk weight of 100% if the prudential underwriting standards are met, in accordance with the overall requirements for real estate exposures, and if a sufficient number of pre-sale/pre-lease contracts exists following (yet to be defined) national requirements.

The CR-SA within the Basel II framework does not explicitly contain a specific treatment of ADC exposures, however, in some jurisdictions they are treated as higher-risk exposures with a corresponding higher risk weight.[13]

Changes to existing Basel II framework, developments during the consultation process and subsequent considerations

The revised capital requirements for real estate exposures had been subject to dramatic amendments in the course of the consultation process, further discussions, and negotiations, respecting both the conceptual approach as well as the quantitative impact.

The Basel II framework differentiates only between residential property (with an implicit loan splitting approach, leading to a 35% risk weight for fully secured exposures) and commercial real estate with a risk weight of 100% that can be reduced to 50% at national discretion (e.g. in some European jurisdictions).

The first consultative paper on the CR-SA revision proposed a calculation of risk weights for claims secured by residential real estate based on a matrix comprising the LTV ratio and the debt service coverage ratio (DSCR). The resulting risk weights ranged between 25% and 100%. As the parameter DSCR proved not to be comparable among different jurisdictions on an international basis, the Basel Committee let go of this approach with its second consultative paper and focused on a LTV-based approach. However, neither consultative paper addressed the loan splitting approach, which was reintroduced in the final framework as an option at national discretion and, furthermore, explicitly defined.

For the commercial real estate exposure class, the first consultative paper contained two options for the future treatment: Option A envisaged treating these claims as unsecured

---

13   The Basel II framework allows national supervisors to include asset classes in the "higher-risk category" if deemed appropriate. In the European Union, for instance, art. 128 (2)(d) lists "speculative immovable property financing" under the corresponding Items associated with particular high risk class, assigning a risk weight of 150%.

and applying a risk weight of 50% at national discretion. Option B was a LTV-based approach with a range of risk weights between 75% and 120%. The second consultative paper focused on Option B, while the final document, apart from lowering the risk weights, reintroduces the possibility of a differentiated risk weighing for secured and unsecured parts of a loan (loan splitting approach).

With the first consultative paper, a concept of aligning the IRB and SA-exposure classes more closely led to the introduction of Income Producing Real Estate (IPRE) and Land Acquisition, Development and Construction (ADC) financing in the SA-CR as specialised lending exposures, which had changed to sub-categories of the real estate exposure class in the second consultative paper.

While ADC is also included in the final document as a new sub-category of the real estate exposure class, the IPRE exposure class has been replaced by a more specific approach focusing on the material dependency of loan repayments on the cash flows generated by the financed property as a criterion for the application of higher risk weights (with additional exemption criteria).

As Figure 1.22 illustrates graphically, both RWA-increasing and RWA-decreasing effects are to be expected from all these changes, depending on the individual risk profile of exposures: in any case, loans secured by residential property with very low LTV ratios receive significantly lower risk weights than under current regulation.[14] The same may hold for respective commercial real estate loans in jurisdictions that apply the Basel II base instead of the preferential risk weight.

However, changes and more precise conditions for the recognition of a property value (e.g. 25% surcharge for junior-lien claims, if applicable, and a new 55% cap for secured exposures under the loan splitting approach) lift the RWA for respective exposures. Further RWA increases can be expected from exposures that are classified as ADC as well as from loans where the repayment materially depends on returns from the financed property.

As a matter of fact, the Basel Committee's initial objective of a more risk-sensitive approach seems to be reflected in decreasing RWA for low-risk exposures, while exposures with high LTV – particularly with LTV > 100% where the loan amount exceeds the actual property value – and loans with riskier characteristics receive higher risk weights. Nevertheless, the latter effect can be eased by national authorities through an implementation of the loan splitting approach.

---

14 In this context, it is worth mentioning that the current EU regulation (CRR), for instance, allows an assignment of the preferential risk weight of 35% to secured residential real estate exposures of up to 80% of the market value or the sustainable mortgage value of the collateral, respectively. Depending on the EU implementation aspects, the Basel IV requirements (20% risk weight for up to 55% of the property value) can lead to higher risk weights compared to the current regulation, particularly for LTV ratios ≥ 80%.

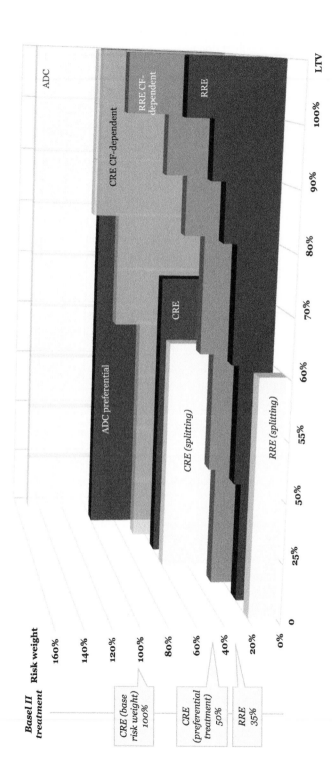

Risk weights for real estate exposures

RRE = Residential Real Estate Exposures; CRE = Commercial Real Estate Exposure; ADC = Land acquisition, development and construction, ADC preferential: preferential risk weight for certain residential ADC exposures; CF-dependent = exposures where the repayment materially depends on cash flows generated by the financed property;

Further explanations: The diagram does not show the capital requirement multiplier of 1.25 for junior lien claims (if applicable); Splitting approaches: The diagram shows only the risk weight for the fully secured part of an exposure (the unsecured part receives the counterparty's risk weight); CRE: The diagram shows only the prescribed risk weight of 60% for LTV ≤ 60%, though a lower counterparty risk weight can be assigned alternatively (if applicable), for LTV >60%, the counterparty risk weight is assigned

Figure 1.22: Overview of risk weights for real estate exposures

1.2.10 Additional risk weights for positions with currency mismatch

In the past, several banks experienced increasing defaults among loans where the repayment currency was different from the currency of the borrower's regular income when there were sudden changes in the exchange rate between these two currencies.

When the Swiss central bank decided in early 2015 to stop taking measures to strictly control the EUR/SFR exchange rate, the value of the Swiss franc suddenly increased against the euro. Borrowers with loans in Swiss francs, who had beenreceiving their main income in the Euro area suddenly faced a sharp increase in their obligations to repay which subsequently led to increased risks and defaults for the lenders.

In the Basel II framework, there is no requirement to anticipate and cover such developments and risks.

In the revised CR-SA an additional risk weight for retail and residential real estate exposures to individuals with a respective unhedged currency mismatch is introduced. It is not calculated by using an add-on of 50%, as discussed earlier in the consultation process, but by applying a multiplier of 1.5 to the risk weight of the position in scope with a 'capped' maximum risk weight of 150%.

Two types of foreign exchange rate hedging prevent exposures in scope from being subject to this additional capital requirement.

- Natural hedge where the borrower receives regular income (e.g. salaries or lease payments) in the currency of the loan.
- Financial hedge where the borrower contractually hedged foreign exchange rate changes with respect to his obligations another currency.

In both cases, at least 90% of the loan instalment have to be covered by the hedging measures to avoid the application of the currency mismatch multiplier. Banks need to ensure that the corresponding hedging measures are recorded, documented and regularly monitored in order to avoid risk weight add-ons in relation to foreign currency loans.

This new feature in the Basel framework had been introduced for retail and residential retail exposures in the Basel Committee's first consultative paper and was extended to corporate exposures in the second consultative paper. However, in the final document the scope was eventually narrowed down again to retail and real estate exposures to individuals.

While the first consultative paper had not specified the amount of the add-on, the second consultative paper proposed an add-on of 50% to the present risk weight (with a maximum of 150%) on unhedged exposures which was replaced by a multiplier in the final revision of the CR-SA.

The market share of foreign currency loans with currency mismatches to individuals varies significantly from one country to another. While loans denominated in Swiss

Franc used to be popular for residential real estate financing in some European countries (often motivated by low CHF interest rates in combination previously stable exchange rates to other European currencies till the central banks' strict exchange rate control suddenly came to an end), such positions are not very common for retail portfolios and residential property financing in other countries, e.g. in Germany.

In general, these financing schemes tend to occur primarily in relation to commercial real estate loans which are now excluded from the requirement to apply additional risk weights.

For said reasons, the quantitative impact on these exposure classes for the entire sector will vary among the jurisdictions with presumably less material impact in many countries.

1.2.11 Off-balance sheet items

Off-balance sheet positions are converted into credit exposures by multiplying the nominal (e.g. committed but undrawn) amount by a credit conversion factor (CCF). Under the new Basel framework, according to the type of exposure and their associated risk, in line with relevant CRR classification, the applied CCFs range from 10% to 100% (Figure 1.23).

This marks an increase of applicable CCF range compared to current Basel II framework and CRR, where positions with a low risk profile – such as commitments that are unconditionally cancellable at any time without any prior notice – receive a CCF of 0%, thus attracting no regulatory capital charge.

In relation to commitments, the new Basel framework applies a standard 40% risk weight, irrespective of the maturity of the underlying facility – with maturity being the differentiator for the applicable risk weight on the existing Basel II rules. In addition, the applicable risk weight for commitments that are unconditionally cancellable at any time by the bank without prior notice, or that effectively provide for automatic cancellation due to deterioration in a borrower's creditworthiness is increased to 10% compared to

	CRR	New Basel framework
Guarantees and other credit substitutes	100%	100%
Undrawn credit facilities commitments, NIFs and RFUs	50%	50%
Short-term self-liquidating letters of credit	20%	20%
Unconditionally cancellable retail credit facilities	0%	10%

Figure 1.23: Selected credit conversion factors (CCF)

the 0% risk weight under Basel II framework. A typical example of the latter category is retail open credit lines, e.g. current accounts which offer overdraft facilities.

Under the new Basel framework, the applicable CCFs for the majority of off-balance sheet exposure types remain unchanged. However, the key impact of new rules is focused on commitments exposures which typically constitute the majority of banks' off-balance sheet positions. For this category, the applicable CCFs will result in increased capital requirements, since banks may have large exposures on commitments that currently receive a CCF of 0% or 20% depending on the type.

1.2.12 Defaulted exposures

While the CRR has already modified the former exposure class "past-due loans" into "defaulted exposures", the Basel regulations still rely on this concept. Under the new framework, the Basel Committee is proposing an alignment of the classification of these loans with the IRB Approach, by replacing the "past due" criterion with the definition of default. While this represents a substantial change in the Basel framework, it does not affect banks under EU regulation as the CRR has already implemented this "alignment".

In the new regulation, the process for assigning risk weights to defaulted exposures remains unchanged compared to Basel II, even though this approach leads to a double benefit since specific provisions both influence the exposure amount and the risk weight.

The net unsecured part of any defaulted exposure – other than qualifying residential real estate – receives a risk weight of 150% if the level of specific provisions applied to this loan is less than 20%. On the other hand, exposures with specific provisions equal to or greater than 20% are assigned a 100% risk weight. As with Basel II, it remains at the national supervisor's discretion to reduce the applicable risk weight to 50% given that specific provisions applied are no less than 50%.

Regarding residential real estate exposures where the repayment is not materially dependent on the cash flows generated by the property, the net unsecured part of the loan is risk weighted at 100% regardless of the level of provisions. This approach differentiates from both Basel II and CRR. Specifically the new framework, introduces a linkage of the purpose of the mortgage with the applicable risk weight and eliminates the option for a reduced risk weight if specific provisions exceed 20%.

Finally, the Basel Committee removed the option to allow for a risk weight of 100% if the defaulted exposure is fully backed with collateral that is not eligible as financial collateral under the standardised approach, and with specific provisions of that exposure that exceed 15%. As this element of the Basel framework was not implemented within EU regulation, no specific effects are to be expected within the CRR.

To conclude, the new regulation preserves the relationship of risk weights with the level of specific provisions applied to the exposure even though the Basel Committee initially removed the linkage during the consultation process by proposing universal risk weights.

1.2.13 Other assets

In terms of other assets, the new Basel framework marks no major changes compared to existing regulations and in particular under the CRR treatment. This exposure class will continue to serve as a residual exposure class for positions that are not subject or do not fit into other exposure classes.

The standard risk weight for all exposures that cannot be classified under a different asset class remains at 100%.

A 0% risk weight will be applied to the following positions:

- cash owned and held at the bank or in transit, and
- gold bullion held at the bank or held in another bank on an allocated basis, to the extent the gold bullion assets are backed by gold bullion liabilities.

A risk weight of 20% will be applied to cash items in the process of collection.

Thus, the new rules are not expected to have an impact on a bank's capital requirements attributable to other assets exposure class.

1.3 Use of external ratings

1.3.1 Recognition process for external ratings by national supervisors

Similar to the existing Basel regulations, external ratings can only be used for regulatory purposes if they meet certain eligibility criteria and are explicitly recognised by the national supervisor. To be eligible, external ratings have to meet the following eight criteria.

1. Objectivity

The methodology for assigning external ratings must be rigorous, systematic, and subject to some form of validation. It has to be established for at least one year (preferably three years) before being eligible for supervisory recognition.

2. Independence

The external rating agency should be independent and especially not subject to political or economic pressure that might influence the rating.

3. Internal access/transparency

In order to allow, at least, a generic understanding of how the external ratings have been derived, the rating agency is required to make certain key elements underlying the assessment publicly available.

4. Disclosure

In order to enable a solid understanding of the rating agency it is required to disclose a number of relevant pieces of information such as its code of conduct, the general nature of its compensation arrangements with assessed entities, any conflict of interest, its compensation arrangements and assessment methodology.

5. Resources

An external rating agency should be able to demonstrate that it has sufficient resources to provide for a high-quality credit assessment and an ongoing contact with the entities assessed

6. Credibility

The credibility of a rating agency is mainly derived by the previous criteria. In addition, the rating agency has to provide evidence that its external ratings are being used by independent parties such as investors and insurances.

7. No abuse of unsolicited ratings

This criteria has been added in the Basel IV regulation. Under current regulation the Basel Committee is expecting only solicited ratings to be used but also allows national supervisors to use unsolicited ratings if these ratings are not used to put pressure on the entities to obtain solicited ratings. Even though this criteria has been added, the requirement does not represent a fundamental change with respect to current regulation.

8. Cooperation with the supervisor

Also this criteria has been added. The Basel Committee now expects that the rating agency notifies the supervisor of significant changes to methodologies and grants access to relevant information. Also this requirement is to be seen as a clarification of the expected form of cooperation between the supervisor and the rating agency rather than a substantial additional eligibility criteria.

In addition to these eligibility criteria, supervisors should also consider the criteria and information provided in the IOSCO Code of Conduct Fundamentals for Credit Rating Agencies when determining ECAI eligibility.

Currently, many national supervisors have performed the recognition process for external rating agencies and have usually recognised the three dominating external rating agencies – Standard and Poors, FitchIBCA and Moodys – as eligible rating agencies. In addition, supervisors may have recognised smaller and more specialised rating agencies. It is to be expected that the range of eligible external rating agencies will not significantly change under Basel IV.

1.3.2 Mapping of external ratings and use of multiple ratings

Once a supervisor has decided on the eligibility of an external rating agency it also has to perform a mapping from the individual grades used by the rating agency to the risk weights in the standardised approach. While doing this mapping it has to be provided with comparable grades from different external rating agencies that result in the same regulatory risk weight.

If a bank intends to use external ratings it has to nominate one or more of the eligible external rating agencies. Once it has chosen the rating agency it has to use the ratings consistently for all types of claim where they have been recognised by their supervisor for both risk-weighting and risk management purposes. In many cases external ratings refer to any senior unsecured debt of the borrower. However, a number of aspects are to be considered in order to identify the correct external rating for the risk weighting.

In order to have the best possible coverage of external ratings, banks usually nominate several external rating agencies. As a consequence, it may happen that a borrower is rated by several of the nominated external rating agencies. Unchanged from current regulation the Basel Committee is prescribing a process by which the applicable rating from a number of available ratings is derived (Figure 1.24).

For determining the correct external rating banks also have to consider whether an issue-specific rating is available for exposure. If an issue-specific rating exists, this rating has to be used (if multiple external ratings exists, the rules for multiple ratings apply). If no issue specific rating is available, the applicable rating is derived by the process illustrated in Figure 1.25.

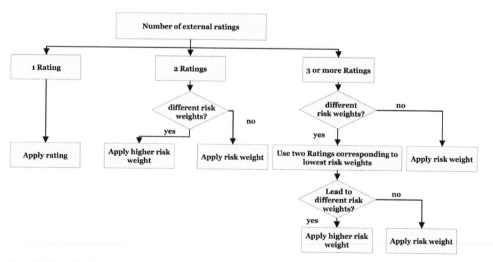

Figure 1.24: Process if multiple external ratings by several ECAIs are available

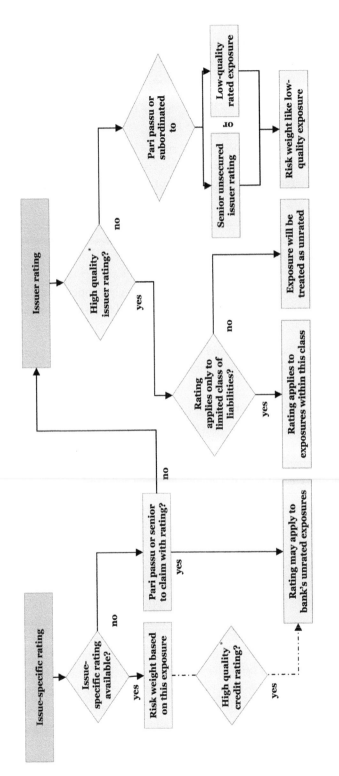

* High quality rating maps into a risk weight lower than that which applies to an unrated claim

Figure 1.25: Issue-specific vs issuer rating

As a third aspect, banks have to differentiate between short-term and long-term ratings. Short-term ratings are deemed to be issue-specific and may only be used for other exposures under restrictive conditions which are unchanged from Basel II. Under no circumstances may a short-term rating be used for long-term exposures.

In general, external ratings for one entity within a corporate group cannot be used to risk-weight other entities within the same group.

With respect to the mapping process of external ratings to risk weights, the use of multiple ratings and the derivation of the applicable risk weight from external ratings, there are no material differences between the current Basel regulations and the regulations under Basel IV.

1.4 Credit risk mitigation techniques

The requirements for credit risk mitigation remain largely identical to the requirements under the current regulation. However, the structure of the wording of the individual has been altered.

With respect to OTC derivatives and SFT counterparties the Basel Committee now explicitly requires banks to devote sufficient resources to ensure an orderly operation of margin agreements.

In terms of the recognition of financial collateral such as cash or debt instruments, however, differences arise with respect to the use of external ratings. In jurisdictions that allow for the use of external ratings the extent of eligible collateral for both the simple and the comprehensive approach remains largely unchanged, only resecuritisations are now explicitly referred to as not eligible financial collateral.

Under the simple approach, the conditions for an exemption from the minimum risk weight of 20 % are now laid out in greater detail – not, however, significantly changing the requirements itself.

With respect to the comprehensive approach the current risk mitigation requirements allow for calculating haircuts based on internal estimates – something which is not in line with the general concept of standardised approaches. As already indicated in the first and second consultative papers the use of internal estimates will not be allowed anymore. Also the use of VaR-Models for certain securities financing transactions (SFT) and the internal models method for SFT and collateralised OTC derivatives, presently available to banks using the standardised approach have been removed for the standardised approach. The table to derive supervisory haircuts in the standardised approach has been modified both in terms of the structure and applicable haircuts (Figure 1.26). The haircuts for main index equities have been increased from 15–20% and for other equities from 25–30%. For other issuers the maturity grading has been altered by introducing maturity bands of 1–3 years, 3–5 years, 5–10 years and more

Supervisory haircuts for comprehensive approach
Jurisdictions that allow the use of external ratings for regulatory purposes

Issue rating for debt securities	Residual maturity	Sovereigns	Other Issuers	Securitisation exposures
AAA to AA−/A−1	≤ 1 year	0.5	1	2
	> 1 year, ≤ 3 years	2	3	8
	> 3 years, ≤ 5 years		4	
	> 5 years, ≤ 10 years	4	6	16
	> 10 years		12	
A+ to BBB−/A−2/A−3 /P−3 and unrated bank securities per para 148(c)(ii)	≤ 1 year	1	2	4
	> 1 year, ≤ 3 years	3	4	12
	> 3 years, ≤ 5 years		6	
	> 5 years, ≤ 10 years	6	12	24
	> 10 years		20	
BB+ to BB−	All	15	Not eligible	Not eligible
Main index equities (including convertible bonds) and gold		20		
Other equities and convertible bonds listed on a recognised exchange		30		
UCITS/mutual funds		Highest haircut applicable to any security in which the fund can invest, unless the bank can apply the look-through approach (LTA) for equity investments in funds, in which case the bank may use a weighted average of haircuts applicable to instruments held by the fund.		
Cash in the same currency		0		

Figure 1.26: Supervisory haircuts using external ratings

than 10 years. Unchanged from Basel II all of these haircuts are based on an assumed holding period of 10 days.

As the comprehensive approach is also an eligible approach in jurisdictions that do not allow the use of external ratings, a revised table for the derivation haircuts has been developed, based mainly on the maturity and the issuer (Figure 1.27).

Unchanged from the current Basel II regulations, the haircut for currency mismatches, i.e. differences in the currency of the exposure and the currency of the collateral is set at 8% and calibrated on a 10-day holding period.

All of these haircuts need to be adjusted in respect of the applicable holding period based on the individual type of collateralised transaction (5, 10 or 20 business days) and the frequency of the revaluation. Unchanged from Basel II regulations, banks need to apply a holding period of 5 days to all repo-style transactions, a 10-day holding period to other capital market transactions and a 20-day holding period to regular secured lending. If the bank does not perform a daily revaluation of the market value of the collateral, the Haircut is to be adjusted based on the formula shown in Figure 1.28.

Supervisory haircuts for comprehensive approach
Jurisdictions that do not allow the use of external ratings for regulatory purposes

Issue rating for debt securities	Residual maturity	Issuer's risk weight (only for securities issued by sovereigns)			Other investment-grade securities, consistent with paragraphs 148(d)(iii)	
		0%	20% or 50%	100%	Non-securitisation exposures	Senior securitisation exposures with risk weight < 100%
Debt securities	≤ 1 year	0.5	1	15	2	4
	> 1 year, ≤ 3 years	2	3	15	4	12
	> 3 years, ≤ 5 years				6	
	> 5 years, ≤ 10 years	4	6	15	12	24
	> 10 years				20	
Main index equities (including convertible bonds) and gold	20					
Other equities and convertible bonds listed on a recognised exchange	30					
UCITS/mutual funds	Highest haircut applicable to any security in which the fund can invest, unless the bank can apply the look-through approach (LTA) for equity investments in funds, in which case the bank may use a weighted average of haircuts applicable to instruments held by the fund.					
Cash in the same currency	0					
Other exposure types	30					

Figure 1.27: Supervisory haircuts without use of external ratings

$$H = H_{10} \sqrt{\frac{N_R + (T_M - 1)}{H_{10}}}$$

H = Haircut

H_{10} = 10 – business day haircut for instrument

N_R = acutal number of business days between remargining
   for capital market transactions or revaluation for secured transactions

T_M = minimum holding period for the type of transaction

Figure 1.28: Calculation of the haircut based on holding period and revaluation

The calculation requirements and formulae and also the options to apply a haircut of zero for core market participants are identical to the current Basel II regulations.

The treatment for security finance transactions covered by master netting has been modified. As already mentioned, the option to use internal models for quantifying the exposure amount in this type of transaction has been removed. The Basel Committee only allows the use of a formula that has been amended in order to better take into account the effect of diversification and correlation.

$$E^* = Max\left\{0;\ \sum_i E_i - \sum_i C_j + 0{,}4 \cdot \underbrace{|\sum_S E_S H_S|}_{\text{net exposure}} + 0{,}6 \cdot \underbrace{\frac{\sum_S E_S |H_S|}{\sqrt{N}}}_{\frac{\text{gross exposure}}{\sqrt{N}}} + \sum_{fx}(E_{fx} \cdot H_{fx})\right\}$$

E^* = exposure value of the netting set after risk mitigation

E_i = current value of all cash and securities lent, sold with an agreement to repurchase or otherwise posted to the counterparty under the netting agreement

C_j = current value of all cash and securities borrowed, purchased with an agreement to resell or otherwise held by the bank under the netting agreement

E_s = The net current value of each security issuance under the netting set (positive value)

H_s = Haircut appropriate to E_s

N = Number of security issues contained in the netting set (except that issuances where the value E_s is less than one tenth of the value of the largest E_s in the netting set are not included the count)

E_{fx} = Absolute value of the net position in each currency fx different from the settlement currency

H_{fx} = haircut appropriate for currency mismatch of currency fx

Figure 1.29: Calculation of the haircut based on holding period and revaluation

Figure 1.29 shows the current standardised formula for calculating repo-style transactions.

The modification has been made in order to better consider diversification effects of the included positions in comparison to the formula being provided by current Basel II regulation.

The second element of the formula, which consists of an add-on to reflect potential price changes in the values of the securities in the netting set, is revised. The portion of the formula weighted with a factor of 0.4 corresponds to the current regulation and allows for negative haircuts ("net exposures"). The newly added portion, which is weighted with a factor of 0.6, takes into account haircuts in the form of add-ons without taking into account if the haircut should be applied as received securities collateral or as a security position established as exposure ("gross exposure"). As a result, higher weighted capital charges, which are divided by the number of exposures contained in the netting set, are calculated in the first step. Overall this results in a more favourable haircut than in the original version. This effect becomes even clearer the more exposures are contained in the netting set.

In jurisdictions that do not allow the use of external ratings, other entities are eligible, as long as they are classified as "investment grade" and meet additional requirements – such as having securities outstanding – and their creditworthiness is not positively correlated with the credit risk of the exposures for which they provided guarantees. Parent, subsidiary or other affiliated companies are also eligible, if their creditworthiness is not positively correlated with the credit risk of the exposure for which they provided for.

With respect to the use of guarantees and credit derivatives in the CRM framework the Basel Committee acknowledges that the range of eligible guarantors/protection providers might differ in jurisdictions that allow the use of external ratings and those jurisdictions that do not allow the use of external ratings and welcome feedback on how to narrow potential differences.

All of the proposed changes to the risk mitigation framework may eventually lead to increased capital requirements for banks. Especially banks using internal estimates that will no longer be allowed, may experience significant increases.

For certain non-centrally cleared SFT with certain counterparties, the Basel Committee introduces a minimum haircut floor. This haircut floor, however, only applies to transactions where cash is provided against collateral other than government securities to counterparties who are not supervised by a regulator that imposes prudential requirements consistent with international norms. This also includes transactions where securities are lent against lower quality securities (so-called "collateral upgrade transactions").

For SFT that meet these requirements ("inscope SFT") the Basel Committee provides a haircut table comparable to the table provided for financial collateral. All transactions that do not meet these haircut floors must be treated as uncollateralised.

As this type of transaction is only relevant for a small segment of the SFT market and current (non regulatory) market standards already contain similar mechanism, the overall effect from this new requirements will probably be quite limited.

With respect to the treatment of guarantees and credit derivatives the Basel Committee does not significantly alter the operational requirements or the range of eligible guarantors or protection providers or the methods to derive the risk weights after credit protection. However, it introduces specific requirements for positions with eligible credit protection where materiality thresholds triggering the payment requirements of the guarantor or protection provider exist. The portion below this minimum amount needs to be risk weighted with 1,250% by the bank purchasing the credit protection.

1.5 Conclusions

The reform of the standardised approach for credit risk is likely to be the most relevant element of Basel IV as it both effects standardised and – via the output floor – IRB-banks. Also credit risk amounts to the vast majority of RWA contribution for nearly all banks regardless of their size and business model.

The consultation process leading to this finalised version was quite intense and demonstrated that the Basel Committee intended to strike a balance between removing deficiencies of the existing approach and increasing risk sensitivity on one side and at the same time offering a standardised approach that would not unduly increase capital requirements for all banks. This process needed two consultative papers and a number of quantitative impact studies and feedback from the industry.

While the intention of the Basel Committee to revise the standardised approach and remove the identified deficiencies was generally welcomed by all market participants, the modifications proposed in the first consultative paper resulted in some unintended consequences, above all an inappropriate increase in capital requirements. Moreover, considerable costs for the implementation of the new procedures, and especially for the replacement of external ratings by risk drivers to be calculated individually, were expected.

With the second consultative paper the Basel Committee showed a clear move back to some existing core elements of the standardised approach – such as the use of external ratings – and complemented these elements with additional requirements. Where available and approved for regulatory purposes, these ratings are used to determine so-called basic risk weights which must be verified by banks in the form of an internal due diligence analyses.

The final rules for the standardised approach mainly follow the concept developed in the second consultative paper. However, there are additional elements in order to avoid detrimental RWA effects or cliff effects without economic basis e.g. the introduction of a 75% risk weight for corporates that have an external rating between BBB+ and BBB– or the possibility of using the loan-splitting approach for real estate exposures that are not materially dependent on cash flows.

The Basel Committee considers that, in aggregate, these modifications between the second consultative paper and the final rules text will – on average – not lead to a significant increase in capital requirements. However, given the large amount of modifications which will in some areas lead to capital reductions and other areas to capital increases, any "average number" will be of limited use for an individual bank.

For banks, the following five areas of modifications are expected to be most relevant.

1. Claims on banks due to the modified regulation on banks without external rating.

2. The newly introduced exposure class of specialised lending, where risk weights above 100% have to be assigned under certain conditions.

3. Exposures secured by real estate (both commercial and residential and both materially depending on cash flows and not materially depending on cash flows).

4. Subordinated debt securities and non-deductible holdings,

5. Risk weight add-ons for currency mismatches.

While a number areas of possibly dramatic capital increases have been altered or removed, the RWA-consequences for an individual bank might still be quite severe. As a consequence, each bank should perform a thorough impact analysis on its individual exposure.

Recommended Literature

Basel Committee for Banking Supervision; BCBS 128 (2006): International Convergence of Capital Measurement and Capital Standards, 2006.

Basel Committee for Banking Supervision; BCBS 205 (2011): Treatment of trade finance under the Basel capital framework, 2011.

Basel Committee for Banking Supervision; BCBS 307 (2014): Consultative Document. Revisions to the Standardised Approach for credit risk, 2014.

Basel Committee for Banking Supervision; BCBS 347 (2015): Second Consultative Document. Standards. Revisions to the Standardised Approach for Credit Risk, 2015.

Basel Committee for Banking Supervision; BCBS 350 (2015): Guidance on credit risk and accounting for expected credit losses, 2015.

Basel Committee for Banking Supervision; BCBS 424 (2017): Basel III: Finalising post-crisis reforms, 2017.

Financial Stability Board; FSB (2012): Principles for sound residential mortgage underwriting practices, 2012.

IOSCO: Code of Conduct Fundamentals for Credit Rating Agencies, 2015.

2 The Future of the IRB Approach

Luís Filipe Barbosa, Kaan Aksel and André Wallenberg

The recent financial crisis has severely impeded the trust that supervisory authorities, and market participants in general, have placed in banks' internal models to calculate capital requirements. The result has been an avalanche of proposals and initiatives by the Basel Committee (BCBS), the European Banking Authority (EBA) and, most recently, the European Central Bank (ECB) – as the competent supervisory authority of the Eurozone countries – to reform the IRB Approach and review its application by banks.

This chapter starts by presenting the key features of an IRB framework brought into life by the Basel II Capital Accord[1] (section 2.1), namely its different variants, the relevant mechanics for the calculation of capital requirements and the minimum conditions required for the adoption and ongoing use of internal models. We keep this chapter rather short for the pupose of highlighting the changes and challenges of Basel IV to the IRB Approach. Nevertheless, there are many requirements unchanged in the IRB Approach that must be considered while implementing Basel IV – in particular, the minimum requirements for entry and on-going use of the IRB Approach.

Moreover, it looks at the final version of the revisions advocated by the Basel Committee, which was published in December 2017 – "Finalising post-crisis reforms" (section 2.2), after an initial consultative document published in March 2016 ("Reducing variation in credit risk-weighted assets – constraints on the use of internal model approaches")[2]. By the 1 January 2022, the new regime should be in place.

In the case of the Eurozone countries, the Basel Committee proposed changes should be considered in combination with the requirements and/or guidance most recently issued by the EBA (as the EU's regulator) and the ECB, as all of them shall be somehow shaping the future of the IRB framework. Only in this way, i.e. by considering the big picture, shall Eurozone banks ensure full compliance with such framework in an efficient and proactive manner. In fact, both actions from the EBA and the ECB are seen as a major contribution to restoring the trust in the use of the IRB models, enhancing comparability across models and reducing the undue variability of capital requirements (i.e. not grounded in different risk profiles), clearly sharing (and complementing) the intentions of the Basel Committee, as they mainly introduce additional detail in the expectations on the core elements of the IRB framework. Indeed, this is the main reason why the chapter includes an extensive description of what both entities have been doing in the last years, anticipating what could be a relevant example for national regulators across the globe.

---

1 See BCBS (2006), "Basel II: International Convergence of Capital Measurement and Capital Standards: A Revised Framework – Comprehensive Version", BIS.
2 BCBS362.

As an integral part of EBA efforts to ensure consistency in model outputs and comparability of RWA, rectifying the issues identified on the comparability of IRB models and providing enhanced clarity on various aspects of the application of the IRB, four EBA documents are covered here. In detail, they clarify the supervisory practices when revising internal models[3] (section 2.3), the features of the new definition of default[4] (section 2.4), as well as the core requirements for the estimation of relevant IRB risk parameters, namely Probability of Default (PD), Loss Given Default (LGD) and the treatment of defaulted assets[5] (section 2.5). These documents are part of the EBA's future of the IRB Approach, which entails several mandates contained in the EU Capital Requirements Regulation (CRR) with the objective of reducing the undue variability of risk-weighted assets (RWA) across IRB banks. It is EBA's expectation that on 1 January 2021 banks will be fully compliant with the new standards and guidelines put forward by these documents.

Finally, in late 2015, the ECB launched the targeted review of internal models (or TRIM), a large-scale project made of horizontal and on-site inspections with the objective of assessing whether the internal models currently used by banks comply with regulatory requirements and, in particular, are reliable and comparable. Moreover, it

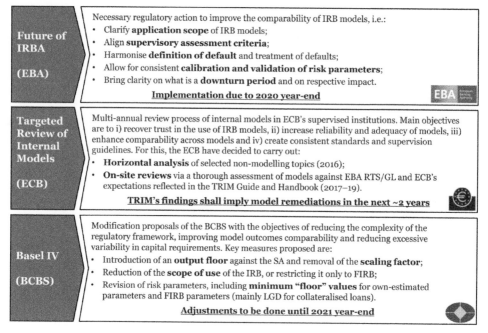

Figure 2.1: The answer to the loss of confidence in the IRB Approach by both regulators and supervisors

---

3   EBA/RTS/2016/03.
4   EBA/RTS/2016/06 and EBA/GL/2016/07.
5   EBA/GL/2017/16.

is ECB's intention to reduce inconsistencies and unwarranted variability when banks use internal models to calculate their RWA. In section 2.4 a short description of this exercise is presented, which should be finalised in 2019.

2.1 Introduction of the fundamentals of the IRB Approach (Basel II)

As mentioned before, the Basel Committee proposes two approaches to calculate credit risk RWA: the Standardised Approach (or SA) and the IRB Approach.

The IRB Approach, which is subject to explicit supervisory approval provided that certain minimum conditions are met, allows banks to use their own internal measures for key drivers of credit risk as primary inputs in determining the capital requirements. Basically, under this approach, exposures have to be classified into seven broad risk classes (Sovereigns, Banks, Corporate, Retail, Equity, items representing securitisation positions and other non-credit obligations assets) and risk weights (RW) are derived from weight functions defined by the Basel Committee, which are fed by the following risk parameters: PD, LGD and maturity (M), giving rise to a range of continuous values. Moreover, to the exposure value, the parameter Conversion Factor (CF) is applied, from which derives the concept of Exposure at Default (EAD) used in the RWA calculation.

For the estimation of those risk parameters, the Basel Committee defines two possible solutions (or variants): the Foundation (F-IRB), which requires banks to use only PD own estimates, relying on supervisory estimates for the remaining parameters, and the Advanced (A-IRB) one, where all parameters are estimated by banks. The credit risk mitigation framework of the Standardised Approach is also applicable to the IRB Approach, with a few additional features, in terms of, for instance, mitigants' eligibility or the possibility of using own-estimated haircuts over financial collaterals.

Another key aspect to emphasise in the IRB Approach is that capital requirements are meant to cover unexpected losses (UL) only, whereas expected losses (EL) are to be covered by loan loss provisions. In order to align both dimensions, it is in fact foreseen that in case of EL being lower than loan loss provisions such difference should be deducted to own funds, while the opposite may contribute to an increase of Tier 2 capital up to 0.6% of RWA.

2.1.1 A non-quantitative introduction to the IRB risk weight formula

As mentioned above, in the IRB Approach the risk weights for the capital requirements are calculated by using internal risk parameters – in comparison to the C-SA, which uses fixed risk weights based on exposure classes and, if applicable, external ratings. The calculation of the IRB risk weight is based on a so-called "Asymptotic Single Risk Factor" (ASRF), which refers to the work of Merton, Gordy and Vasicek.[6]

---

6 BCBS (2005) An Explanatory Note on the Basel II IRB Risk Weight Functions

Many bankers, supervisors or other interested people without a quantitative back-ground, often get a little bit scared when they see the formulas that are used to calculate the risk weights in the IRB Approach. But we believe that it is important to have at least a basic understanding of the theoretical background and the mechanics of the IRB formula. This is why we want to give a brief overview of the components of the IRB formula. We do not want to go into the mathematical detail of the IRB frame-work, but we would like to give a simplified overview of the theoretical background of the IRB framework. Based on our experience, this helps to understand better the inter-dependencies between certain requirements and how the Basel Committee's proposed changes interact with the original framework of 2004.

The overall goal of the IRB Approach is to quantify credit risk and calculate capital requirements that ensure that, even in rare circumstances, the bank has enough regu-latory capital to cover credit risk losses.

Since Basel II it has become standard to quantify credit risk with the calculation of the expected loss (EL). The expected loss is defined as the estimated potential loss for a credit or loan that can occur if the obligor of the position defaults.

Credit risk can be divided into three risk components which are all reflected in the EL:

- default risk,
- recovery risk, and
- exposure risk.

The first component refers to the probability that the obligor does not meet his obliga-tions anymore and fulfils the default definition (see section 2.4). Recovery risk refers to the loss that a bank must suffer in the case that the customer fulfils the definition of default. The loss is measured after collection efforts and is in general lower than the total exposure. The exposure is the maximum amount that a bank can lose in the case of default of a customer/position. Therefore the exposure risk refers to the uncertainty regarding the maximum future exposure that can be lost in the case of default. Since the introduction of Basel II, there is an industry standard of parameters that are used for the measurement of the three above mentioned credit risk/EL components. The three parameters are: the probability of default (PD), the loss given default (LGD) and the exposure at default (EAD). The following chapters include the exact definition for each parameter.

The amount of the expected loss and its components depend on the observed time horizon. The PD becomes higher the longer the observation period is, i.e. the PD in the next 12 month is always lower than that the probability that the obligor defaults in the next 24 month. In general, banks have to reassess the credit risk of a position or customer at least once a year and consider changes in the credit quality in their account-ing. Therefore, this is an industry standard and also adapted by the Basel Committee to consider the PD on a one-year horizon.

The relationship between time and the LGD is more complicated than between time and PD. This is because the LGD depends on several factors like the value of possible collateral that is used and the general economic situation of the obligor. Over time the loss can increase or decrease. Also, the relation between time and the EAD is more complicated. Especially in the case of off-balance sheet exposures like credit limits or guarantees, the amount of the exposure can change over time and therefore the credit risk/EL.

The calculation of EL is based on the following formula:

Equation 2.1

$$EL = PD \times LGD \times EAD \qquad\qquad (2.1)$$

The EL can be calculated both on a single contract level and on the portfolio level. All parameters are measured as averages based on historical default events.

From the perspective of a banking supervisor, the above mentioned EL can only be a first step in the calculation of capital requirements. The EL only quantifies the expected credit risk based on current macroeconomic circumstances. In reality, of course, the actual losses a bank suffers in one year never match the expected loss. It can be higher or lower. If the actual losses are higher than the EL, they are called unexpected losses.

As mentioned above, capital requirements must ensure that banks have not only in the "standard" scenario sufficient regulatory capital but also in "adverse" scenarios. From a supervisory perspective, the capital requirement should equal the unexpected loss or,

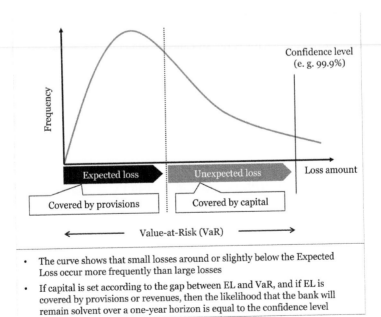

- The curve shows that small losses around or slightly below the Expected Loss occur more frequently than large losses
- If capital is set according to the gap between EL and VaR, and if EL is covered by provisions or revenues, then the likelihood that the bank will remain solvent over a one-year horizon is equal to the confidence level

Figure 2.2: EL vs UL on a portfolio basis

in other words, to the expected loss in an adverse scenario. The big question is, what is an adverse scenario? The Basel Committee defines the adverse scenario for credit risk that should be the basis for the calculation of capital requirements as a macroeconomic scenario with a probability of 0.01% or, in other words, the worst scenario that can happen only once every 1,000 years.

It is not possible to directly estimate the unexpected loss or the components that the unexpected loss would consist of. It is necessary to convert the EL into the unexpected loss based on a model. The Basel Committee has decided to use a model that does not directly convert the EL into the UL, but that can convert one or all parameters of the EL in a way that a confidence level of 99.9% is achieved. This UL can also be considered as the conditional EL. The condition is that the EL is based on a confidence level of 99.9%.

Equation 2.2

$$EL|y = 0.999 = PD|y = 0.999 \times LGD|y = 0.999 \times EAD|y = 0.999 \qquad (2.2)$$

With:

ELy = 0.999: Conditional EL based on a 99.9% confidence interval
PDy = 0.999: Conditional PD based on a 99.9% confidence interval
LGDy = 0.999: Conditional LGD based on a 99.9% confidence interval
EADy = 0.999: Conditional EAD based on a 99.9% confidence interval

The conditional PD can be calculated based on the Asymptotic Single Risk Factor (ASRF) model that is based on the work of Merton, Gordy and Vasicek. The general assumption of the ASRF is that the credit risk (the conditional PD) depends on two factors. The first factor is, of course, the individual credit (default) risk of the customer itself. If the PD of an obligor is already very high, the conditional PD will also be high. The second factor is the so-called systematic factor; the systematic risk factor represents the macroeconomic environment that influences the performance and therefore the credit (default) risk of the obligor. The systematic risk factor could represent industry risk.

Based on the ASRF model the PD of the obligor can be converted into a conditional PD based on the following formula.

Equation 2.3

$$PD|y = 0.999 = \Phi \left(\frac{\Phi^{-1}(PD_i) - \sqrt{\rho_i} \times \Phi^{-1}(0.999))}{\sqrt{1 - \rho_i}} \right) \qquad (2.3)$$

With:

PDy = 0.999: Conditional PD based on a 99.9% confidence interval
Φ: Standard normal distribution function
Φ^{-1}: Inverse standard normal distribution function
ρ_i: Asset correlation for customer i

The conversion of the LGD into a conditional LGD is possible based on the existing model, but according to the Basel Committee, the incorporation of these models into the Basel II framework would lead to too much complexity. That is why the Basel Committee goes for the LGD a more simplified way. The LGD that must be used for the calculation of capital requirements is a downturn LGD (LGD_{DT}) and therefore represents already an LGD in an adverse scenario (see also section 2.4.7).

The EAD is calculated by multiplying the current limit or outstanding amount with a credit conversion factor (CCF). While the CCF for on-balance sheet exposures is always 100% and does not change in different macroeconomic scenarios, the CCF for off-balance sheet exposures can vary between 0% and 100% and can be influenced by different macroeconomic environments. This means that CCFs lower than 100% should be converted into a conditional CCF similarly to the PD and LGD if the UL or the conditional EL has to be calculated.

The same simplification that is applied to the LGD is also applied to the CCF. Banks must always estimate downturn CCFs (CCF_{DT}) that reflect an adverse macroeconomic scenario. No models are applied on the conversion of the CCF into the conditional CCF.

Based on this, formula 2.2 can also be rewritten to:

Equation 2.4

$$EL_i | y = 0.999$$
$$= \left(\Phi \left(\frac{\Phi^{-1}(PD_i) - \sqrt{\rho_i} \times \Phi^{-1}(0.999)}{\sqrt{1 - \rho_i}} \right) \right) \times LGD_{DT,j} \times (E_j \times CCF_{DT,j}) \tag{2.4}$$

With:

ELy = 0.999: Conditional EL based on a 99.9% confidence interval
PD_i: PD of the customer i
$LGD_{DT,j}$: Downturn-LGD of the position j
$CCF_{DT,j}$: Downturn CCF of the position j
ρ_i: Asset correlation for customer i
E_j: Exposure of the position j

As mentioned above, according to the ASRF model, the conditional PD depends on two main components, the individual default risk of the customer (idiosyncratic risk) and the systematic risk. The conditional PD highly depends on how correlated customers are to the systematic risk factor. Not all customers depend in the same way on the systematic risk or macroeconomic environment as others. That is why the correlation parameter ρ_i is not a fixed value for all customers in a portfolio but a function. This function is calibrated differently for different exposure classes. Both intuition and empirical evidence indicate that customers with a higher default risk (PD) are less correlated to the systematic risk factor than customers with lower default risk. That is why the Basel Committee decides to include the PD as the main variable in the correlation functions.

For corporates, central sovereigns and institutions:	$R(PD) = 0.12 * \dfrac{1 - Exp(-50 * PD)}{1 - Exp(-50)} + 0.24 *$ $\left(1 - \dfrac{1 - Exp(-50 * PD)}{1 - Exp(-50)}\right)$
For SMEs	$R(PD) = 0.12 * \dfrac{1 - Exp(-50 * PD)}{1 - Exp(-50)} + 0.24 *$ $\left(1 - \dfrac{1 - Exp(-50 * PD)}{1 - Exp(-50)}\right) - 0.04 * \left(1 - \dfrac{S - 5}{45}\right)$
For retails: secured by a mortgage	$R(PD) = 0.15$
For retails: qualifying revolving	$R(PD) = 0.04$
For other retail	$R(PD) = 0.03 * \dfrac{1 - Exp(-35 * PD)}{1 - Exp(-35)} + 0.16 *$ $\left(1 - \dfrac{1 - Exp(-35 * PD)}{1 - Exp(-35)}\right)$
For specialised lending (high-volatility commercial real estate)	$R(PD) = 0.12 * \dfrac{1 - Exp(-50 * PD)}{1 - Exp(-50)} + 0.30 *$ $\left(1 - \dfrac{1 - Exp(-50 * PD)}{1 - Exp(-50)}\right)$

Figure 2.3: Overview of asset correlation formulas

Figure 2.3 shows the asset correlation equations based on the type of customers. For SMEs, there is a special size factor that must be considered.

For the calculation of capital requirements, the Basel Committee also introduced an adjustment factor for the maturity of a position. The economic rationale behind this maturity adjustment factor is that the credit risk for positions with a longer maturity is higher than for short-term positions. The calibration of the IRB formula assumes an average maturity of 2.5 years. The maturity adjustment factor was calibrated by the Basel Committee in a way that the risk weight increases with longer maturities and because the PD of the customer is also a variable in the adjustment factor, decreases with higher PD values. The maturity adjustment factor is one if the maturity is one.

Equation 2.5

$$MA_j = \frac{1 + (M_j - 2.5) \times (0.11852 - 0.05478 \times ln(PD_i))^2}{1 - 1.5 \times (0.11852 - 0.05478 \times ln(PD_i))^2} \tag{2.5}$$

With:

MA$_j$: Maturity adjustment for position j
  M$_j$: Maturity of position j
PD$_i$: PD of customer i

This adjustment factor is always 1 for retail positions.

We have almost arrived now at the RW formula that was introduced in Basel II. To get to the original formula we must return to the beginning of this chapter. We discussed that the Basel Committee wants to cover the conditionally expected losses for the purpose of capital requirements calculation. But banks already include their unconditional EL in their pricing and their risk provisions. If for capital requirements purposes the conditional EL is used, the EL part of the conditional EL is covered twice, once by risk provisions or interest income and again by the capital requirements.

That is the reason why in the final risk weight formula of the Basel Committee, the EL is deducted from the conditional EL.

The final risk weight formula introduced by Basel II is:

Equation 2.6

$$EL_i|y = 0.999$$

$$= \left(\left\{ \left(\Phi \left(\frac{\Phi^{-1}(PD_i) - \sqrt{\rho_i} \times \Phi^{-1}(0.999))}{\sqrt{1 - \rho_i}} \right) \right) \times LGD_{DT,j} \right\} \right.$$

$$\left. -(PD_i \times LGD_{DT,j}) \right) \times (E_j \times CCF_{DT,j}) \times MA_j \qquad (2.6)$$

With:

$ELy = 0.999$:   Conditional EL based on a 99.9% confidence interval
PD_i: PD of the customer i
$LGD_{DT,j}$:   Downturn-LGD of the position j
$CCF_{DT,j}$:   Downturn CCF of the position j
ρ_i: Asset correlation for customer i
MA_j: Maturity adjustment for position j
E_j: Exposure of the position j

Equation 2.6 still looks quite complicated. But, with the background information provided above, mechanics become hopefully clearer without the need to understand all the mathematical details. If you want to explain the IRB risk weight formula in one sentence (of course without being 100% mathematical) then you might say:

The IRB formula calculates the additional EL that occurs if the macroeconomic environment that influences the credit risk of an obligor or portfolio changes to an adverse scenario that can happen only once every 1,000 years.

2.1.2 The adoption of the IRB Approach

While recognising that for several reasons the IRB Approach implementation across all risk classes and business units at the same time may not be practicable, the Basel Committee introduced in the Basel II framework several flexible conditions as an incentive, namely the possibility of first adopting the IRB Approach for selected, yet material, risk classes or business units as long as all exposures belonging to a risk class in a single business line are submitted to this approach ("cherry picking" prevention), and there is a rollout plan which dictates to what extent and when the IRB Approach is adopted to all risk classes and business units.

Additionally, subject to supervisory approval, some exposures in non-significant business units and risk classes that are immaterial in terms of size, perceived risk profile and number of counterparties may be exempt from the IRB Approach, if it is proved to be unduly burdensome for banks to implement a rating system for these counterparties – the so-called permanent partial use (PPU).

Another lenient condition was set for the Specialised Lending sub-classes where banks unable to meet the PD estimation requirements can map internal grades to five supervisory categories, each of which is associated with a specific RW (usually known as the Supervisory Slotting Criteria Approach – SSCA).

The demarcation made between F-IRB and A-IRB banks reflects the awareness that feasible data limitations can undermine the immediate fulfilment of the minimum standards set for the adoption of own estimates of LGD and CF in all portfolios. Conversely, once a more advanced approach is adopted, the return to a less sophisticated one should be approved by the supervisor.

2.1.3 Calculation of RWA and EL

Under the IRB Approach, RW (and EL) are determined from the following risk weight functions[7] and risk parameters values:

RW applicable to claims on Sovereigns, Banks and Corporates

According to Basel II framework, the RW for the exposure classes sovereigns, banks and corporates are determined as follows.

RW function[8]

Equation 2.7

$$RW = \frac{LGD \times N\left[\frac{G(PD)}{\sqrt{1-R}} + \sqrt{\frac{R}{1-R}} \times G(0.999)\right] - PD \times LGD}{1 - 1.5 \times b}$$
$$\times [1 + (M - 2.5) \times b] \times 12.5 \times 1.06 \tag{2.7}$$

7   See BCBS (2005), "An Explanatory Note on the Basel II IRB Risk Weight Functions", BIS.
8   The equation used in this section is slightly different than in section 2.1.1. This is due to the different purpose of the sections. In section 2.1.1 we give a non-quantitative overview of the IRB risk weight formula, while in this section we want to present all used RW formulas. Therefore we used equations in this section that are in their notation closer to those in the original Basel II paper. Nevertheless the formulas are equivalent.

With:

PD: Probability of default
R: Function of asset correlation (to be determined by exposure/asset class)
LGD: Downturn Loss given default
M: Maturity

$N(x)$ denotes the cumulative distribution function for a standard normal random variable.

$G(Z)$ denotes the inverse cumulative distribution function for a standard normal random variable.

b denotes in Equation 2.7 the maturity adjustment factor, which is defined as

Equation 2.8

$$(0.11852 - 0.05478 \times \ln(PD))^2 \qquad (2.8)$$

With:

PD: Probability of default

For PD = 0, RW is 0. For defaulted exposures (PD = 1), the RW is 0 for banks using regulatory LGD values. In the case of using the advanced IRB Approach, the risk weight must be calculated using this formula.

Equation 2.9

$$RW = Max\{0; 12.5 \times (LGD - EL_{BE})\} \qquad (2.9)$$

With:

RW: Risk weight for defaulted exposures
EL_{BE}: Expected loss best estimate corresponding to the bank's best estimate of EL for defaulted exposures,
LGD: Downturn LGD

The correlation used in above formula (2.7) is a function of the PD.

Equation 2.10

$$R = 0.12 \times \left(\frac{1 - exp\{-50 \times PD\}}{1 - exp\{-50\}} \right) + 0.24 \times \left(1 - \frac{(1 - exp\{-50 \times PD\})}{1 - exp\{-50\}} \right)$$

$$(2.10)$$

With:

PD: Probability of default
R: Asset correlation

For exposures to companies[9] where total annual sales for the consolidated group of which the company is a part is less than 50 million euros, the following correlation formula should be used:

Equation 2.11

$$R = 0.12 \times \left(\frac{1 - exp\{-50 \times PD\}}{1 - exp\{-50\}} \right) + 0.24 \times \left(1 - \frac{(1 - exp\{-50 \times PD\})}{1 - exp\{-50\}} \right)$$
$$- 0.04 \times \left(1 - \frac{S - 5}{45} \right) \tag{2.11}$$

With:

PD: Probability of default
 R: Asset correlation
 S: Size: S is expressed as total annual sales in millions of euros. For sales less than 5 million euros, S shall be 5.

Specialised lending exposures

Specialised lending (SL) exposures should be mapped to five sub-classes: project finance (PF), object finance (OF), commodities finance (CF), income-producing real estate (IPRE), and high-volatility commercial real estate (HVCRE).

Banks not meeting the IRB Approach requirements for PD estimation for the sub-exposure class specialised lending must apply the Supervisory Slotting Criteria Approach (SSCA). This means, they will be required to map their internal ratings grades to five supervisory categories, each of which is associated with a specific RW (except for HVCRE) (see Table 2.1).

Regarding HVCRE, the above stated RW should be that shown in Table 2.2.

Banks that meet the requirements for the estimation of PD are able to use the F-IRB applicable to corporate exposures to derive RW for all classes of SL sub-classes, except

Remaining Maturity	Category 1	Category 2	Category 3	Category 4	Category 5
Less than 2.5 years (national discretion)	50%	70%	115% (only CRR)	250% (only CRR)	0% (only CRR)
Greater than or equal to 2.5 years	70%	90%	115%	250%	0%

Table 2.1: RW for specialised lending (except HVCRE) exposures per category and maturity

---

9 Based on the annual turnover criterion, this condition should be capturing SME only, whose definition for EU countries in stated in Commission Recommendation 2003/361/EC of 6 May 2003 concerning the definition of micro, small and medium-sized enterprises.

Remaining Maturity	Category 1	Category 2	Category 3	Category 4	Category 5
Less than 2.5 years (national discretion)	70%	95%	N/A	N/A	N/A
Greater than or equal to 2.5 years	95%	120%	140%	250%	0%

Table 2.2: RW for HVCRE exposures per category and maturity

HVCRE. At national discretion, banks meeting the requirements for HVCRE exposure are able to use a F-IRB that is similar in all respects to the corporate approach, with the exception of the applied R as described in Equation 2.12.

Equation 2.12

$$R = 0.12 \times \left(\frac{1 - exp\{-50 \times PD\}}{1 - exp\{-50\}} \right) + 0.3 \times \left(1 - \frac{(1 - exp\{-50 \times PD\})}{1 - exp\{-50\}} \right) \quad (2.12)$$

With:

PD: Probability of default

R: Asset correlation

Banks that meet the requirements for the estimation of PD, LGD and EAD are able to use the A-IRB to corporate exposures to derive RW for all classes of SL sub-classes, except HVCRE. At national discretion, banks meeting these requirements for HVCRE exposure are able to use an A-IRB that is similar in all respects to the corporate approach, with the exception of applying the R as presented in Equation 2.6.

RW applicable to claims on retail[10]

According to Basel II framework, the RW for retail exposures are determined as follows.

RW function

Equation 2.13

$$RW = \left\{ LGD \times N \left[\frac{G(PD)}{\sqrt{1 - R}} + \sqrt{\frac{R}{1 - R}} \times G(0.999) \right] - PD \times LGD \right\} \times 12.5 \times 1.06$$

$$(2.13)$$

---

10 To be eligible for the Retail risk class, an exposure should meet the following criteria:
  • Be either to an individual person, or to a SME, provided in the latter case that the total amount owed to the banking group, including any past due exposure, by the obligor client or group of connected clients, but excluding claims or contingent claims secured on residential real estate collateral, shall not, to the knowledge of the bank exceed 1 million euros.
  • Be treated by the bank in its risk management consistently over time and in a similar manner.
  • Not be managed just as individually as exposures in the Corporate risk class.
  • Represent one of a significant number of similarly managed exposures.

With:

PD: Probability of default
R: Function of asset correlation (to be determined by exposure/asset class)
LGD: Loss given default

$N(x)$ denotes the cumulative distribution function for a standard normal random variable.

$G(Z)$ denotes the inverse cumulative distribution function for a standard normal random variable.

For PD = 0, RW is 0. For defaulted exposures (PD = 1), the RW is set by formula 2.3.

Correlation (R)

Exposures secured by mortgages on housing or property for office/commerce: 0.15.

Qualifying revolving retail exposures (QRRE)[11]: 0.04.

For other exposures:

Equation 2.14

$$R = 0.03 \times \left(\frac{1 - exp\{-35 \times PD\}}{1 - exp\{-35\}} \right) + 0.16 \times \left(1 - \frac{(1 - exp\{-35 \times PD\})}{1 - exp\{-35\}} \right)$$

(2.14)

With:

PD: Probability of default
R: Asset correlation

RW applicable to equity exposures[12]

Banks shall determine their RWA for equity exposures, excluding those deducted to own funds, in accordance with the following approaches:

- simple risk weight approach,
- PD/LGD approach, and
- internal models approach.

---

11 Exposures that meet cumulatively the following conditions:
- Are to individuals.
- Are revolving, unsecured, and to the extent they are not drawn immediately and unconditionally, cancellable by the bank.
- The maximum exposure to a single individual in the sub-portfolio is 100,000euros or less.
- The bank can demonstrate that the use of the correlation of this point is limited to portfolios that have exhibited low volatility of loss rates, relative to their average level of loss rates, especially within the low PD bands.

12 In general, equity exposures include both direct and indirect ownership interests, whether voting or non-voting, in the assets and income of a corporate or a financial institution that is not consolidated or deducted to own funds. They should meet all of the following requirements:
- It is irredeemable in the sense that the return of invested funds can be achieved only by the sale of the investment or sale of the rights to the investment or by the liquidation of the issuer.
- It does not embody an obligation on the part of the issuer.
- It conveys a residual claim on the assets or income of the issuer.

A bank may apply different approaches to different equity portfolios where the itself uses different approaches for internal risk management purposes. Where a bank uses different approaches, the choice of the PD / LGD approach or the internal models approach shall be made consistently, including over time, and shall not be determined by regulatory arbitrage considerations.

Simple risk weight approach

The Basel Committee prescribed that a 300% RW is to be applied to equity holdings that are publicly traded and a 400% RW to all other equity holdings. A publicly traded holding is defined as any equity security traded on a recognised security exchange.

There is, however, a significant divergence compared to the CRR, where RW for equity exposures are equivalent to:

- 190% for private equity exposures insufficiently diversified portfolios,
- 290% for exchange-traded equity exposures, and
- 370% for all other equity exposures.

PD/LGD approach

RW are calculated according to the function presented in section 2.1.2.1.

Internal models approach

The RWA amount is the potential loss on the bank's equity exposures as derived using internal Value-at-Risk (VaR) models subject to the 99th percentile, the one-tailed confidence interval of the difference between quarterly returns and appropriate risk-free rate computed over a long-term sample period, multiplied by 12.5.

PD, LGD, CF and M values for F-IRB banks

PD values shall be 100% in case of default and are subject to the general floor of 0.03% in case of exposures to Banks, Corporate and Retail counterparties.

F-IRB banks should use the following LGD values:

- Senior exposures without eligible collateral: 45%;
- Subordinated exposures without eligible collateral: 75%;
- Exposures with funded protection[13]: LGD values can be reduced depending on the type of protection and the collateralisation level.

---

13 To be eligible for recognition the assets relied upon should be sufficiently liquid and their value over time stable enough to provide appropriate certainty as to the credit protection achieved. Moreover, the bank should have the right to liquidate or retain, in a timely manner, the assets from which the protection derives in the event of default, insolvency or bankruptcy of the obligor, or other credit event set out in the transaction documentation and, where applicable, of the custodian holding the collateral.

Remaining Maturity	LGD for senior exposure	LGD for subordinated exposures	Required min. collateralisation level (C*)	Required min. collateralisation level (C**)
Receivables	35%	65%	0%	125%
Residential/ commercial RE	35%	65%	30%	140%
Other collateral	40%	70%	30%	140%

Table 2.3: Minimum LGD for secured parts of exposures

- While in the case of financial collaterals, both the collateral and the exposure (whenever applicable) are subject to a set of volatility adjustments or haircuts (e.g. applicable to the underlying asset, currency mismatch) which can be own-estimated or provided by the CRR (supervisory haircuts), for other funded forms of protection LGD are determined as shown in Table 2.3.[14]

Just to give an example of how C* and C** are applied in practice, please see the following examples.

Consider an exposure (E) of 1.2 million euros to a corporate entity under the F-IRB that is collateralised by a residential real estate property (first lien) with a market value of 1.4 million euros. This means that up to 1 million euros (1.4 million euros divided by the C** of 140%) the applicable LGD is 30%, while for the remaining part of the exposure of 0.2 million euros, a LGD of 45% (for senior unsecured exposures) shall apply.

In the same example, if the market value of another residential real estate property that replaced the previous one in the final loan agreement is of 0.3 million (i.e. below C*, corresponding to 30% of 1.2 million euros), the total exposure of 1.2 million euros should be subject to a LGD of 45%, meaning that no credit risk mitigation effect is to be recognised at all.

- Exposures with unfunded protection[15]: provided certain eligibility and minimum requirements are fulfilled, the PD of the obligor may be replaced by the one of the guarantors.

Regarding CF, depending on the level of risk assigned to each off-balance sheet item, it may range between 0% (low risk) and 100% (high risk).

---

14   Where the required level of collateralisation C** is not achieved in respect of the exposure as a whole, banks shall consider the exposure to be two exposures – one corresponding to the part in respect of which the required level of collateralisation C** is achieved and one corresponding to the remainder. It should be stated that when the ratio of the value of the collateral (C) to the exposure value (E) is below C*, LGD shall be the one applicable for uncollateralised exposures.

15   To be eligible for recognition the party giving the undertaking shall be sufficiently reliable, and the protection agreement legally effective and enforceable in the relevant jurisdictions, to provide appropriate certainty as to the credit protection achieved.

As a general rule, F-IRBA banks should assign an M of 2.5 years,

Equity exposures subject to PD/LGD approach

PD are determined according to the methods for corporate exposures.

All exposures should be allocated an LGD of 90%, with the exception of private equity exposures in sufficiently diversified portfolios, which should be assigned an LGD of 65% (only according to the CRR). M is set at 5 years.

EL

Generally speaking, EL shall equal to the product of PD, LGD and EAD. This amount shall then be compared with the loan loss provisions, meaning that in case of EL is lower than loan loss provisions such difference should be deducted from own funds, while the opposite may contribute to an increase of Tier 2 capital up to 0.6% of RWA.

Regarding SL exposures under the SSCA, EL amount shall be obtained by multiplying 8% by the RWA produced from the below stated RW multiplied by EAD (Table 2.4).

In the case of equity exposures, EL shall be 0 in the Internal models approach and dictated by the CRR in the Simple risk weight approach (0, 0.4%, 2.8%, 8% or 50% depending on the category and remaining maturity). In the PD/LGD approach, PD × LGD × EAD also applies. The main difference in the equity exposures is that EL shall always (entirely) be deducted from own funds.

2.1.4 Minimum conditions for entry and ongoing use

To ensure credibility, consistency, reliability and accuracy of both internal rating systems and risk estimates for each grade or facility, while providing significant comparability across banks, the Basel Committee determined that the IRB Approach permission is continuously conditional on supervisors' satisfaction that the banks' credit risk measurement and management systems are sound and appropriate, implemented with integrity and meet the following standards:

- Rating systems provide for a proper assessment of obligors and transactions characteristics, meaningful risk differentiation and accurate and consistent risk estimates.

SL exposures	Category 1	Category 2	Category 3	Category 4	Category 5
All, but HVCRE	5% (0% national description)	10% (5% national description)	35%	100%	625%
HVCRE	5%	5%	35%	100%	625%

Table 2.4: RW for SL exposures for the calculation of EL

- Internal ratings and estimates of default and loss used in the calculation of capital requirements play a crucial role in risk management, credit approval, internal capital allocation and corporate governance of the bank – the so-called "use test" requirement.
- The existence of an independent credit risk control unit responsible for the rating systems.
- Collection and storage of all relevant data to provide effective support to the credit risk measurement and management processes.
- Adequate internal validation and full documentation of the rating systems.

The fulfilment of these standards should be in accordance with a set of minimum conditions defined by the Basel Committee pertaining to four areas: rating systems, risk quantification, internal validation, and corporate governance and oversights.

Rating systems

Rating dimensions for Sovereigns, Banks and Corporate exposures

A rating system should take into account two separate and distinct dimensions, reflecting:

- The risk of obligor default, meaning that separate exposures to the same obligor should be assigned to the same obligor grade.
- Transaction-specific factors (e.g. collateral, seniority, product type). For F-IRB Approach banks, this condition can be met via the use of a facility dimension, which reflects both obligor and transaction factors. For A-IRB Approach banks, facility ratings should reflect LGD only.

Rating dimensions for Retail exposures

- Banks should consider, at least, the following risk drivers when assigning exposures to a pool: obligor risk characteristics (e.g. obligor type, demographics), transaction risk characteristics, including product and/or collateral types, and delinquency of exposure.

Rating structure for Sovereigns, Banks and Corporate exposures

- The obligor rating scale should have a minimum of seven grades for non-defaulted obligors and one grade for those that have defaulted.
- There should exist a meaningful distribution of obligors across grades (avoiding excessive concentration within a grade), on both its obligor-rating and facility-rating scales.

Rating structure for Retail exposures

- Banks should give quantitative measures of loss characteristics (PD, LGD and CF) per pool.
- The level of differentiation should ensure that the number of exposures in a given pool is sufficient to allow for meaningful quantification and validation of the loss characteristics.
- There should be a meaningful distribution of obligors and exposures across pools.

Rating criteria

Banks should have rating definitions, processes and criteria for assigning exposures to grades within a rating system. The grade definition should include a description of the degree of default risk typical for obligors assigned to that grade and the criteria used to distinguish the level of risk. These criteria should be sufficiently detailed to allow those charged with assigning ratings to consistently assign the same grade to obligors or facilities of similar risk as well as being consistent with the bank's lending policies for handling troubled obligors or facilities.

Use of models

Whenever banks use statistical models or other mechanical methods to assign exposures to grades or pools, they should demonstrate that:

- There is a process for vetting data inputs into the model, which includes an assessment of the accuracy, completeness and appropriateness of the data.
- Data used to build the model are representative of the bank's obligors or facilities.
- Each model has good predictive power, and that capital requirement are not distorted as a result of its use. The variables input to the model should form a reasonable set of predictors.
- There is a regular cycle of model validation that monitors models' performance and stability, reviews model relationships and tests model outputs against outcomes.
- Statistical models are complemented by human judgment and oversight to review the ratings assigned and to ensure that models are used appropriately.

Documentation

Banks should document their rating system's design and operational details, and prove compliance with the IRB Approach conditions. In particular, documentation should address topics such as portfolio segmentation, rating criteria, definition of rating exceptions (including who can approve them), duties of the parties that rate obligors or facilities, frequency of rating reviews and management oversight of the rating process, including the internal control structure.

Rating operations

Minimum conditions for risk rating system operations cover both the rating process and the surrounding environment of the rating system, and include:

- **Rating coverage:** each obligor and recognised guarantor should be assigned a rating/pool and each exposure should be linked to a facility rating as part of the loan approval process.
- **Rating process integrity:** rating assignments and periodic reviews should be approved by a party that does not directly stand to benefit from the extension of credit.
- **Overrides:** when banks use rating models, individuals are generally permitted to override the results under certain conditions and within tolerance levels for frequency. In such circumstances, banks should clearly define the situations in which overrides of the rating process can occur, including how and to what extent they can be used and by whom.
- **Data maintenance:** banks should collect/store data on obligors and facility characteristics (including rating histories and default data) to provide effective support to internal credit risk measurement and management processes, enabling them to meet the other IRB Approach minimum conditions and serve as a basis for supervisory reporting.
- **Stress tests:** banks should carry out stress tests to identify possible events or future changes in economic conditions that could have adverse effects on the banks' credit exposures and the assessment of the banks' ability to withstand such changes.

Risk quantification

Rating quantification is the process of assigning values to the risk components: PD, LGD, CF and M. With the exception of M, the risk components are unobservable and should be estimated or can be provided by the supervisor (regulatory defined parameters).

Overall estimation requirements are that internal estimates:

- Should incorporate all relevant and available data information and methods; yet, the fewer data a bank has, the more conservative it should be in the estimates.
- May be based on internal or external data, provided that, in the latter case, a strong link is proved between i) the bank's process of assigning exposures to a pool and the one used by the external source, and ii) the bank's internal risk profile and the composition of the external data.
- Should be representative of long-run experience.

Other specific requirements for quantifying risk include the following:

- **Definition of default:** a default[16] occurs with regard to a particular obligor when either or both of the two following events have taken place:
  - An obligor is past due more than 90 days on any material credit obligation to the banking group. Overdrafts are past due once the client has breached an advised limit.
  - The bank considers that the obligor is unlikely to pay in full its credit obligations, without recourse to actions such as realising security (if any).
- **Re-ageing:** the criteria for returning to a clean status without the integral payment of principal, interests and fees due should be clearly defined.
- **PD estimation:** PD estimates should be a long-run average of one-year realised default rates for obligors in the same grade. The length of the underlying historical observation period should be at least five years. In this process, banks can use one or a mix of the three specific techniques: internal default experience,[17] mapping to external data,[18] and statistical default approaches.[19]
- **Definition of loss:** LGD should be estimated using the concept of economic loss, which captures the value of recoveries and costs discounted to the time of default.
- **LGD estimation:** banks should estimate LGD for each facility, reflecting economic downturn[20] conditions, where necessary, to capture the relevant risks. LGD cannot be less than the long-run default-weighted average loss rate given default calculated based on the average economic loss of all observed defaults within the data source for that type of facility. Issues such as the control or dependence on the collateral and currency mismatches should be addressed conservatively.
- **CF estimation:** CF should be estimated for each facility on the basis of the long-run default-weighted average, reflecting economic downturn conditions, where necessary, to capture the relevant risks. CF should consider the possibility of additional drawings by the obligor up to, and after, the time a default event is triggered as well as specific policies and procedures related to account monitoring and payment processing.
- **Both LGD and CF estimation:** five and seven years are the minimum data-observation periods allowed for estimates for Retail and for Sovereign, Banks and Corporate exposures, respectively.

---

16 In case of retail exposures, the definition of default may be applied at a facility level.
17 The pool PD for a risk bucket is estimated using historical data on the frequency of defaults among obligors assigned to that bucket.
18 Pool PD are calculated from external data and then mapped to internal grades.
19 Statistical models are used to estimate a PD for each obligor assigned to a risk bucket, being that the pooled PD is then computed as the average (or mean) of the obligor-specific PD.
20 A downturn LGD differs from a realised one in the sense that the latter derives only from observed losses discounted to the time of default for each defaulted exposure in the reference data set, not including any adjustment appropriate for an economic downturn.

Internal validation

Banks are expected to provide continuously sound and accurate predictive and forward-looking estimates of PD, LGD and CF parameters. Thus, they should implement robust systems to validate the rating systems and processes and estimate relevant risk parameters. In addition, supervisors should be satisfied that banks' validation process enables them to assess the performance of rating and risk estimation systems for the risk parameters and the rating process consistently and meaningfully.

Starting with the rating system assessment, the model design validation should include, for instance, a qualitative review of the statistical model building technique, the relevance of the data used to build the model for the banks' specific business segment, the way the risk factors inputs to the models were selected, and whether they are economically meaningful.

In the analysis of PD, LGD and CF estimates, two validation tools acquire relevance:

- **Backtesting:** use of statistical methods to compare realised outcomes (*ex-post*) with estimated (*ex-ante*) parameters (PD, LGD and CF) for a comparable and homogeneous data set.
- **Benchmarking:** comparison of internal estimates across banks and/or with external benchmarks (e.g. external ratings, vendor models, models developed by supervisory authorities).

Focusing on the PD validation, where validation methodologies are still more advanced than those for LGD and CF, three stages should be considered:

- Validating the technique for estimating pooled PD, which depends on the approach(es) used to estimate the pooled PD and has the purpose of assessing the fulfilment of the above-mentioned PD estimation requirements. Moreover, as the dynamic of reported PD is a function of how default events are predicted ("properties of obligor-specific PD")[21] and how the bank assigns obligors to risk buckets ("rating philosophy")[22], both dimensions should be properly dealt with when evaluating the accuracy of reported PD.
- Validating the discriminatory power of a rating system: the discriminatory power expresses the rating system's ability to correctly distinguish *ex-ante* between defaulting and non-defaulting obligors. It can be assessed using a number of statistical measures of discrimination, among which the cumulative accuracy profile

---

21 An obligor-specific PD may include information relevant to assess the obligor's ability to pay its debt as well as information about the economic environment in which the obligor interacts. Thus, obligor's PD can be stressed (stable over the business cycle) or unstressed.

22 It relates to the timing and the context of the information used in assigning ratings to obligors. Ratings can be Point-in-Time (PIT), which tends to change over the business cycle, or Through-the-Cycle (TTC), therefore stable over the business cycle.

(CAP) curve,[23] the Gini coefficient[24] or the Receiver Operating Characteristic (ROC) curve.[25]

- Validating the accuracy of the PD quantification ("calibration"): this involves comparing realised default rates with estimated pool PD to detect if deviations are purely random or occur systematically using statistical techniques. Few approaches are currently being used, such as the binomial tests[26] and the traffic light approach.[27]
- Validating the stability of the rating system, which implies examining the changes in the:
- discriminatory power of a model given forecasting horizons of varying length and in the discriminatory power as loans become older;
- general conditions underlying the use of the model and their effects on individual model parameters and on the results the model generates.

The validation of LGD estimates should center on an assessment of the factors that are needed to estimate LGD. This includes looking at definitions of default and loss used, assumptions made to construct the reference data set, calculation of the realised LGD, an approach for estimating LGD and the compliance with the minimum conditions set for LGD. When validating CF estimates the following qualitative topics should be emphasised: criteria by which CF are estimated, the breakdown of material CF drivers, systems and procedures in place to monitor balances outstanding, and the banks' ability to allow further drawings in the circumstances short of actual default.

Regarding the assessment of the rating process,[28] the following issues should be considered.

- **Data quality:** it is a key issue to ensure accurate and reliable estimation of risk parameters. The validation of data quality requires assessing, among other things, how data are sourced, stored and processed, the data supervision and control system, and the IT infrastructure.

---

23 With all obligors ranked from the worst to the best ratings, the CAP curve is constructed by plotting the cumulative percentage of defaulters on one axis and the cumulative percentage of all obligors on the other. A perfect rating curve would rise linearly and then become horizontal because it would assign the worst ratings to all defaulting obligors and the best ratings to the non-defaulting ones. The closer the CAP curve is to the perfect rating curve, the better the discriminatory power.

24 It gives the proportion of the area under the CAP curve to the area under the perfect curve. This coefficient ranges between 0 (random model) and 1 (perfect model) and depends on the homogeneity of the portfolio (credit quality range) and on the sample size, in particular the number of defaults.

25 Like the CAP, the ROC curve is a visual tool, but of a slightly more complex construction. Based on two representative samples of scores, defaulted and non-defaulted, the concavity of the ROC is equivalent to the conditional probabilities of default being a decreasing function of the underlying scores or ratings and non-concavity indicates sub-optimal use of information in the specification of the score function. The ROC measure (or AUROC) is a linear transformation of the Accuracy Ratio, ranging between 0.5 (random model) and 1 (perfect model).

26 It uses the binomial distribution of default events in different rating grades and compares them with PD estimates to assess calibration.

27 It uses a multinomial distribution of various levels of deviations between predicted and realised default rates over time to infer whether PD are well calibrated.

28 Though quantitative techniques are useful, especially for the data quality assessment, the validation of the rating process is mainly qualitative in nature.

- **Internal reporting:** the reporting system should allow its recipients (e.g. board of directors, originating areas) to carry out a proper analysis of a bank's credit risk profile.

How problems are handled and the rating system is used (use test or "control expectations"): the more internal ratings or scores and IRB Approach estimates are used in a bank's decision-making process, the more confidence management (and supervisors) will have in their reliability. The validation of this requirement should include a full assessment of the divergence detected in estimates for regulatory and economic capital purposes.

Corporate governance and oversight

The conditions set in this field focus mainly on three areas.

- **Corporate governance:** all material aspects of the rating and estimation processes should be approved by the bank's board of directors and senior management. The latter should also have a good understanding of rating systems' design and operation to ensure that all components of the IRB system, including controls, are functioning properly. Information provided to these bodies should be sufficiently detailed to allow them to confirm the continuing appropriateness of the bank's rating approach and to verify the adequacy of the controls supporting the rating system.
- **Credit risk control units:** functionally independent from the staff and management responsible for originating credit exposures, these units are responsible for the design or selection, implementation and performance of internal rating systems.
- **The internal and external audit:** which should review at least annually the bank's rating systems and its operations, including the functioning of the credit risk function and the estimation of PD, LGD and CF.

2.1.5 Approval and post-approval process: Home/host coordination

The supervisory authorities soon faced the reality that in cross-border banking groups, some models were centrally developed based on group-wide principles and guidelines, but (many) others were to be designed for each subsidiary taking into consideration local specificities (e.g. default rates, underwriting standards, legal enforceability, policies and strategies adopted in respect of account monitoring and payment processing). This implies that for getting any approval at consolidated level, the supervisors of all involved geographies have to combine their efforts and harmonise (as best they can) their views and criteria.

At EU level, the CRD IV regulates the supervisory application process in case of EU cross-border groups (or subgroups), requiring supervisors to work together in deciding whether or not to grant the permission sought and defining the terms and conditions, if any, to which the permission should be subject, within a six-month time period. This period starts on the date of receipt of the complete application by the authority responsible for the supervision on a consolidated basis (also called "home supervisor"), which without delay shall forward it to the remaining authorities (the "host supervisors"). Although supervisory authorities are compelled to make their best efforts to reach a joint decision on the application within six months, the absence of a consensus grants the home supervisor the power to decide on the application on its own, with such decision being legally binding for host supervisors.

2.1.6 Decision for application

When deciding whether to target the IRB Approach, banks had to take into account not only the potential impact this decision might have on capital ratios but also several other financial and non-financial issues, including reputation and cultural change. Knowing where the bank stands and the efforts it will be required to make in order to reach (and uphold) a compliant position, along with the many other ordinary changes in the bank's organisation and business, is, thus, the starting point.

The move to an A-IRB Approach entails a significant modification, and with it comes a high cost, dictated by inter alia data availability challenges, documentation creation and collection, complex model requirements and the essential strong co-ordination of internal efforts (e.g. IT, finance, risk, commercial areas). Changes in the IT systems and business policies, processes and procedures, as well as human resources preparation (implying hiring more qualified staff and enhancing training programs), are inevitable and take time. In parallel, two risks should be properly assessed: the risk of failure ("near-compliant IRB Approach") with repercussions in the marketplace, namely stock devaluation and loss of reputation to the regulator and rating agencies, and the risk of rework due to supervisory validation uncertainty. Lastly, once the approval is granted, there are several maintenance costs to be absorbed, since the risk infrastructure has to be kept operating, expecting rising standards in areas such as data quality and integrity, model design, management reports, validation and control environment.

The expectation of capital requirements reduction appears at the front-line of the main advantages of using the IRB Approach. Banks will also be able to build on the reputation of having sound risk-management skills, an increasingly important issue for banks' stakeholders lately. From a strategic perspective, a robust risk framework can provide a source of competitive advantage, as the improvement in data quality and usage, models' predictiveness and risk-reward management culture enhances risk consciousness and, in turn, promotes a better decision-making process. Pricing aligned with the risk incurred, risk mitigation optimisation and client value vis-à-vis portfolio management are drivers of business.

2.2 Basel Committee's initiatives to improve the IRB Approach

2.2.1 Introduction

Starting in 2012, the Basel Committee has been planning to revamp the IRB Approach to capital requirements estimation for credit risk. Maintaining a balance between simplicity, comparability and risk sensitivity has always been the goal of the Basel Committee. The BCBS believes that the IRB Approach has become unduly complex, resulting in negative consequences, which include the following:

- difficulties for internal management in understanding the regulatory regime, the risk profile of the bank and to properly perform capital planning;
- hampering the ability of investors to understand and properly evaluate the risk profiles of banks;
- hampering the ability of regulators to evaluate the capital adequacy of banks;
- increasing the likelihood of false accuracy in the assessment of risk (i.e. model risk);
- opportunities for banks' management and employees to game the regulatory requirements in order to minimise risk-weighted assets;
- diminished comparability of risk estimates.

The aim of the BCBS is to restore credibility in the calculations of RWA and also to simplify the Basel standards and to improve comparability of internal risk estimates. The view that the comparability of internal risk estimates has been undermined was further supported by the results of the Regulatory Consistency Assessment Programme (RCAP), which BCBS began to use in order to monitor the adoption of Basel standards across internationally active banks. The studies conducted as part of the RCAP concluded that there is significant variation in RWA for credit risk among IRB banks, especially for non-retail portfolios (sovereign, bank, corporate). A hypothetical benchmarking exercise concluded that adjusting individual bank risk weights for these portfolios to the median could result in increases or decreases in capital ratios by as much as 1.5–2 percentage units (or 15–20% in relative terms).

Whereas the role of the EBA is to clarify the technical aspects of IRB models within the European Union, the Basel Committee is more focused on clarifying the more general aspects of the IRB framework, especially its scope of application with respect to low-default portfolios. As a result of the shortcomings identified by the Basel Committee and a wide range of stakeholders, there will be a constraint on the use of internal models and also a revised capital floor for IRB-portfolios. The amendments can be broken down into three categories, and are outlined in Table 2.5 and the ensuing sections.

2.2.2 Scope of application of internal models

It is widely understood that the reliability of internal models largely depends on the quantity and quality of underlying data, as well as the modelling choices made by the development team. When data is scarce, general model development techniques that

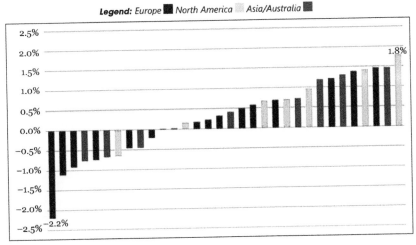

Legend: *Europe* ■ *North America* ▨ *Asia/Australia* ■

Figure 2.4: Change from a 10% hypothetical capital ratio when individual banks' risk weights are adjusted to the median in the sample

Category	Description
Scope of use of internal models	Removing the use of IRB Approach for equities. Removing the use of A-IRB Approach for banks, other financial institutions (including insurance companies) and large corporates (consolidated revenues > 500 million euros). Adoption of IRB Approach by asset classes. QRRE split into sub-classes (transactors and revolvers).
Use of floors on model parameter	Introducing floors for PD and LGD risk parameters in order to ensure a minimum level of conservatism for portfolios where the IRB Approaches remain available
Parameter estimation practices	Providing greater specification of parameter estimation practices to reduce variability in risk-weighted assets for portfolios where the IRB Approaches remain available

Table 2.5: Summary of BCBS amendments

rely on the use of default cases might become unusable. For the PD parameter, the most common modelling approach is to choose and weigh risk factors in a way which differentiates between defaulted and non-defaulted cases. This is typically accomplished using logistic regression, which relies on a large number of defaults and non-defaults to achieve robust statistical results. For the LGD and EAD parameters, data requirements are even more stringent, since these parameters are estimated not by comparing defaults with non-defaults, but rather by studying the defaulted cases in detail. This means that to estimate these parameters on a portfolio level, at the minimum several hundred default cases might be required.

Recognising that the lack of sufficient default data might lead to unreliable estimates of risk parameters, the Basel Committee has limited the scope of application of internal models. The changes affect the corporate, financial institution, specialised lending and equity portfolios, and are outlined below.

- IRB Approach is not permitted for exposure to equities.
- A-IRB Approach would no longer be allowed for (i) banks and other financial institutions including insurance companies, (ii) corporates belonging to consolidated groups with total consolidated annual revenues greater than 500 million euros.
- There are currently no changes to the sovereign portfolios (they are now subject to a separate review).[29]

The limitation of not using A-IRB Approach for the portfolios of large corporate and financial institutions will most probably have minor implications on the risk-weighted assets for the banking sector as a general; it could, however, have more significant effects on certain banks depending on their individual portfolios. Preliminary analysis based on EBA stress test data, outlined in Table 2.6, shows that the average risk weight for the asset class banks and institutions is 22.3% for banks currently using A-IRB Approach and 20.6% for banks using the F-IRB, i.e. in fact, a lower risk weight is obtained by the banks using F-IRB Approach. For the asset class large corporate the average risk weight for banks using A-IRB Approach is 44.7% and 50.5% for those using F-IRB Approach indicating an increase of approximately 6 percentage points.

Of course, it would be wrong to generalise and state that there would always be no RWA impact for the asset class banks and a slight upwards increase in RWA for the asset class corporates. Much would depend on the specific situation of each individual bank. Firstly, the actual composition of the financial institutions and large corporate portfolios would need to be considered, as the effect would depend on starting values of PD and LGD estimates for different counterparts in the portfolio. Secondly, the impact would depend on the size of these portfolios in relation to other portfolios of the bank (e.g. mid-corporates, SMEs, mortgages, retail, etc.). Thirdly, the impact would very much depend on whether or not the banks in question are constrained by the output floor, which is calibrated at 72.5% of the RWA under the

Asset Class	F-IRB Approach	A-IRB Approach
All	27.4%	56.8%
Institutions	22.3%	20.6%
Corporates	43.7%	56.2%
– of which SME	42.5%	64.3%
– of which SL	39.5%	64.7%
–of which large	44.7%	50.5%

Table 2.6: Average risk weights – EBA stress test data 2016

---

29   The BCBS published a discussion paper, 'The regulatory treatment of sovereign exposures', in December 2017 which suggests a removal of the IRB Approach for sovereigns. Comments are published on the website of the Bank for International Settlements – BIS.

standardised approach[1]. Finally, other changes introduced by Basel IV for both the IRB and standardised approaches would also need to be taken into account in order to understand the true impact of the reduction in scope of internal models on RWA.

Let's consider some examples of companies from a hypothetical portfolio of large corporates, presented in Figure 2.5. The PD and LGD risk parameters for this hypothetical portfolio have been modelled using readily available external default and loss data from rating agencies. As can be seen, the Risk Weights for the F-IRB Approach are lower than those for the A-IRB Approach, with the difference of roughly 10–15% depending on the corporate in question. This is due to the fact that the LGD floor in the F-IRB Approach is set at 45% for unsecured exposures to large corporates, whereas a somewhat lower LGD would actually be expected based on historical loss data, taking into account the high probability of cure or restructuring in the event of a default of a large multinational company. Therefore, it would seem as though the transfer of large corporate exposures from the A-IRB to the F-IRB Approach would result in, at most, a 15% increase in the RWA for this portfolio. This is quite sizeable, but could be manageable if the large corporate segment is not a significant share of the total portfolio of the bank.

However, what would happen if the bank in question is constrained by the output floor? The output floor is an aggregate floor, set at 72.5% of the total RWA under the standardised approaches for all asset classes and risk types. If the RWA under the IRB Approach are significantly lower than 72.5% of the RWA under the standardised approaches, the bank in question would have to increase its RWA until it is at the level of 72.5% of the standardised approach.

For large corporates, the standardised Risk Weights depend on external ratings. For Nestlé in Figure 2.5, the standardised Risk Weight is 20%, and the floor based on the standardised approach would be equal to 14.5%. Since this is below the F-IRB Risk Weight of 17%, a bank constrained by the output floor would not need to increase its

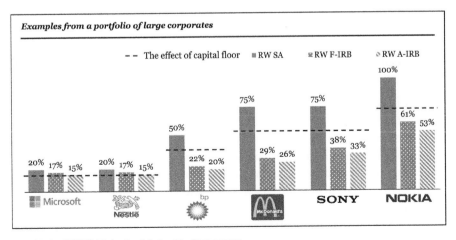

Figure 2.5: Basel IV Risk Weights for a hypothetical portfolio of large corporates

RWA any further than 17% of the exposure amount to this corporate. On the other hand, for McDonald's, the standardised Risk Weight is 75%, and the floor based on the standardised approach would be equal to 54%. The transfer from A-IRB to F-IRB results in an increase in the Risk Weight from 26% to 29%, which is equivalent to 12% in relative terms. However, since the new F-IRB Risk Weight of 29% is much lower than the standardised risk weight of 54%, the bank would actually need to more than double the RWA associated with this exposure (from 26% of the exposure at default to 54% of the exposure at default).

2.2.3 Partial use of the IRB Approach

One key overlooked feature of the Basel IV paper is the ability to choose asset classes for IRB implementation. This could potentially make the IRB Approach much more attractive for standardised banks, which had previously not considered it. It order to understand why this feature could be so attractive to standardised banks, we must first understand how a typical IRB rollout process looked in the past.

According to the initial version of the IRB Approach introduced by Basel II, after a Bank adopts an IRB Approach for a part of its holdings, it has to extend the IRB Approach across the entire banking group for all asset classes over time. After several years from the start of IRB implementation, it is expected that for at least a certain pre-defined percentage of the total portfolio, the RWA are calculated using internal models. This percentage is defined by local supervisors, and in many countries is larger than 85% of the total credit portfolio.

Local supervisors also limit the time frame during which this ratio has to be achieved, typically to 3–5 years from the date of initial IRB implementation. This means that once a bank decides to become an IRB bank, it is expected to migrate the vast majority of its credit portfolio to the IRB Approach over a fairly short period of time. Moreover, it is expected to clearly articulate how this would be achieved to its supervisor in the IRB rollout plan. Of course, there are exceptions, and certain sub-portfolios could be excluded from the IRB Approach altogether, especially if it is not feasible to develop models for them due to data scarcity. However, provided that the portfolio has sufficient data for internal models, it is excepted that it would be transferred to the IRB Approach in due course.

Needless to say, implementing the IRB Approach across all asset classes in a short period of time could be very challenging. This would require a lot of work on the models themselves, but also significant investments in personnel running and using the models, investments in IT infrastructure, and a re-design of internal processes across all business units in order for them to be in line with the IRB requirements. Additionally, at the level of an individual bank, some asset classes would achieve significant RWA reductions from the introduction of the IRB Approach, while for others the effort to develop and implement models would yield little benefit, and in some cases, would even result in increases in RWA.

Based on the Basel IV requirements published in December 2017, banks could now implement the IRB Approach separately for individual asset classes. These include:

- banks,
- corporates (excluding specialised lending and purchased receivables),
- specialised lending,
- corporate purchased receivables,
- retail residential mortgages,
- qualifying revolving retail exposures,
- other retail (excluding purchased receivables), and
- retail purchased receivables.

It is still expected that once a bank decides to implement the IRB Approach for a certain asset class, it has to adopt it for all holdings within that asset class over time. However, it is no longer required to adopt IRB across all other asset classes. This means that standardised banks can now concentrate only on portfolios where the IRB Approach results in the highest benefit and is easiest to implement, leaving other asset classes on the standardised approach.

In order to decide which asset class to migrate to IRB, a bank could consider the potential RWA savings, as well as data availability, quality of IT infrastructure, and the availability of personnel required to implement the IRB Approach. In some banks, it could be the case that for a certain asset class there is already a team working on models for internal credit decision purposes or for reporting purposes.[30] The same team could now re-use the available data for IRB modelling purposes, with much less effort than would have previously been required. Such a bank could implement the IRB Approach in as little as 2–3 years and, after receiving the supervisor's approval, could lower its capital requirements significantly.

Of course, there would be an output floor, which would limit the potential RWA savings (since the minimum RWA is set at 72.5% of the standardised approach, the potential savings are limited to 27.5% of the initial standardised RWA).[31] However, in practice, this could mean that for some banks the permitted RWA savings of 27.5% could be achieved by only moving one or two asset classes to the IRB Approach.

Let's consider the main asset classes, which make up the majority of portfolios of most European banks: retail residential mortgages, corporates and retail exposures. Table 2.7 compares the median standardised and IRB risk weights across different countries in the European Union, as at June 2017.[32] As can be seen, the IRB risk weights are typically a 50–60% lower than the standardised risk weights for each of these asset classes. Of course, with the introduction of additional Basel IV requirements the benefit of the

---

30 Due to the introduction of IFRS9, risk parameters must be used in the calculation of impairment provisions.
31 For details on the output floor, see Chapter 9.
32 Risk weights are calculated per country as the Risk Exposure Amount as a percentage of Exposure Value. Then, the median is taken across countries in the EU, for which data is available. The data is based on disclosures collected for 132 large European banks, collected by the EBA.

Asset Class	SA RW	IRB RW	Relative difference
Mortgages	39%	14%	-63%
Corporates	95%	46%	-51%
Retail	71%	28%	-60%

Table 2.7: Median risk weights – EBA Transparency Exercise, June 2017

IRB Approach could become different, but the IRB Approach is still expected to yield much lower risk weights for many European banks.

Now, let's consider an example (Figure 2.6), in which a standardised bank has found out that for a certain asset class, which makes up 40% of the current aggregate RWA, the IRB Approach would result in an average risk weight, which is 65% lower than the risk weight in the standardised approach. The bank could keep all other portfolios on the standardised approach, and only concentrate on this portfolio in its IRB implementation programme. Once it implements the IRB Approach for only this portfolio – it will have accomplished most of the permitted IRB savings, reducing its RWA by 26% out of the maximum possible value of 27.5%.

Of course, such cherry picking could be viewed negatively by the competent authorities. We will have to see how this new rule will be implemented in different jurisdictions. If supervisors decide that cherry picking should not be allowed, they could opt for a stricter implementation of Basel IV. On the other hand, it could be the case that such an approach would actually be allowed in many jurisdictions. After all, this would encourage smaller banks to use more risk sensitive and advanced credit risk

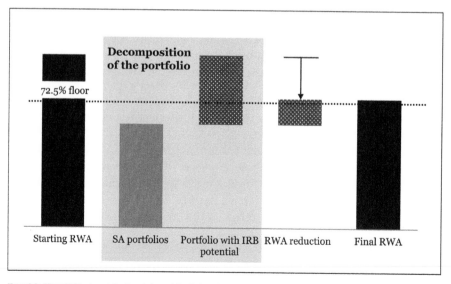

Figure 2.6: Effect of IRB implementation for a single portfolio with the highest IRB potential

management tools. It would also make some of them more competitive in relationship to larger IRB banks. Finally, with the output floor – no matter how much cherry picking the bank would do, at the end, its RWA savings would still be limited to 72.5% of the value calculated under the standardised approach. This should provide some comfort to competent authorities as well.

2.2.4 Risk parameter floors as an instrument of RWA variability reduction

The Basel Committee has decided to introduce additional floors to the capital requirements framework. The floors are introduced to prevent capital requirements from falling too low by limiting the impact of modelling errors or insufficiently conservative modelling practices on RWA. The Committee considered several different types of floors but ended up with an output floor[33] and floors on risk parameters as described below.

Next to the output floor, the second type of floor is the parameter level floor applied on an individual exposure level. Banks would still calculate internal risk parameters (PD, LGD and EAD), but would use the higher of their own internal estimates and the regulatory floors in RWA estimation. In a very rudimentary form, this concept has already been implemented as part of the Basel II framework. Basel II already prescribes a floor for PD estimates of 3 basis points. However, the existing floors are not granular enough, resulting in revisions by the Basel Committee. The new floors are more granular, as they are established on both asset class and product level as presented in Table 2.8.

With the exception of mortgages, the floors also depend on the level of collateralisation of the exposure. This means that the "secured" floors listed in Table 2.8 are applicable only if the exposure is fully secured (i.e. the value of the collateral after the application of collateral haircuts exceeds the exposure value). For a partially secured exposure, the LGD floor is calculated as the weighted average of the unsecured floor and the secured floor, with the weights calculated based on the portion of the exposure which is fully secured after the application of the haircuts. The haircuts for financial collaterals are determined by the comprehensive formula in the standardised approach. For other types of eligible collaterals, the haircuts are set at 40%.

This means, for instance, that for an exposure to a corporate with an exposure amount of 100 CU (currency units), and a real estate collateral value of 100 CU, the LGD floor would be equal to 16%. This is because, after the application of the 40% haircut, the exposure is 60% secured and 40% unsecured, and LGD floors of 10% and 25% are applied to the secured and unsecured portions, respectively.

The established floors will likely increase capital requirements, especially for portfolios subject to the advanced IRB Approach, where the floors for LGD and CF estimates

---

33   For details regarding the output floor, please refer to Chapter 9.

Segment	PD	LGD		EAD/CF
		Unsecured	Secured	
Corporate	5bps	25%	Varying by collateral type: · 0% financial · 10% receivables · 10% commercial or residential real estate · 15% other physical	Sum of: i. the on-balance sheet exposures ii. 50% of the off-balance sheet exposure using the applicable CF in the standardised approach
Retail				
Mortgages	5bps	N/A	5%	
QRRE transactors	5bps	50%	N/A	
QRRE revolvers	10bps	50%	N/A	
Other retail	5bps	30%	Varying by collateral type: · 0% financial · 10% receivables · 10% commercial or residential real estate · 15% other physical	

Table 2.8: BCBS 424 risk parameter floors

would be activated. At the same time, it is worth noting that the level of RWA increase due to these floors will be limited for most banks. This is because the average LGD levels reported by most banks are higher than the LGD floors. Based on a study conducted by the EBA across 39 countries around the world in 2017, most banks report the following average LGD values for various portfolios:[34]

- between 21–50% for corporates, with a weighted average of 35%,
- between 9–27% for mortgages, with a weighted average of 20%,
- between 42–86% for QRRE exposures, with a weighted average of 64%, and
- between 20–57% for other retail exposures, with a weighted average of 42%.

These figures suggest that for most banks, the floors will only affect a small portion of the portfolio. However there will be a small portion of banks (perhaps around 5–10% of all global banks), which will be more heavily affected. It is important that these banks conduct impact studies early on, in order to understand the magnitude of the problem, and to plan possible mitigation actions – such as increasing the level of collateralisation of their portfolios. These banks should also consider other upcoming regulatory changes, especially the changes to the definition of default (described in section 2.3), which can potentially result in significant changes to modelled LGD estimates, and thus can either exacerbate this problem further, or on the other hand, make the impact much smaller.

---

34 EBA Risk Dashboard, Risk Parameters statistics by country of the counterparty for IRB banks, EU and main non-EU countries, 2017 Q3

Clearly, the Basel Committee has tried to ensure that the floors are not too high. High calibration levels of floors would better accomplish the goals of lowering RWA variability and minimising the manipulation of risk weights by banks. At the same time, however, they might incentivise banks to take part in more risky activities by shifting assets into exposures whose risk parameter values are higher than the floors. That being said, some of the banks will be affected by these floors and should start planning mitigating actions.

2.2.5 Parameter estimation practices

The Basel Committee also aims to provide greater specification of parameter estimation practices for portfolios where the IRB Approaches remain available. The specification covers: (i) PD; (ii) LGD; (iii) EAD, including CF; (iv) maturity (M); and (v) credit risk mitigation (CRM), and are summarised in Table 2.9.

Of the changes described above, probably the one having the most potential impact on RWA is the change in the way collateral will be recognised for F-IRB portfolios. According to current requirements introduced by Basel II, the exposure has to be split into a collateralised exposure and non-collateralised exposure, and RWA is calculated separately for the two sub-exposures. Different LGDs are then applied to the collateralised and non-collateralised portions of the exposure. The split is based on minimum and maximum collateralisation levels (C^* and C^{**}), which depend on the collateral type (e.g. for RRE C^* is 30% and C^{**} is 140%):

- When the collateralisation level is below C^*, the entire exposure is classified as non-collateralised.
- When the collateralisation level is above C^{**}, the entire exposure is classified as collateralised.
- When the collateralisation level is between C^* and C^{**}, the exposure amount equal to collateral divided by C^{**} is classified as collateralised, and the remainder as uncollateralised.

Basel IV introduces a new approach, in which a single exposure is used in RWA estimation, but the LGD is calculated as the weighted average of a secured LGD and an unsecured LGD, with the weighting being the portion that is secured. In addition, explicit haircuts are applied to collateral depending on the collateral type prior to LGD estimation. The formula to LGD estimation under the new F-IRB Approach is as follows:

Equation 2.15

$$LGD^* = LGD_U \times \frac{E_U}{E \times (1 + H_E)} + LGD_S \times \frac{E_S}{E \times (1 + H_E)} \tag{2.15}$$

IRB topic	Revisions
Probability of default (PD)	· No significant changes, but rather specifications to ensure consistency (e.g. using through-the-cycle PD, use of downturn years for calibration were already previous requirements)
Loss given default (LGD)	· Changes to the calculation of LGD under F-IRB Approach: – Introducing explicit haircuts for non-financial collaterals and increasing them to 40% for receivables, CRE/RRE and other physical collateral – Decreasing minimum LGD values for fully secured exposures to 20% for receivables and CRE/RRE, and 25% for other physical collateral – Decreasing minimum LGD values for unsecured exposures to corporates from 45% to 40% (banks still remain on 45%) – Removal of minimum collateralisation requirements for non-financial collateral – Gross-up requirement for non-cash exposures secured by non-financial collateral is extended · Changes to the calculation of LGD under A-IRB Approach: – Estimation of the long term LGDs for secured exposures is restricted by a floor varying by collateral type between 0% and 15%
Exposure at default (EAD) & credit conversion factor (CF)	· Banks using F-IRB Approach are required to use supervisory CFs set out in the standardised approach · Estimation of CF using internal models is no longer allowed for non-revolving commitments under A-IRB · Banks using A-IRB Approach are expected to use CFs specified in the standardised approach for a larger range of exposures than is currently required. Modelling the EAD/CF risk parameter is only allowed for exposures that meet the following conditions: – Exposure to a counterparty with available IRB Approach to credit risk (certain corporates and retail) – Exposure is an undrawn revolving commitment – Exposure is not subject to a CF of 100% in the standardised approach · When the conditions specified above are met, additional constraints on EAD/CF estimation practices need to be considered, for example: – EAD/CF models should reflect the product, customer and bank management characteristics of exposures, towards which they are applied – EAD/CF models should conservatively treat facilities which are close to being fully drawn at the reference date – During the construction of the EAD/CF models, the EAD reference data should not be capped at the principle amount outstanding or facility limits – Conservative long-run default-weighted average estimates of EAD/CF must be used – A 12-month fixed horizon estimation approach must be used during the construction of the EAD/CF model – The EAD for each exposure that is used as input into the risk weight formula and the calculation of expected loss is subject to a floor that is the sum of: (i) the on balance sheet amount; and (ii) 50% of the off-balance sheet exposure using the applicable CF in the standardised approach. · In an A-IRB or F-IRB Approach, the EAD for revolving purchased facility is the sum of current amount receivables purchased plus 40% (instead of 75%) of any undrawn purchase commitments minus $K_{Dilution}$.
Maturity (M)	· No change of the fixed 2.5-year maturity parameter under the F-IRB Approach · Determination of maturity parameter under the A-IRB Approach based on the expiry date of a facility (the simple use of the repayment date of the current drawn amount would be prohibited) · The one-year floor does not apply to: i) Short-term self-liquidation trade transactions should be accounted for at their actual remaining maturity; and ii) issued and confirmed letters of credit are short-term and self-liquidating.

Table 2.9: Proposed changes to parameter estimation practices

IRB topic	Revisions
Credit risk mitigation	· Removal of double default treatment for credit derivatives · Under the F-IRB Approach, regarding the recognition of guarantees and credit derivatives, for the covered portion of the exposure only the full substitution approach (PD of the guarantor) shall be allowed · Conditional guarantees are not allowed to be used in the A-IRB Approach, additional guidance is given as to what is considered to be "conditional" · Own estimates of collateral haircuts are not allowed under the F-IRB Approach (as in the case of the new standardised approach) · VaR model approach is allowed for determination of exposures to counterparty credit risk for securities financing transactions · Removal of CRM recognition from first-to-default credit derivatives for underlying exposures under F-IRB Approach; for A-IRB banks only first-to-default credit derivatives can be recognised as part of CRM
Other changes	· The scaling factor of 1.06 in the risk weight formula is removed.

Table 2.9: (continued)

With:

LGD_U: The LGD applicable for an unsecured exposure;

LGD_S: The LGD applicable to exposures secured by the type of collateral used in the transaction;

E: Current value of the exposure;

E_S: Current value of the collateral received after the application of the haircut;

H_E: Haircuts applied to the exposure value.

The introduction of a new formula is, in fact, mostly a presentational change. For instance, the concept of maximum collateralisation levels in Basel II is quite similar to LGD haircuts in Basel IV. Also, splitting the exposure into secured and unsecured parts with different LGDs in Basel II should produce the same result as applying a "weighted average LGD" to the full exposure in Basel IV, if all other things remain equal.

However, there are changes of substance, which could make credit risk mitigation more advantageous under Basel IV (Table 2.10). Firstly, Basel IV introduces a decrease in minimum secured LGDs, which could allow much lower LGDs to be achieved if there is sufficient collateral which is properly stored and managed. Secondly, the removal of the minimum collateralisation level of 30% means that in Basel IV, even a small amount of collateral will begin to reduce risk weighted assets. Finally, there is an increase in collateral haircuts from Basel II to Basel IV, which should have a partially offsetting effect on RWA.[35]

Combined, the changes described above could make it much more beneficial for F-IRB banks to hold many collaterals of high quality. The figure below presents the possible

---

35 In Basel II, implied collateral haircuts could be calculated based on the values of the maximum possible collateralisation levels.

Type of collateral	Minimum secured LGDs		LGD haircuts	
	Basel II	Basel IV	Basel II	Basel IV
Eligible receivables	35%	20%	20%	40%
Eligible RRE / CRE	35%	20%	28.6%	40%
Other physical collateral	40%	25%	28.6%	40%

Table 2.10: Comparison of F-IRB LGDs under Basel II and Basel IV

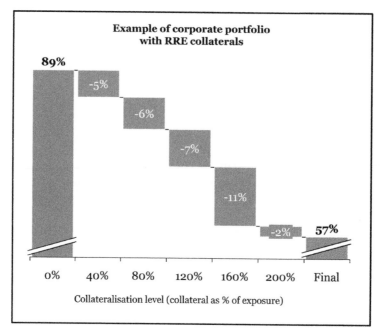

Figure 2.7: Basel IV RWA expressed as a percentage of Basel II RWA at various collateralisation levels under the F-IRB Approach

reductions of risk weights for a corporate portfolio secured by real estate collaterals, depending on the level of collateralisation.[36]

2.2.6 Expected impact on banks

In this section we will first explore the possible magnitude of the quantitative impacts on RWA, and then will discuss other ways in which Basel IV impacts IRB banks, and ways that banks should prepare for these changes.

---

36 Note that in the example there is a reduction in RWA even for unsecured exposures. This is due to the fact that the unsecured LGD for corporates has decreased from 45% to 40%.

Quantitative impact

For the quantitative impact, we will consider two hypothetical portfolios: one on the F-IRB (foundation IRB) approach, and one on the A-IRB (advanced IRB) approach. While these portfolios are hypothetical, they present a common picture that would be experienced by a large number of IRB banks.

Case 1 – Foundation IRB portfolio

In general for the hypothetical corporate RRE/CRE portfolio under the F-IRB Approach there will be a reduction in risk weights that would be largely dependent on the level of collateralisation of the portfolio. Figure 2.8 presents the decomposition of the impact for the non-defaulted portion of the portfolio.

The top bar represents the RWA estimated based on Basel II rules, with following bars showing the marginal impact of each regulatory change, resulting in a relatively smaller RWA according to Basel IV.

As can be seen from the chart the increase of the PD floor does not produce a significant impact since the portion of obligors with PD estimates lower than 5 basis points is quite small across all banks.

The introduction of the haircut concept instead of maximum collateralisation levels results in a slightly higher RWA. The secured part of the exposure still cannot be higher than 100%, meaning there is no impact if the collateral value after the application of the haircut exceeds the exposure amount. At the same time, if the collateral value is lower, then Basel IV results in slightly higher LGDs, since Basel II implied haircuts are lower. The average marginal relative impact on RWA is approximately 2–3%.

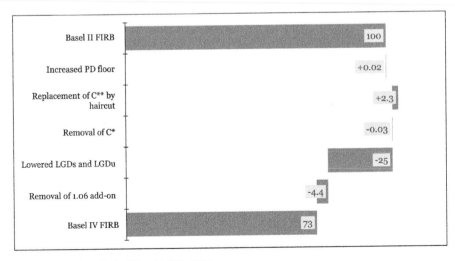

Figure 2.8: Decomposition of the Basel IV impact for FIRB portfolios

The removal of the minimum collateralisation requirement (assuming foundation LGD values for secured and unsecured parts remain the same) does not produce a significant reduction in risk weights, since only exposures with very low collateralisation levels are affected.

The lowered values of LGDs for secured and unsecured portions of the exposure result in a significant reduction of risk weights, with the gains increasing with higher levels of collateralisation. Portfolios with partially secured loans will get a reduction of risk weights from 10–30%, whereas fully and over collateralised portfolios will gain up to a 43% reduction. The dependency is driven by the fact that secured LGDs were reduced more significantly compared to the unsecured LGDs.

Finally, the removal of 1.06 add-on from the risk weight formula results in a fixed 5.66% relative reduction in risk weights.

Overall, the impact of the updated F-IRB Approach for secured non-defaulted portfolios is an approximate reduction of 20%, depending mostly on the level of collateralisation.

The analysis does not include the defaulted exposures, since their share in the portfolio is typically relatively small. For defaults, the reduction in F-IRB LGD parameters will produce a greater reduction in risk weights than for non-defaults, due to the fact that a different risk weight formula is applied for them:

Equation 2.16

$$RW = \max\{0; 12.5 * (LGD - EL_{BE})\} \tag{2.16}$$

Since no changes in EL_{BE} estimate are expected, any reduction in LGDs will correspond to a 12.5 times greater reduction in the risk weight. This means, for example, that an LGD reduction by 5% will result in 62.5% reduction in the risk weight in absolute terms.

The changes in the IRB rules will also impact the IRB shortfall, assuming no changes in the accounting rules for provisions. For non-defaulted portfolios, the EL will generally be reduced under F-IRB, which means that banks can anticipate a reduction in the IRB shortfall.

Case 2 – Advanced IRB portfolio

For the advanced IRB Approach the potential impact is to a higher extent subject to ambiguities connected to the particular risk profile of the portfolio in question, largely driven by own estimates of LGD. Considering the same portfolio under the A-IRB Approach we will assume that LGD estimates are linearly dependent on the level of collateralisation (Figure 2.9).

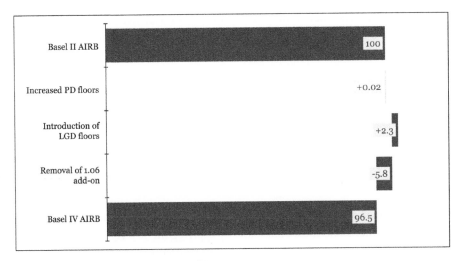

Figure 2.9: Decomposition of the Basel IV impact for AIRB portfolios

Similarly to the F-IRB Approach, the increased PD floor is not expected to have a significant impact on the overall RWA, although it might have a higher relative impact for low default portfolios.

The impact from the introduction of the LGD floors on the A-IRB Approach is highly dependent on the relationship between the LGD and corresponding collateralisation levels. The LGD floor consists of secured and unsecured parts, defined based on the level of collateralisation after application of the corresponding haircut. Consequently, a higher level of collateralisation implies a lower floor.

However, at the same time the LGD estimates are also expected to be lower than under F-IRB and are more likely to hit the floor. Generally, it would be reasonable to assume that own LGD estimates have fairly high variability, meaning that certain portions of the portfolio will be subject to a risk weight increase. However, at the same time this portion of exposures will generally have a better risk profile, meaning that for such loans increase in risk weight would be at most 15–20% in absolute terms. For banks using the IRB Approach for corporate portfolios the own LGD estimates are on average approximately 35%. Considering all of this, on average the overall impact should be limited.

The potential impact from introduction of floors will be reduced by the removal of 1.06 add-on in risk weight formula for non-defaulted exposures. Consequently, overall there is no significant impact expected.

For defaulted exposures the risk weight is more sensitive to changes in LGD estimates. Since no changes in EL_{BE} estimates are expected, the risk weights for defaulted portions of the portfolio would slightly increase.

In terms of the IRB shortfall for the A-IRB portfolio, with an increase in LGD parameters, the regulatory EL will increase as well, resulting in a slightly higher IRB shortfall.

Summary of quantitative impact

As demonstrated in the two cases above, overall the IRB changes described in Basel IV should not result in significant increases in RWA for most banks. For most retail and non-retail portfolios on the A-IRB Approach, the impact should be quite limited. For F-IRB non-retail portfolios, decreases in RWA could be expected, especially for banks which already have – or are planning to increase – the level of collateralisation in their portfolios.

There is of course a caveat. Unfortunately, the IRB portfolios cannot be considered in isolation anymore, and most banks already applying the IRB Approach should not expect significant further reductions in RWA. This is because they now have to consider the standardised risk weights as well – and if they are significantly higher than the IRB risk weights, they will be constrained by the output floor.

On the other hand, for standardised banks which never previously considered to apply IRB, Basel IV presents an opportunity to rethink their past decisions and reconsider implementing internal models.

Other impacts and mitigation actions

Apart from purely quantitative impacts, Basel IV will present a number of operational and strategic challenges to IRB banks. Due to the reduction of scope of use of internal models and changes to parameter estimation practices, banks would have to adjust their strategies for RWA optimisation. This may also imply changes on the business model, including on pricing and risk management practices.

Banks would also have to reconsider their credit risk mitigation policies, practices and types of eligible collaterals. Clearly, Basel IV could be beneficial for IRB banks if they have highly collateralised portfolios with eligible collaterals of high quality. Therefore, banks will have to revise their collateralisation strategies, given the increase in haircuts for non-financial collaterals and decrease in the applied LGD (search for overcollateralisation).

The removal of the A-IRB option for some portfolios and the introduction of internal risk parameter floors would also require the re-development and re-calibration of certain models. For instance, certain loss observations associated with large corporate exposures would have to be removed from historical databases, resulting in the need to re-develop corporate LGD models.

2.2.7 Conclusion

The changes in the IRB Approach for credit risk are not as far reaching as expected and banks still can use this approach for low default portfolios (LDP), although only the foundation approach. Indeed, the earlier proposals from BCBS suggested a removal of the IRB Approach for banks and financial institutions, and large corporates (total assets >50 billion euros). The output floor was also in the meantime clarified and in certain jurisdictions, it shall be of high impact for banks.

The question is whether these changes will make the banking industry less risky? If you listen to the responses of banks to the changes presented by BCBS, it will not increase the quality of risk estimation and would not make the banking industry less risky. Therefore, we will probably continue to receive several updates and further clarifications from both the Basel Committee and competent authorities for the coming years. In the near future, we will also see the comments on the Basel's consultation on sovereign exposures.

2.3 EBA regulatory reform and the revised supervisory assessment methodology

In December 2013, upon request of the European Commission (in sequence of the EU Capital exercise 2011), the EBA published the 'Summary report on the comparability and pro-cyclicality of capital requirements under the Internal Ratings Based Approach in accordance with Article 502 of the Capital Requirements Regulation'.[37] This summary report was prepared with the purpose of analysing the comparability of capital requirements driven by internal models and required from EBA substantial work (in practice, conclusions were driven from an interim top-down report on the consistency of IRB capital requirements, a low default portfolio (LDP) benchmarking exercise, a benchmarking exercise on SMEs and residential mortgages, and a study on supervisory rules and practices).

The results of this study revealed significant discrepancies in the risk estimates and capital requirements across banks that were not originated by differences in the underlying risk profiles. With this background, the EBA was mandated by the CRR to publish a number of additional specifications to reduce the undue variability of RWA. EBA's initial thoughts were presented in March 2015 in the 'Discussion Paper on the future of the IRB Approach' (EBA/DP/2015/01). Since then, the EBA has been publishing detailed regulatory guidance focused on a number of areas identified as potential source of variability due to different interpretations of the regulatory requirements, attempting:

- a uniform application of the IRB requirements, and
- a limit on technical differences in the quantification of risk parameters that do not reflect the real differences in the underlying risk or in the risk management processes at banks.

---

37 In https://www.eba.europa.eu/documents/10180/15947/20131217+Summary+report+on+comparability+and+pro-cyclicality+of+the+IRB+Approach.pdf

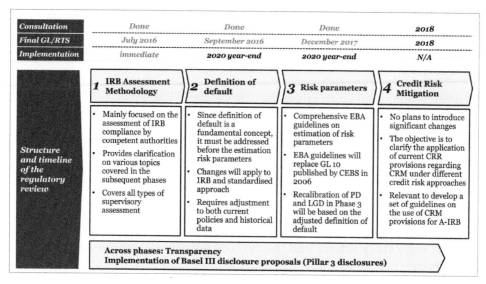

Consultation	*Done*	*Done*	*Done*	**2018**
Final GL/RTS	*July 2016*	*September 2016*	*December 2017*	**2018**
Implementation	*immediate*	**2020 year-end**	**2020 year-end**	**N/A**

Structure and timeline of the regulatory review

1 IRB Assessment Methodology
- Mainly focused on the assessment of IRB compliance by competent authorities
- Provides clarification on various topics covered in the subsequent phases
- Covers all types of supervisory assessment

2 Definition of default
- Since definition of default is a fundamental concept, it must be addressed before the estimation risk parameters
- Changes will apply to IRB and standardised approach
- Requires adjustment to both current policies and historical data

3 Risk parameters
- Comprehensive EBA guidelines on estimation of risk parameters
- EBA guidelines will replace GL 10 published by CEBS in 2006
- Recalibration of PD and LGD in Phase 3 will be based on the adjusted definition of default

4 Credit Risk Mitigation
- No plans to introduce significant changes
- The objective is to clarify the application of current CRR provisions regarding CRM under different credit risk approaches
- Relevant to develop a set of guidelines on the use of CRM provisions for A-IRB

Across phases: Transparency
Implementation of Basel III disclosure proposals (Pillar 3 disclosures)

Figure 2.10: EBA regulatory review since mid-2016

In order to achieve the aforementioned goals, the new regulatory technical standards (RTS) and guidelines consist of the following documents.

- RTS aimed at supervisory authorities in order enable harmonisation of the supervisory assessment methodology across the EU (see below);
- RTS and Guidelines on the default definition, specifying in particular both the quantitative identification of a default (days past due counting and materiality thresholds) and the unlikeliness to pay triggers (discussed in section 2.4); and
- Guidelines on the PD estimation, LGD estimation and the treatment of defaulted assets, and RTS on the specification of the nature, severity and duration of an economic downturn, which is needed for LGD and CF estimation (discussed in section 2.5).

It is thus expected that this new guidance will enhance the robustness and comparability of the internal risk estimates, which are used as the basis for the calculation of capital requirements of European banks. However, it is likely that the compliance with those requirements will result in a significant operational burden, both for banks and competent authorities.

Starting by EBA's mandate to develop RTS to specify the assessment methodology that competent authorities shall follow when assessing the compliance with the requirements to use the IRB Approach ('Final Draft RTS on Assessment Methodology for IRB', EBA/RTS/2016/03), they include standards for when banks initially apply for an IRB application, during the IRB sequential implementation, when carrying out model extensions or applying for model changes, as well as when assessing whether a bank meets the minimum IRB requirements on an ongoing basis. Consequently, these RTS are to be embedded in the day-to-day practices of the supervisory authorities and shall replace the old CEBS 'Guidelines on Validation' (GL-10 CEBS) (April 2006). As a result, it is expected that the implementation of all required changes might result in a significant operational burden for banks.

These RTS provide a mapping of all applicable CRR minimum requirements into 14 chapters across several articles, with each chapter starting with a brief description of the assessment criteria to be used by competent authorities as regards verification requests and of the methods to be used by competent authorities in this context.

In order to structure these RTS, all minimum IRB requirements, as defined in the CRR, have been mapped onto the 14 chapters, covering:

- general rules for the assessment methodology;
- implementation plan and permanent partial use;
- internal governance and validation;
- use test and experience test;
- assignment of exposures to grades and pools;
- definition of default;
- design, operational details and documentation of the rating systems;
- risk quantification;
- assignment of exposures to exposure classes;
- stress tests used in the assessment of capital adequacy;
- own funds requirements calculation;
- data maintenance;
- requirements for equity exposures under the internal models approach;
- management of changes to the rating systems.

Each chapter starts with a brief description of the assessment criteria (including a reference to the CRR requirements), as well as the methods to be used by competent authorities in this context. These requirements focus on the main aspects of the IRB Approach and provide clarification of the CRR requirements.

Table 2.11 presents a summary of the key topics discussed in each of the referred 14 chapters.

2.4 Definition of Default

The purpose of the section below is to summarise and discuss the implications of the EBA's documents on the default definition, namely the 'Guidelines on the definition of default under article 178 of Regulation (EU) No 575/2013' (EBA/GL/2016/07) and the 'Draft regulatory technical standards on the materiality threshold for credit obligations past due under article 178 of Regulation (EU) No 575/2013' (EBA/RTS/2016/06), both published on 28 September 2016. Both documents intend to complement the application of the CRR article 178.

Main Areas	Key topics
General rules for the assessment methodology	– Scope of assessment criteria to be applied by competent authorities.
	– Scope of methods to be applied by competent authorities.
	– Quality and auditability of documentation.
	– Third party involvement.
	– Temporary non-compliance with the requirements of the IRB Approach.
Internal models for equity exposures	– Adequacy of the data used.
	– Adequacy of the models.
	– Comprehensiveness of the stress-testing programme.
	– Integrity of the model and modelling process.
	– Adequacy of the assignment of exposures to the internal models approach.
	– Adequacy of the validation function.
Internal governance and oversight	– Roles of senior management and management body, internal reporting, credit risk control unit and internal audit.
	– Independence of validation function, frequency and completeness of validation process, adequacy of validation methods & procedures, soundness of reporting process and process for addressing conclusions & recommendations.
Use test and experience test	– Internal ratings and default & loss estimates playing an essential role in: – risk management, credit approval and decision making process. – Internal capital allocation. – Corporate governance functions.
	– Previous use of the rating systems.
Definition of Default and loss	– Compliance with the default flagging triggers.
	– Robustness and effectiveness of the process of identifying defaults.
	– Triggers and process for reclassifying obligors into a non-default status.
Risk quantification	– Data requirements, revision of estimates and margin of conservatism.
	– PD: observation period, estimation.
	– LGD: observation period, consistency between PD & LGD, economic downturn, LGD/ELBE/UL estimation for defaulted assets.
	– CF: observation period, estimation, economic downturn, payments monitoring process.
Design, operational details & docs of the rating systems	– Adequacy and completeness of the documentation.
	– Adequacy of the rating systems structure, risk drivers and rating criteria, obligors' distribution in pools/grades, risk differentiation and homogeneity.
	– Data requirements, model design & human judgment.
Assignment of exposures to grades and pools	– Adequacy of definitions, processes and criteria used for assigning/reviewing exposures to grades/ pools.
	– Integrity of the assignment process.
Assignment of exposures to exposure classes	– Assignment methodology and its implementation.
	– Sequence of the process of assigning exposures to exposure classes.
	– Specific segmentation requirements under the Retail and Corporate portfolios.

Table 2.11: Key topics discussed in the EBA/RTS/2016/03

Main Areas	Key topics
Stress tests used in assessment of capital adequacy	– Adequacy of the methods used in designing the stress tests.
	– Robustness of the organisation of the stress tests processes.
	– Integration of the stress tests with the risk and capital management processes.
Own funds requirements calculation	– Reliability of the system used for the capital requirements calculation.
	– Data quality.
	– Correctness of the implementation of the methodology and procedures for different exposure classes.
	– Organisation of the capital requirements calculation process.
Data maintenance	– Quality of the internal, external or pooled data.
	– Data quality management process.
	– Data documentation and reporting.
	– IT infrastructure.
Management of changes to the rating systems	– Responsibilities, reporting and procedures for internal approval.
	– Definitions, methods and metrics to classify the changes.
	– Procedures to identify, monitor, notify and apply for the permission to change.
	– Procedures for implementing the changes.
Implementation plan and permanent partial use	– IRB initial and actual coverage ratio.
	– Gradual implementation (roll-out plan).
	– Conditions for the permanent partial use (PPU).

Table 2.11: (continued)

The following topics are addressed in this section:

- the past-due criterion in the definition of default;
- indications of unlikeliness to pay (distressed restructuring, bankruptcy and others);
- application of the definition of default in external data;
- the consistency of the application of default definition;
- application of default definition for retail exposures;
- criteria for the return to non-defaulted status;
- materiality thresholds;
- implementation of changes;
- impact of the new default definition on RWA.

2.4.1 Past-due criterion in the definition of default

EBA permits banks to consider modifications of schedule in the obligor's payments (including cases when payments are postponed and suspended) as not days past due in the following cases:

- if reasons for these modifications are clarified in the bank's policy;

- if such a right is explicitly stated in a credit arrangement contract;
- if there is a legal allowance to modify/postpone/suspend the payments schedule;
- if there is a dispute between the obligor and the bank regarding the repayment and this dispute has been introduced to a court or another dedicated external body which results in a binding ruling;
- in the specific case of leasing, if a formal complaint has been directed to the bank about the object of the contract, confirmed by an independent internal audit/validation or another comparable independent auditing unit.

However, if the obligor changes the schedule, suspends or postpones the payments, the bank should analyse the reasons for such a change and assess the possible indications of unlikeliness to pay, in accordance with Articles 178(1) and (3) of Regulation (EU) No 575/2013 and Section "Indication of unlikeliness to pay" below.

In the case of an event such as a merger or acquisition, the number of days past due starts from the moment a different person or entity becomes obliged to pay the obligation. However, the counting of days past due should not be affected by a change in the obligor's name.

Classification of the obligor to a defaulted status should not be subject to additional expert judgement; once the obligor meets the past-due criterion all exposures to that obligor are considered defaulted unless either of the following conditions is met:

- Exposures are eligible as retail exposures, and the bank applies the default definition at individual credit facility level;
- A so-called "technical past-due situation" is considered to have occurred (please see description below).

Banks can consider "technical past-due situation" only in the following cases.

- When defaulted status was the result of a bank's data or system error including manual errors, but excluding wrong credit decisions.
- Where defaulted status was a result of non-execution, defective or late execution of the transaction or where there is evidence that the payment was unsuccessful due to the failure of the payment system.
- Where, due to the nature of the transaction, there is a time lag between the receipt of the payment by an obligor and allocation of payment to the relevant account.
- In the several specific cases related to factoring arrangements where materiality threshold is breached, but none of the receivables is past due more than 30 days.

Banks may apply specific treatment for central governments, local authorities and public sector entities where all of the following conditions are met.

- The contract is related to the supply of goods or services, where the administrative procedures require certain controls related to the execution of the contract before the payment can be made.

- Apart from the delay in payment no other indications of unlikeliness to pay as specified in accordance with Article 178(1)(a) and 178(3) of Regulation (EU) No 575/2013.
- The financial situation of the obligor is considered good and stable.
- The obligation is past due not longer than 180 days.

As a consequence, these exposures should not be included in the calculation of materiality threshold and should be clearly documented as exposures subject to specific treatment.

Guidelines separately specify provisions applicable to factoring and purchased receivable. These topics are out of the scope of this section, for details, please refer to paragraphs 27–32 of the Guidelines.

Banks should apply materiality threshold for past due credit obligations set by their competent authorities. Banks may identify defaults based on a lower threshold if they can demonstrate that this lower threshold is a relevant indication of unlikeliness to pay.

2.4.2 Indications of unlikeliness to pay

Non-accrued status

Banks should consider that an obligor is unlikely to pay where interest related to credit obligations is no longer recognised in their income statement due to the decrease of credit quality of the obligation.

Specific credit risk adjustment (SCRA)

All of the following Specific Credit Risk Adjustments (SCRAs) should be treated as an indication of unlikeliness to pay:

- losses recognised in the Profit & Loss account for instruments measured at fair value that represent credit risk impairment;
- losses as a result of current or past events affecting a significant individual exposure or exposures that are not individually significant which are individually or collectively assessed.

The SCRAs that cover the losses for which historical experience, adjusted based on the current observable data, indicate that the loss has occurred, but the bank is not yet aware which individual exposure has suffered these losses ("incurred but not reported losses"), and should not be considered as an indication of unlikeliness to pay for a specific obligor.

Where the bank treats an exposure as impaired such a situation should be considered as an additional indication of unlikeliness to pay.

Where the bank treats an exposure as impaired under IFRS 9, the obligor should be considered defaulted except where the exposure has been considered credit-impaired due to the delay in payment and either or all of the following conditions are met:

- the competent authorities have replaced the 90 days past due with 180 days past due;
- the materiality threshold has not been breached;
- the exposure has been recognised as a technical past-due situation;
- exposure meets the conditions of non-past-due exposures to central governments, local authorities and public sector entities.

Sale of credit obligations

EBA states that if reasons for the sale of credit obligations were not related to credit risk, then this sale should not be considered as an indication of default even where the loss is material. However, there should exist documented justification of the treatment of the sale loss as not credit-related.

If sale loss is considered to be credit related, then it should be compared to a materiality level of 5%. Economic loss is calculated using the following formula:

$$L = \frac{E - P}{E} \tag{2.17}$$

Where L is the economic loss related with the sale of credit obligations; E is the total outstanding amount of the obligations subject to the sale, including interest and fees; and P is the price agreed for the sold obligations.

If the economic loss is higher than this threshold, banks should consider the credit obligations defaulted.

Information about the sale loss should be adequately recorded and stored for the purpose of the estimation of risk parameters.

If the sale of a credit obligation at a material credit-related economic loss occurred before the identification of default on that exposure, the moment of sale should be considered as the moment of default. In the case of a partial sale of the total obligations of an obligor where the sale is associated with a material credit-related economic loss, all the remaining exposures to this obligor should be treated as defaulted, unless the exposures are eligible as retail exposures and the bank can apply the default definition at facility level.

If the price for the total portfolio was determined by specifying the discount on particular credit obligations, the materiality should be assessed individually for each exposure within the portfolio. Where, however, the price was set only at the portfolio level, the materiality may be assessed at the portfolio level and, in that case, if the threshold of 5% is breached, then all credit obligations within this portfolio should be treated as defaulted at the moment of the sale.

Distressed restructuring

Distressed restructuring should be considered to have occurred when concessions have been extended towards a debtor facing or about to face difficulties in meeting its financial commitments. When considering forborne exposures, the obligor should be classified as defaulted only where the relevant forbearance measures are likely to result in a diminished financial obligation. The threshold for the diminished financial obligation is equal to 1%. The diminished financial obligation includes principal, interest and fees and is calculated using the following formula:

$$DO = \frac{NPV_0 - NPV_1}{NPV_0} \tag{2.18}$$

Where DO is the diminished financial obligation; NPV_0 is the net present value of expected cash flows (including unpaid interest and fees) before the changes in terms and conditions of the contract discounted using the customer's original effective interest rate; and NPV_1 is the net present value of the expected cash flows based on the new arrangement discounted using the customer's original effective interest rate.

If DO is above the threshold then diminished financial obligation is considered to be defaulted.

If DO is below the threshold it still has to be checked against other indicators of unlikeliness to pay. The indicators that may suggest unlikeliness to pay include the following:

- a large lump sum payment envisaged at the end of the repayment schedule;
- an irregular repayment schedule where significantly lower payments are envisaged at the beginning of repayment schedule;
- a significant grace period at the beginning of the repayment schedule;
- where the exposures to the obligor have been subject to distressed restructuring more than once.

Any concession extended to an obligor already in default should lead to classifying the obligor as a distressed restructuring. Where any of the modifications of the schedule of credit obligations is the result of financial difficulties of an obligor, banks should also assess whether a distressed restructuring has taken place.

Bankruptcy

Banks should clearly specify in their internal policies what type of arrangement is treated as an order, or as a protection similar to bankruptcy, taking into account all relevant legal frameworks as well as the following typical characteristics of such protection:[38]

---

38 Such legal protections can take different forms and cause significant loss in banks, as the sale of the pledged collateral cannot be enforced for the near future (e.g. Greek mortgage market).

- the protection scheme encompasses all creditors or all creditors with unsecured claims;
- the terms and conditions of the protection scheme are approved by the court or other relevant public authority;
- the terms and conditions of the protection scheme include a temporary suspension of payments or partial redemption of debt;
- the measures involve some sort of control over the management of the company and its assets;
- if the protection scheme fails, the company is likely to be liquidated.

Other indications of unlikeliness to pay

EBA states that banks should assess other indications of unlikeliness to pay per type of portfolio, business line and geographical location and provides a list of examples of possible indications of unlikeliness to pay which could be considered (both from internal and external data sources):

- a borrower's sources of recurring income are no longer available to meet the payments of instalments;
- there are justified concerns about a borrower's future ability to generate stable and sufficient cash flows;
- the borrower's overall leverage level has significantly increased or there are justified expectations of such changes to leverage;
- the borrower has breached the covenants of a credit contract;
- the bank has called any collateral including a guarantee;
- for the exposures to an individual: default of a company fully owned by a single individual where this individual provided the bank with a personal guarantee for all obligations of a company;
- for retail exposures where the default definition is applied at the level of an individual credit facility, the fact that a significant part of the total obligation of the obligor is in default;
- the reporting of an exposure as non-performing in accordance with Annex V of Commission Implementing Regulation (EU) No 680/2014 of 16 April 2014 as amended by Commission Implementing Regulation (EU) 2015/227, except where competent authorities have replaced the 90 days past due with 180 days past due in accordance with point (b) of Article 178(1) of Regulation EU (No) 575/2013;
- significant delays in payments to other creditors have been recorded in the relevant credit register;
- a crisis of the sector in which the counterparty operates combined with a weak position of the counterparty in this sector;
- the disappearance of an active market for a financial asset because of the financial difficulties of the debtor;
- a bank has information that a third party, in particular, another bank, has filed for bankruptcy or similar protection of the obligor.

Banks should specify in their internal policies when the default of one obligor within the group of connected clients has a contagious effect on other entities within this group. Such specifications should be in line with the appropriate policies for the assignment of exposures to the individual obligor to an obligor grade and to groups of connected clients. Where such criteria have not been specified for a non-standard situation, in the case of default of an obligor that is part of a group of connected clients, banks should assess the potential unlikeliness to pay of all other entities within this group on a case-by-case basis.

Where a financial asset was purchased by, or originated from, a bank at a material discount, the bank should assess whether that discount reflects the deteriorated credit quality of the obligor.

With regard to each indication of unlikeliness to pay, banks should define the adequate methods of their identification, including the sources of information and frequency of monitoring.

Banks should have policies in place to identify credit frauds. If the fraud is identified before the default has been recognised, it should be considered as an additional indication of unlikeliness to pay. Banks should establish policies regarding the definition of default in order to ensure its consistent and effective application and, in particular, they should have clear policies and procedures on the application of the criteria for unlikeliness to pay.

2.4.3 Application of the definition of default in external data

In cases where a bank would like to use external data for the purpose of estimating risk parameters, the following conditions should be met:

- definition of default for external data should be consistent with the one implemented by the bank for the relevant portfolio;
- sources of external data and corresponding default definition should be documented;
- impact assessment on whether and to what extent usage of external data may lead to increase or decrease of default rate should be conducted;
- appropriate adjustments should be incorporated to external data or it should be demonstrated that no adjustments are needed in terms of the impact on all risk parameters;
- other relevant regulatory requirements should be met.

When differences in default definitions between external data and the bank's internal one cannot be overcome, an additional margin of conservatism (MoC) should be added to address materiality of remaining differences.

2.4.4 Consistency of the application of default definition

The default of a single obligor should be identified consistently across all a bank's departments and geographies. Banks should implement adequate procedures and mechanisms to ensure default definition consistency. If consistency is not possible to achieve due to different legislation or consumer protection regulation over different geographies, this should be communicated to competent authorities. If the implementation of consistency across all the bank's departments and geographies is very burdensome (e.g. requires the development of a centralised database over different geographies), the bank does not need to apply such mechanisms or procedures if it can demonstrate that the effect of non-compliance is immaterial. In case different default definitions are applied, the scope of application of each default definition should be specified.

If different default definitions are applied across types of exposures, the following conditions should hold:

- the scope of application of each definition is clearly specified;
- definition of default specified for a certain type of exposures, legal entity or geographical location is applied consistently to all exposures within the scope of application.

2.4.5 Application of default definition for retail exposures

For retail exposures, banks may choose to apply the definition of default at the level of an individual credit facility or at the level of a borrower.

In particular, banks may apply the definition of default at the level of an obligor for some types of retail exposures and at the level of a credit facility for others, where this is well justified by internal risk management practices, for instance, due to a different business model of a subsidiary, and where there is evidence that the number of situations where the same clients are subject to different definitions of default at different levels of application is kept to a strict minimum.

Where the definition of default has been applied at the level of an individual credit facility with regard to retail exposures, banks should not automatically consider the different exposures to the same obligor as defaulted at the same time. Nevertheless, banks should take into account that some indications of default are related to the condition of the obligor rather than the status of a particular exposure.

The application of the definition of default for retail exposures at the obligor level implies that where any credit obligation of the obligor meets the conditions of default definition all exposures to that obligor should be considered defaulted.

Banks that decide to apply the definition of default for retail exposures at the obligor level should specify detailed rules for the treatment of joint credit obligations and default contagion between exposures in their internal policies and procedures. Banks should consider a joint credit obligation as exposure to two or more obligors who are equally responsible for the repayment of the credit obligation. This notion does not extend to a credit obligation of an individual obligor secured by another individual or entity in the form of a guarantee or other credit protection.

Where the conditions for default definition are met, with regard to a joint credit obligation of two or more obligors, banks should consider all other joint credit obligations of the same set of obligors and all individual exposures to those obligors as defaulted, unless they can justify that the recognition of default on individual exposures is not appropriate because of at least one of the following conditions:

- The delay in payment of a joint credit obligation results from a dispute between the individual obligors participating in the joint credit obligation that has been introduced to a court or another dedicated external body that results in a binding ruling, and there is no concern about the financial situation of the individual obligors;
- A joint credit obligation is an immaterial part of the total obligations of an individual obligor.

The default of a joint credit obligation should not cause the default of other joint credit obligations of individual obligors with other individuals or entities, which are not involved in the credit obligation that has initially been defaulted; however, banks should assess whether the default of the joint credit obligation at hand constitutes an indication of unlikeliness to pay with regard to the other joint credit obligations.

Banks should conduct a thorough analysis of legislation framework in regards to joint credit obligations and provide in their internal policies procedures for the identification of the obligors that are legally fully liable for certain obligations jointly and severally with other obligors.

2.4.6 Criteria for the return to the non-defaulted status

EBA states that all of the following minimum conditions for reclassification to a non-defaulted status should be met (this does not apply to distressed restructuring):

- no trigger of default continues to apply to a previously defaulted exposure and at least three months have passed since the default event;
- the behaviour and financial situation of a borrower during the period of three months after default should be analysed, and the bank should be satisfied that the improvement in credit quality is factual and permanent;
- conditions stated above should also be met with regard to new exposures to the obligor.

In order to reclassify distressed restructuring defaulted cases as non-defaults, banks should ensure that no triggers of default continue to apply and that at least one year has passed since the latest of the following:

- the moment of extending the restructuring measures;
- the moment when the exposure has been classified as defaulted;
- the end of the grace period included in the restructuring arrangements.

Banks should reclassify the exposure to a non-defaulted status after at least the one-year period referred to in the previous paragraph, where all of the following conditions are met:

- during that period a material payment has been made by the obligor in total equal to the amount that was previously past-due or written off;
- there are no past-due credit obligations according to the schedule applicable after the restructuring arrangements;
- there are no indications of unlikeliness to pay;
- the bank does not consider it unlikely that the obligor will pay its credit obligations in full according to the schedule after the restructuring arrangements without recourse to realising security. In this assessment, banks should examine in particular situations where a large lump sum payment or significantly larger payments are envisaged at the end of the repayment schedule;
- the above conditions should be met with regard to new exposures to the obligor.

2.4.7 Materiality thresholds

The purpose of the section below is to summarise EBA paper "Draft regulatory technical standards on the materiality threshold for credit obligations past due under article 178 of Regulation (EU) No 575/2013" as of 28 September 2016. The section should not be considered as a full reference for the materiality threshold. For a comprehensive default definition, please refer to the above-mentioned document.

EBA states that materiality should result from the combination of absolute and relative thresholds (obligor or transaction are considered defaulted if both absolute and relative limits are breached) to be defined by the competent authority of each jurisdiction (and not by banks).

At obligor level, the relative threshold is set as a percentage of the sum of all credit obligations of the borrower.

At facility level, the relative threshold is set as a percentage of the single credit obligation of the borrower.

The relative threshold should be between 0% and 2.5%, and the following conditions should be considered in the final decision:

- the level of the materiality threshold does not lead to recognition of an excessive number of defaults that result from circumstances other than the financial difficulties of an obligor;
- the level of the materiality threshold does not lead to significant delays in recognition of defaults that result from the financial difficulties of an obligor.

The absolute threshold cannot be higher than 100 euros for retail borrowers and 500 euros for non-retail borrowers. If the absolute threshold is set up in a currency other than euro, and due to volatility of exchange rates threshold does not reflect the equivalent in euro (100 euro for retail loans and 500 euro for non-retail loans), the threshold should remain unchanged unless the competent authority receives approval from EBA that such threshold can be changed.

As said, the competent authorities define the materiality thresholds, meaning that they can vary across jurisdictions due to different economic conditions and price levels.

With the incorporation of the materiality thresholds, EBA also intends to remove discrepancies between banks caused by choice of payment allocation schemes (LIFO, FIFO, etc.). This will have an impact on a significant share of banks in Europe. For example, based on FIFO approach payments are first allocated to the earliest missed instalments, and in the LIFO approach payments are first allocated to the latest missed instalments. This means that the FIFO approach would generally result in earlier identification of defaults compared to LIFO. Additionally, defaults would return to non-defaulted status earlier in the FIFO approach than in the LIFO approach.

The proposed materiality thresholds and the technical analysis of possible approaches to their application for the purpose of the days part due flagging conducted by EBA has resulted in the following technical implementation option to be chosen: "the sum of all amounts past due is used in order to determine the breach of the materiality threshold, but the calculation of days past due starts when the materiality threshold is breached". This means that if the sum is continuously above the materiality thresholds for more than 90 days, a default will be considered to have occurred, irrespective of the arrears of individual credit obligations.

2.4.8 Implementation of changes

EBA confirms that the implementation of these new requirements related to default definition might, in some cases, require significant time and effort, especially in the case of banks that use the IRB Approach, and where the currently used definition of default is significantly different from the proposed rules. These banks will have to change not only their default identification processes and possibly IT systems but also (most probably) to re-estimate, recalibrate or develop their rating systems.

These new requirements described above should be incorporated by banks into their internal policies and IT systems as at 1 January 2021. Competent authorities may accelerate the timeline of this transition at their discretion. IRB banks should adjust their rating systems accordingly so that the estimates of risk parameters reflect the new definition of default by the same date. These adjustments should include at least the following:

- where possible, adjustments of the historical data based on the new definition of default;
- an assessment of the impact on all risk parameters and own funds requirements;

- the inclusion of an additional MoC in rating systems in order to account for the possible distortions of risk estimates resulting from the inconsistent definition of default in the historical data.

Adjustments described above should be verified by an internal validation team, classified as a material change according to the Commission Delegated Regulation (EU) No 529/2014 and, then, approved by the relevant competent authority.

2.4.9 Impact of new default definition on RWA

The impact of the new default definition varies depending on the portfolio and risk profile of each specific bank, and could result in either:

- an increase in PD due to lower materiality thresholds, and corresponding decreases in LGD, because the additional defaults have higher recovery rates;
- a decrease in PD due to the stricter rules related to return from defaulted status, and corresponding increases in LGD because of lower cure rates.

The final effect on RWA is not straightforward, and thus detailed analysis of the impact and of opportunities to optimise capital requirements must be explored by each bank.

In fact, in some cases, the implementation of a compliant default definition may result in lower RWA, as described below.

- In Figure 2.11 a simulation of the new default definition was conducted based on mortgage portfolios.
- Sensitivity analysis is based on different approaches for the default definition implementation.
- Example shows that it is possible to have lower RWA, even with new risk parameter input floors.

2.5 Risk estimates

EBA's new documents ('Guidelines on PD estimation, LGD estimation and the treatment of defaulted exposures', EBA/GL/2017/16, and 'Draft Regulatory Technical Standards on the specification of the nature, severity and duration of an economic downturn in accordance with Articles 181(3)(a) and 182(4)(a) of Regulation (EU) No 575/2013', CP/EBA/2017/02) on risk parameters estimation intend to limit the degree of freedom that banks have previously exercised when developing and calibrating their PD and LGD models.

These new requirements are expected to be fully implemented by the end of 2020 and should be considered together with the regulatory products on the default definition. In other words, banks will first have to adjust their default definition (and historical default data), and will then have to redevelop and recalibrate their risk parameter models. Moreover, banks will have to ensure that, by 2020, the models are properly documented, implemented in their IT systems, approved by senior management and

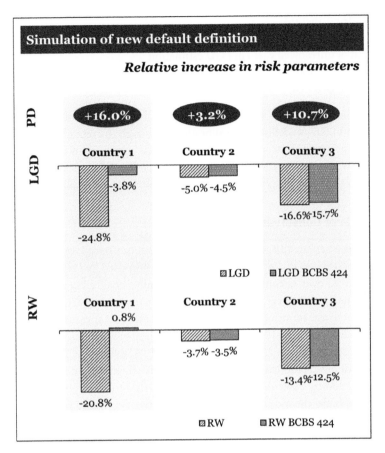

Figure 2.11: Simulation of new default definition impact on RWA

management body and that the supervisory authorities are notified of changes through the submission of detailed and formalised documentation packs. In turn, the supervisory authorities will have to process the wave of notifications and conduct on-site model reviews and approvals.

Considering the number of models in some of the IRB banks (in many cases, over 50 distinct models), the significance of the changes from both a technical and methodological perspective, and the number of steps between the start of work and final supervisory approval, the right time to begin implementing the requirements is now. As banks are finally bringing to an end their IFRS 9 modelling programmes, which in many cases took several years, they will have to reallocate resources quickly to the IRB projects in order to cope with this tough deadline.

The following sections cover some of the more challenging and contentious methodological changes to risk parameter estimation, such as:

- MoC,
- rating philosophy,

- default rate estimation,
- treatment of multiple defaults,
- treatment of unresolved cases in LGD estimation,
- treatment of defaulted exposures and
- downturn adjustment of LGD and CF estimates.

Apart from these, there are a significant number of other less contentious clarifications on the PD and LGD modelling and calibration. Although the remaining clarifications might be fairly straightforward for many banks, their significant number and overarching scope would still require many of the models to be fully redeveloped or at least recalibrated.

2.5.1 Margin of Conservatism (MoC)

From the time when the IRB Approach was first introduced, banks were expected to use conservative estimates of risk parameters. This was proposed by the Basel Committee in order to avoid over-optimism in models, especially considering the fact that their outcome is often prone to error due to deficiencies in underlying data. That being said, in the past, there was no strict guidance for the identification, measurement and incorporation of a MoC into the IRB models. Due to the lack of strict guidance, banks often opted to embed the MoC implicitly into the models. This was done by adjusting some of the methodological modelling assumptions to make them more conservative, rather than actually adding MoC on the top of modelled risk estimates. Such an approach would indeed make the models somehow conservative, but would not provide a clear view of the magnitude of the conservatism to the supervisors. The EBA felt that such an approach was not precise enough, and has thus proposed much more structured guidance on this area.

These new guidelines introduce a structured framework in which all deficiencies must be clearly identified, classified, quantified, mapped into a specific, explicit MoC adjustment, properly monitored and documented. As the first step of the process, banks should have a robust process for identifying all deficiencies and to classify them into distinct categories. These include data and methodological deficiencies (e.g. missing or inaccurate historical information on risk drivers, default triggers, losses), as well as deficiencies due to diminished representation caused by shifts in portfolio risk profiles, changes to internal policies and underwriting standards, or to the overall market or legal environment. Once deficiencies are identified, they must be rectified through appropriate adjustments to the models, whose aim is to correct the deficiencies and ensure that PD and LGD reflect the best estimate view of the true underlying risk.

The purpose of the MoC is to ensure that risk parameters post adjustments are conservative enough, considering that (a) adjustments to data or methodology that attempt to remove deficiencies generally result in increased estimation errors and higher uncertainty and (b) some of the deficiencies might not be corrected via adjustments due to lack of information or a sound technical approach.

Since MoC is now an explicit component that has to be added directly on top of modelled estimates, it must be properly quantified. The EBA explains that the quantification must be performed across several specific categories: (a) MoC related to data or methodological deficiencies, (b) MoC related to relevant changes to underwriting standards, risk appetite, collection and recovery policies and any other source of additional uncertainty, and (c) the general estimation error. The final MoC is the sum of the aforementioned margins of conservatism under each category. While this definitely seems like a sound and structured approach, what the EBA does not explain is how to actually quantify the amount of necessary conservatism depending on the type and severity of the deficiencies. This will be a significant challenge for banks, since the quantification of errors is not always straightforward, and requires the development of new methodological approaches. Moreover, since MoC is a relatively new concept, there is limited information available to benchmark the level of MoC based on the results of other banks. One main reason for that is that most banks cannot provide input as such frameworks do not exist yet.

Besides the proper quantification of MoC, banks are expected to monitor deficiencies and MoC over time, and also develop plans to rectify the deficiencies and reduce the estimation errors within a reasonable timeline. Finally, MoC must be thoroughly documented, with the description of sources and types of deficiencies, adjustments applied to arrive at best estimates, and methods used to quantify and aggregate MoC per each risk parameter and for each of the rating systems.

Combined, all of these facts present a significant challenge for banks, as they will have to create a structured and sound MoC framework for the first time. On the other hand, this is also an opportunity for banks to address model deficiencies, and reduce overall conservatism embedded in the models over time, resulting in more accurate, and possibly even lower RWA.

The implicit conservatism already included in models through underlying assumptions can often result in excessive conservatism. By removing implicit MoC from the model development process and calculating it explicitly (i.e. outside the main model) as an add-on, banks can potentially lower the overall level of risk parameters. Even if this is not the case at the outset, explicit MoC provides better insight into the true source of deficiencies, and the true cost of deficiencies. This will in turn provide an incentive to solve deficiencies over time, resulting in gradual decreases in MoC and reductions of RWA. In addition, the structure of the MoC framework, with clear classification into the discreet types of deficiency, allows better prioritisation of issues, the development of clear timelines for their improvement and assignment of owners responsible for their resolution.

2.5.2 Rating philosophy

Rating philosophy refers to the cyclicality of the PD estimates and consistency of the rating assignment over time. Rating systems are typically classified into Point-in-Time

(PiT), Through-the-Cycle (TtC) or hybrid categories. Banks are required to determine the characteristics of each rating system – whether or not it is PiT, TtC or an in-between rating system, in order to understand the implications on the dynamics and volatility of the own funds.

On the one hand, PiT rating systems produce more accurate one-year forecasts that can significantly deviate from long-run averages at the extremes of the business cycle. This can be achieved, for example, by embedding into the model risk drivers that are more correlated with macroeconomic variables. As the economic situation improves, so do the values of the factors in the models, causing clients to migrate to better ratings, and ultimately resulting in lower portfolio level PD predictions. On the other hand, as the economic situation deteriorates, so do the values of factors in the model, causing migrations to the worst rating grades, and resulting in higher portfolio level PD predictions.

This has its own benefits and costs. While such PD estimates are fairly accurate representations of the expectations one year ahead – which is certainly a benefit when regulatory models are used for internal credit risk management purposes – due to the fluctuations of PD produced by the models from one year to the next, RWA and capital requirements can fluctuate significantly over time as well.

On the contrary, TtC rating systems are more stable, consistently predicting the long run average default rate at the portfolio level. This is achieved by limited highly cyclical factors in the models, which in turn limits the number of rating migrations caused by macroeconomic fluctuations over the rating cycle. Such systems have the benefit of producing stable RWA and capital requirements. However, such systems under- or overestimate the default rates in particular years.

The concepts of PiT and TtC rating philosophies are not new. What is new, however, is that banks now have to thoroughly investigate and monitor to what extent their models are PiT or TtC. Banks must choose their own rating philosophy, and fully understand the implications on the volatility of RWA. Once the rating philosophy is chosen, it must be applied consistently towards the rating system over time. Therefore, monitoring of the rating philosophy appropriateness includes a review of the risk drivers as well as rating migrations and rating yearly default rates. Overall, the rating philosophy requirements would result in more analytical work for banks, more thorough monitoring exercises, as well as a better understanding of the rating systems on the part of senior management and management body.

2.5.3 Calculation of one-year and long-run average default rates

Although the approach to the calculation of one-year default rates is not necessarily technically difficult, it has also been identified as an important driver of differences in RWA. The implementation of the CRR, namely Article 4(78), helps to reduce the variability in the definition of the one-year default rate. However, further alignment is necessary, as significant room for interpretation was observed.

The EBA Guidelines have clarified that default rates should be calculated at the rating grade level using the following equation:

$$DR = \frac{\text{obligors or exposures in dethe nominator that}}{\text{obligors or exposures which are in a portfolio}}$$
$$DR = \frac{\text{defaulted within one year period after cut off date}}{\text{at the beginning of one year period (cut off date)}}$$

In other words, the denominator includes the obligors or exposures which are not in default assigned to that rating grade or pool at the beginning of the one-year period or so-called cut-off, whereas the numerator includes the obligors or exposures considered in the denominator that have defaulted during a period of one year after the respective cut-off date. In case multiple defaults are observed for the same obligor or exposure during the period of one year, a single default with the date of the first observed default is considered. The guidelines also clarify whether or not the calculation must be performed before or after overrides and post-model adjustments, how observations with missing ratings should be treated, as well as observations which have experienced rating migrations.

The EBA has also observed significant differences in the calibration of PD parameters that stem both from the choice of data as well as calibration methods. According to the CRR, PD estimates for each grade or pool should reflect the long run average of one-year default rates in order to ensure that they are relatively stable over time. However, in practice, banks often do not have sufficient data to encompass the whole economic cycle in terms of the cyclicality of major economic factors. In this case, they often apply extrapolation methods to account for the missing data, which can result in an overestimation or underestimation of PD, if they are not performed in a consistent manner across all banks.

The EBA clarifies that, at the very least, five previous years of historical data must be used for PD. Where relevant, additional years must be added to the calibration period as well in order to reflect the likely range of variability of default rates. Where a bank determines that the available historical time period does not cover the full range of likely default rates, then an adjustment must be made to the average of observed one-year default rates. The ECB had for several countries identified the respective historical time intervals so that the effects of the economic recession could be represented in the data series.[39]

Banks can even consider downward adjustments to the average of observed default rates in the event that bad years are over-represented in historical data. However, the possibility to use these downward adjustments is severely limited. A benchmark is

---

[39] The TRIM guide released by the ECB in February 2017 had for Portugal, Greece, Spain and Ireland indicative minimum observation periods.

proposed – equal to the maximum of one-year default rates over the entire historical period and over the last five years. Estimates of long-run default rates below this benchmark are possible but should be fully justified and subject to additional MoC. Needless to say, any deviations should be documented in detail and subject to a thorough review by the competent authority.

2.5.4 Treatment of multiple defaults

In order to ensure consistency between the estimates of various risk parameters, the EBA states that multiple defaults should be treated in a similar manner across the risk parameters.

According to the current understanding of the EBA, a defaulted exposure that is returned to non-defaulted status (i.e. after the probation period) but is then classified as defaulted again in a short period of time (9 months) should be treated as constantly defaulted from the first moment when the default occurred.

Such treatment reflects the real economic meaning of the default experience. At the same time, the treatment of multiple defaults of the same facility as separate defaults might lead to significant errors in risk parameters estimates. Higher default rates would lead to higher PD estimates. LGD values, in this case, would be underestimated. In order to be more specific, the following example is presented:

- The client defaults, afterwards cures, and, in a short time, defaults again.
- The first default of the obligor would be treated as a cured case with a very small loss. In this case, LGD is going to be low. The count of our defaults, in this case, will be increased by one.
- The second default of the same facility will again increase the default counter by one. However, the LGD value, in this case, might be different from that in the first case.

In the aforementioned example, our PD value seems to be overestimated as two default events were counted. LGD might be underestimated, as during the first default event a low observed LGD value was recorded which might not be close to the LGD observed after the second default occurred.

It should also be considered that multiple defaults treatment must be consistent among PD and LGD estimates, both in terms of the recording moment of default and the number of defaults.

In order to solve this issue we, first of all, should refer to the EBA/GL/2016/07 with regards to the probation period concept. The minimum probation period should reflect the time after which the probability of consecutive default is minimised. A reasonably set probation period based on the historical default experience would significantly limit the number of multiple defaults.

In addition to that, at the end of the probation period, the return to non-default status should not occur automatically, but an additional assessment of the payment behaviour and financial situation should first indicate improvement in the counterparty creditworthiness implying a further reduction of multiple default situations.

For a limited remaining number of multiple defaults, the EBA clarifies that default history should not be changed in case of a consequent default. However, in the LGD assessment defaults occurring within 9 months after the return to non-default status, should be treated as one continuous defaulted status starting from the first default date. In this way, the LGD estimate would not be underestimated and would represent the full economic loss associated with a facility.

The consistency between the PD and LGD estimation would be ensured by the use of the same default database for both estimates.

2.5.5 Treatment of unresolved cases in LGD estimation

According to Article 181(1)(a) of the CRR, all observed defaults should be taken into account. Thus both complete and incomplete recovery processes should be considered for LGD estimation. The reasoning behind the inclusion of incomplete processes is to take into account the most up-to-date information about recent recoveries.

In order to obtain a realistic value of the long-run average LGD, the incomplete recovery processes should be included with future recoveries and costs that are expected to be realised or incurred. The value of future recoveries should be calculated as an estimate based on closed recovery processes. As a result, the long-run average of the LGD estimate will also be a measure that is not fully objective, as it contains components that are estimated. To minimise the degree of subjectivity that banks might apply in the estimation of future recoveries, the EBA provides some clarifications of how this process must be conducted.

The expected future recoveries for incomplete processes should be estimated up to a maximum recovery period. In case the workout process already exceeds the maximum workout period expected for the portfolio, the bank cannot assume that additional recoveries will be made in the future.

For cases where there is still an expectation of future recoveries, banks may estimate future costs and recoveries both from the realisation of the collaterals and without the use of collaterals. For the estimation of the future costs and recoveries, banks should analyse and compare the individual realised costs and recoveries with the average costs and recoveries realised during a similar period of time on similar exposures. In other words, any assumptions on future recoveries should be based on historical data associated with exposures, which are similar to those that have not yet recovered.

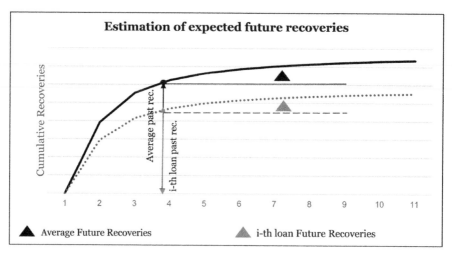

Figure 2.12: Estimation of expected future recoveries

Figure 2.12 is a high-level example of a possible approach which could be used as a basis for estimation of expected recoveries:

1. Estimate average recovery patterns based on historical data.

2. Analyse dependency between past recoveries and future recoveries, e.g. build a regression of the following form:

$$\frac{Future\ recoveries_{i-th\ loan}}{Average\ future\ recoveries} = a + b \left(\frac{Past\ recoveries_{i-th\ loan}}{Average\ past\ recoveries} \right)$$

3. For each loan, compare individual past with average past recoveries in order to forecast individual future recoveries.

The assumptions underlying the expected future costs and recoveries should be adequately justified and back-tested.

2.5.6 Treatment of defaulted exposures

The area of the treatment of defaulted assets is not covered by any specific EBA mandate included in the CRR. However, a lot of significant discrepancies were found between banks' practices and the expectations of the competent authorities, resulting in noteworthy differences in capital requirements, especially since the financial crisis has led to an increase in the size of the defaulted portfolios.

For those reasons, it is important to provide clear interpretations of the CRR requirements. Therefore, the EBA has included in its published guidelines information on the treatment of defaulted assets that covers, in particular, the following:

- LGD for defaulted exposures: the so-called LGD in-default.

- ELBE, as well as the computation of IRB shortfall in accordance with Article 159 of the CRR.
- The difference between EL amounts and credit risk adjustments, additional value adjustments and other own funds reductions for the purpose of own funds recognition (the so-called IRB shortfall).

In the case of the A-IRB Approach the RW of defaulted exposures is calculated according to the following equation:

$$RW = max\{0; 12.5 * (LGD - EL_{BE})\}$$

where:

LGD is the LGD in default parameter, and

EL_{BE} is best estimate of expected loss.

According to Article 181(1)(f) of the CRR, ELBE reflects current economic circumstances and exposure status. LGD in-default should additionally take into account the estimate of the increase of loss rate caused by possible additional unexpected losses during the recovery period. In practice, there are two possible approaches to meet this requirement:

- direct estimation of downturn LGD and ELBE for defaulted exposures;
- direct estimation of ELBE and estimation of LGD in-default as the sum of EL_{BE} and an add-on capturing of the unexpected loss related with exposures in default that might occur during the recovery period.

The EBA Guidelines do indeed provide practical guidance on the relevant calculations and contain numerous specifications on how the LGD-in-default and ELBE risk parameters should be calculated. In fact, the specifications are so far-reaching that, for most banks, they would result in the need to develop new models for defaulted exposures.

For instance, the Guidelines specify that both for modelling and risk parameter application purposes, different reference dates after the date of default can be considered. The goal is always to calculate the value of the risk parameter that is relevant for the current status of the exposures. However, the relationship between risk drivers and expected future recoveries changes throughout the workout period. Some risk drivers may only become relevant after the default event or even after the exposure has been in default for a sufficient period of time. For factors which remain relevant over time, factor values change over time. For instance, information on collateral can change significantly at a certain point of time, when revaluation is performed or after the bank completes a certain stage in the collection process. In addition, time in default, which is often a significant risk driver in itself, is constantly increasing.

Changes in factors over time should be considered both in the estimation of ELBE and LGD-in-default. First, banks have to ensure that they collect information on risk drivers at different points of time after the default event. Second, they must structure the model in such a way that, where relevant, different factors are considered at various points of time. Finally, they must revalue risk parameters at certain points of time after the default event (called reference dates), in order to ensure that they are relevant to the current situation.

At the same time, the Guidelines also specify that the risk parameters for defaulted exposures should be linked to those for non-defaulted exposures to avoid cliff-off events. Thus, there should be a link between the LGD model for performing exposures, and LGD-in-default and ELBE models for defaulted exposures. This would ensure that immediately after the default date, the value of the risk parameters do not change significantly simply due to the transfer of the exposure from one model to the other, and would avoid major fluctuations in capital requirements.

With respect to incomplete recovery processes, the Guidelines specify that the same general requirements as for performing exposures must be adhered to. The Guidelines additionally specify that incomplete recovery processes should be used only in the estimation of risk parameters for those reference dates, for which historical information on recoveries and costs are available for the next reference date. For instance, if an exposure is two years in default, and there were historical observations in the dataset that were in default longer than two years, which experienced recoveries up until the third year, such information can be used in modelling, provided that the next reference date is three years after default. However, if an exposure is three years in default, and no historical observations experienced recoveries past this point, then further recoveries should not be included in the modelling assumptions.

The EBA has also made a number of clarifications with respect to ELBE. First, it has specified that banks cannot simply rely on accounting provisions as the basis for ELBE, as most of them did in the past. The ELBE should be based on a sound model, which is fully compliant with the articles of the CRR and the EBA Guidelines. Some exceptions could still exist, for instance, if the accounting model itself is based on EBA requirements (i.e. if regulatory ELBE is leveraged for accounting purposes), or if the individual assessment is performed for large exposures and is used as an override to modelled ELBE.

Second, the EBA specified how and in which cases ELBE should be modelled. ELBE represents the best estimate view of the EL and should be modelled as an adjustment to the long-run average LGD. To avoid excessive use of adjustments, an adjustment should only be made when the risk estimates produced by the long-run average LGD model component are not sufficiently sensitive to macroeconomic conditions. Where macroeconomic factors are included directly in the long-run LGD estimates or indirectly through risk factors, which are sensitive to macroeconomic parameters, additional adjustments to the long-run LGD estimates are not necessary in order to arrive at ELBE.

The EBA has also clarified the distinction between LGD-in-default and ELBE and explained how they are interrelated. While it is true that LGD-in-default can be calculated either directly or as ELBE and an add-on, it must be made sure that LGD-in-default reflects a possible adverse change in economic conditions, resulting in UL above the best estimate. Moreover, whereas ELBE does not need to take into account any MoC (since it is supposed to reflect a best estimate view), LGD-in-default should include conservatism. Banks are expected to be able to document the relationship between various LGD components, e.g. they must clearly demonstrate the breakdown of LGD-in-default into ELBE and an add-on, and further demonstrate the breakdown of the add-on into its sub-components, namely the downturn adjustment and the MoC.

In practice, this means that for most of the existing LGD models the sub-components and the base LGD model itself would need to be developed from the scratch as most of the existing models will not meet the specific aforementioned criteria. The new LGD models, in turn, should be a compilation of several modelled components which are arranged in a structured way in several distinct steps. The components should reflect differences between pre-default and post-default exposures, the long-run average LGD, ELBE, a downturn adjustment and MoC.

Figure 2.13 displays the possible modelling steps to arrive at a compliant LGD framework. The figure contains all of the relevant modelling components, such as:

- LRA LGD, which reflects the modelled LGD calibrated to the long-run average, where the long-run average is the average of realised closed and incomplete LGD. LRA LGD is a base model for all other components.

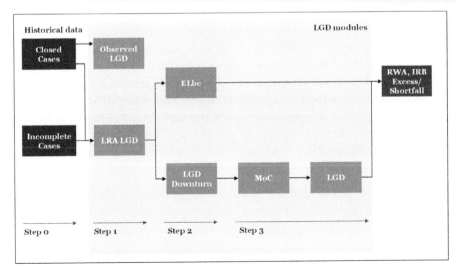

Figure 2.13: Overview of LGD parameters based on EBA requirements

- LGD downturn represents the LGD resulting from the LRA LGD when it is stressed in order to reflect downturn economic conditions. LGD downturn is estimated for both performing and defaulted exposures.
- MoC represents the add-on to reflect the uncertainties and errors in the historical data and other methodological deficiencies.
- LGD represents the final LGD estimates after downturn and MoC adjustments, which are used as the basis for RWA estimation. These estimates should be available for both performing and defaulted portfolios.
- ELBE, which is estimated for only defaulted exposures, reflects best estimates given current economic conditions.
- Finally, ELBE and LGD for defaulted exposures are used as inputs in the calculation of RWA and IRB Excess/Shortfall.

2.5.7 Downturn adjustment of LGD and CF estimates

Currently, the CRR requires that the LGD and CF estimates should reflect the downturn conditions if these are more conservative than the respective long-run average. Despite the fact that the main idea of downturn effect is clear, regulatory requirements still lack detailed rules on what the downturn conditions are, and how to apply them in the risk estimation process. Therefore, a wide variety of approaches is currently used by banks to address an economic recession.

In order to introduce consistency across banks and jurisdictions, Articles 181(3a) and 182(4a) of the CRR require the EBA to develop draft RTS to specify the nature, severity and duration of economic downturn for the purpose of LGD and CF estimation. As at the time of the writing of this book, the draft RTS have already been published by the EBA[40] and are undergoing a consultation and revision period.

2.5.8 Conclusion

Competent authorities will assess in detail the models used by banks for the purpose of the IRB Approach. It will be verified whether the risk parameters are estimated according to the new rules. This verification is going to be done either during the regular review of the IRB Approach or when assessing banks' applications for material changes of models. In most cases, these changes will be classified as a material change in the final risk parameters estimation, prompting supervisory approval before these can be used for regulatory purposes. Additionally, as part of the ECB's TRIM exercise, which is currently being conducted in the SSM, a number of EBA requirements are also already being taken into account by the supervisor (for details see section 2.6).

It is expected that the new technical standards and guidelines could lead to material changes in numerous models. Moreover, the implementation of those rules might appear to be time consuming. With respect to PD models, some may have to be

---

40 CP/EBA/2017/02.

redeveloped, and most will have to be recalibrated, in particular, due to the new default definition. With respect to LGD models, it now seems as most of LGD models will have to be re-developed due to the new modelling requirements.

The overall impact of changes is likely to lead to an increase in RWA, although some banks might experience little change or even decreases in RWA. With respect to defaulted exposures, for some banks, it is possible that the envisaged clarification of the provisions with regard to the calculation of the IRB shortfall might cause a cliff effect on own funds. Therefore, it will be important that both banks and their competent authorities handle such situations in a prudent manner.

2.6 ECB's targeted review of internal models (TRIM)

During the last few years, the reliability of risk models has been seriously questioned by both regulators and supervisors due to significant variation in RWA across EU banks. The main areas of concern were as follows.

- Some banks used internal models to ensure low capital requirements.
- A significant amount of variation was linked to technical modelling choices, and not to differences of risk profiles in the underlying assets.
- Supervisory practices across territories were divergent.

In response to model weaknesses found in the credit risk models of systemically important banks, the ECB launched the Targeted Review of Internal Models (TRIM), which started in late 2015 and is expected to be finalised in 2019. After 2019, TRIM-related activities will be integrated into regular model validation (namely in terms of infrastructure, tools, processes and methodologies).

The ECB is making a large investment in TRIM in terms of its own staff and the cost of external resources, with more than 100 inspectors from its teams and national supervisors being involved.

The on-site missions take place in 2017 and 2018 (with a possible extension into 2019). Each on-site mission requires at least six people to work over a period of at least ten weeks. More than 100 missions commenced in 2017. For each on-site mission, up to half of the workforce will be made up of external consultants. This allows the ECB to maintain its other ongoing supervisory activities.

One of the main objectives of TRIM exercise is the assessment of reliability and comparability of the rating systems across Europe and assurance that risks and capital requirements are calculated correctly. TRIM is led by SSM model experts, involving local regulators and external consultants to support on-site missions.

The TRIM is based on the TRIM Guide[41] published in February 2017. It sets out the ECB's view on appropriate supervisory practices and how regulation is to be applied.

---

41 https://www.bankingsupervision.europa.eu/ecb/pub/pdf/trim_guide.en.pdf

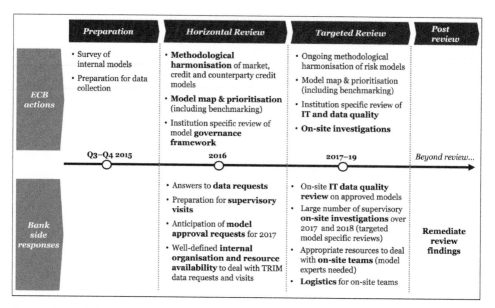

The Guide is also closely aligned with upcoming changes in the regulations on IRB models to speed-up the implementation in the banking industry of new requirements that would come into effect in 2021.

Under the TRIM, IRB models are reviewed in terms of data quality and IT infrastructure, as well as of qualitative and quantitative assumptions and features.

One of the main challenges that banks are facing under TRIM is data quality. Significant amounts of data and documents have to be gathered for the assessment of the data quality governance and management frameworks.

The most frequent issues that banks are facing are as follows: absence of a data quality governance and management policy, lack of automated data quality controls (including reconciliations) for databases and systems in the IRB workflow, disorganised data quality management and reporting processes (the lack of proper data reporting, dashboards), decentralised data storage and inability to trace the data related to key variables back to source systems and absence of (updated) data dictionaries.

Furthermore, banks are being required to provide data templates that need time for data filling-in and quality assurance in order to give comfort to the TRIM's assessment teams on the work done and minimise undue flag alerts.

One of the hot topics is clearly the assessment of IRB models against EBA's newly introduced IRB requirements. Banks were not prepared to implement requirements before the implementation deadline at the end of 2020. New IRB requirements are very complex and in most of the cases require extensive work for models' re-development (particular critical when it comes to estimate LGD, the treatment of defaulted assets and the MoC).

On the quantitative assessment, IRB models are assessed as well with a close look at the level of quality of recent validation reports, including the core components of validation (e.g. quantitative and qualitative assessments, data quality tests, analysis of identified weaknesses and mitigating actions taken to overcome deficiencies, as well as the resulting MoC). It is clear that not only do the validation reports have to be more precise and prove the independence (and right challenge) of the validation function from model development unit(s), but also banks need to formalise triggers of model re-estimation, development and calibration, specifying respective metrics and thresholds, adjusting their validation and monitoring approaches.

Moreover, regarding the qualitative assessment, during the TRIM exercise, attention is focused on the level of quality of models documentation, model changes processes, validation function and methodology, as well as reporting and monitoring processes. It has been evident that banks need to enhance their model risk management frameworks: fractured, out of date or sparsely documented model inventory, model validation with limited challenge, inexistence of a methodology for assessing the materiality of rating systems, and ineffective follow up on model deficiencies are all examples of flaws in this regard.

The timeframe for the TRIM preparation and on-site investigation is very short, during which banks have to manage to deliver a high volume of mandatory data and documentation requests. As a result of TRIM, capital requirements may be directly impacted if the reviews reveal methodological weakness in models. All revisions made in the TRIM context will also be considered as an input in the Supervisory Review and Evaluation Process (SREP) assessment and, therefore, impact on the final grade and respective capital decision.

In line with usual procedure, the ECB will ask banks to address any gaps in their compliance with regulatory requirements directly after completing the on-site missions.

Finally, it should be noted that TRIM is one of the largest EU-wide exercises which the ECB has conducted, both in terms of overall timelines and the resources allocated to this project. This should both alarm banks, and at the same time provide reassurance to them. On the one hand, more in-depth supervisory reviews are an enormous challenge to IRB banks, especially considering that TRIM is happening at the same time as banks are beginning to implement EBA requirements, and as they start to think about Basel IV. On the other hand, the fact that the ECB has invested such an effort into the exercise shows that it still believes in the value of internal models for regulatory purposes, provided that they are developed in a consistent manner across banks and are based on sound data and sound methodological approaches.

Recommended Literature

Basel Committee on Banking Supervision; BCBS 362 (2016): Consultative Document – Reducing variation in credit risk-weighted assets – constraints on the use of internal model approaches, 2016

European Banking Authority; EBA (2013): Summary report on the comparability and pro-cyclicality of capital requirements under the IRB Approach in accordance with Article 502 of the Capital Requirements Regulation; 2013.

European Banking Authority; EBA (2015): Discussion Paper on the future of the IRB Approach"; (EBA/DP/2015/01), 2015.

European Banking Authority; EBA (2016a): Final Draft Regulatory Technical Standards on the specification of the assessment methodology for competent authorities regarding compliance of an institution with the requirements to use the IRB Approach in accordance with Articles 144(2), 173(3) and 180(3)(b) of Regulation (EU) No 575/2013; (EBA/GL/2016/03), 2016

European Banking Authority; EBA (2016b): Final Report: Guidelines on the definition of default under Article 178 of Regulation (EU) No 575/2013; (EBA/GL/2016/07), 2016

European Banking Authority; EBA (2016c): Final Report: Draft Regulatory Technical Standards on the materiality threshold for credit obligations past due under Article 178 of Regulation (EU) No 575/2013; (EBA/RTS/2016/06), 2016

European Banking Authority; EBA (2017a): Guidelines on the estimation of risk parameters under the IRB Approach; (EBA/GL/2017/16), 2017

European Banking Authority; EBA (2017b): Draft Regulatory Technical Standards on the specification of the nature, severity and duration of an economic downturn in accordance with Articles 181(3)(a) and 182(4)(a) of Regulation (EU) No 575/2013; (EBA/CP/2017/02), 2017

European Central Bank; ECB (2017): Guide for the Targeted Review of Internal Models (TRIM); 2017

Commission Delegated Regulation (EU) No 529/2014 of 12 March 2014 supplementing Regulation (EU) No 575/2013 of the European Parliament and of the Council with regard to regulatory technical standards for assessing the materiality of extensions and changes of the Internal Ratings Based Approach and the Advanced Measurement Approach

Commission Implementing Regulation (EU) No 680/2014 of 16 April 2014 laying down implementing technical standards with regard to supervisory reporting of institutions according to Regulation (EU) No 575/2013 of the European Parliament and of the Council

Commission Implementing Regulation (EU) 2015/227 of 9 January 2015 amending Implementing Regulation (EU) No 680/2014 laying down implementing technical standards with regard to supervisory reporting of institutions according to Regulation (EU) No 575/2013 of the European Parliament and of the Council.

3 The New Standardised Approach for measuring Counterparty Credit Risk (SA-CCR)

Fanos Ciftci and Stefan Röth

The Basel Committee's introduction of Basel III rules in 2010 contained significant revisions to the regulatory framework for measuring capital requirements associated with counterparty credit risk. Within Europe, these revisions were implemented on 1 January 2014 with the introduction of CRR and CRD IV, but it wasn't long before further changes were being discussed. In March 2014, the Basel Committee published a new paper (BCBS 279) to introduce a standardised approach for measuring counterparty credit risk associated with OTC derivatives, exchange-traded derivatives and long settlement transactions. This new standardised approach, known as SA-CCR, was designed to replace both the Current Exposure Method (CEM) and the Standardised Method (SM) in the capital adequacy framework. In Europe, the SA-CCR will be introduced as part of the CRR II package.[1] Other countries are also in the final steps of transferring BCBS 279 or the new standardised approach into a binding minimum requirement.

3.1 Counterparty credit risk

3.1.1 Definition of counterparty credit risk

"Counterparty credit risk" (CCR) refers to the risk that a counterparty involved in a transaction defaults and is not able to fulfill the terms and requirements of the transaction. Counterparty credit risk of derivative transactions differs from the more "traditional" kind of credit risk insofar as the potential exposure to the counterparty at default is unknown. Since the market value of a derivative transaction moves with the underlying risk factors, there could be a potential positive or negative exposure to the counterparty at the point of default. In other words, the exposure at default is not deterministic. Compare this with the exposure to counterparties in traditional credit transactions, where the exposure is known from the start and does not change through the life of the transaction. An additional difference between the CCR of derivatives and traditional credit risk is that the CCR inherent in derivative transactions creates a risk for both counterparties involved in the transaction during the entire duration of the agreement. In a traditional credit transaction, the credit risk exists exclusively for the creditor and not for the borrower.

3.1.2 Measuring counterparty credit risk in the EU

The regulatory requirements for measuring CCR are defined in Part 3, Chapter 6 of the Capital Requirements Regulation (CRR). Besides derivatives, additional transactions

---

1 The European Commission published a first draft of the amended CRR ("CRR II") on 23 November 2016 including the SA-CCR framework.

such as repurchase transactions, securities or commodities lending or borrowing transactions, long settlement transactions and margin lending transactions may be treated
according to the CCR framework, if certain methods are used.

The starting point for measuring CCR associated with derivative transactions for the
purpose of calculating regulatory capital charges is the determination of the potential
exposure which exists in the case of a counterparty default. The so-called "Exposure at
Default" (EAD) is the assessment base of the regulatory CCR capital requirement and
therefore one of the most important parameters in CCR measurement for regulatory
purposes. Given that the EAD is not deterministic, the measurement of counterparty
credit risk is complex. The methods set forth in the CRR to determine the EAD are
outlined in Figure 3.1.

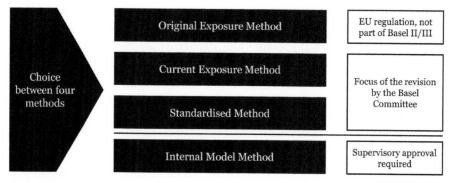

Figure 3.1: Methods to determine the EAD according to CRR

The order of the list is consistent with the models' increasing degree of complexity.
The application of the current "Original Exposure Method"[2] is exclusively granted to
non-trading book institutions. This method is not based on one of the Basel Committee's supervisory standards, rather it is a specificity of EU regulation. The current
exposure method (CEM) was introduced in Basel I back in 1988. Although the standardised method (SM) and the internal model method (IMM) were introduced as
alternatives to the CEM with Basel II, the CEM is the most widely used method to
determine the EAD. This is also due to the fact that the SM exhibits a high degree
of complexity due to the required knowledge of internal modelling of delta equiva-
lents and that institutions need supervisory approval to use the IMM, which comes
hand in hand with significant efforts. As was already mentioned, the "new standardised approach for measuring counterparty credit risk" (SA-CCR) will replace the CEM
and the SM. The IMM will remain in force but IMM banks may be required to calculate
a SA-CCR based floor (see Chapter 9). At least in the European Union, the SA-CCR
will be accompanied by several less complex methods designed to be used by banks

---

2   With the publication of the CRR II draft in November 2016, the current Original Exposure Method had been
    revised.

with smaller derivative portfolios, to replace or enhance the current Original Exposure Method. The replacement of the CEM will have a major impact on the banking landscape as this method is applied by the majority of European banks.

3.1.3 Background and motives for introducing the SA-CCR approach

The final Basel paper for the SA-CCR (BCBS 279) was published in March 2014. At the start of the consultation phase, which started in June 2013 with the first consultative document (BCBS 254), the approach was called the "non-internal model method" (NIMM)[3]. After an impact study in October of that same year, the SA-CCR was ultimately published under its final name taking into account the findings of said study[4].

With the introduction of the SA-CCR, the Basel Committee aimed to accomplish several goals. To start with, it wanted to devise an approach that was suitable to be applied to a wide variety of derivatives – that is for margined and unmargined as well as for cleared and bilateral derivative transactions. Moreover, the SA-CCR should provide a standardised approach that was capable of being implemented simply and uses elements which were already available in the Basel framework (e.g. add-ons, asset classes, asset-class-specific volatility rates, etc.). The approach should also minimise discretionary powers of national supervisory authorities and improve the risk sensitivity with regard to calculations without creating undue complexity. However, one of the most important goals was that the SA-CCR should address known deficiencies of the CEM and the SM. The CEM was criticised mainly because of its economically inadequate representation of netting. Besides an extremely high level of complexity, the SM also was criticised because it required internal methods know-how for computing delta-equivalents. Both methods were criticised because they did not differentiate between margined and unmargined transactions and did not sufficiently capture the level of volatilities as observed over recent stress periods. Figure 3.2 summarises the goals to be achieved by introducing the SA-CCR. The lead time to implement the SA-CCR was generously selected in order to leave sufficient time to prepare for the conversion – especially for smaller banks.

3.2 Side note: Calculating EAD with the current exposure method

Other than the Original Exposure Method, which may only be used by non-trading book institutions, the CEM is the simplest method to determine the EAD. The simplicity is one of the main reasons why the model is so popular and applied by several institutions, especially by smaller banks. The replacement of CEM will have far-reaching effects on the banking landscape. In order to better outline these effects, the regulatory

---

3 Cf. BCBS 254 (2013).
4 The fact that the Basel Committee could not get used to the idea that the name of a standardised approach contained the word combination "internal model" was decisive for the name change. Moreover, the Basel Committee decided that a standardised approach should always be included in a framework.

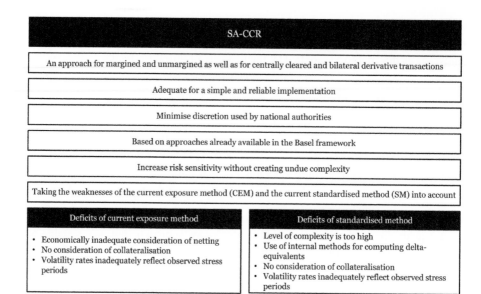

Figure 3.2: Objectives of SA-CCR

requirements and the EAD determination shall be explained in detail in this side note. The procedure to calculate EAD based on the CEM is set forth in Art. 274 CRR.

In case of a default of a counterparty, derivative transactions are usually replaced with identical transactions with another counterparty. This takes place to keep the overall risk profile of a bank's portfolio constant. This one-to-one replacement of defaulted transactions results in replacement costs (RC). The RC value is often used as a proxy of exposure in the event of a default. However, as the replacement costs may vary between the time of EAD calculation and the time at which the counterparty defaults, it is necessary to take account of this potential future change in the replacement costs as well. The CEM reflects this fact in determining EAD by adding a "potential future exposure" (PFE) to the RC value. The PFE represents a so-called add-on for future potential value changes. Equation 3.1 shows how the EAD is determined pursuant to the CEM.

Equation 3.1

$$EAD^{CEM} = RC + PFE \tag{3.1}$$

where:

RC: Replacement Costs

PFE: Potential Future Exposure

The EAD is determined at transaction level, unless an approved netting agreement is available. In order to determine the current RC value for all contracts with positive value, institutions must assign the current market value (V_i) to derivative agreements. Under the CEM method, contractual netting is recognised as risk-mitigating. This allows institutions to offset the negative and positive market values of all derivative transactions within a netting set; this net replacement cost can then be used to determine the RC value. If the result of the offsetting represents a net obligation, the RC value is set to zero.[5] The RC value is subject to a non-negativity condition under the CEM. Equation 3.2 is applied to determine the RC value of a netting set.

Equation 3.2

$$RC^{CEM}_{Netting-Set} = max\left\{\sum_{i=1}^{N} V_i; 0\right\} \qquad (3.2)$$

where:

V_i: current market value that results from offsetting all positive and negative market values of a netting set.

Under CEM, the value of the PFE is determined by multiplying the notional amounts by volatility rates defined by the supervisory authority. These volatility rates differ, on the one hand, depending on the underlying residual maturity of the derivative contract and, on the other hand, depending on the asset class a contract is assigned to. The volatility rates for the asset classes "interest rate", "foreign exchange rate/gold", "equities", "precious metals (except for gold)" and "commodities/other"[6] are displayed in Table 3.1.

The table does not contain volatility rates for credit derivatives, since these rates do not depend on residual maturity. Volatility rates for credit derivatives are, from a regulatory perspective, dealt with separately in Art. 299 CRR and are shown in Table 3.2. When applying volatility rates for credit derivatives the presence of a qualifying or non-qualifying reference obligation is decisive. The volatility rate of a qualifying reference obligation is set at 5%, while for a non-qualifying one it is set at 10%. A qualifying reference obligation refers to a security with a high investment grade.

The PFE component of a netting set is calculated by aggregating the individual PFEs. Since a netting agreement between two counterparties legally ensures that the receivables and payables of both counterparties can be offset, the CRR provides

Residual maturity	Interest rate	Foreign exchange rates/Gold	Equities	Precious metals (except gold)	Commodities/ Others
One year or less	0%	1%	6%	7%	10%
Over one year, not exceeding five years	0.5%	5%	8%	7%	12%
Over five years	1.5%	7.5%	10%	8%	15%

Table 3.1: Volatility rates CEM (without credit derivatives)

5   Cf. Art. 298 (1) (c) (i) CRR.
6   Cf. Art. 274 (2) CRR.

	Protection buyer	Protection provider
Total return swap		
"Qualified reference obligation"	5%	5%
"Non-qualifying reference obligation"	10%	10%
Credit default swap (CDS)		
"Qualified reference obligation"	5%	5%*
"Non-qualifying reference obligation"	10%	10%*

*The protection provider may apply an add-on factor (volatility rate) of 0%, unless the CDS is subject to a close out in the case of the counterparty's insolvency, even if the underlying has not defaulted.

Table 3.2: Volatility rates CEM for credit derivatives

that the PFE value of a netting set can be reduced in accordance with supervisory Equation 3.3[7].

Equation 3.3

$$PFE_{red}^{CEM} = 0{,}4 * PFE_{gross}^{CEM} + 0{,}6 * NGR * PFE_{gross}^{CEM} \qquad (3.3)$$

where:

PFE_{red}^{CEM}:   the reduced figure for potential future exposure for all contracts with a given counterparty included in an eligible netting agreement.

PFE_{gross}^{CEM}:   the sum of the PFEs of all transactions within a netting set.

NGR: [Net-to-Gross-Ratio] the quotient of the net replacement cost (numerator) and the gross replacement cost (denominator).

Figure 3.3 depicts a calculation example including relevant parameters for three transactions of the asset class interest rate.

No.	Transaction type	Maturity	Notional amount	Market value	Volatility rate	Potential Credit Exposure
1	Interest rate swap	10 y	10,000	30	1.5%	150
2	Interest rate swap	4 y	10,000	−20	0.5%	50
3	Swaption	1 y for 10 y	5,000	50	1.5%	75
	Sum		25,000	60		275

EAD	=	Net market value	+	Add-on		
		60		0.4 × 275 + 0.6 × 0.75 × 275	=	293.75

Figure 3.3: Calculation example EAD pursuant to CEM

---

7   Cf. Art. 298 CRR.

The calculation example illustrates the low level of complexity of the CEM. With the option of reducing the PFE component in accordance with Equation 3.3, netting effects can be taken into account, but only in a simplified way of up to 60% of the total PFE component (provided that the net replacement cost is set at zero in the case of a net obligation or an overcollateralisation of market values). It also becomes clear that no differences are made between margined and unmargined transactions.

3.3 Measurement of counterparty credit risk according to SA-CCR

3.3.1 Exposure at Default

EAD according to SA-CCR is calculated in a similar way to the CEM based on two main components, the current replacement cost (RC) and the potential future exposure (PFE)[8]. In addition to the CEM, the SA-CCR contains an α-factor, which is multiplied with the sum of RC and PFE. The α-factor, set at 1.4, was adopted from the IMM. Moreover, a preset *beta*-factor, also set at 1.4, is used in the current SM. Equation 3.4 shows how EAD is determined under SA-CCR.

Equation 3.4

$$EAD_{SA-CCR} = \alpha * (RC + PFE) \tag{3.4}$$

If a netting agreement recognised by the supervisory authority is available, EAD is determined at netting set level; otherwise, EAD is determined at transaction level. Despite the similarities between CEM and SA-CCR which, at first glance, arise from the two main components mentioned above, the SA-CCR contains a completely new methodology. Given that one of the main goals of the SA-CCR consists in better reflecting the effects of collateralisation of derivative transactions, the RC as well as the PFE component take into account whether a transaction is margined or not. Moreover, the PFE component arises from a more comprehensive and elaborate determination than that pursuant to the CEM. In the following, the determination of the RC and PFE components under SA-CCR are explained in more detail.

3.3.2 Current replacement cost

The RC component within the framework of the SA-CCR (similar to CEM) is calculated based on the current market value of the derivative transaction. The calculation of the RC component depends on whether or not the transaction is margined. According to the SA-CCR, unmargined transactions are those for which no variation margin is exchanged. This also applies in the case where a different kind of collateral, such

---

8 Cf. For more detailed information on the derivation of formulas within the SA-CCR: BCBS (2014); Working Paper No 26.

as an initial margin, was provided. Equation 3.5 outlines how the RC component is calculated for unmargined transactions.

Equation 3.5

$$RC_{Netting-Set}^{SA-CCR,unmargined} = max\{V - C; 0\} \tag{3.5}$$

If the calculation of the RC component is based on a netting set, then the RC value is defined as the greater of i) the net replacement costs of the netting set [V], reduced by the net haircut collateral held by the bank for this netting set [C] and ii) zero.

An unilateral collateralisation in favour of the bank's counterparty – that is a bank deposits collateral, but does not receive any from its counterparty – is also treated as unmargined under the SA-CCR. The formula for RC of a margined netting set is shown in Equation 3.6. Here, certain relevant mechanisms or parameters derived from collateralisation agreements are taken into account. The parameters threshold (TH), minimum transfer amount (MTA)[9] and independent amount are included. Equation 3.6 is used to determine the RC value for margined transactions.

Equation 3.6

$$RC_{Netting-Set}^{SA-CCR,margined} = max\{V - C; TH + MTA - NICA; 0\} \tag{3.6}$$

Within the SA-CCR, the so-called NICA term was introduced. NICA stands for "Net Independent Collateral Amount". "Independent Collateral Amount" (ICA) stands for all collaterals that are exchanged due to sensitivity changes in a derivatives portfolio. These are collaterals which, in practice, are generally described as "independent amount" or as "initial margin" within the scope of standard collateralisation documents. The variation margin is not included herein. Given that a bank as well as its counterparty can be asked to deposit an ICA, the term NICA was introduced. NICA is the difference between the ICA received minus ICA provided, which is not bankruptcy remote. NICA describes the collateral amount a bank would need to compensate its exposure in the event of a counterparty default. Bankruptcy remote collateral provided is not taken into account when determining NICA since that amount would be recovered anyway in the case of a default. Using Equation 3.6, the Basel Committee created a method to determine the RC value of a margined netting set that reflects the variations of collateralisation approaches that exist in practice.

---

9   The TH is a threshold, which represents the maximum unmargined exposure that is accepted and for which no collateral must be provided. In determining the TH, a free allowance is set at the same time. Collaterals must only be provided when the predefined threshold is passed. For instance, if parties A and B agree to a threshold of USD 5 million, Party A must only provide collateral if the net market value of the netting set surpasses USD 5 million from the point of view of Party B. The threshold/free allowance can also be seen as a credit line which Party B grants to Party A. The MTA is the minimum amount of collateral to be transferred. Low collateralisation amounts shall be avoided by establishing the MTA. The TH and MTA interact. If the derivative transactions of two counterparties surpass the TH value and the required additional collateral is below the MTA, no measures (i.e. no payments) are made.

3.3.3 Potential future exposure

The PFE component under the SA-CCR is determined very differently from the CEM. This is shown in more detail below. Pursuant to Equation 3.7, the PFE component comprises a so-called "multiplier" and an "aggregated add-on". The add-on is the sum of the add-ons for each asset class where the asset classes prescribed for the SA-CCR are the same as under the CEM: interest rate [IR], credit [CR], equities [EQ], foreign exchange [FX] and commodities [CO].[10]

Equation 3.7

$$PFE^{SA-CCR} = Multiplier * AddOn^{aggregate} \tag{3.7}$$

The multiplier is defined as a function of the three values V, C and the aggregated add-on. Equation 3.8 shows how the multiplier is calculated.

Equation 3.8

$$Multiplier = min \left\{ 1; Floor + (1 - Floor) * exp \left(\frac{V - C}{2 * (1 - Floor) * AddOn^{aggregate}} \right) \right\} \tag{3.8}$$

As long as the value of the collateral held is lower than the positive net replacement costs of the netting set (under-collateralisation) and the numerator in the latter part of the fraction in Equation 3.8 is positive, the multiplier is set to 1. In this case, the total value of the aggregated add-on represents the PFE component. Conversely, in the case of over-collateralisation or a negative value in the numerator, the multiplier is less than 1. In these cases, the multiplier "activates" an add-on reduction. As a result, out-of-the-money transactions and overcollateralised transactions receive a privileged treatment since, from an economic point of view, they do not give rise to an exposure and, consequently, there is no risk that needs to be considered in a bank's risk management. On prudential grounds, the Basel Committee decided to use a multiplier for the PFE component which decreases without reaching zero. The multiplier, therefore, was constructed based on a floor of 5% of the PFE value.

Qualitative requirements on the determination of the PFE

The calculation of the PFE component under SA-CCR basically takes place at four predefined levels: i) Netting set, ii) Asset class, iii) Hedging set and iv) Single Trade level. At each level, the calculation is based on predefined values or supervisory input parameters. The four levels are followed step by step. In the first half of the calculation process: a top-down approach is used to break down the values to the single trade

---

10   At European Level, an additional asset class "other risks" will be added, see European Commission (2016).

level, while they are aggregated up to the netting set level in the second half of the process in terms of a bottom-up approach. At the end of the calculation process, the PFE component of a netting set is obtained. The process described in this paragraph is outlined in Figure 3.4.

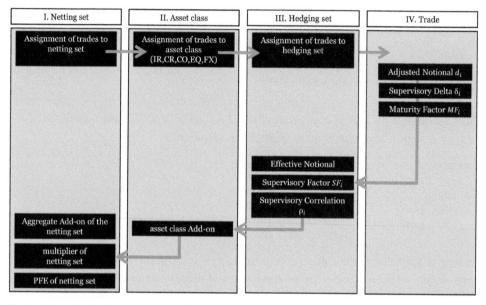

Figure 3.4: Determination of the PFE component according to SA-CCR

Within the scope of the calculation of the PFE component, add-ons take an important role for individual asset classes. This is mainly due to the fact that the method for calculating add-ons is based on a hedging-set concept. This means that similar risks can be aggregated in hedging sets within which a partial or complete offset is permissible. The amount of individual add-ons and, consequently, the amount of the PFE component of individual netting sets varies depending on the hedging effect that can be realised. Table 3.3 summarises how the individual hedging sets in the five asset classes are defined and how the offsetting takes place.

The above outlined hedging-set approach ensures that derivative transactions can only be offset within supervisory limits. For example, within the asset class "commodities" a forward contract on natural gas cannot be used as hedge of a forward contract on grains. Compared to the CEM, the "hedging-set concept" included within SA-CCR is used to achieve a higher degree of risk sensitivity since this concept allows similar and therefore offsetting risks to be (partially) compensated.[11]

---

11 Corresponding to the new asset class "other risks" within the EU, the hedging set concept constitutes supervisory hedging limits for this new asset class.

Asset class	Hedging set	Offset
IR	Currency + maturity bucket (MB) 1. [MB<1 year] 2. [1 year ≤ MB ≤ 5 years] 3. [MB > 5 years]	Complete if same maturity bucket Partial across maturity buckets
FX	Currency pair	Complete
EQ	No defined HS	Complete if same entity Partial if different entity
CR	No defined HS	Complete if same entity Partial if different entity
CO	Commodity classes (energy, metals, agricultural, others)	Complete if same CO type Partial across all CO types

Table 3.3: Hedging-set concept according to SA-CCR

Input parameter defined by the supervisory authority

The input parameters used to calculate the PFE component of the five add-ons according to SA-CCR requirements can be divided into two types. The parameter is either a fixed value that is predefined by the supervisory authority and must be used in the SA-CCR calculations, or a parameter that must be determined based on a formula or procedure described by the SA-CCR. These parameters are illustrated in more detail in the following section.

Maturity parameters

Four different period or date parameters are used in the SA-CCR: M_i, E_i, S_i and T_i.

M_i is the latest date when the contract may still be active. This parameter is used to determine the so-called maturity factor, which is explained below. If a derivative contract has another derivative contract as its underlying, then the maturity of the underlying derivative contract must also be taken into account. In the case of a physically settled European swaption which at its exercise date in six months references at a 5-year interest rate swap, M_i equals 5.5 years. For the same derivative transaction with a cash settlement agreement at the exercise date, M_i equals 0.5 years.

The parameters S_i (start date) and E_i (end date) are exclusively used to determine add-ons for the asset classes interest rate and credit since special adjustments take place depending on the residual term of contracts of these asset classes. S_i represents the time period until the start date and E_i the time period until the end date of a derivate transaction as from the current day. If a transaction references another derivative, S_i and E_i must be determined on the basis of the underlying instrument. In the above mentioned example of a swaption, S_i would be 0.5 years in both cases and E_i 5.5 years. If a derivative transaction has already started, S_i must be set to zero.

T_i (exercise date) is a parameter used to determine option delta. T_i represents the latest contractual exercise date as referenced by the option contract.

In the following, the additional parameters determined within the scope of the PFE component are explained in detail. First, the parameters calculated at trade level will be described. As can be seen in Figure 3.4, these are the adjusted notional, the supervisory delta and the maturity factor.

Adjusted Notional

The so-called "adjusted notional" of transaction [i] belonging to asset class [a] is determined differently for every asset class. For transactions of the asset classes interest rate and credit, it is the product of the notional amount, converted into local currency where necessary, and the so-called "*supervisory duration*", which is calculated according to Equation 3.9. The determination of the adjusted notional is assessed via equation 3.10 respectively.

Equation 3.9

$$SD_i = \frac{\exp(-0{,}05 * S_i) - \exp(-0{,}05 * E_i)}{0{,}05} \tag{3.9}$$

Equation 3.10

$$d_i^{(a)} = \textit{Trade Notional} * \frac{\exp(-0{,}05 * S_i) - \exp(-0{,}05 * E_i)}{0{,}05} \tag{3.10}$$

Equation 3.9 shows that the period parameters S_i and E_i, which were mentioned above, with a floor of 10 days, are used to determine SD_i. The adjustment of notionals using the SD_i factor takes place for interest rate and credit transactions to take residual terms into account. No special adjustment of the notional depending on the residual term is performed for the transactions of the remaining asset classes. The adjustment of foreign currency transactions takes place exclusively through the conversion of the foreign currency leg into local currency. If both legs of an FX derivative contract are in foreign currency, both legs are converted and the higher value shall be used as adjusted notional for further calculations. The product of the current unit price and quantity referencing the respective transaction represents the notional amount for equity and commodity transactions.

Supervisory Delta δ_i

The "supervisory delta" [δ_i] is determined at transaction level as is the adjusted notional. This parameter is used when aggregating the adjusted notional and to determine the so-called "*effective notional*". The calculation of effective notionals, which is done differently for the add-ons of the five asset classes, are described below. δ_i is applied to the adjusted notionals to reflect the position (long/short) and the non-linearity of transactions. In this way, the offsetting of positions is achieved.

In order to assign a delta factor, it is decisive whether one is dealing with a linear or a non-linear derivate transaction and which position the institution holds within

δ_i		
non-option/non-CDO tranche	**Long in the Primary Risk Factor**	**Short in the Primary Risk Factor**
	+1	−1
	Bought	**Sold**
Call Option	$+\Phi(d)$ (3.11)	$-\Phi(d)$ (3.12)
Put Option	$-\Phi(-d)$ (3.13)	$+\Phi(-d)$ (3.14)
CDO tranches	**Purchased (Long Protection)**	**Sold (Long Protection)**
	$+\dfrac{15}{(1+14*A_i)*(1+14*D_i)}$ (3.15)	$-\dfrac{15}{(1+14*A_i)*(1+14*D_i)}$ (3.16)

$$d = \frac{\ln\left(\frac{P_i}{K_i}\right) + 0.5 * \sigma_i^2 * T_i}{\sigma_i^2 * \sqrt{T_i}}$$

Key
P_i: Underlying price
K_i: Strike price
T_i: Last exercise date
σ_i: supervisory option volatility
A_i: Attachment Point of the CDO tranche
D_i: Detachment Point of the CDO tranche

Table 3.4: Supervisory Delta factors under SA-CCR

said transaction. Supervisory prescribed delta formulations are only relevant for derivatives with options and CDO tranches. In the case of linear derivative transactions, the supervisory delta factor of +/− 1 must be applied. If an institution holds the position *"long in the primary risk factor"*, a delta of 1 must be assigned to the transaction. If, on the contrary, the institution holds the position *"short in the primary risk factor"*, a delta of −1 must be applied. In the first category, the market value of the instrument increases if the value of the underlying *primary risk factor* increases (e.g. the floating interest rate of an interest rate derivative) and the second category represents instruments where the market value decreases if the value of the *primary risk factor* increases.

As mentioned above, the SA-CCR provides formulas to determine the supervisory delta factor for options and CDO tranche products. Taking into account all possible variations, Equations 3.11–3.16 in Table 3.4 describe how delta factors are determined for options and CDO tranches.

The calculation of supervisory delta of options is performed similarly to the Black–Scholes option pricing model.[12] It differs, as the SA-CCR does not take into

---

12 For details on delta determination within the Black–Scholes Option Pricing Model: Hull (2014), page 483 et seq.

account the risk free rate in nominator d, which is the case in the Black–Scholes model. Presumably, the purpose was to expose institutions to one less prudential factor. [13]

Maturity Factor

The so-called "maturity factor" describes the last parameter to be determined at transaction level and reflects the time risk horizon of transactions. There are two types of maturity factors according to SA-CCR: one for "margined" and one for "unmargined" transactions. While the unmargined maturity factor is determined for each individual transaction depending on its residual term, the margined maturity factor is based on the so-called "Margin Period of Risk" (*MPOR*) of the underlying collateral agreement. If the collateral agreement is taken into account for the entire netting set, the MPOR is identical for each transaction of the netting set. All transactions of this netting set are evaluated based on the same underlying MPOR. An additional adjustment via the MPOR seems logical from the supervisory point of view since during this period, a bank operates de facto in an unmargined time frame. Despite the existing collateral agreement, risks may still occur during the margin period of risk. Equation 3.17 shows how the maturity factor of margined transactions is calculated.

Equation 3.17

$$MF_i^{(margined)} = \frac{3}{2}\sqrt{\frac{MPOR_i}{1\ year}} \tag{3.17}$$

$MPOR_i$ represents the agreed-upon margin period of risk which applies to transaction i. It is important to note that MPOR obtained from the collateralisation agreement cannot be used for the calculation according to Equation 3.17; it must be adjusted once more pursuant to supervisory requirements. For instance, the MPOR is 10 days in the case of a non-centrally-cleared position subject to daily remargining. This value is reduced to 5 days if the derivative positions are centrally cleared subject to daily remargining. Thus, SA-CCR takes account of the risk reducing effects of daily remargining and central clearing.

The maturity factor for unmargined transactions is shown in Equation 3.18. The smaller value of the residual term (M_i) and one year is used as nominator, where M_i is limited to 10 days. In practice, the business days of one year, which are used to determine the maturity factor, must be calculated taking into account the market conventions of the relevant jurisdiction (e.g. 250d).

Equation 3.18

$$MF_i^{(unmargined)} = \sqrt{\frac{min\{M_i;\ 1\ year\}}{1\ year}} \tag{3.18}$$

[13] For EU legislation purposes it is expected that additional adjustment parameters will be developed and implemented in order to be used within the determination of supervisory delta factors for options and that will allow for a compensation of a negative interest rate environment.

Asset class	Sub-Class	Supervisory Factor	Correlation	Supervisory Option Volatility
Interest Rate	–	0.50%	N/A	50%
Foreign Exchange	–	4.0%	N/A	15%
Credit, Single Name	AAA	0.38%	50%	100%
	AA	0.38%	50%	100%
	A	0.42%	50%	100%
	BBB	0.54%	50%	100%
	BB	1.06%	50%	100%
	B	1.6%	50%	100%
	CCC	6.0%	50%	100%
Credit, Index	IG	0.38%	80%	80%
	SG	1.06%	80%	80%
Equity, Single Name		32%	50%	120%
Equity, Index		20%	80%	75%
Commodity	Electricity	40%	40%	150%
	Oil/Gas	18%	40%	70%
	Metals	18%	40%	70%
	Agricultural	18%	40%	70%
	Other	18%	40%	70%

Table 3.5: Parameters prescribed by the supervisory authority under SA-CCR

Supervisory Factor, Supervisory Correlation Parameter and Supervisory Option Volatility

The "*Supervisory Factor SF_i*", the "*Supervisory Correlation Parameter ρ_i*" and the "*Supervisory Option Volatility σ_i*" vary according to the asset class and the prescribed sub-classes. The supervisory factor is comparable to the volatility rates under the CEM. It transforms the effective notional into an add-on. The supervisory factor values account for the volatilities observed in the latest stress periods.

The supervisory correlation parameters are used to aggregate granular add-ons (ie. entity- and commodity type level) to final add-ons on asset class level. They are exclusively applied for the asset classes credit, equities and commodities. The supervisory option volatility is used to determine the delta factor. Table 3.5 summarises the different values of the supervisory parameters depending on the asset class and sub-classes.

Asset class add-ons

The following section describes in detail how the add-ons for the five supervisory asset classes interest rate, credit, equity, foreign exchange and commodities are determined. The add-on of each asset class is derived in several steps by taking into account various input factors. While the values of the supervisory parameters vary among the different asset classes in order to adequately reflect the risk of each asset class, some features or calculation steps of the add-on determination are identical.

Determination of the add-on for the asset class interest rate

The add-on for interest rate derivatives captures the risk of interest rate derivatives of different maturities. To address this risk, interest rate derivatives are divided into so-called maturity buckets. These maturity buckets are the following:

1. less than one year,

2. between one and five years, and

3. more than five years.

Within interest rate add-ons, the complete offset of transactions assigned to the same maturity bucket is allowed. Moreover, across maturity categories, a partial offset is recognised. After adjusting the notionals, which was already discussed within the section on input parameters, the second step consists of determining the effective notionals of all interest rate derivative transactions to calculate the interest rate add-on. These values are determined via Equation 3.19.

Equation 3.19

$$D_{jk}^{(IR)} = \sum_{i \in \{CCy_j, MB_k\}} \delta_i * d_i^{(IR)} * MF_i^{(type)} \tag{3.19}$$

Equation 3.19 refers to transactions of currency (CCY) j within maturity bucket (MB) k. The effective notional for each maturity bucket within each given currency is the sum of the adjusted notional multiplied by the supervisory delta and the maturity factor. This means that a complete offset of transactions referencing the same currency and assigned to the same maturity bucket takes place at this level.

In the second step, aggregation across maturity buckets (1, 2, 3) is performed using Equation 3.20. Based on Equation 3.20, which allows for a partial offset, the effective notional for each currency j is determined. However, the use of Equation 3.20 is optional: institutions may also calculate the effective notional by adding the absolute values determined in the prior step.

Equation 3.20

$$D_j^{(IR)} = \sqrt{\begin{bmatrix} \left(D_{j1}^{(IR)}\right)^2 + \left(D_{j2}^{(IR)}\right)^2 + \left(D_{j3}^{(IR)}\right)^2 + 1,4 * D_{j1}^{(IR)} * D_{j2}^{(IR)} \\ +1,4 * D_{j2}^{(IR)} * D_{j3}^{(IR)} + 0,6 * D_{j1}^{(IR)} * D_{j3}^{(IR)} \end{bmatrix}} \tag{3.20}$$

In the next step, the add-ons at hedging set level j, that is, at currency level, are determined. This takes place by calculating the product of the supervisory factor and the effective notional amount for each currency. This is shown in Equation 3.21.

Equation 3.21

$$AddOn_j^{(IR)} = SF_j^{(IR)} * D_j^{(IR)} \tag{3.21}$$

Aggregation across hedging-set add-ons is performed via simple summation in the last step. See Equation 3.22.

Equation 3.22

$$AddOn^{IR} = \sum_j AddOn_j^{(IR)} \tag{3.22}$$

Determination of the add-on for the asset class "credit"

After adjusting the notional amounts, the second step is to determine the credit add-ons as well as to calculate the effective notional amounts of all credit derivative transactions using Equation 3.23.

Equation 3.23

$$D_k^{(CR)} = \sum_{i \in \; Entity_k} \delta_i * d_i^{(CR)} * MF_i^{(type)} \tag{3.23}$$

The notation $i \in Entity_k$ describes the consideration of all transactions referencing entity k to determine the effective notional amount. Within the asset class "credit", the effective notional amounts are calculated for each entity as the sum of the adjusted notional amounts multiplied by the supervisory delta factor and the maturity factor. The add-on for all transactions referencing entity k is defined based on Equation 3.24 as the product of the supervisory factor and the effective notional amount.

Equation 3.24

$$AddOn_k^{(CR)} = SF_k^{(Credit)} * D_k^{(CR)} \tag{3.24}$$

The supervisory factor is determined for single name entities through their external ratings and for index entities by distinguishing "*investment grade*" (IG) and "*speculative grade*" (SG). The values prescribed by the supervisory authority for the supervisory factors are given in Table 3.5. In the last step, the add-ons are summed up at entity level based on the single-factor model to obtain the total add-on of the asset class "credit". Within the scope of this calculation, which is shown in Equation 3.25, a differentiation between a systematic and an idiosyncratic component takes place.

Equation 3.25

$$AddOn^{(CR)} = \sqrt{\underbrace{\left(\sum_k \rho_k^{(CR)} * AddOn_k^{(CR)}\right)^2}_{\text{Systematic component}} + \underbrace{\sum_k \left(1 - \left(\rho_k^{(CR)}\right)^2\right) * \left(AddOn_k^{(CR)}\right)^2}_{\text{Idiosyncratic component}}}$$

$$\tag{3.25}$$

Here, ρ represents the supervisory correlation factor for entity k. This correlation factor ensures that both components are weighted to determine the degree of offsetting. The entity add-ons in the systematic component are allowed to offset each other fully while there is no offsetting benefit in the idiosyncratic component.

Determination of the add-on for the asset class "equity"

The procedure to determine equity add-ons shares many similarities with the add-on formula for credit derivatives. The individual calculation steps are shown in Equations 3.26–3.28 taking into account the parameters for the asset class "equity".

Equations 3.26–3.28

$$D_k^{(EQ)} = \sum_{i \in \ Entity_k} \delta_i * d_i^{(EQ)} * MF_i^{(type)} \tag{3.26}$$

$$AddOn_k^{(EQ)} = SF_k^{(EQ)} * D_k^{(EQ)} \tag{3.27}$$

$$AddOn^{(EQ)} = \sqrt{\underbrace{\left(\sum_k \rho_k^{(EQ)} * AddOn_k^{(EQ)} \right)^2}_{\text{Systematic component}} + \underbrace{\sum_k \left(1 - \left(\rho_k^{(EQ)} \right)^2 \right) * \left(AddOn_k^{(EQ)} \right)^2}_{\text{Idiosyncratic component}}}$$

$$\tag{3.28}$$

Determination of the add-on for the asset class "commodities"

The effective notional amounts in the asset class "commodities" are determined based on Equation 3.29. Equation 3.29 is applied to all transactions of commodity type k within the hedging set j. The effective notional amount for transactions of the commodity type k within hedging set j is the sum of the adjusted notional amount multiplied by the supervisory delta and the maturity factor.

Equation 3.29

$$D_k^{(CO)} = \sum_{i \in \ Type_k^j} \delta_i * d_i^{(CO)} * MF_i^{(type)} \tag{3.29}$$

In the next step, the add-ons for the transactions of commodity type k in hedging set j are calculated as the product of the supervisory factor and the effective notional amount based on Equation 3.30.

Equation 3.30

$$AddOn_{Type_k^j}^{(CO)} = SF_{Type_j^k}^{(CO)} * D_k^{(CO)} \tag{3.30}$$

The add-on at hedging set level for the commodity category is calculated in Equation 3.31.

Equation 3.31

$$AddOn_{HS_j}^{(CO)} = \sqrt{\underbrace{\left(\rho_j^{(CO)} * \sum_k AddOn\left(Type_k^j\right)\right)^2}_{\text{Systematic component}} + \underbrace{\left(1 - \left(\rho_j^{(CO)}\right)^2\right) * \sum_k \left(AddOn_{Type_k^j}^{(CO)}\right)^2}_{\text{Idiosyncratic component}}}$$

(3.31)

The individual hedging set add-ons are aggregated using Equation 3.32 to calculate the overall add-on of the asset class "commodities".

Equation 3.32

$$AddOn^{(CO)} = \sum_j AddOn_{HS_j}^{(CO)}$$

(3.32)

Commodity type hedging sets have been defined without regard to characteristics such as quality or location. However, the Basel Committee points out that national supervisors may require banks to use more refined definitions of commodities. The hedging sets for the asset class commodities established in BCBS 279 are summarised in Table 3.6.

Hedging set	Commodity type
Energy	Crude oil
	Natural gas
	Coal
	Electricity
Metals	Silver
	Gold
	...
Agricultural	...
	...
Others	...

Table 3.6: SA-CCR Hedging sets of the asset class Commodity

Determination of the add-on for asset class "foreign exchange"

The effective notional of the asset class foreign exchange is determined using Equation 3.33. The index refers to all transactions of hedging set j. The effective notional of each hedging set, that is for each currency pair, is calculated as the sum of all adjusted notional amounts multiplied by their supervisory delta and the corresponding maturity factor.

Equation 3.33

$$D_j^{(FX)} = \sum_{i \in HS_j} \delta_i * d_i^{(FX)} * MF_i^{(type)}$$

(3.33)

The add-on for each hedging set is determined based on Equation 3.34 as a product of the supervisory factor and the absolute value of the effective notional.

Equation 3.34

$$AddOn_{HS_j}^{(FX)} = SF_j^{(FX)} * |D_j^{(FX)}|$$ (3.34)

In the last step, the add-ons are aggregated at hedging set level using Equation 3.35 to determine the overall add-on for the asset class "foreign exchange".

Equation 3.35

$$AddOn^{(FX)} = \sum_j AddOn_{HS_j}^{(FX)}$$ (3.35)

3.3.4 Calculation example: EAD determination under SA-CCR

Figure 3.5 shows the EAD determination following supervisory SA-CCR requirements. This example is based on same transactions used in section 3.2 for the calculation example under the CEM[14]. Moreover, this example is based on the

No.	Transaction type	Maturity	Currency	Notional in K	Market value in K	Pay Leg	Receive Leg
1	Internet rate swap	10 y	USD	10,000	30	Fixed	Variable
2	Interest rate swap	4 y	USD	10,000	-20	Variable	Fixed
3	Swaption	1 y for 10 y	EUR	5,000	50	Variable	Fixed
	Sum			25,000	60		

No.	Hedging Set	Maturity bucket	Start Date	End Date	SD	Adjusted notional	Delta
1	USD	3	0	10	7.87	78,694	1
2	USD	2	0	4	3.63	36,254	-1
3	EUR	3	1	11	7.49	37,428	-0.27

No.	Maturity factor	Effective notional per maturity bucket	Effective notional per Hedging Set	Supervisory Factor	Add-on of asset class interest rate	α	Multiplier
1		78,694	59,270	0.5			
2	1	−36,254			347	1.4	1
3		−10,083	10,083	0.5			

$$EAD = 1.4 * \begin{bmatrix} \text{Net market value} \\ 60 \end{bmatrix} + 1 * \begin{bmatrix} \text{Aggregated add-on} \\ 347 \end{bmatrix} = 569$$

Figure 3.5: Determination of the EAD according to SA-CCR

14   Example taken from BCBS 279 (2014), page 22 et seq.

assumption that no collateral agreements exist for the transactions. The calculation example includes all the parameters necessary to calculate the EAD according to SA-CCR.

Compared to the CEM, it becomes evident at first glance that the EAD calculation based on SA-CCR requires more parameters, information about the transactions and calculation steps. Moreover, EAD value increases significantly for the transactions (compared to the CEM: approx. 293 K), which can be traced back to the use of additional parameters within SA-CCR. Parameters such as the supervisory duration (SD), the delta parameter, the maturity factor, the alpha factor and the multiplier cause an increase of EAD due to their multiplicative application.

3.4 Use of simplified approaches

As is immediately evident from the above, SA-CCR increases the complexity of EAD calculation as compared to the CEM and original exposure method. While this is on the one hand side part of the supervisory motivation for its introduction, it may cause some challenges especially for smaller institutions with less complex derivative portfolios. To address their concerns, it seems likely that supervisors will provide them with simplified approaches that offer reduced complexity at the price of a more conservative calibration. The following section describes the European Union's proposals for two simplified approaches that will be implemented together with the SA-CCR as part of the CRR II reforms. These two approaches are labelled as the simplified SA-CCR and the revised original exposure method respectively.

Institutions may use either of these two approaches if the volume of their derivatives remains below the following thresholds which have been defined and implemented by the European Commission into the CRR II draft. Based on end-of-month values and supervised on a monthly basis, the size of the on- and off-balance sheet derivative business must be equal to or less than both of the thresholds shown in Figure (3.6):

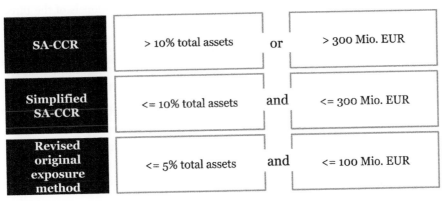

SA-CCR	> 10% total assets	or	> 300 Mio. EUR
Simplified SA-CCR	<= 10% total assets	and	<= 300 Mio. EUR
Revised original exposure method	<= 5% total assets	and	<= 100 Mio. EUR

Figure 3.6: Thresholds for simplified approaches

3.4.1 Simplified SA-CCR

The simplified SA-CCR, as its name suggests, is based on the SA-CCR described above (so-called "*Full SA-CCR*"), subject to some modifications in order to reduce the complexity of the approach in the full version. These modifications are described in turn:

Similarly to the SA-CCR, EAD is calculated as the sum of replacement costs and potential future exposure, weighted with an alpha-factor of 1.4. The replacement cost component for positions not subject to a variation margin agreement is calculated as the larger of the derivatives current market value (in case of a netting agreement: the net market value of all derivatives contained in said netting set) or zero. Other collateral such as independent amounts are not taken into account to reduce the current market value. If a variation margin agreement exists or in case of centrally cleared or exchange traded derivatives, the replacement costs are calculated as the sum of threshold and minimum transfer amount, once again without taking into account other types of collateral and therefore omitting the NICA parameter.

While the construction of hedging sets basically remains as under SA-CCR, some exceptions for specific cases such as transactions referencing volatility or basis risk as the main risk driver are omitted as well.

The multiplier is set to 1 in order to prevent a reduction of the PFE component in case of over-collateralisation or negative market values.

Under simplified SA-CCR, when calculating the effective notionals, some input parameters are calculated in a more simplified way. For example, the supervisory delta used to capture the effects of non-linearity in options and CDO-tranches is set to $+1/-1$. Similarly, the calculation of the supervisory duration is abbreviated and simply refers to the difference between a transaction's start date (S_i) and end date (E_i). Also, the maturity factor (MF) is set to 1 in case of netting sets not subject to a variation margin agreement and 0.42 in all other cases. And finally, for interest rate derivatives, the effective notional of hedging set (j) is not calculated according to Equation 3.20 but as the simple sum of the absolute values of the effective notionals of the three maturity buckets.

Similarly, when calculating asset class level add-ons, a simplification is introduced by omitting the differentiation between the systematic and idiosyncratic components for credit, equity and commodity derivatives as described in Equations 3.25, 3.28 and 3.31.

As a result, calculating EADs according to the simplified SA-CCR will result in higher values as compared to the SA-CCR and this effect will be more pronounced the more the described simplifications impact the calculation. For example, the presence of options, independent collateral amounts and over-collateralisation all tend to increase the advantage of the SA-CCR as compared to its simplified sibling. It remains to be seen if the more simplified calculation is seen as an adequate payoff for these higher EADs by institutions.[15]

3.4.2 Revised original exposure method

The revised original exposure method as contained in the CRR II draft shows even more similarities to the CEM than to its namesake. As the simplified SA-CCR, it calculates EAD as the sum of replacement costs and potential future exposure, multiplied by the alpha factor of 1.4. While the calculation of replacement costs is identical to the simplified SA-CCR, the potential future exposure is calculated as in the CEM, by multiplying the derivative's notional with a supervisory provided volatility rate (see Table 3.7):

Interest rate	Credit risk	Foreign exchange	Electricity	Other commodities	Equities
0.5% × residual maturity	6% × residual maturity	4%	40%	18%	32%

Table 3.7: Volatility rates revised OEM

In case of transactions subject to a variation margin agreement, the resulting potential future exposure is to be multiplied by a factor of 0.42.

In the most simple cases (no netting, no collateral, no options …) it can be shown that SA-CCR, simplified SA-CCR and revised OEM lead to the same results. However, given that supervisors put more and more emphasis on netting and collateral agreements, the revised OEM as the simplified SA-CCR will create larger EADs and risk weighted assets at the price of some reduced complexity.

3.5 Expected impact on the banking industry

With the SA-CCR the Basel Committee has developed an approach that will be applied by many banks and for several regulatory topics. On the one hand, SA-CCR will replace the widely used CEM and therefore will have to be implemented by a majority of banks. As it is also used for the calculation of capital floors, IMM banks also will have to be able to calculate EADs according to SA-CCR. On the other hand, SA-CCR is not only relevant for the determination of risk weighted assets for counterparty credit risk, but impacts other regulatory frameworks such as the Credit Valuation Adjustment, central counterparties, the leverage ratio and the large exposure framework as well.

Although the SA-CCR is more complex than the CEM, it is easy to use and allows for the risk-sensitive calculation of EAD. It captures netting and hedging effects better than the CEM which was illustrated with the calculation examples in sections 3.2 and 3.3.4.

---

15 Results of a comparison between SA-CCR and simplified SA-CCR are presented by Ciftci/Röth (2017).

While the effects of netting are only captured up to a maximum of 60% of the total PFE component under CEM, a complete offset of derivative transactions is possible in certain circumstances under SA-CCR. Moreover, the EAD-reducing effects of the presence of collateral are captured by the SA-CCR.

However, the positive effects of a risk-sensitive EAD determination by using the SA-CCR also create huge challenges. The new data requirements constitute one of the main challenging effects on the banking industry. The new parameters, transaction information and calculation steps within SA-CCR call for a high implementation and restructuring effort with regard to front office as well as back office systems. In addition, through the privileging effects of collateral exchange, incentives are created to enter into margining agreements. As a result, special attention has to be paid to the bank's liquidity and collateral management. An impact study of the SA-CCR approach was carried out in its final version within the scope of the 2015 Basel III monitoring. The Implementation of SA-CCR requirements on EU level is expected for 2020 at the earliest.

Recommended Literature

Basel Committee on Banking Supervision; BCBS (2015): Basel III: The standardised approach for measuring counterparty credit risk exposures: Frequently asked questions, 2015

Basel Committee on Banking Supervision; BCBS 254 (2013): Consultative Document: The non-internal model method for capitalising counterparty credit risk exposures, 2013

Basel Committee on Banking Supervision; BCBS (2014): Working Paper No 26 – Foundations of the standardised approach for measuring counterparty credit risk exposures, 2014

Basel Committee on Banking Supervision; BCBS 279 (2014): The standardised approach for measuring counterparty credit risk exposures, 2014

Capital Requirements Regulation; CRR (2013): Regulation (EU) No 575/2013 of the European Parliament and of the Council of 26 June 2013 on prudential requirements for credit institutions and investment firms and amending Regulation (EU) No 646/2012

Ciftci, Fanos and Röth, Stefan (2017): 'Vereinfachte Messverfahren im Gegenparteiausfallrisiko', in: RisikoManager 09/2017, pp. 41–44.

European Commission (2016): Proposal for a Regulation of the European Parliament and of the Council amending Regulation (EU) No 575/2013

Görg, Andreas (2014): SA-CCR. The standardised approach for measuring counterparty credit risk exposures, available under: http://www.nagler-company.com/fileadmin/Unternehmen/Themen/SA_CCR.pdf

Hull, John (2014): Optionen, Futures und andere Derivate [Options, futures and other derivatives], Pearson editorial, (Munich), 2014

4 The new securitisation framework

Dr. Wolfgang Frank and Dr. Philipp Völk

4.1 Introduction

Under the Basel framework, capital requirements for credit risk are calculated using the Standardised Approach or the Internal Ratings Based Approach (see Chapters 1 and 2). Similarly, capital requirements for the credit risk of securitisation positions under the Basel framework depend on whether the institution uses the Standardised Approach or the IRB Approach. Prior to Basel IV, there are different methods for each approach (see section 4.2.3).

The Basel guidelines were adopted in the Capital Requirements Regulation (CRR) at the European level without major differences and have been applicable in the current form for European banks since 1 January 2014.

Since securitisations have been considered a primary factor contributing to the financial crisis started in 2007/2008, the BCBS intends to strengthen the capital requirements for securitisation positions held in the banking book (there are also new rules for securitisation positions in the banking book under the FRTB, see Chapter 6). For this purpose, it aims to eliminate weaknesses in the applicable rules for RWA calculation and to establish criteria that identify less complex securitisations which are suitable for the development of a sustainable securitisation market and therefore receive lower risk weights.[1] The starting point of these considerations are the documents "Revisions to the securitisation framework" issued on 11 December 2014[2] and the "Criteria for identifying simple, transparent and comparable securitisations" issued in July 2015.[3] In addition, the BCBS published another consultation paper in November 2015,[4] which contained proposals for the adaptation of the criteria for qualified securitisations as well as of the risk weights applicable to them. The final version of the document "Revisions to the securitisation framework (BCBS 374)" published in July of 2016 incorporated the capital treatment for "simple, transparent and comparable (STC)" securitisations.

The implementation of the revised securitisation framework is being executed in two steps by the BCBS. In a first step, the intention is to change the existing securitisation standards, in particular in the area of capital requirements for originators, sponsors and investors in order to deal with a number of weaknesses acknowledged in the existing securitisation framework, including:

- the mechanistic reliance on external ratings when determining capital requirements,
- the insufficient risk-sensitivity due to the negligence of certain risk drivers, and
- the existence of "cliff-effects" with pro-cyclical impact.

---

1   Cf. BCBS 374 (2016)
2   Cf. BCBS 303 (2014).
3   Cf. BCBS 332 (2015).
4   Cf. BCBS 343 (2015).

In a second step, the Basel Committee defined criteria of STC securitisations and attach lower risk weights to them. Thus it intends to set incentives to all market participants to implement STC securitisations.

The BCBS has announced that the revised framework will come into force as of the beginning of 2018. The new framework for securitisations in the EU, being the adaptation of the Basel provisions into European law, was finalised in December 2017 and will apply as of 1 January 2019 with a transitional period until 1 January 2020 for existing transactions.

4.2 The securitisation framework under Basel II

4.2.1 Scope and definitions

Basel II first required institutions to apply the securitisation framework for determining the capital requirements for exposures arising from securitisation transactions. In order to define the scope of these requirements, the first requirement in this context is to determine what a securitisation structure is. As there are different types of securitisations, the capital treatment of a securitisation exposure must be determined based on its economic substance rather than its legal form. Nonetheless, the framework provides definitions for both general types of securitisation – traditional[5] and synthetic.[6] The definitions remain unchanged under Basel IV.

According to the Basel II Securitisation Framework, a traditional securitisation is described as a structure where the cash flows from an underlying pool of assets are used to service at least two different stratified risk positions or tranches reflecting different degrees of credit risk. Payments to the investors depend on the performance of the specified underlying exposures, as opposed to being derived from an obligation of the institution originating those exposures. The stratified or tranched structures characterise a securitisation structure. Those stratified or tranched structures differ from ordinary senior or subordinated debt instruments in that junior securitisation tranches can absorb losses without interrupting contractual payments to more senior tranches and that the tranches of a securitisation are limited in their right to specified cash flows from a clearly defined portfolio of underlying assets, which is not the case with sub-debt. By contrast, subordination in a senior or subordinated debt instrument structure is a matter of priority of rights to the proceeds of liquidation.

A synthetic securitisation is a structure with at least two different stratified risk positions or tranches that reflect different degrees of credit risk. Credit risk of an underlying pool of exposures is transferred, in whole or in part, through the use of funded credit derivatives (e.g. credit-linked notes), unfunded credit derivatives (e.g. credit default

---

5   A structure where the credit risk of the underlying pool is transferred through a true sale of the underlying exposures.
6   A structure where the credit risk of the underlying pool is transferred through credit derivatives.

swaps ...) or guarantees that hedge the credit risk of the underlying pool of exposures. Accordingly, the investors' potential risk is dependent on the performance of the
underlying pool from an economic point of view, similar to a traditional securitisation.

The basic concept of a traditional securitisation is illustrated in Figure 4.1.

4.2.2 Exclusion of securitised exposure from the calculation of risk-weighted exposure amount

Securitisation is a flexible, efficient and cost-effective way of raising funds and transferring credit risk. From the originating institution's point of view, the main advantage for
regulatory capital purposes is the exclusion of the securitised exposures from the calculation of risk-weighted exposure amounts. In order to exclude underlying exposures
from the calculation of risk-weighted assets, the originator of a traditional or synthetic
securitisation has to achieve the recognition of a significant risk transfer of the credit
risk of the underlying exposures to a third party. The Basel II Securitisation Framework
(unchanged in BCBS 374) sets out the operational requirements for the recognition of
significant risk transfer, applicable to both the standardised and IRB Approaches, for
traditional and synthetic securitisations. If an originator does not meet the operational
requirements for the recognition of risk transfer, the underlying exposures must be
treated as if they were not securitised. Nonetheless, if an originator institution meets
the requirements for the recognition of significant risk transfer, it must still hold regulatory capital against any retained securitisation position.

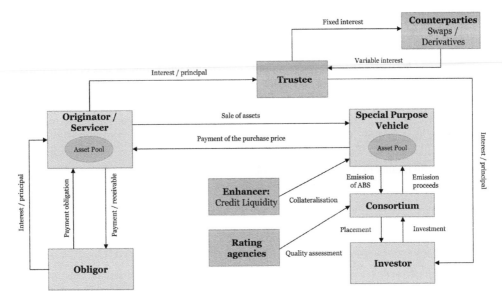

Figure 4.1: Basic concept of a traditional securitisation

Operational requirements for the recognition of risk transfer for traditional securitisations

To fulfil the requirements of a significant risk transfer for traditional securitisations[7], the following conditions have to be met cumulatively:

- Significant credit risk associated with the underlying exposures has been transferred to third parties. There is no definition of the transfer of significant credit risk in the Basel II Securitisation Framework. However, the retaining or repurchasing of significant securitisation exposures, depending on the proportion of risk held by the originator, might undermine the intent of a securitisation transaction to transfer credit risk. For example, the repurchasing of a whole tranche or positions bought for market making purposes, which are not resold within an appropriate period can hinder the transfer of a significant credit risk[8] (see also section 4.2.2.2).
- The transferor does not maintain effective or indirect control over the transferred exposures.
- The transferor is deemed to have maintained effective control over the transferred credit risk exposures where it is able to repurchase from the transferee the previously transferred exposures in order to realise their benefits or it is obliged to retain the risk of the transferred exposures. The condition is fulfilled when the assets are legally isolated from the transferor in such a way that the exposures are put beyond the reach of the transferor and its creditors, even in bankruptcy or receivership.
- The securities issued are not obligations of the transferor and investors only have claim to the underlying pool of exposures.
- The transferee is an SPE, and the holders of the beneficial interests in that entity have the right to pledge or exchange them without restriction.
- Clean-up calls must be at the discretion of the originating bank, not be structured to avoid losses for the investors and only exercisable when 10% or less of the original underlying reference portfolio value remains.
- The securitisation does not contain clauses that require the originating bank to alter the underlying exposures such that the pool's credit quality is improved, to increase the first loss position or credit enhancement or to increase the yields payable to investors or providers of credit enhancements in response to deterioration in the credit quality of the underlying pool.

---

7 While the operational requirements for traditional securitisations primarily aim at the transfer of the underlying assets the operational requirements for synthetic transactions primarily aim at the use of the credit risk mitigation and can also be found at BCBS 128 (2006) page 123 f.

8 According to the requirements set out in Art. 243 (2) CRR a significant credit risk shall be considered to have been transferred if the originator holds no more than 50% of the mezzanine securitisation positions. If the securitisation has no mezzanine securitisation positions, it must be proven that the exposure values of the securitisation positions to be deducted from the CET1 or to be assigned with a risk weight of 1,250% are significantly higher than the loss actually expected to arise from these securitisised exposures. Furthermore, the originator may hold no more than 20% of the exposures of the forementioned securitisation positions.

Circumstances that hinder the recognition of significant risk transfer

The Basel II Framework provides examples of cases that hinder the significant risk transfer. For example, the above mentioned retaining or repurchasing of significant amounts of risk or "cherry picking" of the exposures to be transferred via a securitisation. Another implication of realising only a non-significant risk transfer, especially if related to good quality unrated exposures, is that both the poorer quality unrated underlyings and most of the credit risk embedded in the exposures underlying the securitised transaction are likely to remain with the originator. Further, the provision of implicit (or non-contractual) support, as opposed to contractual credit support (i.e. credit enhancements), raises significant supervisory concerns. For traditional securitisation structures the provision of implicit support undermines the clean break criteria, which - when satisfied - would allow banks to exclude the securitised assets from regulatory capital calculations. For synthetic securitisation structures, it negates the significance of risk transference. By providing implicit support, banks signal to the market that the risk is still with the bank and in effect has not been transferred. The institution's capital calculation, in this case, understates the real risk.

4.2.3 Treatment of securitisation exposures

While the subject of the exclusion of securitised exposures from the RWA calculation is addressed mainly from the originator institutions viewpoint, the regulatory treatment of securitisation exposures primarily affects the point of view of investors (i.e. note-holders) in securitised assets.

The Capital treatment under the Basel II securitisation framework includes provisions for the calculation of the risk weighted assets under the Standardised Approach (SA) and the Internal Ratings-Based Approach (IRBA).

When using the SA for the calculation of credit risk of securitisation positions, the following rules apply (see Figure 4.2):

- If the securitisation position possesses an external rating, the standardised approach is used (risk weight of position taken from a look-up table).
- If the securitisation possesses no external rating but the institution knows the underlying portfolio's composition at all times, it uses the look-through approach (risk weight of position calculated as product of weighted-average risk weight of underlyings assets and concentration ratio).
- In all other cases the securitisation position must be deducted from capital.
- There are exceptions from deduction for qualified liquidity facilities to ABCP structures and for senior and some second-loss positions in an ABCP structure.

When using the IRBA for the calculation of credit risk of securitisation positions, the following rules apply:

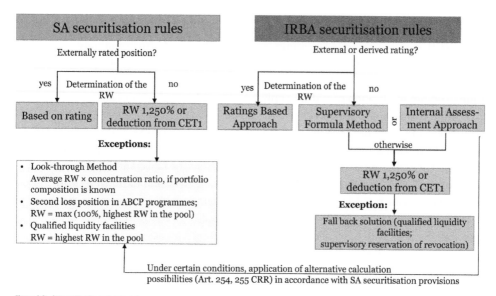

Figure 4.2: Systematic of current approaches

- If the securitisation position possesses an external rating or that rating may be inferred, the ratings based approach (RBA) is used (risk weight of positions taken from a look-up table).
- If the securitisation position possesses no external rating the supervisory formula approach (SFA) may be used if the institution knows the parameters (risk weight calculated with a formula approach).
- If the securitisation position refers to an ABCP structure, the institution may use the Internal Assessment Approach (IAA) provided supervisory approval has been granted.
- In all other cases the securitisation position must be deducted from capital.
- The exceptions from deduction of the SA approach apply accordingly.

4.3 Revisions to the securitisation framework under Basel IV

4.3.1 Criticism of the existing rules

The current provisions for determining the risk weights for securitisation positions of the Basel rules do not differ substantially from those of Basel II. The fact that the calculation rules were not decisively revised when Basel III or, for example, CRR[9] (as the European implementation of Basel III) were introduced may in some way be understood as a "precaution". After the experiences of the global financial crisis of 2007–2008, the introduction of new approaches was needed in order to increase the resilience of the financial market based on the crisis lessons.

---

9   Regulation (EU) No 575/2013 of the European Parliament and of the Council of 26 June 2013

The BCBS's analysis of the financial crisis highlighted the shortcomings of the Basel II securitisation framework (BCBS 303). There were major concerns that the calculation methods for determining risk weights and their calibration could generate insufficient capital requirements for certain exposures. In addition, particular doubts were raised on the mechanistic reliance on external ratings in determining capital requirements. Insufficient risk sensitivity was particularly the result of the absence of adequate risk parameters within the approaches used to determine risk weights and pro-cyclical "cliff effects" in the capital requirements.

For these reasons, the BCBS issued its own view proposing to reduce mechanistic reliance on external ratings and enhance risk sensitivity of the framework by revising the applicable risk weights and introducing new approaches which are more prudent in terms of their calibration. In the proposed approaches, other risk drivers that significantly influence the risk of a securitisation position – such as the tranche maturity – are also taken into consideration. The BCBS also sought to reduce the occurrence of cliff effects, which can arise due to the fact that minor downward changes in the underlying portfolio can cause significant shifts in the external ratings, and thus can lead to sharp step-ups of the applicable risk weights for securitisation positions (e.g. the risk weight jumping up from 350% to 1,250% because of the migration of the rating class from CC– to C– under the SA). This last point was found to be especially harmful during the financial crisis since rating downgrades for securitisation positions were frequent and led to sudden disproportionate jumps in capital requirements for securitisation positions. In the future, part of the mitigation of these cliff effects will be achieved by including the maturity of the securitisation tranches (M_T) in the calculation of risk-weighted exposure amounts.

A further criticism of the Basel securitisation framework was the lack of differentiation of the regulatory treatment between securitisations with simple structures on the one hand and complex transactions on the other. In the future, this will be considered through the introduction of specific criteria which – if fulfilled – will lead to the classification of a securitisation position as simple, transparent and comparable (STC). For this purpose, the BCBS launched a consultation on 11 December 2014 and published the final document with concrete STC criteria in July 2015. This was followed by a further round of consultations from November 2015 until the beginning of February 2016, with the objective to determine the risk weights for STC securitisations. BCBS 303 was revised taking the results of this consultation into account and, in July 2016, BCBS 374 was published, presenting the final capital treatment for non-STC and STC securitisation positions. In addition, BCBS 413 and BCBS 414 presenting rules for the capital treatment of STC-compliant short-term/ABCP securitisations was issued for comments in July 2017, which were followed by the final documents BCBS 441 and BCBS 442 in May 2018.

The timing of the revision of the securitisation framework is shown in Figure 4.3.

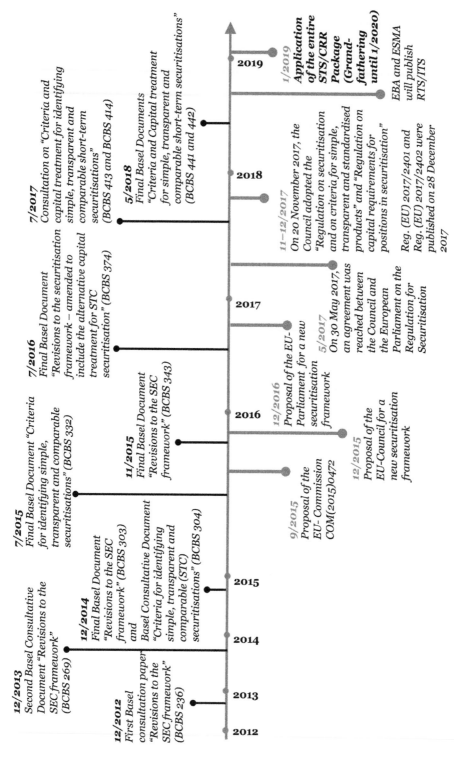

Figure 4.3: Basel documents on revisions to the securitisation framework and STC criteria

4.3.2 New approaches and a revised hierarchy for the determination of risk-weighted exposure amounts

New approaches for the determination of risk-weighted exposure amounts

In order to reduce the mechanistic reliance on external ratings, the Basel Committee has revised the hierarchy of approaches for the calculation of the risk weighted exposure amounts of securitisation positions and added additional risk drivers. It has also limited the number of applicable approaches and simplified their use by establishing one single hierarchy for all institutions and portfolios (Figure 4.4).

The hierarchy of approaches prescribed by the Basel rules depends on the approach used for credit risk of the underlying securitised exposures and the availability of external ratings for securitisation positions and must be strictly followed. This means that the role of the bank as an SA or IRBA institution is no longer decisive. Instead, for each specific securitisation, it must use the highest approach in the hierarchy for which all input parameters are available or which is otherwise feasible. At the top of the revised sequential hierarchy of approaches stands the SEC-IRBA. This approach – similar to the current SFA – must be applied by the institutions if they use one or more internal models for the assets underlying the securitisation which have obtained supervisory approval for assessing credit risks (IRB Approach approval). This rules out the application of the SEC-IRBA for Securitisations with underlying SA assets because the bank does not possess the required IRB input parameters. If the bank doesn't use any internal models for the underlying assets and the securitisation tranches are externally rated, SEC-ERBA as the subsequent approach must be used. If no external ratings for the

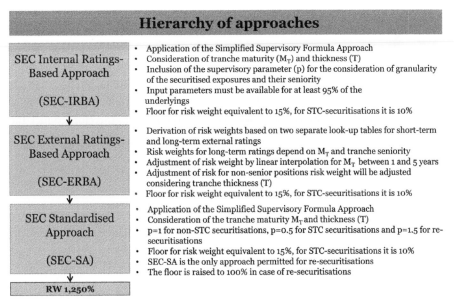

Figure 4.4: The revised hierarchy and new approaches for the calculation of risk weights

tranches are available, but the bank knows the SA parameters as well as the delinquency ratio of the underlying exposures, SEC-SA must be applied. This approach is intended to be used in jurisdictions where the use of external ratings is not allowed. It is also the only approach allowed for re-securitisations. Under all approaches, the risk weight is subject to a floor of 15% for non-STC securitisation positions in senior tranches, whereas, for STC-securitisations, floors of 10% for senior and of 15% for non-senior tranches apply. If none of the three approaches can be calculated, a risk weight of 1,250% must be assigned to the securitisation position or the position must be deducted from the institutions CET 1 (we will subsequently not differentiate between these two alternatives).

Example: Representation of a transaction

The impact of the new approaches will be illustrated below on the basis of a sample transaction. The fictional AAA bank (total assets approx. EUR 130 billion) mainly grants loans to small and medium-sized German companies. The AAA bank uses the advanced IRB Approach to determine the RWA for the credit risk. To actively manage its balance sheet it has securitised a wholesale credit portfolio of receivables on companies (no re-securitisations, no non-performing or defaulted exposures) through a special purpose vehicle. The portfolio consists of 100 individual exposures with an EAD totalling EUR 200 million and a total maturity of 10 years. The special purpose vehicle issues three sequentially repaid tranches (A to C). Further details on these three tranches are shown in Table 4.1.

The tranching of the transaction is illustrated in Figure 4.5.

SEC-IRBA

The SEC-IRBA is based on the Simplified Supervisory Formula Approach (SSFA), whose introduction had already been proposed in the first consultative document on "Revisions to the securitisation framework". The main difference between the SSFA and the SFA under the Basel IV rules is the consideration of the maturity of the securitisation tranches as a key risk driver by the former. Therefore, under the

	Tranche A	Tranche B	Tranche C
External rating	AAA	BBB	Unrated
Maturity	7 years	10 years	10 years
Volume	EUR 130 million	EUR 60 million	EUR 10 million
Attachment Point	35%	5%	0%
Detachment Point	100%	35%	5%
Tranche thickness (T)	65%	30%	5%

Table 4.1: Tranching of the transaction of the AAA bank

Tranching – waterfall

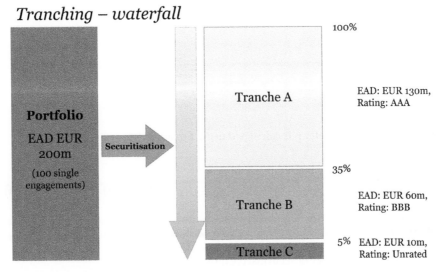

Figure 4.5: Tranching of the transaction of the AAA bank

SEC-IRBA the calculation of the risk weight is carried out according to Equation 4.1 (which is a modified version of the SSFA):

Equation 4.1

$$RW = \left[\left(\frac{K_{IRB} - A}{D - A}\right) \cdot 12.5\right] + \left[\left(\frac{D - K_{IRB}}{D - A}\right) \cdot 12.5 \cdot K_{SSFA(K_{IRB})}\right] \tag{4.1}$$

where:

RW	= Risk weight
K_{IRB}	= Capital charge of the underlying pool according to the IRB Approach
A	= Attachment point (the threshold for loss allocation)
D	= Detachment point (the threshold for the total loss of the tranche)
$K_{SSFA(K_{IRB})}$	= IRBA capital requirement per unit of a securitisation exposure

The determination of K_{IRB} requires an authorised IRB model for the exposures in the securitisation pool. The capital requirements pursuant to K_{IRB} result from dividing the risk-weighted assets under IRB by the total exposure value multiplied by 8%

$K_{SSFA(K_{IRB})}$ is determined as follows in accordance with Equation 4.2:

Equation 4.2

$$K_{SSFA(K_{IRB})} = \frac{e^{a \cdot u} - e^{a \cdot l}}{a(u - l)} \tag{4.2}$$

Where e is the base of the natural logarithms which equals ~2.7.

Variables a, u and l are determined depending on K_{IRB} and p:

$$a = -\frac{1}{p * K_{IRB}}$$

$$u = D - K_{IRB}$$

$$l = \max(A - K_{IRB}; 0)$$

The supervisory parameter p is calculated using Equation 4.3:

Equation 4.3

$$p = \max\left[0.3; \left(A + B * \left(\frac{1}{N}\right) + C * K_{IRB} + D * LGD + E * M_T\right)\right] \qquad (4.3)$$

where:

N $\quad$ = Effective number of securitised exposures

LGD = Exposure-weighted average loss ratio in case of default

M_T $\quad$ = Tranche maturity

The formula components A to E are five supervisory parameters that are provided in a look-up table (see Table 4.2). They depend on N, seniority and whether the underlying pool consists of wholesale or retail exposures.[10]

M_T can be determined either as the weighted average maturity of the contractual cash flows over the tranche's lifetime (Method 1) or by performing a supervisory discount to the legal remaining maturity of the securitisation tranche (Method 2). A floor of one year and a cap of five years apply in both cases. Both Methods of the calculation of M_T apply identically for all approaches (SEC-IRBA, SEC-ERBA and SEC-SA).

Method 1: Determination of M_T through the calculation of the weighted average maturity of the cash flows (Equation 4.4):

		A	B	C	D	E
Wholesale	Senior, granular (N ≥ 25)	0	3.56	−1.85	0.55	0.07
	Senior, non-granular (N < 25)	0.11	2.61	−2.91	0.68	0.07
	Non-senior, granular (N ≥ 25)	0.16	2.87	−1.03	0.21	0.07
	Non-senior, non-granular (N < 25)	0.22	2.35	−2.46	0.48	0.07
Retail	Senior	0	0	−7.48	0.71	0.24
	Non-senior	0	0	−5.78	0.55	0.27

Table 4.2: Parameters for the calculation of the supervisory parameter (p)

---

10 $\quad$ In this respect, there is a dual assignment of the letters A and D. Detailed remarks on the input parameters Attachment Point (A) and Detachment Point (D) are contained above in this chapter.

Equation 4.4

$$M_T = \sum_t t \cdot CF_t / \sum_t CF_t \qquad\qquad (4.4)$$

where:

CF_t = Cash flows (principal, interest and fees) in period t

   t = Period in which the cash flows (CF_t) must be paid

Method 2: Determination of M_T based on the remaining legal maturity (Equation 4.5):

Equation 4.5

$$M_T = 1 + (M_L - 1) * 80\% \qquad\qquad (4.5)$$

Under both methods, M_T will have a floor of one year and a cap of five years.

In order to apply SEC-IRBA, the institution must fundamentally be able to determine all required input parameters. In mixed pools (the underlying assets consisting of IRB- and SA-exposures), the IRB-exposures must represent at least 95% of the underlying exposures in the pool, and the institution must know the relevant parameters for those exposures for the institution to be allowed to apply SEC-IRBA to the pool. If this threshold is not reached, the bank is obliged to apply a subsequent approach (SEC-ERBA, SEC-SA or 1,250% risk weight). If it is a securitisation with highly complex or high-risk characteristics, the supervisory authorities may forbid the institutions to use SEC-IRBA in particular cases.

As is the case when using the current SFA for IRB-exposures under Basel III rules, the parameters N, LGD (formerly ELGD) and K_{IRB} are required for calculating risk weights using the SEC-IRBA. The determination of the parameters does not differ from the way in which they are determined using the SFA in accordance with BCBS 128. In the following example, these parameters are:

N   = 98.78 (effective number of securitised exposures)

LGD = 33.87% (exposure value weighted average loss ratio in case of default)

K_{IRB} = 6.46% (relation of IRB capital requirement for the underlying exposures to the sum of the portfolio's exposure values)

The parameters p and M_T must be separately determined for each tranche. The supervisory parameter p is used as a factor for the scaling of K_{IRB}. The parameters for the determination of p are shown in Table 4.2.

p is floored at 0.3 and acquires the values shown in Table 4.3 for the individual tranches of the example.

Tranche	Parameter p
A	0.45
B	0.54
C	0.54

Table 4.3: Supervisory parameter p of the tranches

Tranche	M_T
A	5
B	5
C	5

Table 4.4: Tranche maturities

Furthermore, the effective remaining maturity M_T of each tranche must be determined. Using Method 2, the individual tranches get the following M_T values (after application of floors / caps) as shown in Table 4.4.

The risk weights for the individual tranches are calculated by implementing parameters a, u and l in Equation 4.2 (see Equations 4.6–4.8):

Equations 4.6–4.8

$$K_{SSFA(K_{IRB})A} = \frac{e^{-34.18\cdot0.94} - e^{-34.18\cdot0.29}}{-34.18(0.94 - 0.29)} \tag{4.6}$$

$$K_{SSFA(K_{IRB})B} = \frac{e^{-28.47\cdot0.29} - e^{-28.47\cdot0}}{-28.47(0.29 - 0)} \tag{4.7}$$

$$K_{SSFA(K_{IRB})C} = \frac{e^{-28.47\cdot-0.01} - e^{-28.47\cdot0}}{-28.47(-0.01 - 0)} \tag{4.8}$$

The approach used to calculate the risk weight RW for each tranche D (detachment point) and A (attachment point) to K_{IRB} and is determined as follows:

For $D \le K_{IRB}$: $RW = 1{,}250\%$

For $A \ge K_{IRB}$: $RW = K_{SSFA(K_{IRB})} * 12.5$

For $A < K_{IRB}$ and $D > K_{IRB}$ RW is calculated by applying parameters K_{IRB}, $K_{SSFA(KIRB)}$, A and D to Equation 4.6 (see Equations 4.9–4.11):

Equations 4.9–4.11

$$RW_A = \left[\left(\frac{6.46\% - 35\%}{100\% - 35\%}\right)\cdot 12.5\right] + \left[\left(\frac{100\% - 6.46\%}{100\% - 35\%}\right)\cdot 12.5 \cdot 0{,}00026\%\right] \tag{4.9}$$

Tranche	Risk weight
A	15%
B	207%
C	1,250%

Table 4.5: SEC-IRBA risk weights of tranches

$$RW_B = \left[\left(\frac{6.46\% - 5\%}{35\% - 5\%}\right) \cdot 12.5\right] + \left[\left(\frac{35\% - 6.46\%}{35\% - 5\%}\right) \cdot 12.5 \cdot 12\%\right] \qquad (4.10)$$

$$RW_C = \left[\left(\frac{6.46\% - 0\%}{5\% - 0\%}\right) \cdot 12.5\right] + \left[\left(\frac{5\% - 6.46\%}{5\% - 0\%}\right) \cdot 12.5 \cdot 124\%\right] \qquad (4.11)$$

Using SEC-IRBA, the risk weights summarised in Table 4.5 are obtained (including the application of the floor for Tranche A as required by the rules).

SEC-ERBA

Under the SEC-ERBA, the risk weight is determined based on external ratings. In this regard, this approach is comparable to the ratings-based Approach under Basel II. Different from the latter, the maturity of the securitisation position (M_T) is taken into account when determining the risk weights for tranches because it was judged to be a significant risk driver by the Basel Committee (whereas before it was judged to be already considered in the rating itself). Moreover, the tranche thickness (T) is also included in the calculation of risk weights of non-senior securitisation tranches. The effective number of securitised exposures (N), a relevant criterion under the IRBA in use, is omitted since the Basel Committee is of the opinion that it is already sufficiently considered by the rating agencies.

In order to apply the SEC-ERBA, external or at least derived ratings must be available for the securitisation positions to be weighted. As stated above, the SEC-ERBA may only be used if the bank cannot apply the SEC-IRBA and as long as the corresponding tranche or inferred ratings are available. If short-term ratings are available, the risk weights can be determined based on a separate mapping table. In the case of long-term ratings, a table containing the risk weights for senior and non-senior tranches with a remaining maturity (M_T) of one or five years is also provided. The risk weights for maturities between one and five years must be determined using linear interpolation (Table 4.6).

For non-senior tranches, the risk weight under the SEC-ERBA is determined by utilising Equation 4.12, where the risk weight is multiplied by a scaling factor of at least 0.5 and always less than 1 (the risk weight of subordinated tranches under the SEC-ERBA never reaches 1,250%):

Rating	Senior tranche Tranche maturity (M_T)		Non-senior (thin) tranche Tranche maturity (M_T)	
	1 year	5 years	1 year	5 years
AAA	15%	20%	15%	70%
AA+	15%	30%	15%	90%
AA	25%	40%	30%	120%
AA–	30%	45%	40%	140%
A+	40%	50%	60%	160%
A	50%	65%	80%	180%
A–	60%	70%	120%	210%
BBB+	75%	90%	170%	260%
BBB	90%	105%	220%	310%
BBB–	120%	140%	330%	420%
BB+	140%	160%	470%	580%
BB	160%	180%	620%	760%
BB–	200%	225%	750%	860%
B+	250%	280%	900%	950%
B	310%	340%	1,050%	1,050%
B–	380%	420%	1,130%	1,130%
CCC(+/ /–)	460%	505%	1,250%	1,250%
Below CCC–	1,250%	1,250%	1,250%	1,250%

Table 4.6: SEC-ERBA risk weights for long-term ratings

Equation 4.12

$$RW = [\text{risk weight from table after adjusting for maturity}] * [1 - \min(T;\ 50\%)]$$

$$(4.12)$$

Example: Regulatory treatment of a transaction under the SEC-ERBA

The risk weights under the SEC-ERBA are determined according to external ratings of the tranches given in Table 4.1. In addition, the parameters rank (senior or non-senior) and the remaining maturity M_T must be taken into account. Table 4.7 provides an overview of the input parameters.

Tranche	Rank	Effective remaining maturity (M_T)	External rating
A	Senior	5	AAA
B	Non-senior	5	BBB
C	Non-senior	5	unrated

Table 4.7: Determination of risk weights under the SEC-ERBA

In determining the risk weight of non-senior tranches B and C, the tranche thickness $(T=D-A)$ must be taken into account using Equation 4.14. By inserting the risk weights pursuant to Table 4.6 (after adjustment by linear interpolation, the result being the "risk weight after adjusting for maturity" of Equation 4.14) and thickness (T) of the individual tranches into Equation 4.12, the following risk weights are obtained (Equations 4.13–4.15):

Equations 4.13–4.15

$$RW_A = 20\% \tag{4.13}$$

$$RW_B = 310\% * [1 - \min(30\%;\ 50\%)] \tag{4.14}$$

$$RW_C = 1{,}250\% * [1 - \min(5\%;\ 50\%)] \tag{4.15}$$

In this case, the scaling factor is applied to tranches B (RW = 310%) and C (RW = 1,250%), where tranche thickness is 30% for tranche B and 5% for tranche C respectively.

Table 4.8 illustrates the risk weights under SEC-ERBA.

SEC-SA

The calculation method of the SEC-SA is comparable to that of the SEC-IRBA and is mainly intended for underlying pools of SA assets in transactions without tranche ratings. It is also the only approach for institutions in jurisdictions where the use of external ratings is not permitted short of applying 1,250% risk weight.[11] To determine the risk-weighted exposure amounts, a modified version of the SSFA is applied.

The calculation is performed comparably to the SEC-IRBA while using different parameters (Equation 4.16):

Equation 4.16

$$RW = \left[\left(\frac{K_A - A}{D - A} \right) * 12.5 \right] + \left[\left(\frac{D - K_A}{D - A} \right) * 12.5 * K_{SSFA(K_A)} \right] \tag{4.16}$$

Tranche	Risk weight
A	20%
B	217%
C	1,188%

Table 4.8: SEC-ERBA risk weights of tranches

---

11   Cf. Chapter 4.3.2 on the application requirements.

where:

$K_{SSFA(K_A)}$ = SA capital requirement per unit of the securitisation exposure

K_A is determined based on Equation 4.17:

Equation 4.17

$$K_A = (1 - W) \cdot K_{SA} + W \cdot 0{,}5 \tag{4.17}$$

where:

W = Ratio of delinquent exposures in the underlying pool

K_{SA} = Capital charge of the underlying pool under the Standardised Approach to Credit Risk

The formula used under SEC-IRBA is also applied to determine $K_{SSFA(KA)}$ (Equation 4.18):[12]

Equation 4.18

$$K_{SSFA(K_A)} = \frac{e^{a \cdot u} - e^{a \cdot l}}{a(u - l)} \tag{4.18}$$

Variables a, u and l are determined depending on K_A and p:

$$a = -\frac{1}{p * K_A}$$

$$u = D - K_A$$

$$l = \max(A - K_A; 0)$$

The supervisory parameter p is set to 1 for the determination of the risk weight of a securitisation position (no calculation using a separate formula as in SEC-IRBA).

The capital requirements pursuant to K_{SA} result from dividing the risk-weighted assets under SA by the total exposure value multiplied by 8%. The parameter (W) equals the ratio of the sum of all delinquent exposures to all exposures in the pool. Delinquent exposures are underlying exposures that are 90 days or more past due, subject to bankruptcy or insolvency proceedings, in the process of foreclosure or in default where the default is defined within the securitisation deal documents.[13] The bank must be able

---

12 Cf. 4.3.1.1 on SEC-IRBA for a detailed explanation of the input parameters.
13 A difference compared to the current proposals of the Basel Committee regarding the definition of default under the Standardised Approach for credit risk can be observed here. In said case, the following requirements must be met: a default in payment of over 90 days or the debtor is a so-called "defaulted borrower", see BCBS 347 (2015), page 16 in connection with page 39.

to determine for at least 95% of the exposures whether they are delinquent exposures (an adapted version of the SEC-SA-formula is used if W can be determined for exactly 95%[14]). If W is known for less than 95%, a risk weight of 1,250% is assigned to the securitisation positions.

SEC-SA is also the only admissible approach for re-securitisation positions. Within the scope of the calculation, W is set to 0. The supervisory parameter p is set to 1.5. A floor of 100% is applied to the resulting risk weight.

Example: Regulatory treatment of a transaction under the SEC-SA

In order to determine the risk weights of individual tranches under the SEC-SA, the parameters K_{SA} and W, as well as the tranche thickness T (T = D–A), are required.

The value of the individual parameters is:

$$K_{SA} = 7\%$$
$$W = 0\% \text{ in the example.}$$

K_A must be determined based on the parameters K_{SA} and W. K_A is the capital charge under consideration of the delinquent exposures in the pool (Equation 4.19):

Equation 4.19

$$K_A = (1 - 0\%) \cdot 7\% + 0\% \cdot 0{,}5 \tag{4.19}$$

K_A is included in the calculation of $K_{SSFA(K_A)}$ (see Equations 4.20–4.22):

Equations 4.20–4.22

$$K_{SSFA(K_A)A} = \frac{e^{-13.56\cdot0.93} - e^{-13.56\cdot0.28}}{-13.56(0.93 - 0.28)} \tag{4.20}$$

$$K_{SSFA(K_A)B} = \frac{e^{-13.56\cdot0.28} - e^{-13.56\%\cdot0}}{-13.56(0.28 - 0)} \tag{4.21}$$

$$K_{SSFA(K_A)C} = \frac{e^{-13.56\cdots-0.02} - e^{-13.56\cdot0}}{-13.56(-0.02 - 0)} \tag{4.22}$$

The parameter $K_{SSFA(K_A)}$ indicates the capital requirements of the Standardised Approach for one unit of the securitised portfolio. It is used when determining the risk weight (RW) of each tranche.

---

14   Cf BCBS 374 (2016), page 29.

The risk weight RW for the individual tranches depends on the ratio of D and A to K_A and is calculated as follows:

For $D \leq K_A$: RW $= 1{,}250\%$

For $A \geq K_A$: RW $= K_{SSFA(K_A)} {}^{*} 12.5$

For $A < K_A$ and $D > K_A$ RW is calculated pursuant to Equation 4.16 using the parameters A, D, K_A, $K_{SSFA(K_A)}$ (Equations 4.23–4.25):

Equations 4.23–4.25

$$RW_A = \left[\left(\frac{7\% - 35\%}{100\% - 35\%} \right) * 12.5 \right] + \left[\left(\frac{100\% - 7\%}{100\% - 35\%} \right) * 12.5 * 0.3\% \right] \qquad (4.23)$$

$$RW_B = \left[\left(\frac{7\% - 5\%}{35\% - 5\%} \right) * 12.5 \right] + \left[\left(\frac{35\% - 7\%}{35\% - 5\%} \right) * 12.5 * 26\% \right] \qquad (4.24)$$

$$RW_C = \left[\left(\frac{7\% - 0\%}{5\% - 0\%} \right) * 12.5 \right] + \left[\left(\frac{5\% - 7\%}{5\% - 0\%} \right) * 12.5 * 118\% \right] \qquad (4.25)$$

The risk weights listed in Table 4.9 arise under SEC-SA.

Conclusions

The determination of capital requirements for securitisation positions will be significantly more risk sensitive and also more conservative using the new approaches. In addition, the required effort on the part of affected institutions will increase given that not only the number of input parameters but also the complexity of the calculations increases. The application of the SEC-IRBA can be expected to be mainly reserved to securitising institutions (originators) since, for example, an investor may not be able to access the required level of granularity and data quality of the underlying exposures. Moreover, it will be especially hard for smaller institutions to depict the enhanced complexity of the calculations.

Based on the transaction of the AAA bank used as an example, we have shown that the new approaches have a considerable impact on capital requirements for securitisation positions. This becomes especially clear when comparing the results under the

Tranche	Risk weight
A	15%
B	399%
C	1,250%

Table 4.9: SEC-SA risk weights of tranches

approaches currently in force under CRR and the new approaches of the Basel Committee. The risk weights are compared below.

Under the assumption that the underlying portfolios are pure Standardised Approach portfolios, the respective risk weights for the different approaches are outlined in Table 4.10.

The increase of the risk weights for the mezzanine tranche in particular when using the new approaches becomes apparent in this example. Although we show that in case of SEC-SA there is a decrease in RW due to the fact that the floor applies. Figure 4.6 shows the changes for each tranche in detail.

Under the assumption that the underlying portfolios are pure IRB Approach portfolios, the resulting tendency is comparable to that of an SA portfolio. In this case, the

	Basel III (ERBA)	Basel IV (SEC-ERBA)	Basel IV (SEC-SA)
RW_A	20%	20%	15%
RW_B	100%	217%	399%
RW_C	1,250%	1,188%	1,250%

Table 4.10: Risk weights of SA securitisation positions

Risk weights for the SA portfolio under different approaches

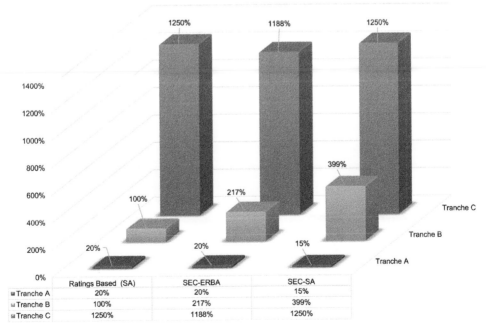

	Ratings Based (SA)	SEC-ERBA	SEC-SA
Tranche A	20%	20%	15%
Tranche B	100%	217%	399%
Tranche C	1250%	1188%	1250%

Figure 4.6: Risk weights of the SA portfolios of the AAA bank

risk weights for the senior and mezzanine tranches also increase significantly. The risk weight under the SEC-SA is especially high (Table 4.11).

The increase of risk weights becomes particularly clear in the graphical representation of risk weights shown in Figure 4.7.

4.3.3 Risk weights for securitisation positions when complying with STC criteria

The financial crisis showed that the risk related to entering securitisation positions, especially in the case of extremely complex and opaque structures, is hard to assess for investors. However, even simple and transparent securitisations may render it unfeasible to recognise risks if they arise from inappropriate eligibility criteria or inadequate control mechanisms. Therefore, the goal of the Basel Committee is to make risk assessment easier for investors before they decide to invest in a securitisation position. For this purpose, the Basel Committee issued the final paper "Criteria for identifying simple, transparent and comparable securitisations" in July 2015.[15] In this paper, the Basel

	Basel III (ERBA)	Basel III (SFA)	Basel IV (SEC-IRBA)	Basel IV (SEC-ERBA)	Basel IV (SEC-SA)
RW_A	7%	7%	15%	20%	15%
RW_B	75%	99%	207%	217%	399%
RW_C	1,250%	1,250%	1,250%	1,188%	1,250%

Table 4.11: Risk weights of IRB Approach securitisation positions

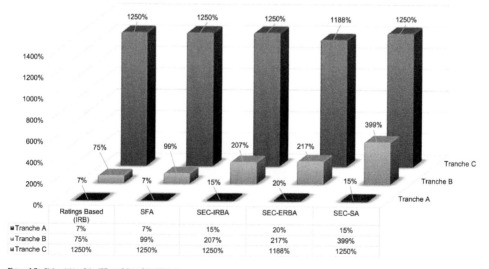

Figure 4.7: Risk weights of the IRB portfolios of the AAA bank

15 Cf. BCBS 332 (2015).

Committee identifies so-called STC criteria which can be assigned to three overarching risk categories: asset risk, structural risk and fiduciary and servicer risk.[16] These criteria were defined in detail by setting forth specific requirements.[17]

The Basel Committee published an additional consultation paper titled "Capital treatment for 'simple, transparent and comparable' securitisations (BCBS 343)" in November 2015, the consultation phase of which lasted until 5 February 2016.[18] The purpose of this consultation paper was to discuss the adjustment of the approaches to determine risk weights for securitisation positions defined in BCBS 303. The fulfilment of the STC criteria should not only alleviate investment decisions for investors but also bring along lower risk weights for securitisation positions. Thus, compliance with STC rules will result in "qualified securitisations", for which privileging can be justified in terms of capital charge.

The December 2014 framework did not capture certain features of securitisation structures found in the marketplace. Therefore the Committee included the July 2015 STC criteria and supplemented them with the so-called "additional criteria" for capital purposes as the fourth overarching risk category.[19]

Definition of the STC criteria

Asset risk

The Basel Committee deals with the asset risk first. It comprises risk directly related to credit claims or receivables (especially the risks of delinquency and default as well as the lack of legal enforceability). The criteria to meet this risk type are described in the following:

- Regarding the nature of the assets underlying the securitisation, these should be homogeneous as to the asset type, jurisdiction, legal system and currency.
- Contractually agreed-upon periodic payments must be made.
- Regarding the asset performance history: delinquency and default data must be available over an appropriately long period of time.[20] Credit claims or receivables being transferred to the securitisation may not include obligations that are in default or delinquent at the time of inclusion in the pool. On the contrary, at least one payment should have been made at the time of their inclusion in the pool.[21]

---

16 Cf. BCBS 332 (2015), page 6 et seq.
17 The BCBS released on 6 July 2017 a consultative document (BCBS 414 (2017)) regarding the "Criteria for identifying simple, transparent and comparable short-term securitisations". The design of the short-term STC criteria follows the STC criteria published in July 2015 for term securitisations. While all principles underlying the STC criteria for term securitisations are relevant for short-term securitisations, some criteria have been amended to reflect specific aspects of ABCP conduits.
18 Cf. BCBS 343 (2015).
19 Cf. BCBS 374 (2016). Those additional criteria already were included in the consultation paper BCBS 343
20 A period of time of at least seven years is considered "appropriate" for non-retail exposures, while five years is expected for retail exposure. Cf. BCBS 374 (2016), page 48.
21 Cf. BCBS 374 (2016), page 49.

- The originator should demonstrate that any credit claims or receivables have been originated in the ordinary course of business to materially non-deteriorating underwriting standards. So-called "originate-to-distribute securitisations" are excluded from the scope of STC requirements.[22]
- Active portfolio management is not allowed; the selection of credit claims or receivables should satisfy clearly defined eligibility criteria.
- The availability of sufficient granular data must be ensured before and after issuance.

Structural risk

The Basel Committee identified the so-called structural risk as the second overriding risk category. All risks arising from the structure of securitisation transactions shall be adequately secured against interest rate and credit risks. Moreover, the Basel Committee pays special attention to the requirements on cash flow waterfalls. The paper demands full transparency over priority of payments, especially with regard to note classes. All triggers affecting the cash flow waterfall should be clearly disclosed to the investors in offering documents and in investor reports. In the case of revolving transactions, rules on the early termination and the termination of the revolving phase must be available. Cash flow models should be made available to investors before pricing and on an ongoing basis. To help ensure clarity for investors of their rights to control and enforce on the underlying credit claims or receivables upon insolvency of the originator or sponsor, all voting and enforcement rights should be transferred to the securitisation. The pertinent documentation shall be made available to the investor prior to pricing, which should be reviewed by a third party legal practice. It must be ensured that the originator or sponsor retain the legal material net economic exposure.

Fiduciary and servicer risk

The Basel Committee identifies the fiduciary and servicer risk as another overriding risk category. This shall be minimised by means of the following measure: the servicer managing securitised credit claims or receivables should be able to demonstrate expertise in this area and be supported by a team with extensive industry experience. The contractual obligations, duties and responsibilities of all key parties should be defined clearly both in the initial offering and all underlying documentation. Provisions should be documented for the replacement of servicers, bank account providers, derivatives counterparties and liquidity providers in the event of non-performance or insolvency. All payments such as scheduled interest, redemption principal, prepaid principal and compensations must be identifiable for investors.

Additional criteria for capital purposes

The Basel Committee added two completely new criteria in BCBS 374 to address the credit risk of underlying assets and the granularity of the pool.

---

22 Cf. BCBS 374 (2016), page 48.

- To help ensure that higher-risk underlying exposures would not be able to qualify for alternative treatment as STC-compliant transactions, transactions are excluded if risk weights for the underlying exposures under the standardised approach exceed certain levels (depending on the exposure class and after credit risk mitigation).
- At the portfolio cut-off date, the aggregated value of all exposures to a single obligor shall not exceed 1% of the aggregated outstanding exposure value of all exposures in the portfolio. This shall ensure that granular asset portfolios would be at a level where statistical approaches to model losses can be employed, as opposed to having to review the credit quality of individual exposures.

Risk weight adjustments when complying with STC criteria

Based on the STC benchmark set forth in BCBS 332[23], the Basel Committee included in the BCBS 374 adjustments to the approaches for securitisations, which fulfil the STC criteria by taking into account the comments received on the consultative documents and the results of a QIS study[24]. On the one hand, the minimum risk weight (floor) is set to 10% for senior and 15% for mezzanine securitisation tranches. On the other hand, the supervisory parameter p is reduced.[25] The overall conservative orientation of the new approaches is therefore partially reduced in favour of STC securitisations, although there is still a step-up in risk weights (floor increases from 7% to 10% for senior tranches of the best rating class). In addition, there are proposed rules for the calculation of risk weighted exposure amounts for short-term ABS / ABCP programs.[26] The general tendency is to treat exposures to STC ABCP structures in the same manner as term securitisations without increasing the operational burden on the banks in calculating capital requirements for them. RWA calculation for synthetic securitisations is mainly out of the scope of the STC securitisations (with the exception of certain senior tranches of SME securitisations).[27]

SEC-IRBA and SEC-SA

Under the SEC-IRBA, the formula for the calculation of the supervisory parameter p is supplemented by the factor x, equalling 0.5 (see Equation 4.26). Consequently, p is lower compared to non-STC securitisations (x equalling 1 for non-STC-securitisations), which c.p. results in lower risk weights. The remaining technical input parameters (A to E) needed to determine p are identical to those used for non-STC securitisations.

23   Cf. above under 4.3.3
24   At the EU level, the new proposals in BCBS 374 were adapted into European law through Regulation (EU) 2017/2401 and Regulation (EU) 2017/2402 without substantial modifications in December 2017. One difference to Basel framework is in the naming convention for STC qualified securitisations, such securitisations are called "simple, transparent and standardised" (STS) in EU. Another difference is in the hierarchy of approaches, an Europe SEC-SA will be applied before SEC-ERBA, whereas under certain conditions the hierarchy suggested by Basel is also valid in EU.
25   Cf. BCBS 374 (2016), page 34 and page 36.
26   Cf. BCBS 413 (2017), the final version of this consultative document was not finalised at the release date of this book
27   Cf. BCBS 374 (2016), page 33

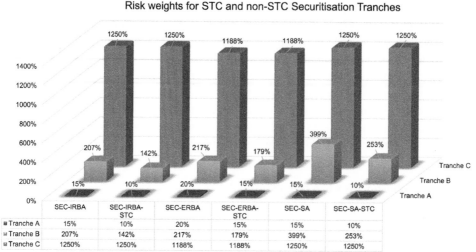

Figure 4.8 shows the effects on the risk weights on all tranches of the AAA Bank's sample securitisation under the assumption of STC-compliance and non-compliance

	SEC-IRBA	SEC-IRBA-STC	SEC-ERBA	SEC-ERBA-STC	SEC-SA	SEC-SA-STC
Tranche A	15%	10%	20%	15%	15%	10%
Tranche B	207%	142%	217%	179%	399%	253%
Tranche C	1250%	1250%	1188%	1188%	1250%	1250%

Figure 4.8: Risk weights on all tranches of the AAA bank's sample securitisation under the assumption of STC-compliance and non-compliance

Equation 4.26

$$p = \max\left[0,3; \left(A + B * \left(\frac{1}{N}\right) + C * K_{IRB} + D * LGD + E * M_T\right) * [x]\right] \quad (4.26)$$

Under the SEC-SA, p acquires a value of 0.5.[28]

Figure 4.8 shows the effects on the risk weights on all tranches of the AAA Bank's sample securitisation transaction assuming that they comply with the STC criteria. It can be observed that for each approach the risk weights on the senior and mezzanine STC tranches are lower compared to a non-STC transaction. This example illustrates the beneficial capital treatment of STC compliant securitisations, especially for senior and mezzanine tranches.

SEC-ERBA

Senior tranches with an AAA rating are subject to risk weight reductions of between 5% and 10% compared to non-STC-securitisations. Risk weights for non-senior tranches with a rating of BBB range between 180% and 225% and are thus between 40% and 55% lower than those required for non-STC securitisations (before application of Equation 4.12 for non-senior tranches). Senior tranches with ratings below CCC– (or below B– in the case of non-senior tranches) are subject to a 1,250% risk weight. Senior securitisation positions are subject to a minimum risk weight of 10%. Table 4.12 shows the risk weights for STC-securitisations under the SEC-ERBA.

---

28   Cf. BCBS 374 (2016), page 36.

Rating	Senior tranche		Non-senior (thin) tranche	
	Tranche maturity (M_T)		Tranche maturity (M_T)	
	1 year	5 years	1 year	5 years
AAA	10%	10%	15%	40%
AA+	10%	15%	15%	55%
AA	15%	20%	15%	70%
AA−	15%	25%	25%	80%
A+	20%	30%	35%	95%
A	30%	40%	60%	135%
A−	35%	40%	95%	170%
BBB+	45%	55%	150%	225%
BBB	55%	65%	180%	255%
BBB−	70%	85%	270%	345%
BB+	120%	135%	405%	500%
BB	135%	155%	535%	655%
BB−	170%	195%	645%	740%
B+	225%	250%	810%	855%
B	280%	305%	945%	945%
B−	340%	380%	1,015%	1,015%
CCC(+/ /−)	415%	455%	1,250%	1,250%
Below CCC−	1,250%	1,250%	1,250%	1,250%

Table 4.12: SEC-ERBA risk weights pursuant to long-term ratings

Conclusions

Compared to the risk weights originally proposed within the framework of BCBS 303, substantial relief is granted to qualified securitisation positions which also leads to a reduction of capital requirements compared to the first ideas of the Basel Committee (including a floor of 20%). An increase of the floor from 7% (current floor) to 15% still means that the risk weights more than double in the best case (senior tranche with AAA rating and maturity of 1 year) considering the final requirements.

With regard to STC securitisations, a certain relief compared to the strong increase of risk weights for non-qualified securitisations can be observed. There, an increase of the present floor of 7% to a future floor of 10% is an increase of more than 40%. From the implementation date onwards, this should represent a significant incentive for originators and sponsors to implement STC requirements.

4.4 General Conclusions

With BCBS 374 and its predecessors a comprehensive set of regulations on securitisation exists, which also completely reforms the approaches to the credit risk of securitisation positions contained in Basel II. Compared to the current approaches, a strong increase of the risk weights should be expected in all of the three new approaches; however, compared to the previous consultative papers, some relieve has been achieved. At the same time, the effort also increases for originators and investors as well. For both, given that the approaches are more complex compared to the CRR regulations currently in force, for the originators when incorporating the STC-criteria into the structuring of future transactions.

Institutions should therefore make good use of the time remaining until the implementation of the new regulation in order to adapt their data systems and internal procedures as well as to perform test calculations to determine the expected impact on capital requirements. As a result thereof, they should adjust their securitisation positions in a timely manner, if necessary.

Recommended Literature

Basel Committee on Banking Supervision; BCBS 128 (2006): International Convergence of Capital Measurement and Capital Standards, A Revised Framework Comprehensive Version

Basel Committee on Banking Supervision; BCBS 236 (2012): Consultative Document. Revisions to the Basel Securitisation framework, 2012

Basel Committee on Banking Supervision; BCBS 303 (2014): Basel III Document. Revisions to the Securitisation framework, 2014

Basel Committee on Banking Supervision; BCBS 304 (2014): Consultative Document. Criteria for identifying simple, transparent and comparable securitisations, 2014

Basel Committee on Banking Supervision; BCBS 332 (2015): Criteria for identifying simple, transparent and comparable securitisations, 2015

Basel Committee on Banking Supervision; BCBS 343 (2015): Consultative Document. Capital treatment for "simple, transparent and comparable" securitisations, 2015

Basel Committee on Banking Supervision; BCBS 347 (2015): Second Consultative Document. Standards. Revisions to the Standardised Approach for credit risk, 2015

Basel Committee on Banking Supervision; BCBS 374 (2016): Basel III Document. Revisions to the Securitisation framework, 2016

Basel Committee on Banking Supervision; BCBS 413 (2017): Consultative document. Capital treatment for simple, transparent and comparable short-term securitisations, 2017

Basel Committee on Banking Supervision; BCBS 414 (2017): Consultative document. Criteria for identifying simple, transparent and comparable short-term securitisations, 2017

Basel Committee on Banking Supervision; BCBS 441 (2018): Capital treatment for simple, transparent and comparable short-term securitisations, 2018

Basel Committee on Banking Supervision; BCBS 442 (2018): Criteria for identifying simple, transparent and comparable short-term securitisations, 2018

Capital Requirements Regulation; CRR (2013): Regulation (EU) No 575/2013 of the European Parliament and of the Council of June 26, 2013 on prudential requirements for credit institutions and investment firms and amending Regulation (EU) No 646/2012.

European Banking Authority; EBA (2016): Guidelines on implicit support for securitisation transactions (EBA/GL/2016/08), 2016 Commission Implementing Regulation (EU) 2016/1801 of 11 October 2016 on laying down implementing technical standards with regard to the mapping of credit assessments of external credit assessment institutions for securitisation in accordance with Regulation (EU) No 575/2013 of the European Parliament and of the Council

Gordy, Michael (2004): Model Foundations for the Supervisory Formula Approach in Structured Credit Products in Pricing, Rating, Risk Management and Basel II, RiskBooks (London), 2004

5 Capital Requirements for Bank's Equity Investments in Funds

Andrea Schnoz and Natalia Dmitrieva

5.1 Overview

As part of the work by the Financial Stability Board to strengthen the oversight and regulation of the shadow banking sector, the Basel Committee for Banking Supervision (BCBS) revised the risk-based capital requirements for banks' exposures to funds effective 1 January 2017 (BCBS 266).

This initiative was undertaken to clarify the existing treatment of such exposures in the Basel II capital adequacy framework, and also to achieve a more internationally consistent and risk-sensitive capital treatment for banks' investments in the equity of funds, reflecting both the risk of the fund's underlying investments and its leverage.

The European Central Bank (ECB) also identified these potential risks and attributes the growth of the shadow banking sector within the Eurozone mainly to the strong increase of cash inflow into investment funds (without money market funds).[1]

Even though funds licensed for sale (in Europe, for example) are strongly regulated, and specific financial instruments or activities are restricted or not allowed under investment law,[2] the actual risk taken by investing in a fund is not always clearly recognisable or measurable for the investor including for investing banks.

Therefore, the variety of bank-like activities that funds are allowed to carry out (e.g. securities lending and repurchase agreements, gearing, acquisition of credit default risks and granting of loans[3]) caught the attention of both the FSB and the ECB.

The new framework for capital requirements for bank's equity investments in funds does not differentiate between (regulated) investment-based funds and other undertakings that collect capital to collectively invest it following a fixed investment strategy (e.g. private equity holding, venture capital holding).

The need for a policy framework for capital requirements for bank's equity investments in funds and the look-through approach to identify underlying assets as a general principle were also introduced in other frameworks of the Basel Committee.[4] Namely, these are the large exposures framework and the revised minimum capital requirements for market risks. In the latter, the trading book vs banking book boundary needs to be

---

1 Cf. ECB (2015).
2 Cf. AIFMD (2011), Directive 2009/65/EU (2009).
3 Granting of loans on behalf of AIF by changing the administrative practice to grant loans of 12 May 2015 also possible in Germany, cf. WA 41-WP2100 2015/0001
4 For additional details within the framework of large exposure: BCBS 283 (2014) and Chapter 9 of this book. For additional details within the market risk: BCBS 352 (2016) and Chapter 5 of this book.

understood to scope the application of this framework (details on this can be found in Chapter 6).

5.2 Trading book vs banking book boundary

By revising the framework for minimum capital requirements for market risks (BCBS 352), the Basel Committee created a new regulatory framework which affects a bank's treatment of equity investments in funds.

For the purposes of the designation of trades to the trading books vs the banking book (TB vs BB boundary), the Basel framework previously relied on the intent of a bank to trade the respective positions and to embed this in the bank's general trading strategy. In the absence of objective criteria, solely the subjective definition for allocation to one of the books was decisive.

Within the scope of the revised capital requirements for market risks, the Basel Committee introduced additional criteria for the allocation of positions to the trading book and the banking book, respectively.[5]

The standard lists several positions with mandatory allocation to one of the books but also a list of positions for which a bank can deviate from the presumptive allocation to the trading book; this, however, only in exceptional cases with the prior approval of national supervisors. Equity investments in funds, which the bank cannot look through daily or where the bank cannot obtain daily real prices for its equity investment, are part of this list.

The BCBS recognised in its March 2018 proposed revisions to the minimum capital requirements for market risk (BCBS 436) that in some cases financial instruments can be both in the list of instruments that must be in a particular book, and in the list that are expected to be in the other book. In these cases, it may not be clear which requirement takes precedence.

The BCBS therefore proposed amendments to this part of the standard to clarify the approach in these situations.

The March 2018 proposed revisions also clarify under what conditions equity investments in funds (e.g. exchange-traded funds) can be included in the trading book (Figure 5.1). Under the proposals, banks may assign to the trading book funds:

a) for which daily price quotes are available;
b) which track a non-leveraged benchmark; and
c) which demonstrate a tracking difference, ignoring fees and commissions, for which the absolute value is less than 1%.

---

5   For additional details within the standard on capital requirements for market risks, see Chapter 6 of this book.

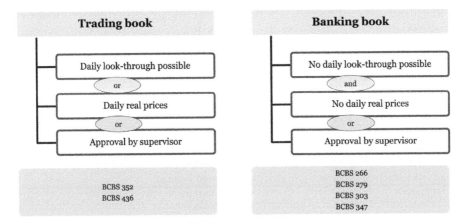

Figure 5.1: Treatment of equity investments in funds

The tracking difference must be checked at regular intervals of no more than one year and is defined as the annualised return difference between the fund and its tracked benchmark over the last 12 months of available data (or a shorter period in the absence of a full 12 months of data).

It can be assumed that mainly ETFs will be assigned to the trading book should the proposal be finalised in its current form while all other equity investments in funds will be subject to banking book rules and, as such, to this framework for equity investments in funds.

5.3 Own funds requirements for funds in the banking book

5.3.1 Scoping and hierarchy of approaches

The following paragraphs only apply to a bank's equity investment in a fund held in the banking book.

Positions or funds that are subject to a capital deduction under the deduction framework should be excluded from this framework. Here we mainly refer to indirect investments in the equity of banking and finance entities which are subject to either full or threshold deductions from regulatory capital under the Basel III framework.

The framework comprises a hierarchy of approaches for banks' equity investments in funds:

- **The Look-through Approach (LTA)** is the most granular approach. Subject to meeting the conditions set out for its use, banks employing the LTA must apply the risk weight of the fund's underlying exposures as if the exposures were held directly by the bank.

- **The Mandate-based Approach (MBA)** provides an additional layer of risk sensitivity that can be used when banks do not meet the conditions for applying the LTA. Banks employing the MBA assign risk weights on the basis of the information contained in a fund's mandate or in the relevant national legislation.
- **The Fall-back Approach (FBA)** must be used when neither of the above approaches is feasible. The FBA applies a 1,250% risk weight to a bank's equity investment in the fund.

The revised framework for funds in the banking book provides stronger incentives for the use of the look-through approach and for mapping the funds' underlying risks in the bank's internal processes and risk management system.

The framework for capital requirements for a bank's equity investments in funds distinguishes between regulations for investments under the standardised approach (SA) and the internal ratings-based approach (IRB).

Accordingly, revisions to the SA and IRB approaches that the BCBS finalised in December 2017 are applicable to both of the look-through approaches available for banks for their equity investments in funds. This means that due diligence needs to be applied before an external rating and can be applied to risk-weight a credit risk exposures and constraints apply on the model inputs used for IRB calculations.

5.3.2 Funds under the standardised approach

Figure 5.2 shows at a glance how equity investments in funds under the credit risk standardised approach will be treated in the Basel framework.

The granularity and, therefore, the knowledge of the underlying risk positions in the funds decrease with each level. This lack of knowledge in relation to the fund's actual

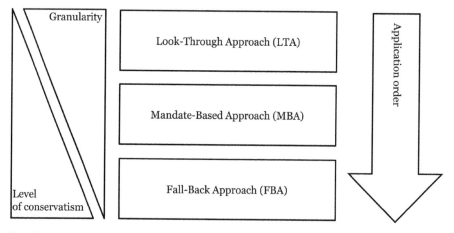

Figure 5.2: Three-step approach under the standardised approach

risk composition results in an increasing level of conservatism. A combination of these three approaches is possible.

The basic principle of the three-step approach has already been implemented in European law with the CRR1. Nevertheless, the new BCBS provisions differ to some extent from the CRR1 provisions.

As part of the CRR2 reforms, the European Commission is in the process of adapting CRR1 to the BCBS framework for capital requirements for banks' investments in the equity of funds. This means in essence that all the BCBS 266 requirements are expected to apply under CRR2.

However, the current super-equivalence of CRR1 with respect to, for example, equivalence of the regulations applicable to the fund manager will continue to exist as a fundamental principle of the implementation of the BCBS standards in EU regulations.

Look-through approach (LTA)

The LTA requires a bank to risk weight the underlying exposures of a fund as if the exposures were held directly by the bank. This is the most granular and risk-sensitive approach. It must be used when:

a) there is sufficient and frequent information provided to the bank regarding the underlying exposures of the fund; and
b) such information is verified by an independent third party.

To satisfy condition (a) above, the frequency of financial reporting of the fund must be the same as, or more frequent than, that of the bank's and the granularity of the financial information must be sufficient to calculate the corresponding risk weights. However, a financial audit is not required.

To satisfy condition (b) above, there must be verification of the underlying exposures by an independent third party, such as the depository or the custodian bank or, where applicable, the management company.

All underlying exposures of the fund include underlying exposure arising from the fund's derivatives activities and the associated counterparty credit risk (CCR) exposure.

This means that, under the LTA, a bank will have to calculate CCR a fund is exposed to under SA-CRR (BCBS 279) for derivatives and the revised exposure calculations for SFT transactions (BCBS 424).

Instead of credit valuation adjustment (CVA) capital requirements, banks multiply the above-mentioned CCR capital requirements by a factor of 1.5. This can either apply to both derivatives and SFT transactions depending on whether the responsible supervisory authority includes SFT transactions in the scope of the CVA volatility capital requirements.

The look-through approach is already established in Germany for collective investment undertakings (CIUs)[6] at the level of asset management companies and eventually also at the level of the asset management company of the respective target funds. The new framework provides that the calculation of the average risk weight by third parties is sanctioned with increased risk weights of 20%, i.e. the risk weight applied to each single investment of the fund is 1.2 times higher when determined by a third party.

For an example of how to calculate risk-weighted assets using the LTA, please refer to the example calculation BCBS 266 provides.

The latter shows that the underlying risk of derivatives (equities) needs to be included in the calculation of risk-weighted assets as equities are also included in the Pillar 1 capital requirements for credit risks. Accordingly, the same logic would for example apply to sold credit derivatives and guarantees in the banking book for which a capital requirement for credit risks applies.

However, importantly, the BCBS does not seem to require capitalisation of interest rate risks and foreign currency risks entered by the fund.

On interest rate risks, these are not captured in the Pillar 1 regime of banking book rules and, as such, are consistently (alongside other banking book items) not capitalised by a bank if indirectly entered by a fund.

On foreign exchange risks no look-through is applied. A bank would simply include its investment in the equity of the fund in its market risk capital requirements which apply to its entire on- and off-balance sheet.

The above are key differences in the resulting capital requirements between funds held in the banking book vs trading book.

Mandate-based approach (MBA)

The MBA can be used when the conditions for applying the LTA are not met.

Under the MBA banks may use the information contained in a fund's mandate or in the national regulations governing such investment funds.

To ensure that all underlying risks are taken into account and that the MBA renders capital requirements no less than the LTA, the risk-weighted assets for the fund's exposures are calculated as the sum of the following three items:

1. Risk weighting of the fund's assets assuming the portfolio is invested to the maximum extent allowed under the fund's mandate in those assets attracting the highest capital requirements, and then progressively in those other assets with lower capital requirements. If more than one risk weight can be applied to a given exposure, the maximum applicable risk weight must be used.

---

6   Cf. Art. 4 par. 1 no. 7 CRR.

2. Risk-weighting of the notional amount of the derivative position and off-balance sheet exposure in the underlying assets.

3. The CCR associated with the fund's derivative exposures is calculated using SA-CCR (BCBS 279) according to footnote 12 of BCBS 266. If the CCR exposure is unknown, the notional amount is used as a proxy.

Consistently with the LTA, instead of determining a CVA charge, a factor of 1.5 is applied to the CCR exposure.

Refer to the Annex for an example provided by the BCBS of how to calculate risk-weighted assets using the MBA.

Fall-back approach (FBA)

Provided that the treatment of equity investments in funds is not feasible under the above described approaches, then the so-called fall-back approach (FBA) is applied. Following the logic of the approaches' decreasing granularity, this approach is subject to the highest level of conservatism. As a result, the FBA applies a 1.250% risk weight to the equity investments in the fund.

This means in effect that the bank must back an investment in the equity of a fund with more capital than its carrying value once all the buffers are considered.

For example, a bank with a minimum total capital requirement of 10% would risk-weight an investment of 10 with 1250% and then apply a capital requirement of 10%, i.e. holds regulatory capital of 12.5.

The introduction of the FBA means, for banking operating under regulatory capital constraints, that a bank will have no choice but to dispose of an investment in the equity of a fund, or to implement either the LTA or MBA.

5.3.3 Funds under the internal ratings-based approach (IRB)

BCBS 266 does not provide for noteworthy differences with regard to the use of the IRB, except for the possible use of the MBA. The treatment of equity investment in funds under the IRB pursuant to the Basel framework can be outlined as shown in Figure 5.3.

Under the IRB, the first step is to verify if a complete look-through of the equity investments in the fund by the investing bank is possible.

In practice, we seldom expect this to be because of the requirements on data and model validation that banks need to comply with to obtain IRB model approval.

In theory, however, under the **LTA**, the underlying on-balance sheet, off-balance sheet and derivatives exposures of the fund must be treated like exposures held directly by the bank.

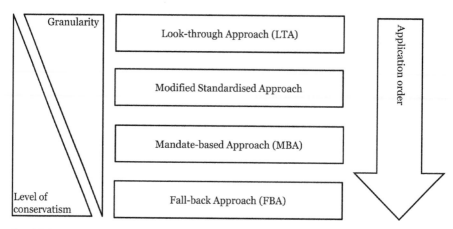

Figure 5.3: Four-step approach under the IRBA

Banks using an IRB approach may use the Standardised Approach for credit risk when applying risk weights to the underlying components of funds if they are permitted to do so under the partial use provisions set out in paragraphs 256 to 262 of the Basel II framework in the case of directly held investments.

In addition, when an IRB calculation is not feasible (e.g. the bank cannot assign the necessary risk components to the underlying exposures in a manner consistent with its own underwriting criteria), IRB banks shall also use the SA risk weights.

However, under the finalised post crisis reforms of the BCBS issued in December 2017 banks must apply the simple risk weight method for equity exposures in the banking book. For securitisation positions, the ratings-based approach mandatorily applies.

Under the **MBA,** banks using an IRB approach must apply the standardised approach risk weights. This conversely means that a bank that wishes to use its approved IRB approach for its investments in funds will have to use the LTA.

If none of the mentioned approaches can be used, a risk weight of 1,250% applies to the funds in accordance with the FBA.

5.3.4 Leverage adjustment under the LTA and the MBA

Since the procedures described above only take into account a fund's assets, the BCBS also introduced a leverage adjustment.

To account for a possible leverage of the fund, the adjustment works similarly to pro-portional consolidation (total assets/total equity). It increases the risk-weighted assets by the share of the fund's debt financing in relation to its assets (sum of risk-weighted assets * assets/equity).

An example of how the leverage adjustment works is provided by the BCBS.

In Germany, the calculation of an average risk weight for a fund under the LTA has already been established. It is common practice to calculate the average risk weight by setting the risk-weighted assets in relation with the share value (net asset value) of the fund. Under this calculation method, the leverage adjustment, which is newly introduced by the Basel Committee, is already taken indirectly into account as can be seen in the example contained in Table 5.1.

The examples show that the calculation pursuant to Basel (including leverage adjustment) and the common practice in Germany lead to the same results.

5.3.5 Treatment of funds that invest in other funds (target funds, fund of funds)

When a bank has an investment in a fund (e.g. Fund A) that itself has an investment in another fund (e.g. Fund B), which the bank identified by using either the LTA or the MBA, the risk weight applied to the investment of the first fund (i.e. Fund A's investment in Fund B) can be determined by using one of the three approaches set out above.

For all subsequent layers (e.g. Fund B's investments in Fund C and so forth), the risk weights applied to an investment in another fund (Fund C) can be determined by using the LTA, under the condition that the LTA was also used for determining the risk weight for the investment in the fund at the previous layer (Fund B). Otherwise, the FBA must be applied.

The example in Table 5.2 clarifies the impact on the average risk weight of a fund that invests 10% of its asset value in target funds for which the LTA cannot be applied.

Position	Market value	Risk weight	Risk-weighted assets	Risk-weighted assets in percentage of the net asset value[8]
Bank balances	5	20%	1	1.25%
Shares	55	250%	137.5	171.88%
Equity investments in funds	10	1,250%	125	156.25
Government bonds	30	20%	6	7.5%
Liabilities	−20			
Sum **(Fund volume)**	**80**			**336.88%**

Table 5.1: Calculation of the average risk weight[7] (Germany)

---

7   The CRR does not provide for the calculation of the average risk weight, the representation reflects common practice.
8   Percentage according to German practice.

Position	Market value	Risk weight		Risk-weighted assets (shares in the fund)	
		new	old	new	old
Bank balances	5	20%	20%	1%	1%
Equity investments in funds	10	1.250%	100%	125%	10%
Corporates	85	50%	50%	42.5%	42.5%
Liabilities	0				
Net Asset Value	**100**				
Fund's average risk weight (standardised approach)				**168.50%**	**53.50%**

Table 5.2: Calculation of the average risk weight including FBA for target funds

5.4 Summary and conclusion

To summarise, the revisions of the Basel requirements aimed at the risks of banks inter-acting with shadow banking entities affect banks' investments in funds as follows:

- Investments in all types of funds are affected, including funds of funds.
- The revised boundary between trading and banking book (BCBS 352) and (BCBS 436) will likely only allow ETFs and other index-tracking funds to be assigned to the trading book and therefore increase the scope and number of equity investments held in the banking book subject to this framework.
- New grades of investments in funds are driven by level of granularity of informa-tion available and promote and incentivise stronger internal processes and internal risk management frameworks (BCBS 266), including imposing additional capital charges for using third parties inputs.
- The approaches LTA/MBA/FBA are supposed to reflect the risk of a fund underlying investments, imposing higher capital requirements if no sufficient transparency is achieved.
- The above approaches are applicable to both banks following standardised and inter-nal risk-based approaches.
- Capital requirements are affected by the fund leverage.

At the international level, the look-through approach for funds has gained importance within the framework of Basel IV. In Germany, however, the look-through principle has long constituted a regulatory requirement. Institutional investors have been receiving information of the fund composition and/or the already prepared regulatory ratios (e.g. amount-weighted average risk weight of a fund, foreign currency positions, large exposure reporting) on a monthly basis.

The European implementation of Basel III via the CRR[9] complemented the trans-parency requirements for funds with additional topics such as holdings in financial

---

9   BCBS 189 (2010).

sector entities, the geographical location of risk positions, haircuts for CIU positions or the calculation of the CVA risk capital charge at fund level. To account for the increased transparency requirement down to the level of the (lowest) target fund, asset management companies developed a widespread system to exchange data on regulatory ratios and fund composition. This system allowed banks to take into account all exposures contained in a fund according to the corresponding provisions that apply to the underlying exposures.

The CRR also provides for an external confirmation of certain ratios[10] in order to enable banks to consider these aggregated indicators without additional verification steps or due diligence requirements to determine capital requirements.

By contrast, the Basel Committee's intention with these measures is to set clear incentives for banks, to consider not only the risks taken through the fund in determining capital requirements, but also in setting internal processes and internal risk management frameworks, as if these were direct investments.

An immediate implementation of the Basel provisions would significantly impact the processes currently established used for data preparation (e.g. for the calculation of capital requirements for a fund's underlying exposures through third parties) and would most likely require substantial changes from their present form.

The FBA, as proposed, would result in a conservative, general risk weight of 1,250%, which might not adequately reflect the investment profile and characteristics of the funds.

It might be more adequate and therefore preferable to use more differentiated risk weights, taking into account the maximum leverage of borrowed capital and the use of derivatives so that the required capital can be reduced. This will however require an investment in processes and reporting infrastructure to be made. Therefore, we expect banks that operate under regulatory capital constraints to either make these investments or to sell their investments in the equity of funds.

Recommended Literature

Alternative Investment Fund Managers Directive, AIFMD (2011): DIRECTIVE 2011/61/EU OF THE EUROPEAN PARLIAMENT AND OF THE COUNCIL of 8 June 2011 on Alternative Investment Fund Managers and amending Directives 2003/41/EC and 2009/65/EC and Regulations (EC) No 1060/2009 and (EU) No 1095/2010

BCBS 04 (1988): Basel I: International Convergence of Capital Measurement and Capital Standards, 1988.

---

10 Risk weights (SA, IRBA), foreign currency positions, deductions for UCIs (liquidity).

BCBS 128 (2006): Basel II: International Convergence of Capital Measurement and Capital Standards, 2006.

BCBS 189 (2010): Basel III: A global regulatory framework for more resilient banks and banking systems, 2010.

BCBS 219 (2012): Consultative Document. Fundamental Review of the Trading Book, (2012).

BCBS 257 (2013): Consultative Document. Capital requirements for banks' equity investments in funds, (2013).

BCBS 265 (2013): Consultative Document. Fundamental Review of the Trading Book: A revised market risk framework, 2013.

BCBS 266 (2013): Capital requirements for banks' equity investments in funds, (2013).

BCBS 279 (2014): The standardised approach for measuring counterparty credit risk exposures, 2014.

BCBS 283 (2014): Standards. Supervisory framework for measuring and controlling large exposures, 2014.

BCBS 303 (2014): Revisions to the Securitisation framework, 2014.

BCBS 347 (2015): Second Consultative Document. Standards. Revisions to the Standardised Approach for Credit Risk, 2015.

BCBS 352 (2016): Minimum capital requirements for market risk, 2016.

BCBS 424 (2017): Basel III: Finalising post-crisis reforms

BCBS 436 (2018): Revisions to the minimum capital requirements for market risk – consultative document

Bundesanstalt für Finanzdienstleistungsaufsicht, BaFin [Federal Financial Supervisory Authority] (2015): Auslegungsentscheidung. Änderung der Verwaltungspraxis zur Vergabe von Darlehen sowie zur sog. "Restrukturierung" und Prolongation von Darlehen für Rechnung des Investmentvermögens, 2015. [Interpretation decision. Change in German adminstrative practice to the granting of loans as well as so-called "restructuring" and prolongation of loans to calculate investment assets.] Available under: https://www.bafin.de/SharedDocs/Veroeffentlichungen/DE/Auslegungsentscheidung/WA/ae_150512_kreditfonds_aif.html

Bundesverband Investment und Asset Management e. V., BV (2014): BVI's position on the Consultative Document of the Basel Commitee on Banking Supervision: Capital requirements for bank's equity investments in funds, 2014.

Capital Requirements Regulation; CRR (2013): Regulation (EU) No 575/2013 of the European Parliament and of the Council of 26 June 2013 on prudential requirements for credit institutions and investment firms and amending Regulation (EU) No 646/2012

Commission Delegated Regulation (EU) No 1187/2014 of 2 October 2014 supplementing Regulation (EU) No 575/2013 of the European Parliament and of the Council as regards regulatory technical standards for determining the overall exposure to a client or a group of connected clients in respect of transactions with underlying assets.

DIRECTIVE 2009/65/EC OF THE EUROPEAN PARLIAMENT AND OF THE COUNCIL of 13 July 2009 on the coordination of laws, regulations and administrative provisions relating to undertakings for collective investment in transferable securities (UCITS)

European Central Bank, ECB (2015): Financial Stability Review, 2015. Available under: http://www.ecb.europa.eu/pub/pdf/other/financialstabilityreview201505.en.pdf?3cd887eb74f562fc8db70554df5b01ca

Financial Stability Board (2012): Consultative Document. Strengthening Oversight and Regulation of Shadow Banking: An Integrated Overview of Policy Recommendations, 2012. Available under: http://www.fsb.org/wp-content/uploads/r_121118.pdf

Regulation (EU) 2015/2365 of the EUROPEAN PARLIAMENT AND OF THE COUNCIL of 25 November 2015 on transparency of securities financing transactions and of reuse and amending Regulation (EU) No 648/2012.

6 Fundamental Review of the Trading Book: A New Age for Market Risks

Marius M. Schulte-Mattler, Anne Leonhardt, Matthias Ohliger, Philipp Schröder, Lars Norup, Manuel Plattner and Sebastian Gerigk

6.1 Introduction

The financial crisis 2007/2008 identified apparent weaknesses regarding the provisions to determine capital requirements for risks arising out of trading activities. Those provisions had already been discussed in previous years since the available capital had not been sufficient to absorb losses. The Basel Committee on Banking Supervision (BCBS) was aware of this fact and published the first revision of the market risk framework within the context of Basel II.5 in July 2009 to increase the banks' resilience in times of crisis. In 2012, the Basel Committee published the first consultation paper with significant changes in the risk assessment of market price risks. Two additional consultation rounds followed as well as four quantitative impact studies.[1] After the last publication in 2016, the Basel Committee continued monitoring the implementation status and the impact on banks of the market risk standard as well as market risk capital requirements. Finally, the Group of Governors and Heads of Supervision (GHOS), has decided an extension of the implementation date to 1 January 2022. While on the other hand in March 2018 another consultation document was published by the Basel Committee on the "Revisions to the minimum capital requirements for market risk".[2]

The market price risk is one of the most important risk types for banks, and mainly describes the risk of losses as a consequence of an adverse change in prices for an item, based on a change in the underlying risk factors (such as exchange rates, stock prices or interest rates). Together with credit and operational risks, market risks constitute the principal regulatory risks for which banks must fulfil minimum capital requirements within the scope of effective banking supervision under Pillar I. Open positions with market risks must, therefore, be backed by regulatory capital since Basel 1.5.[3]

The Basel framework must be adopted into national banking supervision law. In the EU, for example, the market risk provisions for European banks are outlined in the Capital Requirements Regulation (CRR). Article 4 (1) (86) CRR establishes that all positions held for trading must be assigned to the trading book and are consequently subject to the respective regulatory requirements. With the comprehensive review of the current market risk regulations, which must be incorporated into national

---

1   Cf. BCBS 265 (2013) and BCBS 305 (2014).
2   Cf. BCBS 436 (2018). In the consultation paper, the prior discussed reduced sensitivities-based method (BCBS 408) is replaced by a recalibrated version of the Basel II standardised approach.
3   Cf. BCBS 24 (1996).

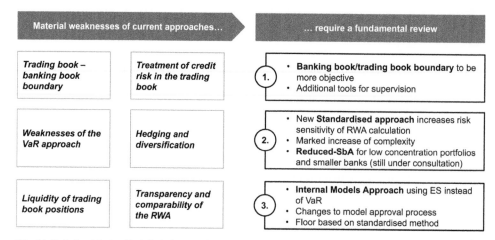

Figure 6.1: The fundamental review of the trading book – an overview

regulation,[4] the Basel Committee intervenes in the banks' organisational structure. The main three areas of change are outlined below and summarised in Figure 6.1.[5]

1. A precise definition of the trading book.

2. New standardised approach for all market risk areas.

3. Review of the internal models approach (contemplation of market illiquidity as well as adjustments of the risk metrics in the case of internal models).

The chapter is structured as follows: Section 6.2 provides an overview on how the trading book will, in the future, be delimited from the non-trading book, also called banking book. Section 6.3 then describes the new standardised approach in the market price risk area to determine minimum capital requirements (Sensitivities Based Approach – SBA) as well as the Simplified alternative to the standardised approach[6] which was first discussed by the BCBS[7] in a separate consultative document (named Reduced Sensitivities-based Method, R-SbM). Section 6.4 outlines the innovations about internal models. In addition, Sections 6.2 to 6.4 give an outlook on the EU implementation. Finally, Section 6.5 analyses the impact on business and market implications while Section 6.6 elaborates on possible optimisation approaches. In conclusion, Section 6.7 presents an overall analysis and identifies challenges.

6.2 Revised trading book boundary

Probably the biggest problem of the current regulations is the imprecise boundary criteria to classify positions as either trading book or non-trading book positions since

---

4   The implementation into European Regulation through a CRR amendment (CRR II) by the European Commission is already under the consultation of the European Parliament and Council.
5   Cf. BCBS 352 (2016), marginal no. 44.
6   Cf. BCBS 436 (2018).
7   Cf. BCBS 408 (2017).

they facilitate several possibilities for regulatory arbitrage. The solution to this problem was not included in the reform packages Basel II.5 and Basel III and is, therefore, one of the three major topics of the comprehensive review of the trading book. Consequently, the allocation criteria for risk positions of both books are defined in more detail.

The Basel Committee concretised the allocation criteria for both books since it is the belief that the previous procedures – i.e. focus only on the banks' trading intent when delimitating positions – often led to false incentives due to their subjectivity and different capital requirements for individual risk positions in the particular book. Moreover, the Committee mentions example products for the respective books. Said examples aim at establishing a shared understanding of the requirements of supervisory authorities across different jurisdictions. A consistent application of requirements among different banks shall also be promoted thereby.

Imposing strict limits on the movement between books mitigates supervisory arbitrage. The Basel Committee thereby seeks to achieve a consistent allocation to the respective book. Capital reduction incentives, which would otherwise make frequent movements between books more attractive, shall be eliminated by reducing the substantial differences, which currently exist as regards the level of capital requirements for positions depending on the book they are assigned to.

6.2.1 Revised boundary of the trading and banking books

To the most significant extent, the Basel Committee bases its revisions to the trading book boundary on the existing methodology, which was predominantly driven by the "intent to trade". The Committee extends said boundary by specific allocation criteria for the trading book as well as example products for both books. The first proposals of the Basel Committee – the Trading Evidence-Based Approach and Valuation-Based Approach – were comparatively extremely radical. In comparison, the final provisions present an attenuated mix of the first two draft proposals (see Figure 6.2).

The differentiation among instruments that must be assigned to the trading book in every case and those which can also be assigned to the banking book with the approval of the supervisory authority constitutes an innovation. The new comprehensive requirements also serve the purpose of concretising the concept "intent to trade", which was not sufficiently defined before. Moreover, it should help to determine when an "intent to trade" is assumed from the supervisory point of view ensuring a consistent allocation of instruments to the trading or the banking book (see Figure 6.2).

The Basel Committee defines several lists of positions and the purpose for which they are being held. The allocation of positions to the trading or the banking book must result from such lists. Figure 6.2 provides a decision tree for the initial allocation of positions to either the banking book or trading book. It also shows that the requirements for allocation of instruments are divided into four categories.

The first category defines specific trading purposes for which instruments are held and which require – if met – an allocation to the trading book. Instruments held for

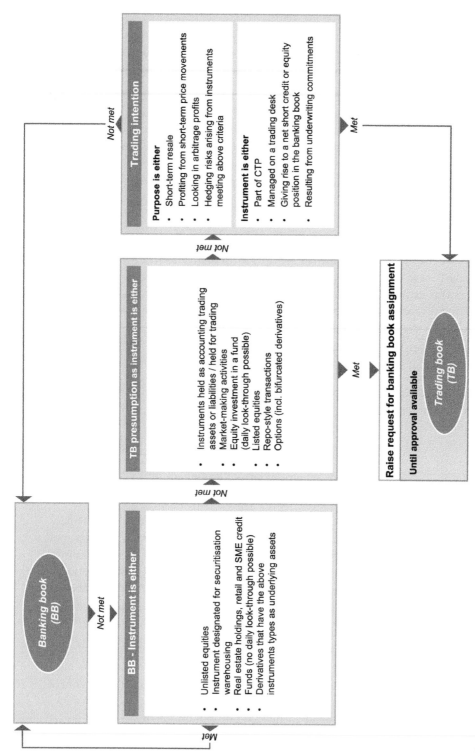

Figure 6.2: Decision tree for banking and trading book allocation

short-term resale or for locking in arbitrage profits are assigned to the trading book. These purposes coincide with the general allocation criteria for the trading book, which are already known from the consultation phase as well as from the CRR. Moreover, the list of different purposes to hold instruments is broadened by an enumeration of instruments that must compulsorily be allocated to the trading book. Thus, all positions of a trading desk must be assigned unconditionally to the trading book.

The third delimitation area for the trading book represents a significant innovation of the new Basel standards compared to the second consultation paper. In exceptional cases, substantiated by the bank and approved beforehand by the responsible supervisor, the positions listed in this area must not be assigned to the trading book. These include equity investments in a fund with daily look-through, instruments held as accounting trading assets or liabilities and listed equities. Options including bifurcated embedded derivatives from instruments that relate to credit or equity risks are a new addition.

Instruments that are not held for trading book purposes, or are not explicitly included in the list of the supervisory authority, must be assigned to the banking book. The Basel standard provides a list of example products that must be compulsorily allocated to the banking book. Positions assigned to the banking book can be traced back in most of the cases to lack of liquidity or difficulties in performing a daily evaluation. The goal of the supervisory authority is to consider all relevant pieces of information, if possible, about the positions of the bank's risk management. Further qualitative requirements on trading book positions are outlined in Figure 6.3.

The revisions may lead to significant changes in the banks' portfolio structure. Non-trading book institutions will most likely continue to be subject to materiality

---

Trading book institutions need strategies, procedures and controls regarding the management of the trading book

General requirements	Valuation of trading book positions
• Business strategy (instruments/positions/portfolios, accepted holding periods) • Active position management (admissible products, limits, reporting channels, trade ability/ hedging) • Anti-fraud procedures and controls • Matching positions with the business strategy	• At least daily valuation of all trading book positions using prudent valuation • Documentation regarding valuation procedures, assumptions and data sources • Independent validation of the valuation procedure, esp. in the case of mark-to-model; regular review and backtesting; explicit model change process required • Include/ inform senior management, esp. on the scope of the mark-to-model valuation and the limits and risks of the procedure used • If possible, use mark-to-market, conservative consideration of bid/ask spreads • Mark-to-model must be used conservatively by recognised models and procedures • At least monthly independent price verification, independently of the front office • Valuation adjustments, esp. in the case of concentrations, illiquid positions, complex and exotic product such as "stale positions"
Management of the trading book	
• Policies and procedures for allocation to the trading book (regularly verified by internal audit) • Determine business activities • Scope of the mark-to-market and mark-to-model valuation • Independent valuation validation • Legal and operational restrictions on trade ability and hedging • Active risk management for trading positions	

Figure 6.3: Qualitative requirements on trading book positions

thresholds at a national level. Said institutions are encouraged to analyse, at an early stage, whether they surpass these thresholds or not.

In the consultation paper published in March 2018, the BCBS provides clarification on the boundary requirements in order to ensure their intended impact and consistent implementation.[8] Especially in the case of instruments that can be allocated to both the trading book and the banking book, the Committee clarifies which requirements take precedence. In this context, the Committee gives more weight to the trading purposes as a criterion for differentiation. Furthermore, it is clarified that equity investments in funds for which daily price quotes are available, which track a non-leverage benchmark and which demonstrate a tracking difference for which the absolute value is less than 1% are included in the trading book.

6.2.2 Reallocation of positions between books

The switching of positions between books ("reallocation") is based on strict regulatory requirements. Besides, the supervisory authority reserves the right to determine real-location of individual positions at any time. This sharply reduces the banks' own power to make decisions regarding the movement between books. The Basel Committee explicitly sets forth that changed market conditions or changed intents to trade are no longer sufficient to perform switches and shall only be admitted in exceptional cases (just as the task of a trading desk). If the capital charge is reduced, as a result of a switch, the difference may be imposed on the bank at any time as a capital surcharge.

The new trading book boundary will lead to greater involvement of the responsible supervisory authority in the banks' internal strategic decisions. Therefore, a switch between books must not only be authorised by the management in the future but also requires the explicit approval of supervisors. Moreover, the requirements for public disclosure at the next reporting deadline as well as the prohibition to reverse the switch are introduced.

The new Basel standard also contains additional requirements regarding trading desks (Figure 6.4), documentation and data availability. The classification of positions and the procedure in the case of possible switches must be included in internal guidelines, be updated on a yearly basis and presented to the supervisors as well as to the internal review. For each trading desk, the following information must be prepared daily and transmitted to the supervisors, if necessary. The information includes the following: limits, limit breaches and follow-up actions, assessment of market liquidity, and inventory ageing reports. The purpose hereof is to identify which positions have been held over a more extended period.[9]

---

8   Cf. BCBS 436 (2018), pp. 35–38.
9   Cf. BCBS 352 (2016), marginal no. 22–25.

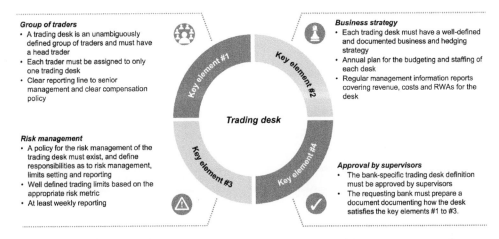

Group of traders
- A trading desk is an unambiguously defined group of traders and must have a head trader
- Each trader must be assigned to only one trading desk
- Clear reporting line to senior management and clear compensation policy

Business strategy
- Each trading desk must have a well-defined and documented business and hedging strategy
- Annual plan for the budgeting and staffing of each desk
- Regular management information reports covering revenue, costs and RWAs for the desk

Risk management
- A policy for the risk management of the trading desk must exist, and define responsibilities as to risk management, limits setting and reporting
- Well defined trading limits based on the appropriate risk metric
- At least weekly reporting

Approval by supervisors
- The bank-specific trading desk definition must be approved by supervisors
- The requesting bank must prepare a document documenting how the desk satisfies the key elements #1 to #3.

Key element #1 — Key element #2 — Key element #3 — Key element #4

Trading desk

Figure 6.4: Requirements for the trading desk

Based on the observations during the started implementation phase of FRTB, the Basel Committee is proposing specific provisions to the trading desk requirements.[10] Of note is the requirement for a single head trader per desk and the restriction that a trader may only be assigned to a single trading desk; this could lead to an unwanted conflict with the trading desk organisation of the institution. Thus, those requirements are reworded in a less binding and strict way.

6.2.3 Internal risk transfer

Besides concretising the actual definition of the trading book and the requirements regarding a switch between the trading book and the banking book, the Basel Committee also specifies special requirements on the internal risk transfer (IRT).[11] It aims to develop a treatment which balances the need for effective risk management and does not compromise the revised trading book and banking book boundary (Figure 6.5).

One example of this is that a bank's internal risk transfer can be divided into two steps (Figure 6.6). Thereby an internal derivative transaction between the trading book and the banking book takes place (internal risk transfer) that is later hedged by offsetting it with an external counterparty. This kind of hedge could be recognised as risk mitigation for banking book positions. Based on this procedure, the Basel Committee distinguishes between two different approaches regarding credit, equity or interest rate risks as well as relating to the direction of the risk transfer between the trading book and the banking book.

---

10   Cf. BCBS 436, p. 30.
11   According to BCBS 352 (2016, p. 11) "an internal risk transfer is an internal written record of a transfer of risk within the banking book, between the banking and the trading book or within the trading book (between different desks)."

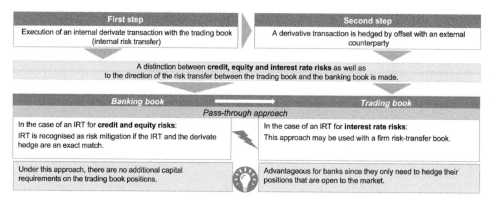

Figure 6.5: Overview of the internal risk transfer (IRT)

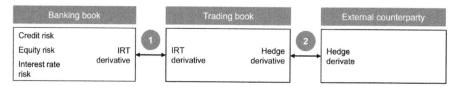

Figure 6.6: Internal risk transfer in detail

In the case of internal risk transfers from the banking to the trading book, the "pass-through" approach is introduced for credit and equity risks. Under this approach, the internal risk transfer in the banking book would be recognised as risk mitigation if the trading book engages in a derivative transaction with an external counterparty that is an exact match of such internal risk transfer. In this case, there is no capital requirement for the trading book position. This method may be used for interest rate risks by using a firm risk-transfer book.

This pass-through approach is also advantageous for many banks since they only need to hedge those positions that are open to the market. How this approach will interact with the IRRBB requirements remains to be seen.[12] Contrary thereto, the risk transfer between trading desks in the Internal Models Approach and the standardised approach within the FRTB framework is not subject to any limitations.

There is no regulatory capital recognition for internal risk transfers from the trading book to the banking book. This means that such internal risk transfers do not reduce regulatory capital requirements.

6.2.4 Example for national implementation: Boundary requirements and thresholds in the EU

The EU Commission states that implementation of the FRTB in the Union should need to "preserve the good functioning of financial markets in the Union." Even though

---

12   Cf. BCBS 319 (2015).

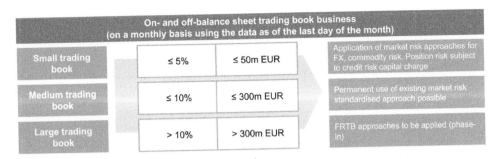

Figure 6.7: New thresholds under CRR II

CRR II mainly adopts the requirements laid out by the Basel Committee, it introduces different thresholds to account for a "proportional" treatment for market risks within the EU. Regarding the detailed requirements of the trading book boundary, the EU Commission formulates more comprehensive and stricter rules.

For institutions with limited trading book activities, two possible treatments are proposed, depending on the size of their trading book as shown in Figure 6.7. Banks with a small trading book according to the thresholds laid out by CRR II are still allowed to apply the credit risk framework for banking book positions. Also, institutions with a medium-sized trading book are allowed to use a simplified standardised approach,[13] which is in line with the approach currently in use under CRR. All other banks need to apply the approaches that are defined through the FRTB.

According to the proposals, CRR II allows institutions to use combinations of the three approaches subject to the following restrictions (current standardised approach according to CRR, standardised approach as proposed under FRTB, Internal Models Approach – IMA – as proposed under FRTB). In case the FRTB-IMA is used, it has to account for more as 10% of all market risk capital requirements. No combination of current standardised approach and FRTB approaches is allowed.

6.3 The revised standardised approach for market risks

The revised standardised approach for market price risks should provide a simple method for calculating capital requirements for the given market risk areas (interest rate, credit, equity, commodities and foreign exchange risk). In the view of the BCBS, banks with less complex business models and small trading books can and should make use of this method. The fact that the revised method has a strong focus on risk sensitivity contradicts the goals of "greater simplicity" and "more transparent models".[14] The purpose of the revised approach is to make market risk reporting more manageable and comparable.[15]

---

13   CRR II proposes to use the current CRR standardised approach for market risks as a simplified alternative to the FRTB methodology.
14   Cf. BCBS 258 (2013) and Chapter 8 on floor regulations.
15   Cf. BCBS 352 (2016).

The approach shall also serve as a fall-back, benchmark and recalibration basis for regulatory bank-internal models. The financial crisis highlighted a series of weaknesses of banks using internal models. The purpose hereof is to attenuate these shortcomings using a capital floor based on the new standardised approach, on top of the actual review of the Internal Models Approach (IMA). The floor regulation[16] – as well as the revised Basel standard – underscores that all banks must calculate the respective amounts according to the standardised approach. This comprises an increased effort on the part of model banks since they will be forced to perform a parallel calculation by means of the new standardised approach in addition to implementing the new Internal Models Approach.

The revised Basel standardised approach, also called sensitivities-based approach (SBA), was initially suggested by the Canadian Bankers Association.[17] In the revised standardised approach, the minimum capital requirements in the market risk area are composed of the sum of partial requirements for the sensitivities-based method (delta, vega and curvature risks), default risk charge and residual risk add-on. In addition to a requirement for the "pure" market price risk (delta risk) for all positions, further requirements are added in the case of optionality risk components: curvature risk (change of the delta risk) and vega risk (volatility risk). In the case of positions with issuers, e.g. interest rate and equity positions, additional capital requirements are implemented through the credit spread risk and the default risk charges. For all risks that cannot be captured by the mentioned elements, the "residual risk add-on" is introduced. The total capital requirement is a simple sum of these five components, which are outlined in Figure 6.8.

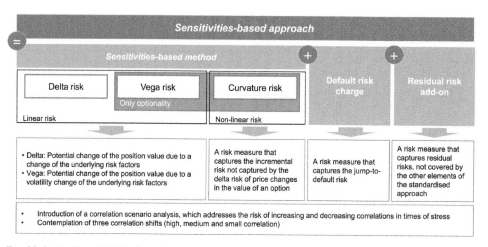

Figure 6.8: Overview of the sensitivities-based approach

---

16   Cf. BCBS 306 (2015).
17   Cf. BCBS 305 (2014), Annex 2, SBA, p. 1.

6.3.1 Linear and non-linear price risks

In the revised market risk standardised approach, a distinction is made between the linear risks "delta" and "vega", and the non-linear "curvature" risk. Delta describes a potentially negative effect on the position value due to changes regarding the risk factors that have an impact on the position. Vega describes a potentially adverse effect on the position value due to a volatility change of the risk factors that have a bearing on the position. The curvature risk comprises the effects caused by the fact that all relevant linear risks change if the risk driver changes.

To determine the risk content of positions, seven risk classes are used that are subject to so-called risk buckets used as basic categorisation to assess the risk. Table 6.1 shows the risk classes in more detail.

1. General interest rate risk (GIRR),
2. Credit spread risk: non-securitisation (CSR),
3. Credit spread risk: securitisation/non-correlation trading portfolio (nCTP),
4. Credit spread risk: securitisation/correlation trading portfolio (CTP),
5. Equity risk,
6. Commodity risk and
7. Foreign exchange risk.

Table 6.1: Detailed risk classes

Compared to previous consultation papers, the Basel Committee did not make any changes to the final classification of the individual risk classes. The conventional differentiation of the market risks into four risk classes is kept and complemented by three new credit spread risk classes. Moreover, a correlation scenario analysis is introduced, which addresses the risk of increasing and decreasing correlations in times of stress. Banks are required to take into consideration three correlation shifts (high, medium and low). Compared to the initial proposal of correlation shifts of the final FRTB paper, the BCBS has observed that the "low correlations" scenario can lead to capital requirements that are overly conservative. Thus, in its latest consultation paper of March 2018, it is proposing revisions to this specific correlation parameter by limiting the reduction.[18] The necessary procedure for determining capital requirements for linear and non-linear risks resembles the current procedure closely. Besides the gamma risk, additional non-linear risks are added.

Basic procedure to determine capital requirements for linear risks

The basis for risk assessment for the delta and vega risks are the sensitivities of the individual positions regarding a change of the risk factors established by the Basel Committee. Figure 6.9 summarises the main risk factors by classifying them into the seven risk classes within the FRTB framework. Offsetting is allowed for positions

---

18   Cf. BCBS 436 (2018), p. 15.

Risk class of the risk factor	Delta	Vega	Curvature
General interest rate risk (GIRR)	• Two-dimensional risk factors: risk-free interest rate curve (for each currency separately) as well as vertices between 0.25 years and 30 years • Contemplation of market-implicit inflation rates • Contemplation of a "cross-currency-basis risk factor" for each currency	• Implied volatility defined based on two dimensions: Maturity and residual term of the option based on vertices between 0.5 years and 10 years	• Risk factors are defined based on the risk-free interest rate curve
Credit spread risks (CSR): non-securitisation	• Two-dimensional risk factors: the relevant credit spread curve of the issuer as well as the maturities between 0.5 years and 10 years	• Implied volatility that is referred to based on the issuer's name. • Contemplation of the option's maturity based on vertices between 0.5 years and 10 years	• Risk factor defined based on the credit spread curve of the issuer.
Credit spread risks (CSR): securitisation non-correlation trading portfolio (nCTP)	• Two-dimensional risk factors: the relevant credit spread curve of the tranche as well as the maturities between 0.5 years and 10 years	• Implied volatility that refers to the nCTP credit spreads as underlying • Contemplation of the option's maturity based on vertices between 0.5 years and 10 years	• Risk factor defined based on the credit spread curve of the tranche.
Credit spread risks (CSR): securitisation correlation trading portfolio (CTP)	• Two-dimensional risk factors: the relevant credit spread curve of the underlying as well as the maturities between 0.5 years and 10 years	• Implied volatility that refers to the CTP credit spreads as underlying • Contemplation of the option's maturity based on vertices between 0.5 years and 10 years	• Risk factor defined based on the credit spread curve of the underlying.
Equity risks	• Equity spot price • Equity repo rates	• Implied volatility that refers to the equities spot price as underlying • Contemplation of the option's maturity based on vertices between 0.5 years and 10 years	• Equity spot price
Commodity risks	• Commodity's spot price depending on the contract grade of the physical commodities • City of delivery • Maturity of the traded instrument (0 years – 30 years)	• Implied volatility that refers to the commodity's spot price as underlying • Contemplation of the option's maturity based on vertices between 0.5 years and 10 years	• Commodity spot price
Foreign exchange risk	• Exchange rate between reporting currency and currency of the respective instrument	• Implied volatility that refers to exchange rates • Contemplation of the option's maturity based on vertices between 0.5 years and 10 years	• Exchange rate between reporting currency and currency of the respective instrument

Figure 6.9: Risk factors and risk classes under the SBA

that fall under the same risk factor. The cash value of a position, discounted by the appropriate returns based on the maturity or the nature of the transaction, is recognised. For those risk classes where vertices are defined by the BCBS, the use of linear interpolation is allowed.

The central sensitivity indicator of a net position i (s_{ik}) expresses a shift in the market value of the position (V_i) which results from a change of the underlying risk factor (k).[19] This value change is determined by a revaluation of the position and should assess the impact of a "marginal" change of the underlying risk factor. Figure 6.10 exemplifies the sensitivity calculation of the equity risk in three steps.[20]

The vega sensitivity is based on the multiplication of the respective position's vega and the implied volatility. In cases in which the vega sensitivity is strongly negative or positive, the position value is very sensitive to volatility changes.[21]

---

19 If the valuation of the position is based on formulas (e.g. in the case of bond positions), BCBS prescribes a change of risk factor by one basis point and by 1 percent in all other cases.
20 BCBS 395 (2017) and BCBS 437 (2018) clarify that the banks are allowed to use "sensitivities based on pricing models that the bank's independent risk control unit uses to report market risks or actual profits and losses to senior management."
21 Cf. Hull (2015).

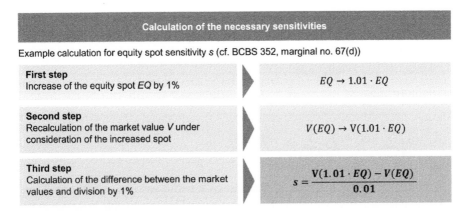

Figure 6.10: Example calculation of delta sensitivity

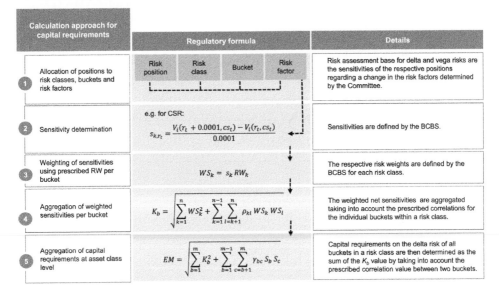

Figure 6.11: Calculation approach for linear risks

Figure 6.11 illustrates the calculation approach for linear risks. The actual value change that is assumed by the regulator is expressed in risk weights. For each bucket within the seven risk classes, the Basel Committee assigned individual regulatory risk weights (RW).

In order to determine the weighted net sensitivities (WS_k), one needs to multiply the net sensitivities (s_k) for open positions within a bucket by the respective risk weights (RW_k). Equation 6.1 shows this calculation:

Equation 6.1

$$WS_k = s_k \, RW_k \tag{6.1}$$

To determine the capital requirements for each bucket b (K_b) within a risk class, one needs to aggregate the weighted net sensitivities within a bucket using the corresponding correlation (ρ_{kl}). K_b is calculated using the portfolio formula of Harry M. Markowitz[22] shown in Equation 6.2:

Equation 6.2

$$K_b = \sqrt{\sum_{k=1}^{n} WS_k^2 + \sum_{k=1}^{n-1}\sum_{l=k+1}^{n} \rho_{kl}\, WS_k\, WS_l}$$ (6.2)

K_b is a risk metric from the Value-at-Risk indicator family and expresses the total sensitivity in bucket b. In other words, K_b is the potential loss that would arise due to the change of the risk factors in the bucket.

The capital requirement for the delta risk of all buckets within a risk class (EM_{Delta}) is then determined by aggregating the K_b values using the corresponding correlations between buckets b and c (γ_{bc}). Equation 6.3, which is very similar to the portfolio formula, is utilised for this purpose.

Equation 6.3

$$EM_{Delta} = \sqrt{\sum_{b=1}^{m} K_b^2 + \sum_{b=1}^{m-1}\sum_{c=b+1}^{m} \gamma_{bc}\, S_b\, S_c}$$ (6.3)

where:

$$S_b = \sum_{k=1}^{n} WS_k \text{ for all risk factors in bucket } b \text{ and}$$

$$S_c = \sum_{k=1}^{n} WS_k \text{ for all risk factors in bucket } c.$$

Since – compared to the portfolio formula in Equation 6.2 – for Equation 6.3 it is not mathematically ensured that the sum under the radical sign will be positive. A particular rule has to be taken into account in the case of a negative sum.

In order to determine capital requirements for the vega risk in all risk classes, the aggregation formulas shown in Equations 6.1 to 6.3 are used. Nonetheless, capital requirements on delta and vega risks must be calculated separately, since vega applies price risks based on volatility changes in the risk factors. Diversification effects between the delta and vega risk factors are not taken into account. Specific particularities exist in the individual risk classes when assessing linear risks. The conversion of the

22   Cf. Markowitz (2014), Formula 8, p. 43.

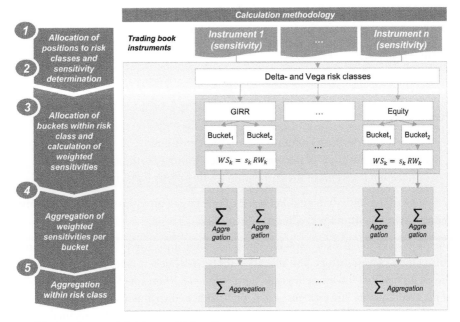

Figure 6.12: Schematic overview of calculation approach for linear risks

regulatory calculation formulas for linear risks into a more schematic approach is illustrated in Figure 6.12.

Specifics within the respective risk classes in determining linear risks

Interest rate risk

Within interest rate risk, risk positions are considered separately for each currency (risk buckets). Within a bucket, ten vertices between 0.25 years and 30 years are defined, which are assigned to specific risk weights. The risk weight level shifts between 1.5 and 2.4 percent. Further reductions of risk weights by 20% to 40% are possible based on the recent consultation paper of the BCBS.[23] To determine sensitivities, a change of the respective underlying interest rate shall be subject to one basis point.

For the aggregation of weighted sensitivities within the risk buckets, the BCBS prescribes a correlation matrix, which values need to be determined beforehand with a supervisory formula. On the one hand, the formula takes into account that the hedging effect of offsetting positions decreases when the difference between the residual terms of the positions increases. On the other hand, it takes into account that the diversification effect of offsetting positions increases in such situations. Afterwards, the risk positions and the sums of weighted sensitivities are aggregated across all

---

23   Cf. BCBS 436 (2018), p. 19.

buckets by taking into account the correlations to determine capital requirements. The Basel Committee sets forth a correlation factor of 50 percent.

Credit spread risks

Within the scope of credit spread risks, interest rate net positions are divided into three subcategories. A separate calculation of capital charges is performed for each subcategory (Figure 6.13):

- credit spread risks (CSR) of non-securitisation positions,
- securitisation positions of the non-correlation trading portfolio (nCTP), and
- securitisation positions of the correlation trading portfolio (CTP).

A change of the underlying market value of one basis point is assumed to determine the sensitivities within the credit spread risk class.

The provisions to calculate capital requirements for unsecured CSR positions distinguish among seven sectors. The allocation to the risk buckets takes place according to the credit quality ("investment grade" and "high yield/non-rated"). Within the scope of the credit quality "investment grade", secured debt instruments are also included in a separate bucket. Moreover, an additional bucket comprises all "other sectors" where no distinction is made regarding credit quality.

To these sixteen buckets risk weights ranging from 0.5 percent (states, investment grade) to 12 percent (financial sector, high yield/non-rated, among others) are assigned. When aggregating the weighted sensitivities within the buckets of credit risk positions, a correlation value, which results from multiplying three factors, is applied. The factors take into account whether the sensitivities refer to identical positions, as well as if the tenor and the basis of the sensitivity coincide. The bucket for "other sectors" is an exception. In this case, the correlation is determined as a simple sum of the net-weighted sensitivities of the respective positions of the bucket.

To determine capital requirements for non-securitisation CSR positions, the risk positions and the sums of the weighted sensitivities across all buckets are aggregated taking into account the respective correlations. The Basel Committee defined a formula to

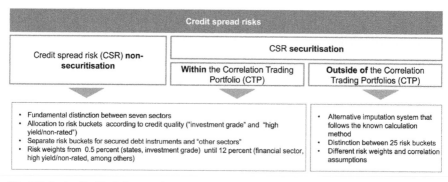

Figure 6.13: Overview of the distinction between credit spread risks

determine correlation. It is the result of multiplying the given correlation parameters according to rating and sector.

The correlation trading portfolio constitutes an exception within credit spread risks and is subject to unique criteria and requirements. Said portfolio holds securitisation and the corresponding hedges, which are subject to strict requirements. These positions cannot be re-securitised and must not be associated with underlying retail instruments or special purpose vehicles, among others.

The definition of the correlation trading portfolio gains importance especially in connection with the trading book requirements for securitisation positions. The credit spread risk for securitisation positions of the correlation trading portfolio is determined with a similar methodology as that used for non-securitisation CSR positions. A distinction is made among the same risk buckets; however, risk weights for securitisation positions of the correlation trading portfolio are usually higher as those positions face longer liquidity horizons and higher basis risks.

In the case of securitisation CSR positions that do not fall under the definition of the correlation trading portfolio, the Basel Committee suggests an alternative calculation approach that is based on the methodology for credit spread risks. The main difference is the classification of positions into twenty-five risk buckets which are divided into four sectors (senior investment grade, non-senior investment grade, high yield/non-rated as well as other sectors). Other changes arise from the risk weight level and the correlation assumptions. The correlations are calculated by multiplying three factors (tranche, tenor and basis). The parameter for correlations among the different buckets is set to zero percent.

Equity risk

The current provisions on equity risk, which group positions according to their national market, are fundamentally changed by the introduction of eleven different equity classes (buckets). The allocation of an equity position to a bucket depends on the criteria of the industry affiliation, market capitalisation and region. Five branches, as well as a high and a low market capitalisation, are defined (relevant limit EUR 2 billion). Furthermore, a distinction is made between advanced economies and emerging countries about affiliation to a specific region. To allocate equity of corporations that are active in several regions or several sectors, one needs to pay particular attention to the main market and sector. Within the buckets, long and short positions of the same instruments are offset against each other.

To determine sensitivities, a 1% change of the underlying equity price or, in the case of repos, a change of the repo term structure of interest rates (RTS) by one basis point is assumed. The resulting potential change in the value of the position is divided by 1% (equity) or by 0.01% (repos). The eleven buckets are assigned risk weights ranging from 30 to 79 percent for equity positions and 0.3 to 0.7 percent for repo positions. Further reductions of risk weights by 25% to 50% might be possible based on the recent consultation paper of March 2018.[24] Equity positions of corporations with a small market capitalisation and corporations from emerging countries are assigned higher risk weights than corporations with a high market capitalisation or corporations from developed countries.

The weighted sensitivities of equity or repos positions are summed up by taking into account the rule of signs for long and short positions and the correlations defined by the supervisory authority for delta positions of the buckets. This means that capital requirements for delta risks in the equity risk class can be calculated by summing up the delta risk positions and the sum of the weighted sensitivities across all equity classes (buckets) by taking into account the correlations.

Commodity risk

Within the commodity risk area, eleven commodity classes determine the respective risk buckets. Within the buckets, a distinction of the commodities based on the type, delivery date, place of delivery or other criteria is made. The commodity prices constitute the risk factors. To determine the sensitivities, a 1 percent change in the underlying commodity price is assumed. Risk weights ranging from 20 percent (precious metals) to 80 percent (freight) are assigned to the eleven buckets.

When the weighted sensitivities are aggregated within the buckets to risk positions, a correlation value determined by multiplying three factors is applied to the commodity risk class. Said factors take into account whether goods are identical and if the goods' delivery time, quality and place of delivery coincide. If the goods are not identical, a correlation value for each of the eleven commodity classes, which ranges from 15 to 95 percent, is defined. If the delivery times differ, a factor of 99 percent must be applied. If the quality or the place of delivery do not match, the factor is set at 99.9 percent. If the commodity positions fulfil all three criteria mentioned, then all factors equal one.

The risk positions and the sums of the weighted risk sensitivities are aggregated across all classes of goods (buckets) taking correlations into account to determine capital requirements. The Basel Committee specifies a correlation of 20 percent for classes of goods 1 to 10 and a correlation of 0 percent for the class of goods 11 (other goods). The new procedure is structured similarly to the current maturity ladder approach. The breakdown of goods and the repeated consideration of given correlations in adding up partial risks is, however, considerably more complicated than CRR provisions.

Foreign exchange risk

In the foreign exchange risk area, the individual currencies define the relevant risk buckets. The exchange rates of the currency used for accounting are the risk factors used to determine the positions' sensitivities. The Committee assumes a 1 percent change of the underlying exchange rate. A fixed value amount of 30 percent shall be used as risk weight. A reduction of risk weight to values between 15% – 22.5% as well as

---

24 Cf. BCBS 436 (2018), p. 19.

amendments to the risk factor definition are possible based on the consultation paper of March 2018.[25] Specific currency pairs, which are defined by the Committee, are assigned a lower risk weight of 21.21 percent (30% divided by the square root of 2) and are currently in further consultation.

When aggregating the weighted sensitivities within the buckets, a correlation value of one must be applied to the foreign currency area. This correlation value decreases to 60 percent when aggregating weighted sensitivities across all buckets. The revised procedure increases in complexity compared to the current multiplication procedure, as this does not explicitly consider correlations when adding partial amounts. Figure 6.14 shows an example calculation of the delta risk charge calculation for FX.

Vega risk

Within the context of the vega risk, the relevant risk buckets of the risk areas described for the delta risk are widely replicated. The vega sensitivity is determined by multiplying the vega of the risk factor with the implicit volatility of the option. Additional differences compared to the delta risk parameters arise in the area of the vega risk weights and correlation assumptions. The risk weights that are necessary to determine the weighted vega sensitivity will be calculated based on a formula introduced by the Committee. This formula takes into account market illiquidity based on specific liquidity horizons for each risk area (ranging from 20 in the case of large-cap equity to 120 in the case of CSR). The basis risk weight relevant for the formula equals 55 percent. Calculation requirements defined by the BCBS, which are mainly based on the terms of the options and the underlyings, are also imposed for the calculation of vega correlations.

Basic procedure to determine capital charges for non-linear risks

As with the vega risk, only instruments of the trading book with explicit or embedded options are subject to additional capital requirements on non-linear risks. The so-called curvature risk is not a second-order approximation like the gamma risk. It is a full revaluation that determines the capital requirement on the non-linear risk. The calculation method differs from the method used for the delta and the vega risk in that the convex relation between the risk factor and the position value is taken into account instead of the linear relation between the risk factor and the sensitivity.

First, the curvature risk exposure (curvature risk charge, CVR) of the risk factor k is determined for all risk classes with Equation 6.4.

Equation 6.4

$$CVR_k = -min \begin{bmatrix} \sum_i \left\{ V_i(x_k^{(RW^{(curvature)}+)}) - V_i(x_k) - RW_k^{(curvature)} s_{ik} \right\} \\ \sum_i \left\{ V_i(x_k^{(RW^{(curvature)}-)}) - V_i(x_k) + RW_k^{(curvature)} s_{ik} \right\} \end{bmatrix} \qquad (6.4)$$

25   Cf. BCBS 436 (2018), pp. 17–19.

Calculation approach — Example FX

1 Sensitivity determination

Find sensitivities across instruments to each risk factor k.

2 Calculation of weighted sensitivities

Facilitation for risk weight?	Bucket	Net sensitivity	Applicable risk weight	Weighted sensitivity
yes	€/GBP	109.00	21.21%	23.12
yes	€/JPY	-44.00	21.21%	-9.33
no	€/AED	30.00	30.00%	9.00

Privileged RW for specific currency pairs according: Division of RW by $\sqrt{2}$.

3 Aggregation of weighted sensitivities per bucket

Bucket b	Capital charge per bucket	for step 4
€/GBP	23.12	534.65
€/JPY	-9.33	87.12
€/AED	9.00	81.00
	Sum ($K_b{}^2$):	**702.77**

The square of the capital charge of each bucket is needed to calculate the overall capital charge across buckets

4 Aggregation within risk class

kb	c*γ_{bc}	€/GBP	€/JPY	€/AED
23.12	€/GBP	0%	60%	60%
-9.33	€/JPY	60%	0%	60%
9.00	€/AED	60%	60%	0%

Capital charge for FX

€/JPY – €/GBP	-258.98
€/AED – €/GBP	249.72
€/AED – €/JPY	-100.81
Sum γ_{bc}*S_b*S_c	**-110.07**
Sum ($K_b{}^2$)	702.77
Delta capital charge FX correl. parameter = 1:	**24.35**

- Correlation parameter = 60%
- Calculation step needs to be repeated for each correlation scenario

Figure 6.14: Example calculation: Delta risk charge for FX

where:

i is an instrument subject to the risk factor k,

x_k is the current level of risk factor k, $V_i(x_k)$ is the price of instrument i depending on the current level of risk factor k,

$V_i(x_k^{(RW^{(curvature)}+)})$ and $V_i(x_k^{(RW^{(curvature)}-)})$ denote the price of the instrument i, after x_k is shifted and

s_{ik} is the delta sensitivity of instrument i with respect to the curvature risk factor k.

Second, the curvature risk exposures must be aggregated within a bucket using the corresponding correlation ρ_{kl} as set out in Equation 6.5.

Equation 6.5

$$K_b = \sqrt{max\left(0,\ \sum_k max(CVR_k, 0)^2\right) + \sum_k \sum_{k \neq l} \rho_{kl} CVR_k CVR_l \psi(CVR_k, CVR_l)}$$

(6.5)

where:

$\psi(CVR_k, CVR_l)$ is a function that takes the value 0 if CVR_k and CVR_l both have negative signs.

In all other cases, $\psi(CVR_k, CVR_l)$ takes the value 1.

Finally, the capital requirements on the curvature risk across buckets within each risk class ($EM_{Curvature}$) are determined by aggregating the k_b value under consideration of the correlation factors defined by the Committee between buckets b and c (γ_{bc}). Equation 6.6 displays the corresponding supervisory formula.

Equation 6.6

$$EM_{Curvature} = \sqrt{\sum_b k_b^2 + \sum_b \sum_{c \neq b} \gamma_{bc} S_b S_c \psi(S_b, S_c)}$$

(6.6)

where:

$S_b = \sum_k CVR_k$ for all risk factors in bucket b and

$S_c = \sum_k CVR_k$ for all risk factors in bucket c.

$\psi(S_b, S_c)$ is a function that takes the value 0 if S_b and S_c both have negative signs. In all other cases, $\psi(S_b, S_c)$ takes the value 1.

The conversion of the regulatory calculation formulas for non-linear risks into a more schematic approach is illustrated in Figure 6.15.

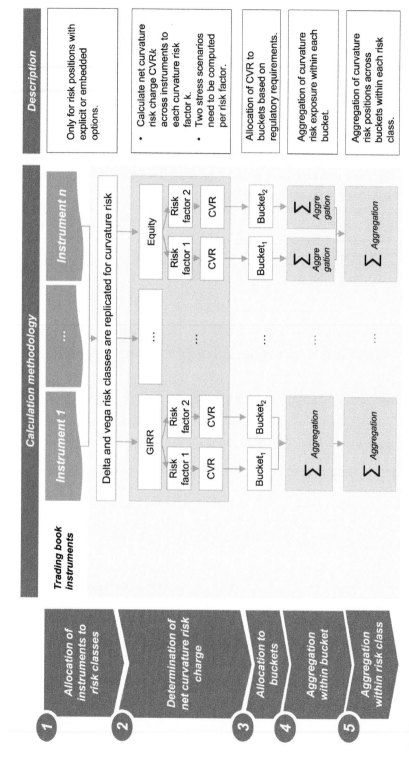

Figure 6.15: Schematic overview of calculation approach for non-linear risks

In the consultation paper as of March 2018, certain revisions to the described curvature risk methodology are proposed by the BCBS. In detail, they are focusing on three aspects. First, the BCBS suggests amending the application of shock scenarios in such a way that consistent scenarios are applied to risk factors within the same bucket. Therefore, clarifications and amendments to Equation 6.4 and its components are made. Regardless of this, the BCBS is considering an alternative approach that is focusing on a sector definition per bucket in order to apply shock scenarios on that level.

Second, the formula used to calculate aggregate capital requirements is proposed to be floored in order to fix potential cliff effect that arises from the use of an alternative specification that institutions need to use when curvature risk positions are negative. Finally, the Basel Committee raises the issue of a potential double-counting effect for FX options where none of the underlying currencies of a particular instrument is the bank's reporting currency. If this effect is found to be material, the application of a scalar needs to be defined in the further consultation process.[26]

Specifics within the respective risk classes in determining non-linear risks

The granular requirements to determine the capital charge in the area of curvature risk rely on the described methodology for delta and vega risks. For instance, the defined delta and vega risk classes and risk buckets are also applied to curvature risks.

However, when looking at the curvature risk weights and the curvature correlations, differences can be identified. In the area of the equity and foreign currency risks, delta risk weights are applied since these are equated with curvature risk weights as a relative shock. For the remaining risk classes, the curvature risk weight is contemplated as a parallel shift of all vertices of the relevant curves, which are based on the highest delta risk weight for each risk area.[27]

The correlations among curvature risk positions are also based on the delta correlations of the respective risk areas. Though, the Basel Committee demands that the correlation parameter is squared. For example, this results in a correlation of 25 percent ($= 0.5^2$ percent) when taking two GIRR positions (CVR_{EUR} and CVR_{USD}).

6.3.2 Default risk charge

Within the scope of the default risk charge, the so-called jump-to-default risk (JTD risk)[28] has to be estimated (Figure 6.16). For the default risk charge, the Basel Committee distinguishes among different requirements for non-securitisation and securitisation positions of the non-correlation and the correlation trading portfolio.

---

26   Cf. BCBS 436 (2018), pp. 15–16.

27   BCBS 395 (2017) and BCBS 437 (2018) clarify in reference to para. 132 BCBS 352 (2016) that "the risk weight for the curvature risk charge should be the highest delta risk weight for each of the delta risk factors which are shocked together to determine the curvature risk charge."

28   The "jump-to-default risk" is a risk of a counterparty or issuer's sudden default before the market had time to take the higher default risk into consideration (cf. Regulation 153/2013 Art. 1 marginal no. 4).

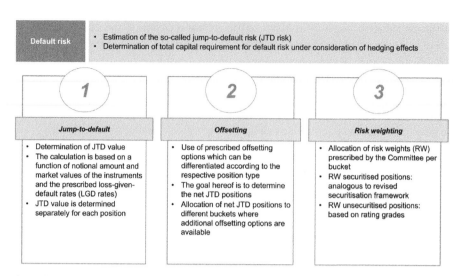

Figure 6.16: Overview of the default risk charge calculation

The method to determine the default risk charge can be divided into three steps: In the first step, JTD amounts are determined. The calculation is based on a function of notional value and market value of the instrument and the given loss-given-default ratio (LGD ratio). The JTD value is determined separately for each position.[29] The second step comprises the use of offsetting rules, which vary according to the instrument type. The offsetting goal is to determine the net JTD position per bucket. The net JTD risk positions are then allocated in the last step to buckets, where additional offsetting options are available. Risk weights defined by the Committee are available for each bucket and are based on the revised securitisation framework for securitised positions and are assigned to non-securitised positions based on rating grades.[30]

To determine the total capital requirement for the default risk, the capital requirement for each bucket is calculated first. For non-securitisation and securitisation non-correlation trading portfolios, the default risk charge is the simple sum of bucket level default risk charges. For the correlation trading portfolio, offsetting can still take place to contemplate hedging effects. As a result, the default risk charge is the simple sum of the bucket level default risk charges when they are positive, and half the bucket level default risks when they are negative.

6.3.3 Residual risk add-on

The residual risk add-on shall include the risk of all instruments, which have not yet been included in another risk factor or another risk class of the standardised procedure. The goal of the add-on is to introduce a conservative and straightforward method

---

29 Cf. BCBS 352 (2016), marginal no. 57 (a).
30 Cf. BCBS 352 (2016), marginal no. 57 (b) – 57 (c).

that also takes into account complex and exotic instruments pragmatically within the standardised approach without increasing the complexity of the approach.

The add-on is calculated by multiplying the sum of the gross notional amount of the instruments with a given risk weight. For exotic underlyings (such as the weather, natural disasters or longevity), a risk weight of one percent is suggested. The Basel Committee defines a risk weight of 0.1 percent for all other cases.[31]

The FRTB standard provides a non-exhaustive list of other risk types that may fall within the criteria applicable to residual risks. Considering detailed requirements, these include the gap risk, the correlation risk of positions with different underlyings or the behavioural risk. The given list stands opposite to a list of risk types according to which instruments are not automatically subject to the residual risk add-on. For instance, this second list includes the smile risk, a unique form of the inherent volatility risk in the case of options and the dividend risk.[32]

6.3.4 Simplified alternative to the standardised approach

In June 2017, the Basel Committee on Banking Supervision (BCBS) published a proposal[33] for a simplified alternative to the primary component of the standardised approach described in the previous chapters, namely the sensitivities-based method (SbM) as shown in Figure 6.8. The proposal of a "reduced" sensitivities-based method (R-SbM) should aim to decrease the complexity of the approach in order to reduce implementation challenges for banks with a low concentration of trading book activities as well as smaller banks. In doing so, the R-SbM makes some significant simplifications in comparison to the SbM, including the removal of capital requirements for vega and curvature risks as well as reductions in risk factor granularity. Besides, the correlation parameters, as well as risk weights, increase compared to the SbM.

Overall, the reduction of complexity comes at a price. Test calculations show that the capital charge under the R-SbM doubles compared to the SbM. Thereby, the capital driver is the generalised risk weight of 5% in the context of GIRR. This assessment is also reflected in the comments the BCBS received on their draft. Thus, the Basel Committee proposes in its publication as of March 2018 to dismiss the R-SbM methodology and apply a recalibrated version of the Basel II standardised approach as a simplified alternative for smaller or less complex institutions.[34] This approach is already reflected in the CRR II drafts on the European level and is now adopted and clarified by the BCBS.

For recalibration the BCBS suggest applying multipliers in each risk class of the Basel II standardised approach without any further adjustments to the initial methodologies. In detail, the following multipliers are suggested and are subject to calibration

---

31 Cf. BCBS 352 (2016), marginal no. 58 (c).
32 Cf. Basel Committee on Banking Supervision (2016), marginal no. 58 (e) – 58 (h).
33 Cf. BCBS 408 (2017).
34 Cf. BCBS 436 (2018), p. 39.

during the ongoing consultation: General and specific interest rate risk with a multiplier between 1.50 and 2.00, general and specific equity risk with a multiplier between 3.00 and 3.50, commodity risk with a multiplier between 1.50 and 2.50 as well as FX with a multiplier between 1.25 and 1.50. The overall capital requirement is the simple sum of the recalibrated capital requirements arising from each of the four Basel II risk classes.

The aim is that the recalibrated Basel II standard is slightly more conservative than the revised full standardised approach under FRTB. The BCBS is not proposing eligibility requirements, however, and states that the approach is not appropriate for G-SIBs, or institutions that use the Internal Models Approach or hold any correlation trading positions.

Proposal of the reduced sensitivities-based method in detail

The application of the R-SbM is based on specific qualitative as well as quantitative requirements that need to be assessed on a quarterly basis. The approach is only available to institutions that apply no internal models approach and that are not global systemically important banks (G-SIBs) or domestic systemically important banks (D-SIBs). Furthermore, it is required that banks do not engage in writing options and do not hold any correlation trading positions, as the corresponding capital charges and requirements are removed from the approach. Exceptions to these requirements are back-to-back options and covered options whereby the bank owns the securities it may need to deliver under the terms of the option.

From a quantitative perspective, explicit requirements apply. The bank's total non-derivative trading book assets and liabilities plus the sum of the gross fair value of its trading book derivative assets and liabilities are below 1 billion EUR. The division of market risk RWA under the R-SbM by its total RWA is below 5% as well. The aggregate notional amount of non-centrally cleared derivatives is below a threshold that is not quantified so far.

For banks that fulfil the quantitative and qualitative requirements and received supervisory approval for adopting the R-SbM, the total capital charge for market risk will be the sum of the following three components (see Figure 6.17): the R-SbM as described by BCBS 408, the default risk charge as described by BCBS 352, and the Residual risk add-on as described by BCBS 352.

The structure of the R-SbM is solely driven by the delta risk capital charge. For that, the aggregation formulas, as well as calculation steps, are almost identical to the SbM. Furthermore, the definitions as laid out in BCBS 352 apply. Figure 6.18 indicates a comparison of the risk weights between the SbM and the R-SbM. It becomes clear that through the reduction of granularity for the risk factors and risk classes higher risk weights apply. For example, the delta risk weight for FX increases from 30% to 45%.

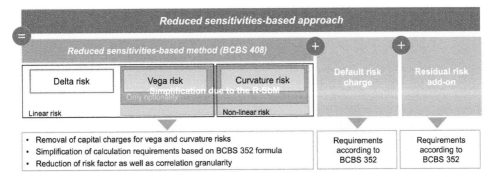

Figure 6.17: Overview of the reduced sensitivities-based method

6.3.5 Example for national implementation: The implementation of the SBA in the EU

Similar to the revised trading book boundary, the requirements set out by the BCBS for the sensitivities-based approach were largely adopted by the EU Commission in its draft for CRR II (2016). In the on-going consultation phase certain details are under discussion and subject to change.[35] Timewise, the aggregation of risk-class specific own funds requirements for delta, vega and curvature risks under the different correlation scenarios was discussed. Nevertheless, in the latest drafts (March 2018), there is no change to the approach set out by the BCBS (see Article 325i CRR II). Moreover, the EU Commission revised certain elements of the FRTB approach set out by the BCBS. In detail, CRR II clarifies that an institution may, subject to the approval from competent authorities, use alternative definitions of delta risk sensitivities in the calculation of the own fund requirements of a trading book position (see Article 325u CRR II). Furthermore, there are changes to some calculation factors and risk factors throughout the FRTB-SA methodology, e.g. Article 325l CRR II (underwriting positions) or Article 325n CRR II (credit spread risk factors for non-securitisation). Also, CRR II suggests minor revisions to certain computation formulas (e.g. Article 325s CRR II, delta risk sensitivities) or Article 325x CRR II (gross jump to default amounts). Last but not least, CRR II stated different risk weights as well as correlation factors (e.g. Article 325ag CRR II to Article 325az CRR II). The reasons for the adjustments are not always apparent in detail.

It is expected that due to the on-going discussions further details will be changed compared to the finalised FRTB standard by the BCBS to make the framework best applicable to certain particularities within the EU. In this regard, it will be interesting to what extent the latest proposal of the BCBS in March 2018 – regarding changes to the FRTB framework as well as the simplified alternative to the standardised approach – will be transferred into the final CRR II standard.

---

35 The comparison relates to CRR II drafts as of 2016 and 2017.

Sensitivities-based method (BCBS 352)

	Risk factor	RW	
GIRR	0.25 / 0.5 / 1 / 2 / 3 / 5 / 10 / 15 / 20 / 30 years	1.5%–2.4%*	
	INF / CCY	2.25%*	

	Risk factor	non-sec	secCTP
Delta CSR	B1: IG - Sov.	0.5%	
	B2: IG - Local government	1.0%	4.0%
	B3: IG - Financials	5.0%	8.0%
	B4: IG - Basic materials	3.0%	5.0%
	B5: IG - Consumer goods	3.0%	4.0%
	B6: IG - Technology	2.0%	3.0%
	B7: IG - Health care	1.5%	2.0%
	B8: IG - Covered bonds	4.0%	6.0%
	B9-B15: HY&NR	3.0%–12%	10%–16%
	B16: Other sectors	12.0%	13.0%

	Risk factor	RW	
Delta CSR sec nCTP	B1 - B3: Senior IG - RMBS	0.9%–2.0%	
	B4: Senior IG - CMBS	2.0%	
	B5 - B7: Senior IG - ABS	0.8–1.4%	
	B8: Senior IG - CLO nCTP	1.4%	
	B9-16: RW B1-B8 multiplied by	Fact. 1.25	
	B17-24: RW B1-B8 multiplied by	Fact. 1.75	

	Risk factor	Spot price	Repo rate
Equity	B1 - B4: Large MC - EME	45%–60%	0.45%–0.60%
	B5 - B8: Large MC - AE	30%–50%	0.30%–0.50%
	B9: Small MC - EME - Along B1 - B4	70%	0.70%
	B10: Smalls MC - AE - Along B5 - B8	50%	0.50%
	B11: Other sector	70%	0.70%

	Risk factor	Spot price
Commodity	B1 - B3: Energy	30%–60%
	B4 - B10: Further commodities	20%–80%
	B11: Other commodity	50%
FX	FX sensitivities / exposures	30%*

Reduced sensitivities-based method (BCBS 408)

Risk factor	RW
≤ 5 years / >5 years	5%
INF / CCY	3%

Risk factor	non-sec
B1: IG - Sov.	1% / 5%
B2: IG - Financials	10%
B3: Other sector	15%
B4: HY&NR - Sov.	5% / 10%
B5: HY&NR - Fin.	25%
B6: HY&NR - Other	30%

Risk factor	RW sec
B1: Senior IG - RMBS	2.0%
B2: Senior IG - NM retail securitisation	5.0%
B3: Senior IG - CMBS	5.0%
B4: Senior IG - Other	10.0%
B5-B8: Non-Senior IG	5%–12.5%
B9-B12: HY&NR	3.5%–17.5%

Risk factor	Spot price
B1 - B2: Large MC - EME	60%
B3 - B4: Large MC - AE	40%–50%
B5: Small MC - EME - All	70%
B6: Small MC - AE - All	60%

Risk factor	Spot price
B1 - B3: Solid combustibles	40%–70%
B4 - B10: Further commodities	30%–90%
B11: Other commodity	60%
FX sensitivities	45% / 32%**

* for selected currencies: RW/square root of 2

** for selected currencies

INF = Inflation; CCY = Cross currency; IG = Investment grade; HY & NR = High yield & non-rated;

Figure 6.18: Comparison of risk weights between SbM and R-SbM

6.4 Internal Models Approach for market risk (IMA-TB)

This part of the chapter is dedicated to the Internal Models Approach for market risk (IMA-TB) within the context of the revised provisions on capital requirements for market risk in the trading book.[36] We also discuss the changes proposed by the BCBS in March 2018.[37] Furthermore, we consider an example for national implementation of the IMA-TB. For this example we use the CRR II/CRD V draft published by the European Commission.

Section 6.4.1 outlines the shortcomings of the existing framework from the regulator's point of view and the changes and goals in relation hereto. In the following, the procedural and organisational challenges are dealt with in Section 6.4.2. The methodological novelties and the challenges arising in connection hereto are described in Section 6.4.3. We also summarise the recent discussion about the problem of backtesting expected shortfall. Section 6.4.4 depicts possible consequences for capital requirements of market risks in the trading book resulting from the revised provisions.

6.4.1 Regulatory background and goals

As of 2009, regulators paid particular attention to the Internal Models Approach for market risk used predominantly by larger financial institutions. During this process, the Basel Committee identified the following main issues in the current regulatory regime which shall be addressed with the aid of the revised models-based approach.[38]

a) The first issue is the use of the VaR as a risk metric. The BCBS highlights several shortcomings simultaneously such as the lack of sensitivity of the VaR vis-à-vis so-called tail events. In this context, tail events refer to risks or losses, respectively, which occur with a probability of less than 1 percent within the observed 10-day time frame. Since the prescribed regulatory VaR does not comprise these risks, banks are incentivised to run such risks specifically since they do not increase capital requirements. Moreover, compared to the expected shortfall used in the IMA-TB, the VaR is not a *coherent* risk metric since it lacks the necessary subadditive characteristic.[39] This means that the VaR of a compound portfolio is not necessarily lower or equal to the sum of the VaRs of its components (Figure 6.19). This contradicts the intuition that the risks of a portfolio cannot increase through diversification.

---

36 Final framework BCBS 352 (2016) based on BCBS 265 (2013).
37 Revisions to the minimum capital requirements for market risk (BCBS 436, 2018)
38 Cf. BCBS 219 (2012), page 8 et seq. and BCBS 265 (2013), page 3 et seq.
39 Cf. Acerbi/Tasche (2002).

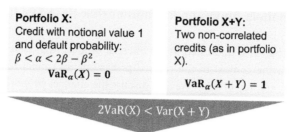

Not sub-additive

Figure 6.19: VaR: Incoherent risk metric since it is not sub-additive

b) The holding period of 10 days, which is assumed for all products, is an additional weakness of the regulatory VaR. Especially complex and structured products, which cannot be sold or secured by hedging within the assumed holding period in the event of a crisis, are consequently not covered with sufficient capital. The third point of criticism is the use of a one-year time frame as a basis to calibrate the VaR model. This induces a strong procyclicality which could entail worsened predictive power of the VaR model. Lower capital requirements, which would most likely not be sufficient in a crisis, typically accrue in calm market situations. This also explains several backtesting breaches during the financial market crisis.

c) An additional cause pertains to the strongly different results of banks' internal models among them and compared to the standardised approach. As the results of several "Quantitative Impact Studies" (QIS)[40] showed, internal models of different credit institutions lead to very different capital requirements even for the same benchmark portfolios.

The goal of the revised provisions on the IMA-TB is to remedy these causes and weaknesses. In the following, the procedural as well as the organisational challenges and the new approval process within the context of the IMA-TB are discussed in detail.

6.4.2 Procedural and organisational challenges

A significant change is an approval for the IMA-TB at trading desk level. The first challenge lies in evaluating the organisational infrastructure which comprises the definition and structure of a credit institute's trading desk. The BCBS applies the criteria set forth in Appendix A of the BCBS 352.[41]

---

40 Cf. Quantitative Impact Study (2014) and Quantitative Impact Study (2015).
41 Cf. BCBS 352 (2016), Appendix A.

To obtain an IMA-TB approval for individual trading desks, various requirements must be fulfilled. These requirements comprise backtesting and "Profit & Loss" (P&L) attribution at trading desk level,[42] among others.

6.4.3 Methodological amendment

Under the current Basel framework, capital requirements for market risk when using internal models are mainly based on three indicators. These indicators lie at the heart of the revised provisions in connection with the IMA-TB and are thus briefly outlined below.[43]

a) **Value-at-Risk (VaR):** Capital requirements result from the VaR with a 99% level of confidence and a holding period of 10 days multiplied by a defined factor. The factor is determined within the course of backtesting and is based on the number of events, where of the actual losses are beyond forecasted losses within a one-year period (VaR breaches).

b) **Stressed VaR (SVaR):** Calculated in a similar way to the VaR with the difference that a model calibration for a period of severe stress for the current portfolio. The analysed stress period must be reviewed on a yearly basis.

c) **Incremental Risk Charge (IRC):** An additional capital requirement on the default and migration risk of trading book positions that are subject to a capital requirement for the special interest rate change risk. The losses based on defaults and rating migration must be measured with the Internal Model used with a 99.9% level of confidence over a one-year time horizon. This indicator must be determined at least weekly.

Within the context of the revised provisions, the VaR and the SVaR are replaced by a new indicator, which is based on the expected shortfall (ES) with a confidence level of 97.5%. In addition, the IRC is replaced by the Default Risk Charge (DRC). Besides this methodical change, additional challenges arise from changes and new requirements on data history and quality. Figure 6.20 outlines said changes.

Expected shortfall as a new risk metric

The VaR and SVaR indicators of the current regulatory framework are replaced in the revised approach by a standardised ES with a 97.5% level of confidence that is calibrated based on a stress period. Mathematically, the ES is defined as a random variable X at a quantile α (Equation 6.7):

Equation 6.7

$$ES_\alpha(X) = \frac{1}{1-\alpha} \int_\alpha^1 VaR_\gamma(X)d\gamma \qquad (6.7)$$

---

42 Compare Section 6.4.3.5
43 Cf. Art. 364–376 CRR.

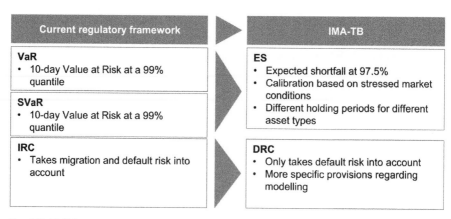

Figure 6.20: IMA-TB changes

where VaR_γ is the Value-at-Risk at a quantile γ. The expected value of the "tail" is established here, that is the events that occur with a probability lower than $1 - \alpha$.

To define the stress period, a one-year period between 2005 and now, in which the current portfolio would have suffered the greatest loss, must be found. This period must be adjusted on a monthly basis as well as ad-hoc in the event of significant changes in the risk factors in the portfolio. The new approach allows for the use of an alternative procedure since data history is not available for all risk factors regarding the necessary lengths and quality. The identified reduced set of risk factors must be able to explain a minimum of 75% of the variation of the full model. This reduced set of factors is subject to supervisory approval. After approval, the ES can be determined using Equation 6.8:[44]

Equation 6.8

$$ES_B = ES_{R,S} \cdot \frac{ES_{F,C}}{ES_{R,C}} \tag{6.8}$$

$ES_{R,S}$ refers to the expected shortfall in terms of the reduced set of factors R and is calibrated with respect to the above-mentioned stress period, $ES_{R,C}$ refers to the ES for the current one-year period for the reduced set R and $ES_{F,C}$ to the expected shortfall including all risk factors for the current one-year period. The stressed ES is therefore scaled with the reduced risk factors in relation to the current expected shortfalls taking into account all risk factors. Moreover, the Committee established that the relation arising out of $ES_{F,C}$ and $ES_{R,C}$ should not fall below 1.

---

44   Cf. BCBS 352 (2016), p. 53.

In the current regulatory framework it was still possible to scale the required 10-day VaR based on a 1-day VaR based on the so-called "square-root T rule" (Equation 6.9):[45]

Equation 6.9

$$VaR_{10T} = \sqrt{10}\, VaR_{1T} \tag{6.9}$$

This is no longer allowed under the revised approach. Instead, overlapping 10-day changes of the risk factors must be used. Furthermore, the new approach shall better outline the varying liquidity of the different risk factors. For this purpose, the defined risk factors are divided into five categories with different liquidity horizons. Table 6.2 provides an overview of these five categories.

By means of the prescribed liquidity horizons, the expected shortfall is scaled based on Equation 6.10 on the liquidity-adjusted ES':

Equation 6.10

$$ES' = \sqrt{(ES_{T,F})^2 + \sum_{j=2}^{5}\left(ES_{T,j}\sqrt{\frac{LH_j - LH_{j-1}}{T}}\right)^2} \tag{6.10}$$

LH_j is the liquidity horizon j,

T is the length of the base horizon of 10 days,

j	Liquidity horizon (in days)	Risk factors
1	10	· Interest in the bank's currency such as EUR, USD, GBP, AUF, JPY, SEK, CAD · Equity (in main index) · Exchange rate (major currency pairs)
2	20	· Interest in other currency · Equity (not in main index) · Equity volatility (in main index) · Exchange rate (other currency pairs) · Energy, precious metals (price) · Credit spread states (investment grade)
3	40	· Interest volatility · Exchange rate volatility and other FX factors · Energy, precious metals (other risk factors) · Credit spread states (high yield) · Credit spread corporations (investment grade)
4	60	· Equity volatility (not in main index) and other equity risk factors · Credit spread corporations (high yield) · Other commodities (price) · Commodities (other risk factors)
5	120	· Other credit spread (including all structured products and CDS)

Table 6.2: Liquidity categories and associated risk factors

---

45   Cf. Art. 186 a) CRR.

$ES_{T,F}$ is the expected shortfall at horizon T, which includes shocks to all risk factors, and

$ES_{T,j}$ is the expected shortfall at horizon T which only includes shocks to risk factors of the liquidity class j.

Backtestability of expected shortfall

Backtestability is a necessary feature for a regulatory standard because it is questionable whether a model that can't be validated is reasonable. Since proposing to replace the VaR in favour of the ES, there has been a controversial debate whether the ES is backtestable. The discussion about backtestability of the ES started with the finding that ES is not elicitable[46] followed by arguing that it is therefore not backtestable.[47]

Roughly speaking, a test statistic $Y(X)$ is said to be elicitable if it can be expressed as the minimiser of the expectation of a scoring function $S(y, x)$, i.e.

$$Y(X) = \arg \min_y E[S(y, X)].$$

Elicitability is important because it immediately allows to say something about the (relative) quality between different models only based on the forecasts of $Y(X)$ and realisations of X. A model is better than a second one if its mean score $\overline{S}$ defined as

$$\overline{S} = \frac{1}{T} \sum_{t=1}^{T} S(y_t, x_t)$$

is lower.

A popular example of a scoring function is the mean with $S(y, x) = (y - x)^2$. As an example of the quality assessment of models, we draw 250 samples of X which have a standard normal distribution, i.e. with mean one and standard deviation one. To forecast the mean we consider two models where the first model forecasts the correct mean plus some normally distributed noise with standard deviation 0.1 and a second model with more noise where the noise has a standard deviation of 0.5. Since the forecasting of the first model is more precise, it should have a lower mean score $\overline{S}$ than the second model. Running this simulation 50 times we get the expected results as shown in Figure 6.21.

However, it is unclear if elicitability is a necessary condition for backtestability. Acerbi and Szekely (2014) argue that elicitability is rather important for model selection and not model validation. For instance, the backtest for VaR is not based on the scoring function for VaR. The test statistic for VaR is even model-independent (binomial distributed) making VaR a unique case among all risk measures. Thus, we have a zoo of

---

46   Cf. Gneiting (2011).
47   Cf. Carver (2013).

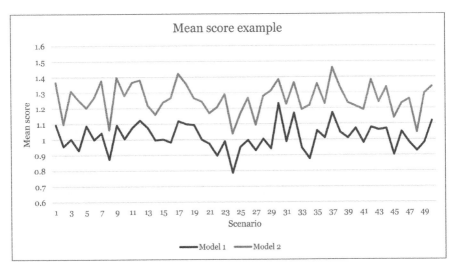

Figure 6.21: Mean score example

proposed backtests for ES taking different approaches (e.g. Acerbi and Szekely 2014; Corbetta and Peri, 2016; Emmer et al 2015; Righi and Ceretta 2013; Du and Escanciano 2016). However, none of the proposed backtests has been convincing enough to become the standard backtest for ES. Many tests are sensitive to the VaR leading to rejection of models giving correct predictions for ES and no rejection of models giving false predictions for ES. Other tests are for the whole distribution or the tail of the distribution rather than specifically for ES.

Whereas ES alone is not elicitable it is jointly elicitable with VaR[48] which is similar to the variance which is also only jointly elicitable with the mean. Building on this property Acerbi and Szekely (2017) propose a framework for backtestability. They argue that, given a single model, the mean score shown above does not give an indication about the absolute quality of the model. It is rather a procedure for model selection than model validation. Additionally, the mean score test might favour models underestimating ES to models overestimating ES which might be undesirable regarding prudent goals of risk management. Their definition of backtestability is closely related to elicitability but eliminates the weaknesses of the scoring function. The subsequently resulting approach for backtesting ES is called ridge backtest of ES.

Currently, there is no regulatory proposed backtest for ES and it remains unclear whether this will change in the future. As described in Section 6.4.3.6, the new IMA-TB introduced by BCBS 352 still uses a traffic-light approach to backtesting based on the VaR. Backtesting ES is possible but either only jointly with VaR or indirectly by testing the whole distribution or its tail.

---

48   Cf. Fissler, Ziegel, Gneiting (2015)

Non-modellable risk factors (NMRF)

A key new concept in the revised Internal Models Approach is that of non-modellable risk factors (NMRF).[49] Risk factors that do not have at least 24 "real" prices within one year, with a maximum period of one month between two consecutive observations, are not considered in the ES calculation described above.[50] According to the banks' comments, this applies mainly to rarely traded stocks. After quite a lot of criticism from the financial industry, the BCBS proposed some changes to the treatment of NMRF.

A distinction is made between specific credit risk ("idiosyncratic risk") and other risk factors. For the specific credit risk, losses from the stress scenario ($ISES_j$) may be aggregated as long as the bank can prove that the correlation is negligible. In the case of other risk factors, no diversification is permitted when aggregating losses under the stress scenario (SES_j). The total capital requirements for non-modellable risk factors result from Equation 6.11:[51]

Equation 6.11

$$ SES = \sqrt{\sum_{i=1}^{L} ISES_i^2 + \sum_{j=1}^{K} SES_j} \tag{6.11} $$

where

L represents the number of risk factors aggregated with zero correlation and

K the number of non-modellable risk factors.

The stress scenario must be calibrated to at least one loss at a 97.5% confidence threshold over a period of extreme stress for the given risk factors.[52] Moreover, the applied liquidity horizon must be greater than the largest time interval between two consecutive price observations. An additional task for banks lies in the identification and documentation of non-modellable risk factors as well as in the selection of adequate stress scenarios for individual representatives. Notably, it must be taken into account that the Committee includes options under which it can reject stress scenarios suggested by banks. If this is the case, the maximum possible loss must be used instead of a loss under a stress scenario. As a result, the selection of stress scenarios constitutes a real challenge for banks in the context of the introduction of the IMA-TB.

As there is no special treatment of idiosyncratic equity risk, banks complained that the method described in Equation 6.11 leads to an undue increase of capital requirements. In response to this criticism, the Committee asked for comments on the following changes: The assumption of zero correlation may also be applied for idiosyncratic equity risk.

---

49   Cf. BCBS 352 (2016), pp. 57 et seq.
50   Cf. BCBS 352 (2016), p. 58.
51   Cf. BCBS 352 (2016), p. 65.
52   Cf. BCBS 352 (2016), page 64.

Equation 6.12

$$SES = \sqrt{\sum_{i=1}^{I} ISES_{CS,i}^2} + \sqrt{\sum_{Eq,j=1}^{J} ISES_j^2} + \sum_{k=1}^{K} SES_k \qquad (6.12)$$

where

I represents the number of idiosyncratic *credit spread* risk factors aggregated with zero correlation,

J represents the number of idiosyncratic *equity risk* factors aggregated with zero correlation and,

K is the number of other non-modellable risk factors.

To show that the zero correlation assumption holds, banks may use factor models and demonstrate that the residuals are homogeneous within each residual distribution and heterogeneous against others. In addition, they must not display serial correlation in the time series. However, it is worth stressing again that this change in the treatment of idiosyncratic equity risk is not a proposed change yet but only included in the paper for banks in order to give feedback. The committee even states that if there is no "compelling evidence" that this change solves the issue pointed out by banks, the method of Equation 6.11 is going to stay.

Another point addressed by the recent paper concerns seasonal markets such as those for certain agricultural commodities. For those, it is not too uncommon to have longer periods, i.e. longer than one month, without any quote even though for the rest of the year there is sufficient liquidity. The committee asks banks to provide proof that such risk factors have indeed been sufficiently liquid during recent times of stress. If this is the case, and there is enough evidence, the conditions on modellability might be relaxed.

Notwithstanding the proposed changes, there are substantial challenges stemming from the topic of non-modellable risk factors. The key task is the definition of risk factors. After surveying the risk factor universe of the bank, one can get a shortlist of possible NMRFs based upon the existence of real prices and continuous availability. Apart from their own prices, banks might want to rely on data obtained via data-pooling from other banks and on quotes received from data vendors who are at the moment starting to define suiting offers. The derivative association ISDA also participates in these efforts.

In a next step, an analysis should be performed as to which risk factors need to be considered at all. The criteria for P&L attribution do not require all risk factors to be included but only enough to fulfil the requirements detailed in Section 6.4.3.5. This induces an interdependency between different parts of the IMA-TB implementation: The definition of risk factors and materiality considerations will not only have an impact on the capital of NMRF but also the outcomes of P&L attribution tests. Thus, NMRF, P&L attribution and backtesting have to be considered concurrently as these tests/processes are dependent on each other.

If a risk factor is then identified as being both non-modellable and having a material contribution to the P&L, there exists another possibility to reduce the impact of the stress scenario connected to this risk factor: The risk factor can be decomposed as a sum (or a linear combination) of proxy which is a modellable risk factor and a basis risk factor as a residual which is non-modellable. As the basis risk factor should have smaller changes in the stress scenarios, the total impact can be notably reduced. Figure 6.22 shows the most common examples of possible NMRFs and their corresponding basis risk factors.

When selecting a suitable proxy there is an important trade-off to face. A proxy closer to the desired risk factor (Figure 6.23, left side) will lead to a smaller stress impact of

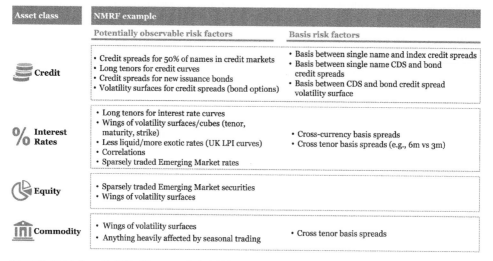

Figure 6.22: Examples for possible NMRF and the corresponding basis risk factors

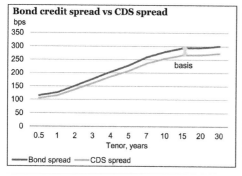
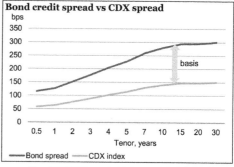

Figure 6.23: Two possible choices of basis risk factor for the same NMRF

the basis risk. However, it might be less liquid than a more general proxy (Figure 6.23, right side) which might lead to the proxy to become non-modellable itself.

Default Risk Charge

The IRC applied so far is replaced by the DRC. Since the migration risk is included under the ES, the DRC refers exclusively to the default risk in order to avoid the possibility of the mitigation risk being taken into account twice. On top of enhanced requirements on the correlation calibration documentation, for instance, a two-factor model is prescribed for the DRC. This could require substantial adaptation from some banks. Moreover, it must be taken into account that probabilities of default (PDs) lower than 0.03% are not allowed for any debtor. This floor was strongly criticised during the consultation phase,[53] since the default rates of AAA and AA debtors (especially sovereigns) are greatly overestimated.

Calculation methods for capital requirements

The aggregation of capital requirements to the overall amount *ACC* is slightly more complex compared to the existing framework, but still not a big challenge. The value *ACC* is calculated as in Equation 6.13:[54]

Equation 6.13

$$ACC = C_A + DRC + C_U, \tag{6.13}$$

where C_A represents the aggregated capital requirements of all trading desks with IMA-TB approval, *DRC* is the capital requirement for the Default Risk Charge and C_U is the aggregated capital requirement for trading desks without approval.

The capital requirements for trading desks with IMA-TB approval are calculated as in Equation 6.14:[55]

Equation 6.14

$$C_A = \max\{IMCC_{t-1} + SES_{t-1}; m_c \cdot IMCC_{avg} + SES_{avg}\} \tag{6.14}$$

The index "$t-1$" refers to the value of the respective amounts of the previous day und the index "avg" refers to the 12-week average. The variable *SES* indicates the sum of capital requirements for the scenario losses for non-modellable risk factors *SES*. The factor m_c amounts to 1.5 at least and can increase up to 2.0 within the course of backtesting, depending on the number of VaR breaches. In the above mentioned formula, *IMCC*

---

53   Cf. Deutsche Bank (2015).
54   Cf. BCBS 352 (2016), p. 64.
55   Cf. BCBS 352 (2016), pp. 54 and 63–65.

refers to the aggregated capital requirements on the modellable risk factors, which are calculated as in Equation 6.15:

Equation 6.15

$$IMCC = \rho \cdot ES_B + (1 - \rho) \cdot \sum_i ES_{i,B} \qquad (6.15)$$

In this formula, $ES_{i,B}$ refers to the expected shortfall, which has to be calculated in the same manner as ES_B, whereby only the risk factors of a specific desk are taken into account. The underlying intention of the above formula to calculate $IMCC$ is to limit hedging effects among the individual trading desks. The value of ρ is set to 0.5 in the above formula. The aggregation logic is outlined in Figure 6.24.

Besides the above-described requirements, there are additional ones arising out of the requirements on the already mentioned backtesting as well as on P&L attribution.

Backtesting and additional requirements

Backtesting is the main procedure used to measure model performance ex-post. This is why backtesting plays an important role under the IMA-TB. As described in Section 6.4.3, the backtesting result defines the value of the multiplication factor m_c and, as a consequence, directly determines capital requirements.

At present, there are controversial discussions as to whether the option of performing backtesting for the expected shortfall persists and, if so, to what extent.[56] Consequently, in the revised provisions of the IMA-TB, backtesting is still based on the VaR. Within

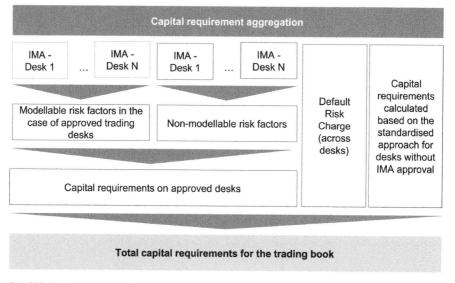

Figure 6.24: Capital requirement aggregation

56   See Carver (2014).

Quantile	Thresholds for backtesting overshootings (in one year)
97.5%	30
99%	12

Table 6.3: Thresholds for backtesting overshootings (VaR breaches)

the scope of backtesting, in addition to the 99% quantile, a 97.5% quantile was intro-duced for the VaR. In order to avoid distortions due to portfolio changes, a holding period of one day is used, and backtesting is performed against two different P&L vari-ants.[57] On the one hand, the actual trading outcome, which also depends on business transactions during the observed day, is used. On the other hand, the hypothetical trading outcome of the portfolio value for the positions at the end of the day must also be applied. In cases where the bank does not determine the hypothetical trading out-come up to now, costs regarding the system implementation will arise. An additional point to be taken into account is that backtesting must be carried out at trading desk level. If the number of backtesting breaches overruns the threshold value set forth in Table 6.3, the model approval for the respective desk is not granted or it is withdrawn and the capital requirements must be calculated based on the standardised approach mentioned in Section 6.3.

An additional condition for IMA-TB approval exists, besides general requirements and the above-explained backtesting. Said additional requirement consists of two criteria based on P&L attribution, which must also be applied at desk level. These criteria serve to verify if an ES model adequately models all relevant risk factors of the respective trading desk. In this context it can be simultaneously verified if the pricing models used by the risk management function provide reasonably similar results compared to the ones used in the front office systems. This could be a challenge, especially for exotic options or structured products. The two criteria based on P&L attribution are complied with (Equations 6.16/6.17) if:[58]

Equations 6.16/6.17

$$P\&L_1 := \left| \frac{\frac{1}{K} \sum_{i=1}^{K} \Delta_i - \delta_i}{\sqrt{\sigma^2(\delta)}} \right| \le 10\% \tag{6.16}$$

and

$$P\&L_2 := \frac{\sigma^2(\Delta)}{\sigma^2(\delta)} \le 20\% \tag{6.17}$$

---

57   Cf. BCBS 352 (2016), p. 73.
58   Cf. BCBS 352 (2016), pp. 57 and 71.

In the above formulas, Δ_i refers to the hypothetical change of the value of the portfolio with constant portfolio composition observed from day i to the next work day. δ_i denotes the portfolio value change that results from the observed risk factors in the ES model. Risk factors classified as non-modelable must also be taken into account. $\sigma^2(\cdot)$ is the respective P&L variance over the daily data of the past 12-month period. Both P&L metrics $P\&L_1$ and $P\&L_2$ must be calculated and reported on a monthly basis for each trading desk. If one of the two P&L indicators surpasses its limit of 10% or 20%, respectively, more than 4 times a year, the IMA-TB approval is withdrawn and the relevant trading desk must be capitalised based on the standardised approach.[59] The efforts that banks will face are determined by two factors. On the one hand, by the complexity of the traded instruments and, on the other, by the efficiency of the risk management system. If necessary, new risk factors will have to be defined – a task that is not negligible – and integrated into the existing systems in order to comply with model approval requirements.

The BCBS's consultative document of March 2018 replaces the two criteria of Equations 6.15/6.16 by two new methods which should be performed on a quarterly basis with data from the preceding twelve-month period. The first is based on the "Spearman correlation metric" which checks if the daily changes from the hypothetical P&L are ordered in the same fashion as the ones from the risk model. The second criterion is based on a straightforward similarity test of the hypothetical P&L and the risk P&L. The committee has provided two methods for discussion: The first alternative used the Kolmogorov-Smirnov, the second the Chi-squared test metric.

Furthermore, the new tests will not have a single pass/fail-threshold but feature two thresholds yielding a green zone (test result below the first threshold), an amber zone (result between the thresholds), and a red zone (result above the second threshold). If one or both of the tests give a result in the amber zone, the bank might still use the internal model but the desk will be subject to a capital charge depending on the corresponding capital requirements calculated with the standardised approach.

Additionally, after ongoing discussion with the industry the committee acknowledged that the purpose of the P&L attribution test is not to test for differences in market data, and therefore allowed market data transformations when calculating the risk-theoretical P&L.

6.4.4 Impact on capital requirements

The results of the "Interim Impact Analysis" carried out by the BCBS make an impact analysis of the new capital requirements possible. Within the course of this analysis, a total of 78 banks provided data. Table 6.4 shows the changes regarding capital requirements for individual risk factor classes.[60] As multiplier m_c, the same value of a bank's

---

59 Cf. BCBS 352 (2016), p. 57.
60 Cf. BCBS 346 (2015), p. 7.

Risk type	Change in capital requirements (existing IMA to IMA-TB)
Interest rate	−20%
Credit spreads	+48%
Equity	+29%
Commodity	+22%
Foreign exchange	+15%

Table 6.4: Results of the Interim Impact Analysis

current VaR model was used. It must be taken into account that the variation among the values reported by the banks is very large. The standard deviation for all risk types is larger than the absolute average change.

Against the backdrop of liquidity horizons, the results are not surprising. If a single trading desk, that only trades products which belong to the same liquidity group j, is observed, capital requirements for risk factors with longer liquidity horizons increase disproportionately. The reason hereof is the scaling method introduced with the third consultation paper. Furthermore, the calculations for the "Interim Impact Analysis" were carried out with the values of the third consultation paper instead of with the final values for liquidity horizons.[61] In the third consultation paper, 10, 20, 60, 120, and 250 days were still used as liquidity horizons which were then adjusted to the values in the final version (Table 6.5).[62] In order to estimate the differences between these two versions, Table 6.5 shows the approximate effects of changes on capital requirements. The "square-root T rule" was used for this purpose.

The risk metric shift from VaR to ES has less impact on the results than the introduction of the differentiated liquidity horizons. For risk factors that are modelled using a normal distribution, and portfolios where the value change depends linearly on the risk factor change, $ES_{97,5\%} \approx VaR_{99\%}$ applies. If $VaR_{99\%}$ or $ES_{97,5\%}$ is greater depends on the loss distribution, besides the non-linearity of the portfolio.

J	Liquidity horizon LH (third consultation paper)	Liquidity horizon LH (final paper)	Changes in capital requirements
1	10	10	0%
2	20	20	0%
3	60	40	−18%
4	120	60	−29%
5	250	120	−31%

Table 6.5: Comparison of liquidity horizons

---

61   Cf. BCBS 305 (2015).
62   Cf. Deutsche Bank (2015) and Barclays (2015).

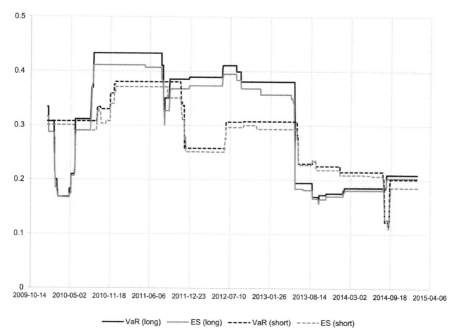

Figure 6.25: 99% VaR and 97.5% ES for two hypothetical portfolios

Figure 6.25 compares the $VaR_{99\%}$ and $ES_{97,5\%}$ for a holding period of 10 days. This graph is based on two hypothetical portfolios with a 10-year swap rate as only one risk factor and gamma equal to zero. The first portfolio is "long", the second is "short" in this risk factor. It can be observed that even in the case of these two very simple portfolios, the difference between $VaR_{99\%}$ and $ES_{97,5\%}$ changes signs several times.

As described in Section 6.4.2, the new rules regarding model approval can lead to substantial expenses. In order to be able to estimate if a model approval for a new trading desk should be aimed at, the necessary costs to achieve this should be compared to the spared cost of equity. The results from the "Interim Impact Analysis" show that the standardised approach leads to significantly larger capital requirements than the IMA-TB.[63] Table 6.6 outlines the corresponding results.

In the proposed translation of BCBS 352 into European law,[64] the European Commission introduced only minor changes: The applicable liquidity horizons for credit spreads of European governments and for covered bonds issued by banks in the EU were reduced. This leads to reduced capital requirements for banks with larger activities in the respective sector. In addition, the EU text mandates the EBA to issue detailed guidelines for the treatment of non-modellable risk factors in the form of an ETS. It is worth noting that it is still unclear how the EU commission will incorporate the

63   Cf. BCBS 346 (2015), page 9.
64   Cf. "Proposal to amend rules on banking prudential requirements" (2016)

Risk type	Average increase
Interest rate	+1,024%
Credit spreads	+335%
Equity	+837%
Commodity	+579%
Foreign exchange	+364%

Table 6.6: Increase of capital requirements under the standardised approach compared to the IMA-TB

proposed changes made by the Basel Committee in BCBS 436. This is especially relevant for the topic of non-modellable risk factors and for the P&L attribution tests.

6.5 Business implications and impact in the financial markets

The simultaneous introduction of the FRTB together with the rest of the Basel IV regulation in a "Big Bang" has – together with the implementation of other regulations relevant for the markets space like MiFID II – created a very different business environment and this chapter shall attempt a holistic look at the future business implications for banks in this important part of their operations.

In the wake of the Global Financial Crisis 2007–2009, significant losses were experienced among private individuals, corporates, banks and even states. At the G20 meeting in 2009 a number of regulatory initiatives were outlined to prevent this from happening again. Some of the guiding principles outlined included a wish for more transparency, better investor protection, improved risk management capabilities and better and more consistent supervision. This was especially the case in the financial markets space as the high gearings and volatility spikes seen in the aftermath were markedly bigger than predicted by the models and risk management methodologies employed by most of the banks active as market makers. This problem has often been termed the "underestimation of the fat tails issue" in the Value at Risk model and is – together with a tougher definition of market liquidity for existing positions – the key reasons for the switch to the use of the expected shortfall approach in the new Internal Models Approach. Investor protection and safeguarding client assets were other important areas, where the financial markets in many people's eyes had room for improvement and these issues were also duly addressed in the MiFID II regulation.

As a consequence, the markets area has seen the introduction of several pieces of new regulation that have combined to create a completely new environment for banks to operate in and have necessitated a fundamental rethink of their markets divisions. Without wishing to provide a historical chronology of the various relevant pieces of regulation, the following shall strive to provide a combined summary of some of the key business consequences and trends including how these are already starting to affect the financial environment banks are operating within, with a special focus on banks' markets divisions.

6.5.1 Market microstructure

The market microstructure was first rocked by the introduction of MiFID II that came into effect on 3 January, 2018, and further disruption as a consequence of the roll out of the FRTB and Basel IV regulation as agreed on 7 December, 2017, can now be foreseen. Please see also the previous Sections 6.1–6.4 on the subject of a more detailed description of what FRTB entails.

Some of the key characteristics of this business disruption is evident, particularly the product offerings and the market depth and risk appetite.

The cost of capital involved in holding market risk (see sections 6.3 and 6.4) shall increase further and the impact especially on the OTC derivatives markets will be quite substantial. MiFID II has reduced the number of banks acting as market makers in OTC derivatives, and FRTB/Basel IV shall further exacerbate this trend. A significant number of banks shall be forced to act solely as brokers and/or provide white label platform solutions.

As outlined in Section 6.2, the FRTB requires a much clearer trading desk definition, including the relevant group of traders, risk management policies, business strategy and supervisor approval. The supervisor shall thus have a much more active involvement in a bank's markets operation and daily reporting of limits, limit breaches and risk positions is a key requirement. A trading desk needs to have clearly designated traders, including a head trader, a well defined risk management policy and an equally well defined and documented business strategy. The correct structuring of, and number of, trading desks is one of the areas, where optimisation possibilities exist. This optimisation exercise is described in more detail in Section 6.5.3 on possible solutions and workarounds. The bank-specific trading desk definition must be approved by the relevant national supervisor and the bank is also obliged to document how it meets the above three big picture criteria (see also Section 6.2.2 and Figure 6.4).

Corporate treasury functions will have fewer banks to choose amongst that are willing (and capable) of bearing the additional capital requirements. Over the last 5 years, the total amount of market risk managed by banks has, according to *Risk* magazine, been reduced by more than 50%.

Concentration risks amongst counter-parties capable of transacting in size will increase, while the ability to hedge portfolios quickly and efficiently will get severely limited, as banks increasingly reduce or outright relinquish their roles as market-makers. This is a problem currently much discussed among European institutional investors and sovereign debt agencies, as well as other major users of the financial markets. Since 2015, a number of non-regulated hedge funds have increasingly competed with banks in the role of market makers and this trend is bound to continue.

Maintaining bond inventories in the trading book under the FRTB framework will incur higher capital charges – banks will no longer be able to offset against the banking book leading to decreased inventories and hence significantly reduced liquidity in the markets.

Coupled with increased risk weights, wider bid-offer spreads will become the norm as banks will look to be compensated for the additional capital requirements, as well as the additional regulatory risks that must be factored in.

Pricing of existing products shall suffer as complexity in the new standard approach increases, and internal models for market, credit and CVA risks get capped or "outlawed".

6.5.2 The competitive landscape

The classic European corporate banking model – subsidising term lending with attractive and highly profitable ancillary products – shall be hit by a double whammy over the course of the next two to three years.

Market risk on average becomes more expensive by a factor 2–3 and term lending to large corporates also becomes drastically more expensive, as the minimum capital requirements reflect the coming cyclical buffers in Basel III, as well as the RWA increases in the coming Basel IV. Though the effect globally is limited, the European banks in particular will be affected as the financial structure in Europe has 70+% of corporate financing running through banks' balance sheets.

In particular, the large corporates just below the blue-chip top segment become a lot less attractive from a banking perspective; they require substantial amounts of term financing and the re-priced future revenue stream from ancillary products cannot any longer subsidise this increasingly expensive lending activity.

Historically, the key ancillary products have typically been OTC hedging products in Foreign Exchange, Interest Rates, Credit and Equity plus M & A advisory and Debt Capital Management, i.e. mainly typical markets products.

New regulatory environment including SBA, the new Standard Approach (see Section 6.3), and IMA, the new Internal Model (see Section 6.4) applying expected shortfall methodology, shall make for much increased complexity, more demanding data quality and -quantity – see the discussion of NMRF in Section 6.4 - and thus result in significantly tougher economics in servicing corporate and institutional customers with their hedging needs and requirements.

Looking to white label solutions, and strategic/tactical co-operations with major league banks, are some of the obvious responses. A continuation of the European bank consolidation seen since 2007 shall in most of the recently published research on the future of the banking industry be accelerated even further in the coming five years.

The size and significance of this trend are reflected in a number of studies by both investment banks and academia, where the conclusions typically predict that more than 20% market share in both CIB and Business Banking – somewhat less in Retail/Private Banking – shall change hands before the end of 2020. Within the markets space specifically, the shift in market share is predicted to be even higher – potentially in excess of 30%, largely due to the dramatic drop in average markets ROIC for European Tier 1 banks from around 30% in 2010 to around 10% in 2017(Bloomberg data, February, 2018).

The amount and complexity of the existing and coming regulation shall – all other things being equal – give bigger banks some competitive advantages in several product areas. An increased concentration of market share in some key product areas is the expected outcome, mainly for the remaining OTC products and the more bespoke markets offerings. Tier 1.5 and Tier 2 banks are the most vulnerable.

The dramatically increasing compliance costs from MiFID, and other already implemented markets relevant regulation, shall provide a further and more immediate argument for economies of scale and reduce the viability of running a market making operation at many Tier 2 banks. The increased complexity of both the new Internal Model and the new Standard Approach shall pull in the same direction.

Capital requirements for all derivatives will rise, and the Default Risk Charge and illiquidity charge captured as Add-On risk cause havoc for several SA/SBA banks (see the discussion in Section 6.3.2). The expected shortfall model that shall be the methodology for the new IMA approach, poses several challenges and requires much more preparatory work and investment (see the discussion in Section 6.4.3). The introduction of a capital floor limiting the capital utilisation advantage of applying an internal model is also widely expected to reduce the number of banks aiming to use the new expected shortfall IMA methodology as opposed to the new SBA Standard Approach.

The pricing of pretty much all financial assets and instruments shall change; some perhaps not too dramatically, others fundamentally.

A lot of Tier 2 banks shall focus on only owning and providing the best customer experience and in-source the products and required trading platforms, to keep their chosen longer-term targeted customers happy.

6.5.3 Possible solutions and workarounds

A number of workaround solutions can be identified but one should realise that considerable investments are required to make these feasible and have them implemented in time. Timing is also crucial, as a lot of detailed impact assessments and preparatory initiatives need to be initiated long before FRTB/Basel IV enters into force on the 1 January 2022.

The *right* changes and adjustments can lead to the bank having a more clearly defined and well-described business model, capital structure, customer and product focus.

A number of possible optimisation and workaround possibilities should be investigated in detail and efforts made to implement the chosen solutions quickly, so as to reduce the future ROE squeeze.

Some of the solutions for the markets space include rethinking the tasks a bank is prepared to outsource and the entire required framework for this process, development of standardised and simplified CSA-light families for different key customer segments, expanding/establishing existing product segments/sub-segments, where a pull/push synergy potentially makes sense. As experienced up to the introduction of MiFID II, a number of product areas probably would have to be exited, but care should be given to identifying long-term viable products and not just applying short-term thinking based upon existing market conditions and the current macro economic market environment.

For banks choosing to opt for the new IMA, deciding the structure and optimal number of trading desks is a key element and many views have been expounded on this subject.

Though the optimal solution does vary from bank to bank, depending upon the overall business model, including customer and product mix, a couple of more definite observations and recommendations can be made.

As the approval for the Internal Models Approach (IMA) is now given on a single trading desk basis, and the approval process has intensified, with some very stringent and difficult to satisfy requirements like the P&L attribution test, the number of possible combinations increase very rapidly. Applying an iterative process in seeking to optimise the overall trading desk structure, can be recommended.

This process can be structured in different ways but should generally contain the following five elements.

1. **Strategy set-up.** Banks set their own priorities. For example, minimising the capital charge.

2. **Definition of limitations**. The fact that there are many combinations of trading desk set-ups does not mean all of them are relevant. In this phase, some limitations are set. For example, those desks for which approval of IMA is very unlikely, should be eliminated a priori from the range of possible choices and be directly assigned to the Standardised Approach (SBA).

3. **Charge breakdown**. Each product is analysed to identify which components of the capital charge it would be subject to under each of the approaches.

4. **Products' assignation**. Based on the mapping done in the previous step, products are assigned to a group with other homogeneous products, e.g., those which are subject to all three charge components – a general market risk component (either sensitivity

based or expected shortfall based), a default risk charge for instruments subject to jump-to-default risk and finally an add-on, based on the residual risk - and under both approaches.

5. **Pattern identification**. In each of the groups established, the charge is calculated under both approaches, to identify patterns of "better" behaviour. For example, exotic equity options might receive a lower charge in general under the IMA. These patterns will guide the choice of which products should be assigned to which desks and which approach to use for these desks.

The approach described above is relatively quick and more statistically solid than a brute force one, which tries all combinations, but does also require a certain degree of iteration.

For more about specifically the optimal split between IMA and SBA trading desks see Section 6.6 below on optimisation considerations.

Identifying and implementing all the optimal workaround solutions for a given bank is not a trivial exercise and necessitates a thorough understanding of the bank, it's chosen business model, customer characteristics and behaviour, as well as how the market's space *per se* is going to change over the coming years.

As many of the more effective and long-term promising workaround solutions in the markets space, require considerable investment in skillsets, systems and the building of long term partnerships, this is not an exercise that can be counted on to have a quick implementation period.

Choosing the right workaround solutions should also ideally be seen as a supporting element in a bank's overall business strategy and not as just a quick fix to a short-term problem in the markets area.

6.6 Optimisation considerations

Under the new regulation of BCBS 352,[65] it is allowed to nominate only a subset of trading desks for IMA, whereas the rest of the desks will still be capitalised using the SBA. In this Section, we will see that this new rule opens up new opportunities, but also bears risks.

Overall IMA capital requirements are expected to be lower than those using the SBA. Therefore the initial thought is to receive IMA approval for all trading desks. But the implementation of an IMA also triggers additional costs such as the development of an ES model itself and the fulfilment of the requirement of a sophisticated data structure, which must be sufficient for a desk to pass eligibility testing, i.e. P&L attribution and backtesting (initial set-up and maintenance).

---

65   Cf. BCBS 352 (2016).

Therefore, the evaluation of the benefits in cost of capital for an IMA implementation and recurring implementation and maintenance costs is required for sound decision-making. These benefits and costs might heavily differ from trading desk to trading desk, which leads to the utilisation of a selective IMA desk structure, where only a subset of trading desks is nominated for IMA.

6.6.1 Selective IMA – general aspects

For the purpose of regulatory capital calculations, a "trading desk" is defined as a group of traders or trading accounts that implements a well-defined business strategy, operating within a clear risk management structure, defined by the bank but with the definition approved by supervisors for capital purposes (see also Section 6.1). While nominating trading desks for IMA, meeting these qualitative criteria seems rather easy; the final selection is definitely not. An IMA desk selection cannot just be leveraged from operational desk definitions but must be defined in agreement with economic capital and cost-saving considerations which have to be performed for each trading desk.

When evaluating which desks to opt for IMA, positive and negative selection criteria have to be compared carefully. However, as so often, the devil is in the detail. On the one hand, it seems favourable to choose desks which currently show a high capital charge, have a high proportion of modellable risk factors, do not demand default risk charge (DRC) or do not diminish any diversification benefits. On the other hand, meeting the strict criteria for risk factors considered to be modellable is not easy, and their calibration is calculation-intense. Furthermore, it is the extra capital charge for non-modellable risk factors which are driving the desk's regulatory capital costs for which the market data modellability is not just straightforward. Last but not least, being confident in passing the eligibility tests for backtesting and P&L attribution is crucial as failing my occur from one day to another and, hence, having a solid strategic capital allocation planning in place is of high importance buffering possible switches to SA.

In addition to the individual desk optimisation, there is of course also further optimisation potential among different desks that should be investigated. To give an example, internal risk transfers or inter-desk-hedges might help to further improve the desk set-up or reduce capital costs by consciously concentrating specific risk classes on a dedicated IMA desk from other SBA desks where certain risks unintentionally occur as a by-product from their daily trading activities.

At the bottom line, a thorough evaluation may lead to an adjustment of the trading desk hierarchy. Furthermore, a complete business case evaluating the benefits in cost of capital against IMA implementation and maintenance costs is required for a well-founded desk structure, and the IMA trading desk hierarchy must be chosen such that diversification effects are correctly taken into account.

6.6.2 Example I: Diversification benefit realisation

In order to better understand the possible loss of diversification benefits when applying a selective IMA, it is instructive to have a closer look at the following trading book model: Suppose the trading book is partitioned in a sufficiently high number of trading desks, N. Each of these desks yields an individual capital requirement under SBA of C^{Desk}. If applying IMA, this requirement can be reduced to ηC^{Desk}. Furthermore, we assume that having two desks on SBA, a diversification benefit of D can be realised. If those desks are on IMA, the diversification benefit is assumed to be ξD. Let β be the fraction of desks whose capital requirements are determined using the IMA. The overall capital requirements $C_{\xi,\eta}(\beta)$ can then be estimated by

$$C_{\xi,\eta}(\beta) \approx NC^{\text{Desk}}[1 - (1 - \eta)\beta] - \frac{N^2 D}{2}[(1 - \beta)^2 + \xi \beta^2]$$

It is not difficult to see that for $\beta = 0$ one obtains $NC^{\text{Desk}} - \frac{N^2 D}{2}$, which, for large N, is approximately the capital requirement under pure SA. On the other hand, taking $\beta = 1$, yields approximately the IMA capital requirement, $C_{\xi,\eta}(1) \approx \eta NC^{\text{Desk}} - \xi \frac{N^2 D}{2}$.

An equivalent form of the above equation is

$$C_{\xi,\eta}(\beta) \approx C^{\max} \left[\frac{2}{1 + \eta} - \frac{1 - \eta}{1 + \eta} \frac{1 - (1 + \xi)\beta\,(2\beta_0 - \beta)}{1 - (1 + \xi)\beta_0} \right]$$

where $\beta_0 = \dfrac{1 - \frac{1 - \eta}{N} \frac{C^{\text{Desk}}}{D}}{1 + \xi}$.

It is important to note that, for certain choices of the parameters, $C_{\xi,\eta}(\beta)$ has a maximum at β_0 within the interval between 0 and 1. This implies that, starting from a pure SA trading book at $\beta = 0$, moving the first desk to IMA will *increase* the overall capital requirement for the trading book. Only if a sufficient number of desks, $\beta > 2\beta_0$, is nominated and eligible for IMA, a capital benefit is realised (Figure 6.26).

One way to mitigate this methodological artefact is to choose a trading desk structure in the first place that minimises the inter-desk diversification benefit, referred to as D in the high-level model above. If D is sufficiently small, $C_{\xi,\eta}(\beta)$ will be monotonically decreasing and a capital benefit can be realised even with a small number of desks on IMA.

Admittedly, this model does not represent the complexities of an actual trading book scenario. However, it does show that moving towards IMA requires adaptions of the trading desk structure and trading process in order to achieve capital benefits. One particularly important aspect is risk factor clustering to reduce inter-desk diversification effects.

6.6.3 Example II: Optimisation of risk factors

Based on the above mentioned aspects, a reasonable desk to be set under IMA would be an FX desk trading mostly vanilla products. The risk factors can be expected to qualify

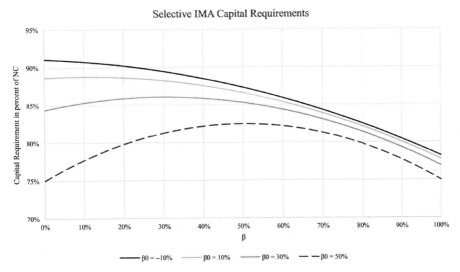

Figure 6.26: Selective IMA capital requirements

as modellable, and there is no need for a default risk charge. Furthermore, a vanilla FX desk can be assumed to pass eligibility testing easily.

It is instructive to have a closer look at the capital requirements of a vanilla FX desk: The EURUSD exposure is attributed a risk weight of roughly 21% in the SBA. This should be compared with the effective risk weight resulting from the IMA, i.e. the stressed liquidity-horizon adjusted expected shortfall of the EURUSD rate, of less than 10%. As a consequence, it can be estimated that the capital requirements for a bank's EURUSD exposure can be halved by nominating it for IMA.

This observation holds for other currency pairs as well. A small overview of effective risk weights for the main currency pairs are given in the list below.[66]

- effective IMA risk weight of EURUSD ≈ 9%
- effective IMA risk weight GBPUSD ≈ 15%
- effective IMA risk weight CHFUSD ≈ 16%

6.7 Conclusions

As a consequence of the new trading book provisions, the management is stripped of competences that usually fall within their field of action. The shift between books is only accepted under extraordinary circumstances and requires supervisory approval. The challenge, therefore, is to make active management decision possible despite restrictions. The requirements regarding daily look-through of funds could bring about unwanted incentives. Banks could establish a unit of funds that are not subject to

66   Data Source: FRED – Economic Data, St. Louis FED, empiric ES with moving one-year window.

a daily look-through and deliberately prevent a fund from falling under the definition of the trading book. The shifting of business activities in funds and the camouflaging of the trading outcomes result is precisely what the Committee is trying to avoid.

Immediate needs for action and optimisation opportunities exist above all in the area of position management and adjustment of business strategy. The effects of innovations should be analysed by banks at an early stage to make timely strategic decisions and be able to recognise necessary changes over time. This would ensure that adjustment is efficiently implemented.

The adequacy of the previous **standardised procedure** in different risk areas has already been put into question by several scientific studies. The risks arising from business activities are too complex to be evaluated using simple and standardised methods. Rossignolo et al (2012) are of the opinion that capital requirements are not acceptable and far from covering losses that occur in crisis situations.[67] Prescott (1997) obtained similar results. In his analyses, standardised procedures achieved the worst performance within a series of alternative approaches.[68]

Banks with small to medium business transactions, that will mainly apply the SBA, could face problems in determining the necessary sensitivities for all their positions due to the approach's greater complexity.

Reports to the supervisors will take place on a monthly basis in the future. Details on the actual scope of the report are currently not known. The present requirements within the framework of Basel III monitoring provide a first impression. It remains to be seen to what extent these proposals will be implemented at national level. It can be assumed that the reporting duty will reflect the structure of the standardised approach as well as its main components. A requirement leap as from Basel I to Basel II for credit risk could also be conceivable.

Within the framework of the regulatory consistency assessment programme (RCAP), it was determined based on a sample of banks that the supervisory **disclosure for the trading book** must be adjusted and considerably improved.[69] The requirements of the trading book compared to the banking book are significantly less severe. The Basel Committee addresses the composition of the trading book, its boundary to the banking book and the composition of the banks' trade area in the new provisions. For details, the Basel Committee remits to a separate document since this topic is not taken up in the final framework (see also the chapter on disclosure).

The new **Basel Standard for market risks** confronts banks with a series of adjustments and changes about the determination of minimum capital requirements for price risks arising from open positions. From the results of the performed quantitative impact study (QIS), it can already be inferred that the new requirements can bring about a

---

67 Cf. Rossignolo/Fethi/Shaban (2012), page 1331.
68 Cf. Prescott (1997).
69 Cf. BCBS 240 (2013).

significant increase of capital requirement for market price risks depending on the trading strategy.[70] Compared to the current market risk framework, the increase of the average weighted capital requirements – according to the Basel Committee – amounted to 40 percent. However, these numbers do not yet reflect calibration by the final framework. Recent test calculations show a much more diverse picture. Similar to the other new approaches proposed by the Basel Committee, the capital requirement can increase for certain portfolios and products, but can also decrease for some banks.

Based on this outlook, banks will have to brace themselves for a future capital requirement adjustment. Except for the expected capital requirement increase, generalised statements cannot be made on the revised standardised approach. The effects of the risk-sensitive approach will vary depending on the portfolio, business model and size of the bank. Based on early test calculations and analyses at trading desk level, individual impacts can be estimated.

The increased complexity of the standardised approach impacts a series of strategic and procedural aspects. For example, gap analyses help appraise if the requirements on data availability and quality are complied with. Moreover, banks will most likely also face adjustments regarding the IT infrastructure to ensure reporting capacity over a standard reporting software. If a manual reporting process is inevitable during the transition phase, it should be planned and implemented at an early stage. This is also associated with extra costs in the implementation phase.

The revised provisions on the **IMA-TB** entail different consequences for credit institutes. In the future, IMA-TB approval shall take place per trading desk, which provides banks with greater flexibility; however, the requirements for the use of internal models for market risk are significantly more severe. Compliance with the increased requirements is partially connected to a considerable amount of effort that is bank-specific. This could go as far as putting the profitability of internal models for market risk of some banks in question. Banks should analyse in advance which positions or portfolios an IMA-TB approval pays off compared to the standardised approach. It must be taken into account that not only under the IMA-TB but also under the SBA, the level of detail and the complexity clearly increased compared to the present regulatory framework.

Moreover, some banks will face challenges in terms of risk management of portfolios with less liquid positions due to the new liquidity horizons. Consequently, the revised provisions could, for example, make specific existing hedging relations disadvantageous from the regulatory point of view and thus create incentives not to secure certain positions in the future. In consequence, some banks will most likely have to adapt risk management to specific positions or portfolios or, alternatively, review their business model and possibly give up specific segments. This will probably go hand in hand with a significant need for adaptation. The revised provisions on IMA-TB could

---

70   Cf. BCBS 346 (2015) and Basel Committee on Banking Supervision (2016).

bring about significant negative impacts on the liquidity of specific markets or market segments as, for instance, in the sovereign debt market.

Recommended Literature

Acerbi, C./Tasche D. (2002): Expected Shortfall: A natural coherent alternative to value at risk, Economic Notes, Vol: 31, 2002, S. 379–388.

Barclays (2015): Re – Fundamental review of the trading book: outstanding issues (d305); available under: http://www.bis.org/bcbs/publ/comments/d305/barclays.pdf

Basel Committee on Banking Supervision; BCBS (2014): Instructions for Basel III Monitoring (Quantitative Impact Study (QIS)).

Basel Committee on Banking Supervision; BCBS (2015): Instructions for Basel III Monitoring (Quantitative Impact Study (QIS)).

Basel Committee on Banking Supervision; BCBS (2016): Explanatory note on the revised minimum capital requirements for market risk.

Basel Committee on Banking Supervision; BCBS 24 (1996): Amendment to the Capital Accord to incorporate Market Risks, 1996.

Basel Committee on Banking Supervision; BCBS 158 (2009): Revisions to the Basel II market risk framework, 2009.

Basel Committee on Banking Supervision; BCBS 219 (2012): Fundamental review of the trading book, 2012.

Basel Committee on Banking Supervision; BCBS 240 (2013): Regulatory consistency assessment programme (RCAP) – Analysis of risk-weighted assets for market risk, 2013.

Basel Committee on Banking Supervision; BCBS 258 (2013): Discussion Paper, The regulatory framework: balancing risk sensitivity, simplicity and comparability, 2013.

Basel Committee on Banking Supervision; BCBS 265 (2013): Fundamental review of the trading book: A revised market risk framework, 2013.

Basel Committee on Banking Supervision; BCBS 305 (2014): Fundamental review of the trading book: Outstanding issues, 2014.

Basel Committee on Banking Supervision; BCBS 306 (2015): Capital floors: The design of a framework based on standardised approaches, 2015.

Basel Committee on Banking Supervision; BCBS 319 (2015): Interest rate risk in the banking book, 2015.

Basel Committee on Banking Supervision; BCBS 346 (2015): Fundamental review of the trading book – interim impact analysis, 2015.

Basel Committee on Banking Supervision; BCBS 352 (2016): Minimum capital requirements for market risk, 2016.

Basel Committee on Banking Supervision; BCBS 395 (2017): Frequently asked questions on market risk capital requirements, 2017.

Basel Committee on Banking Supervision; BCBS 408 (2017): Consultation document - Simplified alternative to the standardised approach to market risk capital requirements, 2017.

Basel Committee on Banking Supervision; BCBS 436 (2018): Consultative Document - Revisions to the minimum capital requirements for market risk, 2018.

Basel Committee on Banking Supervision; BCBS 437 (2018): Frequently asked questions on market risk capital requirements, 2018.

Carver, L. (2014): "Back-testing expected shortfall: mission possible?", published 17 October 2014 on Risk.net, available under: back-testing-expected-shortfall-mission-possible

Capital Requirements Regulation; CRR (2013): Regulation (EU) No 575/2013 of the European Parliament and of the Council of 26 June 2013 on prudential requirements for credit institutions and investment firms and amending Regulation (EU) No 648/2012.

CRR II (2016): Proposal for a Regulation of the European Parliament and of the Council amending Regulation (EU) No 575/2013 as regards the leverage ratio, the net stable funding ratio, requirements for own funds and eligible liabilities, counterparty credit risk, market risk, exposures to central counterparties, exposures to collective investment undertakings, large exposures, reporting and disclosure requirements and amending Regulation (EU) No 648/2012. COM(2016) 850 final, Brussels, 23.11.2016.

CRR II (2017): Comments by the Council of the European Union on the Proposal for a Regulation of the European Parliament and of the Council amending Regulation (EU) No 575/2013 as regards the leverage ratio, the net stable funding ratio, requirements for own funds and eligible liabilities, counterparty credit risk, market risk, exposures to central counterparties, exposures to collective investment undertakings, large exposures, reporting and disclosure requirements and amending Regulation (EU) No 648/2012, Brussels, 05.11.2017.

Commission Delegated Regulation (EU) No 153/2013 of 19 December 2012 supplementing Regulation (EU) No 648/2012 of the European Parliament and of the Council with regard to regulatory technical standards on requirements for central counterparties.

Deutsche Bank (2015): Deutsche Bank's (DB) response to the Basel Committee on Banking Supervision consultative document on the Fundamental Review of the Trading Book; available under: http://www.bis.org/bcbs/publ/comments/d305/deutschebank.pdf

Hull, J. C. (2015): Options, Futures und andere Derivate [Options, Futures and other Derivative]. Pearson, 2015.

Markowitz, H. (2014): Risk-return analysis – The Theory and Practice of rational investing. McGraw-Hill, 2014.

Prescott, E. C. (1997): The precommitment approach in a model of regulatory banking capital. Economic Quarterly, 83 (1), Federal Reserve Bank of Richmond, Virginia, 1997.

Rossignolo, A. F., Fethi, M. D., & Shaban, M. (2012): Market crises and Basel capital requirements: Could Basel III have been different? Evidence from Portugal, Ireland, Greece and Spain (PIGS). Journal of Banking and Finance, 37 (5), 1323–1339, 2012.

Acerbi, C., Szekely, B. (2014): Backtesting Expected Shortfall. MSCI Inc.

Gneiting, T. (2011): Making and Evaluating Point Forecasts. Journal of the American Statistical Association (106), pp. 746–762.

Carver, L. (2013): Mooted var substitute cannot be back-tested, says top quant. Risk magazine.

Corbetta, J., Peri, I. (2016): A New Approach to Backtesting and Risk Model Selection. Ecole des Ponts ParisTech, University of Greenwich.

Emmer, S., Kratz, M., Tasche, D. (2015): What Is the Best Risk Measure in Practice? A Comparison of Standard Measures. Journal of Risk 18(2), pp. 31–60.

Righi, M. B., Ceretta, P. S. (2013): Individual and flexible expected shortfall backtesting. Journal of Risk Model Validation, 7(3), pp. 3–20.

Du, Z., Escanciano, J. C. (2016): Backtesting expected shortfall – accounting for tail risk. Management Science.

Acerbi, C., Szekely, B. (2017): General properties of backtestable statistics. MSCI Inc.

Fissler, T., Ziegel, J. F., Gneiting, T. (2015): Expected Shortfall is jointly elicitable with Value at Risk – Implications for backtesting. Risk magazine.

7 CVA Risk Capital Charge Framework

Fanos Ciftci, Jasmin Pandya and Anne Leonhardt

The regulatory framework for the treatment of Credit Valuation Adjustment (CVA) risk was published in 2010 within the Basel III framework.[1] Identified weaknesses and inadequately contemplated aspects in the existing regulatory CVA framework as well as the further development of the topic within the accounting frameworks motivated the Basel Committee for Banking Supervision (BCBS) to submit the existing regulatory CVA framework to a fundamental revision, only one year after it was implemented at European level in 2014. As part of the new Basel IV package, on 1 July 2015 a new consultation paper, in which the Basel Committee describes the planned restructuring of the regulatory CVA framework, was published. Afterwards, the BCBS conducted quantitative impact studies (QIS)[2], made final adjustments to approaches and risk weights and eventually finalised the revised CVA risk capital framework in December 2017 together with the standardised approach to credit risk, the IRB Approach and operational risk requirements.[3] In line with those approaches, the revised CVA risk capital charge is expected to enter into force on 1 January 2022.[4]

This chapter on the revised CVA framework is divided into four sections. The first, "Credit Valuation Adjustment" presents the background and the content of the regulatory CVA framework as well as the definition of the term and provides a brief overview of available approaches in the final Basel IV standard. Sections 7.2 and 7.3 focus on the two main approaches "SA-CVA" as well as "BA-CVA" and outline in detail the Basel standard including the associated regulatory requirements. The chapter is wrapped up with section 7.4 "Additional aspects and expected effects".

7.1 Credit Valuation Adjustment

7.1.1 Definition of the term "Credit Valuation Adjustment"

Credit Valuation Adjustment (CVA) refers to the value adjustment of derivative transactions under consideration of counterparty credit risk. The CVA is also often referred to as the price to be paid to take account of changes in the creditworthiness of the counterparty in a derivative transaction. Within the management of counterparty credit risk, CVA plays an important role. CVA allows the inclusion of the creditworthiness of the counterparty in the valuation of a derivative transaction. When defining the CVA for supervisory purposes, the Basel Committee points out potential mark-to-market losses associated with a deterioration in the creditworthiness of a counterparty.[5] From the supervisory point of view, only the negative value

1 Cf. BCBS 189 (2010), page 31ff.
2 Cf. BCBS CVA QIS (2016).
3 Cf. BCBS 424 (2017).
4 Cf. BCBS 424 (2017), page 2.
5 Cf. BCBS 189 (2010), page 4, marginal no. 14b).

adjustments, which lead to a loss in the balance sheet and the P&L statement and therefore in the regulatory capital, are taken into account.

Several possibilities exist in practice to determine CVA. A differentiation is made between unilateral and bilateral CVA. In the first case, the bank only takes the creditworthiness of the counterparty into account. In the bilateral approach, however, the bank's own default risk is included in CVA calculation. CVA can be determined at portfolio level, at counterparty level, at netting-set level or at individual transaction level.[6]

Credit Valuation Adjustments have gained in importance in the wake of the recent financial crisis (2007–2009) when the financial system nearly collapsed. At that point in time, several banks had considerable losses in their OTC derivative portfolios that were less driven by actual counterparty defaults, but rather by the deterioration of the counterparty's creditworthiness and the subsequently necessary credit valuation adjustments (CVA) of the OTC derivative transaction.[7] The topic was immediately included in the agenda of accountants and supervisors and turned into a permanent task for financial institutions with IFRS 13 and Basel III at the latest. Within the scope of the international accounting standards (IAS 39/IFRS 9/IFRS 13)[8], the default risk is a factor to be taken into account within the fair-value pricing of derivatives and CVA determination. Due to the effects on regulatory capital requirements which resulted thereof, Basel III implemented the regulatory framework to treat the CVA risk and the regulatory capital charge for this risk.[9]

7.1.2 Background of the regulatory CVA

Since the implementation of Basel III, the CVA risk capital charge constitutes an additional regulatory capital requirement to cover mark-to-market losses on the expected counterparty risk for OTC derivatives besides capital requirements on counterparty credit risk (default risk).[10] Pursuant to the Basel standard, the regulatory requirements to treat the CVA risk is limited to the so-called unilateral CVA at counterparty level. According to the final Basel IV standard " ... CVA reflects the adjustment of default-free prices of derivatives and securities financing transactions (SFTs) [...] due to a potential default of the counterparty. Regulatory CVA may differ from CVA used for accounting purposes as follows (i) regulatory CVA excludes the effect of the bank's own default; (ii) several constraints reflecting best practices in accounting CVA are imposed on calculation of regulatory CVA".[11] Furthermore, in the context of regulatory

---

6   Cf. Talkenberger/Wehn (2012), page 9 et seq.
7   Additional information on the background of the CVA introduction from the regulatory point of view: BCBS 189 (2010), page 4, para. 14b).
8   CVA accounting was already required under IAS 39; IFRS 13 requires a more differentiated and broadened contemplation.
9   Cf. BCBS 189 (2010).
10   Cf. BCBS 189 (2010), page 37, para 99.
11   Cf. BCBS 424 (2017), page 109, para 1.

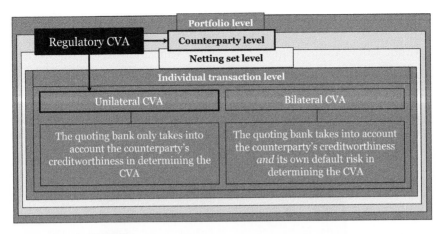

Figure 7.1: Unilateral and bilateral CVA

requirements for CVA risk, CVA is specified at a counterparty level. Figure 7.1 outlines the different forms of CVA and shows the relationship to regulatory CVA.

7.1.3 Revision of the CVA framework

The current CVA framework under Basel III admits two methods to determine the CVA risk capital charge. On the one hand, the "advanced method" for banks with IMM (internal model method) approval for counterparty credit risk and approval to use the market risk internal models approach for the specific interest-rate risk of bonds. On the other hand, there is the "standardised method" which can be applied without any further restrictions.[12] Both methods are designed in such a way that the counterparty's credit spread risk is the only CVA risk driver contemplated. Consistently, under the current CVA framework, only those hedging measures that hedge the credit spread risk are admissible for regulatory purposes. This includes single name CDS or single-name contingent CDS, which reference the counterparty directly, as well as Index CDS under certain conditions.[13]

An important driver of the CVA risk, namely, the exposure component, is currently not covered by the regulatory CVA framework. The exposure component in its role as exposure value, however, is directly linked to the price of all the transactions that are within the scope of the CVA risk capital charge. As these prices are sensitive to variability in underlying market risk factors, the CVA also materially depends on those factors.[14] Similarly, hedging measures of the exposure component, which are commonly used in practice to actively manage the CVA risk, are left out of consideration. The apparent weaknesses of the existing regulatory CVA framework

---

12   Cf. BCBS 189 (2010), Part VIII A and B, pages 31ff.
13   Cf. BCBS 189 (2010), page 34, para 102f.
14   Cf. BCBS 424 Summary (2017), page 7.

outlined here motivated the Basel Committee to carry out a substantial review of said framework. The regulatory requirements, which arise from the revised CVA framework, were finalised within the final Basel IV standard (BCBS 424) in December 2017. The Basel Committee pursues the following three goals with the review of the regulatory CVA framework (Figure 7.2):

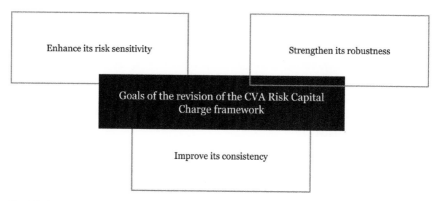

Figure 7.2: Goals of the revision of the CVA framework

- Enhance its risk sensitivity: The current CVA framework does not cover an important driver of CVA risk, namely, the variability of the exposure component. The exposure component, which depends on market risk factors, influences the CVA risk capital charge significantly. The revised CVA framework takes into account the exposure component of CVA risk along with its associated hedges of the market risk factors.
- Strengthen its robustness: In the opinion of the Basel Committee, CVA risk is a complex risk that cannot be modelled in a robust and prudent manner. Therefore, the final Basel standard does not include an internal model approach for CVA risk. Furthermore, the Basel Committee included a simplified approach for banks with a small non-centrally cleared derivative portfolio.
- Improve its consistency: Since the CVA is an adjustment to the price of a fair-valued derivative instrument, the regulatory capital charge for the CVA risk should be closely linked to the capital charge for market risk. Consequently, and for consistency purposes, the revised CVA framework is also based on the revised framework for the regulatory treatment of market risk (FRTB), which focuses on sensitivities of market risk factors.

With the revision of the CVA framework, the Basel Committee aims at determining CVA risk capital charges for all derivative transactions that are subject to the risk that a counterparty could default. Whether transactions are margined or not shall not play a role. It is clarified that instruments held in the banking book for the purposes of hedge accounting (e.g. interest rate derivatives in the banking book), shall also be subject to the CVA risk capital charge. In addition, the Basel Committee also provides that fair-valued securities financing transactions (SFTs) shall be encompassed in the

CVA risk capital charge. The sole exception included in the revised framework by the Basel Committee are transactions cleared through a qualified central counterparty. The revised scope of application for the CVA risk capital charge suggested by the Basel Committee is broader compared to the previous provisions set forth in the Basel III framework. This is due to the fact that the determination of CVA risk capital charge under the current Basel III treatment is limited to OTC derivatives and includes SFTs only if a bank's CVA losses from SFTs are deemed material.[15]

7.1.4 Hierarchy of approaches

The revised CVA framework consists of two approaches as well as a simplified method for calculating CVA capital. On the one hand, the standardised approach (SA-CVA), which adopts various elements from market risk requirements of the "Fundamental Review of the Trading Book (FRTB)". On the other hand, there is the so-called Basic CVA approach (BA-CVA). In its first consultation paper (BCBS 325), the Basel Committee considered the implementation of an internal model approach consistent with the FRTB as well.[16] The Basel Committee decided to drop the IMA-CVA approach due to its complexity and the entailed model risk.[17] Figure 7.3 outlines the two approaches as well as the simplified method of the revised CVA framework pursuant to the Basel IV final standard.

The Standardised Approach for CVA (SA-CVA) is designed for banks that can determine CVA based on the sensitivities of credit spreads of its counterparties. It can only be applied with the supervisor's approval. Banks must demonstrate to the satisfaction of their supervisors that they meet several regulatory requirements in terms of the calculation and risk management of the regulatory CVA. These are outlined in more detail in section 7.2.

The Basic CVA Approach (BA-CVA) can be applied by all banks that do not have approval to use the SA-CVA approach. The BA-CVA approach is basically an enhanced version of the current Basel III standardised CVA risk capital charge and can be divided into a reduced version (without consideration of hedges) as well as a full version (with recognition of hedges). The BA-CVA is described in more detail in section 7.3.

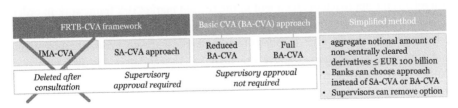

Figure 7.3: The revised CVA framework (BCBS 424)

---

15 Cf. BCBS 189 (2010), page 31, para 97.
16 Cf. BCBS 325 (2015), pages 9 and 25 – 27.
17 Cf. BCBS D424summary (2017), page 7; BCBS 362 (2016), page 4.

Moreover, the Simplified Method introduced in the final Basel IV standard is available to banks whose aggregate notional amount of non-centrally cleared derivatives is less than or equal to 100 billion euro (materiality threshold). Those banks may choose to set its CVA capital equal to 100% of capital requirements for counterparty credit risk. In this method, hedges are not recognised and supervisors may withdraw this option if the CVA risk is a material risk driver for a certain bank.

The SA-CVA and the BA-CVA can be applied simultaneously for different portfolios, e.g. if a bank does not fulfill the requirements to use the SA-CVA for some netting sets. These netting sets must be carved out from the SA-CVA and the BA-CVA must be used. The simplified method must be used for a bank's entire portfolio instead of the SA-CVA or BA-CVA.

In terms of capital floors, all approaches and methods described above are classified as "standard approaches". Hence, the use of a more advanced approach to calculate CVA capital can reduce overall risk weighted assets subject to the output floor. For a detailed description of the output floor, please refer to Chapter 9.

7.2 FRTB-CVA framework

7.2.1 Regulatory requirements for the application of the FRTB-CVA framework

In contrast to the consultation paper, where the Basel Committee sets forth two different methods to calculate the regulatory FRTB-CVA risk capital charge, credit institutions now face only one possible procedure under the FRTB-CVA. The final approach available within the FRTB-CVA framework, namely, the SA-CVA, is broken down into the following two main points:

- determination of the exposure component for the regulatory CVA, and
- determination of specific risk factor sensitivities to which the regulatory CVA reacts.

Although the internal model approach (IMA-CVA) for calculating the regulatory CVA risk capital charge was rejected during the consultation phase, the Basel Committee still retains the approach of alignment to the revised market risk framework in order to obtain consistency. Unlike the standardised approach under the revised market risk framework, the SA-CVA is subject to compliance with supervisory requirements and approval. As mentioned above the BA-CVA is mandatory for all banks that do not have approval to use the SA-CVA. In addition to this, the BA-CVA has to be calculated for any netting sets that the bank may wish to exclude from the SA-CVA calculation.

The application requirements address the following range of topics:

- minimum requirements,
- regulatory CVA calculation,

- eligible hedges, and
- multiplier.

Minimum requirements: Since the modelling and simulation of exposures and sensitivities are highly complex, the minimum requirements set forth that a bank must be able to model exposures and regularly calculate (at least monthly, and on supervisory demand) the CVA risk capital charge and CVA sensitivities. Within the portfolios, numerous drivers exist, which influence the exposure component and sensitivities. Some of them are hard to observe, difficult to measure and volatile.

Furthermore, the minimum requirements demand that a CVA desk (or a similar function) responsible for the risk management and hedging of regulatory CVA is established.

Exposure component for regulatory CVA: The regulatory CVA provides the basis for calculating the CVA risk capital charge under the SA-CVA which must be done for each counterparty with which the bank holds at least one covered position. BCBS 424 determines that only the accounting-based CVA method can be applied for the creation of discounted exposure profiles while the second IMM-based CVA calculation method of the consultation paper was rejected.

Since the determination of the exposure component is an important topic within the context of the revised CVA framework, it will be discussed in detail in the following chapter.

Eligible hedges: All transactions used for the purpose of mitigating CVA risk can be eligible hedges under the SA-CVA framework. This covers both – hedges of the counterparty credit spread as well as the exposure component. Instruments that cannot be included in the Internal Model Approach for market risk (IMA-TB) cannot be eligible hedges. This includes *inter alia* tranched credit derivatives. Non-eligible CVA hedges are treated as trading book instruments and are capitalised via market risk rules for the trading book. On the other hand, all instruments eligible as hedges for the regulatory CVA risk are not taken into account when calculating capital charges for the trading book or the banking book.

Multiplier: Compared to the market value of trading book instruments and the respective sensitivities, the calculation of CVAs and CVA sensitivities are subject to a higher level of model risk. To compensate for this risk, the expected shortfall measure used in the SA-CVA is scaled up via a multiplier m_{CVA}. In BCBS 424, the multiplier has a default value of 1.25. However, the default value of the multiplier can be increased by the bank's supervisory authority if it determines that the CVA calculation model used is subject to increased model risk. Figure 7.4 outlines the application requirements for the FRTB-CVA framework.[18]

---

18   In order to analyse the impact of setting the multiplier to 1, this point has been considered within a quantitative
     impact study conducted by the Basel Committee during 2016.

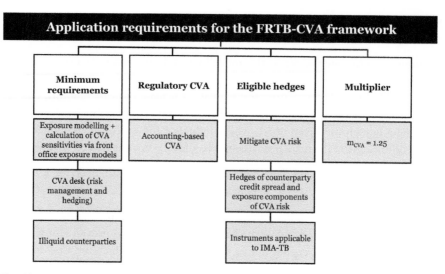

Figure 7.4: Application requirements for the FRTB-CVA framework

7.2.2 Exposure value for the FRTB-CVA

As was already briefly mentioned in section 7.2.1, the Basel Committee decided to discard the Internal Model Method (IMM)-based approach for generating scenarios for discounted exposure profiles since the complexity of the risk was not reflected in large parts of the positions in banks' trading books. Therefore, BCBS 424 leaves the banks with the accounting-based approach where exposure profiles are obtained via exposure models (the same data and procedures) used by a bank for calculating accounting and front office CVA. The purpose of this is to increase the convergence between accounting and regulatory CVA. According to BCBS 424, better alignment with the economic risk would result in a better recognition of hedging strategies used for accounting CVA and for the regulatory CVA risk capital charge. A complete convergence with the accounting CVA risk, however, is not possible since the consideration of their own default risk is not admissible in the regulatory context.

Although no explicit specifications are outlined for calculating the scenarios for discounted exposure profiles, BCBS 424 lays down three principles that must be followed when calculating CVA. All principles are unified by the use of up-to-date market data to the largest extent possible. The first principle is the use of the term structure of market-implicit probabilities of default. Second, market-consensus expected loss given default (ELGD) and third simulated paths of discounted future exposure must be used as input for the calculation of the expectation of future losses.

Moreover, with regard to the first principle, a bank must have a methodology in place to determine the credit spreads of illiquid counterparties. Credit spreads represent a risk factor within the calculation method of the FRTB-CVA framework, for which sensitivities must be determined. The following regulatory requirements must be complied with when determining credit spreads of illiquid counterparties:[19]

a) The credit spread curves of illiquid counterparties should be estimated from credit spreads observed in the markets of its liquid peers taking into account at least the rating, industry and region.
b) In certain cases, proxies may be developed based on market observation (e.g. country for regional government), although this must be justified in every case.
c) When no time series of credit spreads is observed in any of the counterparty's liquid peers (e.g. project finance, funds), a bank is allowed to use a more fundamental analysis of credit risk to proxy the spread. However, the resulting spread cannot be based solely on historical PD, but must relate to credit markets.

Nevertheless, some additional regulatory requirements must be complied with, such as:[20]

- For the margin period of risk a floor of $9 + N$ (N is equal to the re-margining period) business days must be applied.
- A market-implicit (risk-neutral) model calibration shall be used. Historical calibration is only permissible where a risk-neutral calibration is not possible due to the lack of market data.
- The distribution of modelled risk factors must account for the possible non-normality of the distribution of exposures, including the existence of leptokurtosis (also called "fat tails"), where appropriate.

Besides these rather technical or quantitative requirements, a series of additional qualitative requirements are mentioned in BCBS 424. Examples include:

- accounting-based exposure models must be independently validated,
- must be part of a CVA risk management framework, and
- the bank must have a process in place for ensuring compliance with a documented set of internal policies, controls and procedures concerning the operation of the exposure calculation engine.

7.2.3 Standardised approach for CVA (SA-CVA)

The standardised approach to determine the CVA risk capital charge within the FRTB-CVA framework (SA-CVA) is an adaptation of the standardised approach for market risk within the FRTB (SBA). This is the so-called sensitivity-based approach which uses the sensitivities of the regulatory CVA on credit spreads of counterparties and market risk factors prescribed by the Basel Committee as input. Basically, the calculation of the CVA risk capital charge within the SA-CVA takes place in four

---

19 Cf. BCBS 424 (2017), marginal no. 30.
20 Cf. BCBS 424 (2017), page 116.

sections: **risk class, risk type, risk factor and aggregation**. Within these four sections several calculation and aggregation steps take place to add parameters prescribed by the regulator, such as correlation factors and risk weights. The procedure within the mentioned sections is discussed below.

Risk class (delta and vega): The SA-CVA capital requirement is calculated as the simple sum of the capital requirements for delta and vega risks calculated for the entire CVA book (including eligible hedges). The capital requirement for delta and vega risks is calculated as the simple sum of the regulatory capital requirements for the risk types prescribed by the supervisors. A more detailed description of the designed calculation steps will be given below.

Risk Type: Within the section "risk type", the instruments and hedges of the CVA book are assigned to the following risk types prescribed by the supervisory authority: counterparty credit spreads, interest rate, foreign exchange, reference asset credit spreads, equity and commodity. The risk type counterparty credit spread is not taken into account in the calculation of the vega risk since it is approximately linear.

Risk factor: Sensitivities of the instruments and hedges contained in the CVA book regarding risk factors prescribed by the supervisory authority are determined in this section. For an interest rate transaction (in local currency) or the leading international currencies (USD, EUR, GBP, AUD, CAD, SEK, JPY), the risk factor is the risk-free yield curve (with the specified time horizons 1, 2, 5, 10 and 30 years) and the absolute change of the inflation rate. Other currencies to the ones specified above are treated differently, as the absolute change in the inflation rate and the parallel shift of the entire risk-free yield curve are set as the risk factors. Within the risk type counterparty credit spread, the absolute shift of credit spread of the counterparty (within the prescribed tenors of 0.5, 1, 3, 5 and 10 years) represents the regulatory risk factor. In addition, sensitivities are weighted within prescribed "buckets" via prescribed risk weights.

Aggregation: Taking into account the correlation parameter and the multiplier (see section 7.2.1), weighted sensitivities are aggregated in the aforementioned "buckets" and risk classes. The following buckets are prescribed by the supervisory authority for each risk type:

Interest rate: individual currencies in different maturity brackets;

FX: all individual currencies, except a bank's domestic currency;

counterparty credit spread: credit quality and sector;

reference asset credit spread: credit quality and sector;

equity: size, region and sector;

commodity: commodity groups.

Figure 7.5 shows the calculation steps under the SA-CVA.

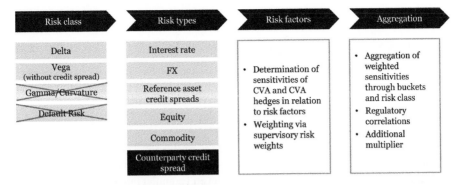

Figure 7.5: Calculation steps under the SA-CVA

To clarify the procedure under the SA-CVA, an overview of the main calculation and aggregation steps as well as of the use of regulatory parameters is illustrated in the following based on the formulas to be applied. After calculating the sensitivities of the aggregated CVA S_k^{CVA} and of all eligible hedges S_k^{Hdg} for each risk factor k in the risk type, these are weighted with the prescribed risk weights. The result of the sum of the weighted sensitivities is the net-weighted sensitivities for each risk factor. Equations 7.1–7.3 show the described calculation steps:

Equations 7.1–7.3

$$WS_k^{CVA} = RW_k * s_k^{CVA} \tag{7.1}$$

$$WS_k^{Hdg} = RW_k * s_k^{Hdg} \tag{7.2}$$

$$WS_k = WS_k^{CVA} + WS_k^{Hdg} \tag{7.3}$$

The weighted sensitivities for each risk factor must be aggregated into a capital charge K_b within each bucket b according to Equation 7.4. As can be observed in formula (4),[21] the correlation parameter ρ_{kl} is applied here. It indicates the degree of correlation among the individual risk factors. Moreover, parameter R, set at 0.01, prevents the possibility of perfect hedging of CVA risks.

Equation 7.4

$$K_b = \sqrt{\left[\sum_{k \in b} WS_k^2 + \sum_{k \in b} \sum_{l \in b; l \neq k} \rho_{kl} * WS_k * WS_l \right] + R * \sum_{k \in b} \left[\left(WS_k^{Hdg} \right)^2 \right]} \tag{7.4}$$

Bucket-level capital charges are then aggregated across buckets within each risk type K based on Equation 7.5. The regulatory correlation parameters prescribe the degree of correlation among individual buckets γ_{bc}. Moreover, multiplier m_{CVA} presented in section 7.2.1 is applied here.

---

21 This equation has been revised during the quantitative impact study in 2016.

Equation 7.5

$$K = m_{CVA} * \sqrt{\sum_b K_b^2 + \sum_b \sum_{c \neq b} \gamma_{bc} * K_b * K_c} \tag{7.5}$$

Even though the risk factors and sensitivities within the SA-CVA are determined based on the definition and validation requirements of the FRTB,[22] the SA-CVA differs from the SBA in some essential aspects.[23] The main differences are as follows.

a) **Reduced granularity of market risk factors:** within the FRTB, granular market risk factors are applied. For instance, within the risk type interest rate, the number of the maturity brackets is decreased. While eleven (granular) maturity brackets (risk factors) are prescribed within the FRTB, only four maturity brackets are used under the SA-CVA.

b) **Absence of default and curvature (gamma) risks:** The non-contemplation of the default risk is due to the fact that it is already taken into account by the provisions on capital charge for the counterparty credit risk. In terms of the gamma risk, the Basel Committee aims at reducing calculation efforts.

c) **Use of a conservative risk aggregation:** the risk that the non-contemplation of the gamma risk and the reduced market risk factor granularity inadequately depict the risk is compensated by a conservative risk aggregation within SA-CVA compared to the SBA. Within the conservative risk aggregation, no diversification effects between delta and vega risks are permissible and a complete hedging offset is prevented by parameter R in formula 4.

d) **Use of multiplier m_{CVA}:** the multiplier set at 1.25 is used to reflect existing model risks.

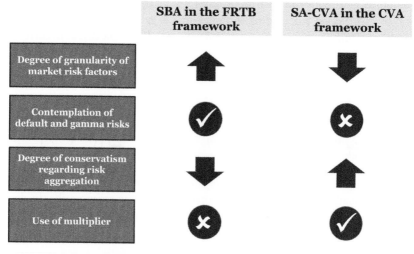

Figure 7.6: Differences between the SBA and the SA-CVA

---

22   Cf. BCBS 352 (2016).
23   Please refer to Chapter 6 for a presentation of the revised standardised approach for market risk.

Figure 7.6 shows the main differences between the SA-CVA and the sensitivities-based approach of the FRTB framework.

7.3 Basic CVA framework

7.3.1 Side note: Calculation of the CVA Risk Capital Charge under the current standardised method according to Basel III

The current Basel III CVA framework already provides for a standardised method to determine the CVA risk capital charge.[24] It is applied by all those institutions that do not comply with the requirements for the advanced method to calculate the CVA risk capital charge in accordance with paragraph 98 of BCBS 189. Similarly, within the scope of the revised Basel IV CVA framework, the BA-CVA approach represents the method used by all those institutions that are not allowed to, or do not want to, apply the SA-CVA approach. Against the backdrop that the circle of users of the current standardised method will most likely apply the new BA-CVA approach, it is considered worthwhile to explain the regulatory requirements that arise from the use of the current standardised method in detail at this point in order to specify the differences between these two methods.

Following the current standardised method, the capital requirement for the CVA risk of all counterparties (K) is determined at portfolio level based on Equation 7.6.

Equation 7.6

$$K = 2{,}33 * \sqrt{h} * \sqrt{\left(\sum_i 0{,}5 * w_i * (M_i * EAD_i^{total} - M_i^{hedge} B_i)\right)^2 + \sum_i 0{,}75 * w_i^2 * (M_i * EAD_i^{total} - M_i^{hedge} B_i)^2} \qquad (7.6)$$

where:

h: the one-year risk horizon (in units of a year); h = 1
w_i: the weight applicable to counterparty i, which shall be mapped based on an external credit rating

The weighting rates to be used for each external credit rating are outlined in Table 7.1.

In the event that no external credit rating is available for a counterparty, the Basel III rules text (BCBS 189) requires from banks using the IRB (internal rating-based

---

24   Cf. BCBS 189 (2010), para 104.

Credit Quality Step	weight (w)
1	0.7%
2	0.8%
3	1.0%
4	2.0%
5	3.0%
6	10.0%

Table 7.1: Weighting rates depending on the credit rating

approach) to match the internal assessment of a counterparty to an external credit rating subject to supervisory approval.[25]

$EAD_{i,total}$: The EAD (Exposure at Default) component (summed across all netting sets with the counterparty) is determined pursuant to the mark-to-market/current exposure method, the standardised method or the internal model method (IMM). Non-IMM banks must discount the EAD using a prescribed discount factor that is also used for B_i and B_{ind}.

Equation 7.7

$$EAD\ Discount\ Factor_{Non-IMM\ banks} = \frac{1 - e^{-0.05*M_i}}{0.05 * M_i} \qquad (7.7)$$

B_i: The notional of purchased single name CDS (summed if more than one position) referencing counterparty (i) and used to hedge CVA risk. That notional amount shall be discounted by applying the prescribed discount factor using $M_{i,hedge}$.

B_{ind}: The full notional value of one or more credit index default swap of purchased protection used to hedge CVA risk. That notional amount shall be discounted by applying the prescribed discount factor using M_{ind}.

At this point it should be pointed out that where a counterparty is included in an index on which a credit default swap used for hedging counterparty credit risk is based, the institution may subtract the notional amount attributable to that counterparty in accordance with its reference entity weight from the index CDS notional amount (B_{ind}) and treat it as a single name hedge (B_i) of the individual counterparty with maturity based on the maturity of the index.[26]

w_{ind}: The weight applicable to index hedges. It shall be determined by calculating a weighted average of w_i that is applicable to the individual constituents of the index i.e. w_i is based on the average spread of index 'ind'.

---

25   Within the European Union, this requirement was specified in more detail also for banks using the standardised approach for credit risk and included specific requirements for positions with high risk (please refer to Art. 384 CRR). Banks using the standardised approach apply a risk weight w_i of 1% for unrated counterparties. Furthermore, for items "associated with a particular high risk", in the sense of Art. 128 CRR under the standardised approach, a risk weight of 3% is applied.
26   Cf. BCBS 189 (2010), page 35, para 104.

M_i: The effective maturity of the transactions with counterparty (i). The Basel II accord provides for a specific calculation of this parameter depending on the method applied to determine EAD. IMM banks determine the effective maturity pursuant to the formula provided in Annex 4, paragraph 38 Basel II accord.[27] Non-IMM banks calculate the effective maturity in accordance with the third bullet point of para 320 of the Basel II accord as notional-weighted average maturity of a netting set.[28] M_i shall not be capped at 5 years.

$M_{i,hedge}$: the maturity of the hedge with notional B_i (the quantities $M_{i,hedge}$ B_i are to be summed if there are several positions).

M_{ind}: the maturity of the index hedge. In the case of more than one index hedge position, M_{ind} is the notional-weighted maturity.

Within the current CVA framework under Basel III, the same requirements on hedging transactions apply under the advanced as well as under the standardised method. Pursuant to paragraph 103 Basel III accord, single name CDS, other equivalent hedging instruments referencing the counterparty directly and, under specific circumstances, index CDS shall be eligible instruments for the purpose of calculating the CVA risk capital charge.

In Figure 7.7, is an example calculation representing the standardised method to determine the CVA risk capital charge. The basis of this example is an interest rate swap for which the EAD component was determined based on the current exposure method (CEM). The value of the EAD component was already discounted by the regulatory discount factor (disc. EAD).The residual term is four years, assuming that no hedging transactions were closed. The resulting CVA risk capital charge under the premises set forth herein is also outlined (Figure 7.7).

Transaction data:
- Instrument: IR Swap
- Notional value   100,000,000
- Rating: AA
- Maturity: 4 years
- Collateral: not specified
- Market value: 0

CEM			CVA (Basel III)	
Market value		0	Disc. EAD	453,173
Volatility		0.50%	Maturity	4
AddOn		500,000	Weight	0.70%
EAD		**500,000**	**CVA**	**29,565**

Figure 7.7: Example calculation - current CVA Risk Capital Charge (1/2)

27 Cf. BCBS 128 (2006), page 262.
28 Cf. BCBS 128 (2006), page 75.

Transaction data:
- Instrument: IR Swap
- Notional value   100,000,000
- Rating: AA
- Maturity: 10 years
- Collateral: not specified
- Market value: 0

CEM			CVA (Basel III)	
Market value		0	Disc. EAD	1,180,408
Volatility		1.50%	Maturity	10
AddOn		1,500,000	Weight	0.70%
EAD		**1,500,000**	**CVA**	**192,524**

Figure 7.8: Example calculation – current CVA Risk Capital Charge (2/2)

In the next step, the maturity of the analysed interest rate swap transaction will be increased to ten years in order to demonstrate the severe impact the maturity has on the CVA risk capital charge. The result is shown in Figure 7.8.

As can be observed in Figure 7.8, the maturity is a significant driver of the CVA risk capital charge. The maturity is reflected, on the one hand, in the assessment basis (EAD) under CEM by a higher volatility rate (1.5% instead of 0.5%) and, on the other, in the maturity parameter M_i within the CVA risk capital charge calculation based on formula (6).

7.3.2 Regulatory requirements for the application of the basic CVA framework

The basic CVA framework (BA-CVA) represents a significant progression of the current standardised method and can be applied by banks that do not have an approval for the application of the SA-CVA framework either for the entire portfolio or at least some netting sets and do not use the simplified method described in section 7.1. Compared to the SA-CVA, no inherent sensitivities must be determined for market risk factors within the scope of the BA-CVA.

7.3.3 Exposure value for the basic CVA

Within the BA-CVA framework, the exposure component can be determined either based on the new standardised approach for counterparty credit risk (SA-CCR)[29] or based on the Internal Model Method (IMM).[30] While banks require the approval of

---

29 See the chapter on SA-CCR (Chapter 3) in this book for detailed information on regulatory requirements for the SA-CCR.
30 Cf. SA-CCR: BCBS 279 (2014) and IMM: BCBS 128 (2006), Annex IV.

supervisors to apply the IMM, within the scope of which exposures are determined based on derivative transactions using simulation procedures, the SA-CCR method can be applied without any further restrictions.

7.3.4 Determination of regulatory capital requirements based on the basic CVA framework

The BA-CVA approach is available in both full and reduced versions. The full version is designed for banks that hedge CVA risk, the reduced version does not take into account hedging and is obtained from the full version by eliminating the hedging parameters.

The reduced BA-CVA is based on the stand-alone CVA capital charge for counterparty c ($SCVA_c$) as well as a supervisory correlation parameter ρ and is determined based on the following Equation 7.8:

Equation 7.8

$$K_{reduced} = \sqrt{\left(\rho * \sum_c SCVA_c \right)^2 + (1 - \rho^2) * \sum_c SCVA_c{}^2} \qquad (7.8)$$

The application of correlation factor ρ (set at 50%) reflects the degree of correlation set by the supervisory authority between the credit spread of a counterparty and the systematic factor. The $SCVA_c$ is the CVA capital a counterparty would receive if considered on a stand-alone basis and depends on three input parameters: The risk weight of counterparty i RW_i, the remaining maturity of a netting set M_{NS}, and the discounted Exposure at Default of a netting set. The calculation of $SCVA_c$ is outlined in Equation 7.9.

Equation 7.9

$$SCVA_c = \frac{1}{\alpha} * RW_c * \sum_{NS} M_{NS} * EAD_{NS} * DF_{NS} \qquad (7.9)$$

RW_c represents the risk weight of the counterparty and is based on a combination of sector and credit quality of the counterparty c as shown in Table 7.2. The risk weight of the Basel IV CVA risk capital charge differs from the risk weight of the Basel III CVA risk capital charge (w_i) in the following aspects:

- The risk weight (RW_c) is more risk sensitive as it takes not only the external rating into account but also the sector of the counterparty. For example, an AA– rated financial institution received a 0.7% risk weight according to Basel III (w_i) but receives a 5% risk weight (RW_c) within the Basel IV treatment. On the other hand, an AA–rated sovereign received a 0.7% risk weight according to Basel III and will benefit from a lower risk weight (0.5%) according to Basel IV.

Sector of Counterparty	Investment Grade	High Yield and Non-Rated
Sovereigns including central banks, multilateral development banks	0.5 %	3.0 %
Local government, government-backed non-financials, education and public administration	1.0 %	4.0 %
Financials including government-backed financials	5.0 %	12.0 %
Basic materials, energy, industrials, agriculture, manufacturing, mining and quarrying	3.0 %	7.0 %
Consumer goods and services, transportation and storage, administrative and support service activities	3.0 %	8.5 %
Technology, telecommunications	2.0 %	5.5 %
Health care, utilities, professional and technical activities	1.5 %	5.0 %
Other sector	5.0 %	12.0 %

Table 7.2: Risk weights BA-CVA

- The risk weight (RW_c) differentiates between investment grade (IG) and non-investment grade (high yield – HY) and non-rated only.[31] Therefore, the risk weight is less dependent on marginal rating migrations compared to the Basel III risk weight that distinguishes between 6 credit quality steps.

EAD_{NS} represents the exposure component that, as was already mentioned, is determined according to the SA-CCR or the IMM method. At this point attention is drawn to the fact that even if within formula (8) hedging instruments are not explicitly taken into account, some hedging transactions are already implicitly taken into account as the exposure component is calculated according to the SA-CCR. This is due to the fact that transactions with identical offsetting risks are offset within the SA-CCR. CVA hedges are not taken into account within the reduced version. Ultimately, the division by the alpha factor (1.4) within formula (9) serves the purpose of removing the multiplier from the exposure component used to determine the CVA risk charge. The alpha factor is applied within the scope of the SA-CCR as well as within the IMM in order to convert the EEPE (Expected Effective Positive Exposure) into an EAD. However, the regulatory framework on the CVA risk takes the EEPE into account instead of the EAD.

DF_{NS} is a supervisory discount factor and derived according to formula (7) in section 7.3.1. Therefore, the same EAD discount factor for Basel III and Basel IV CVA risk capital charge is used.

Finally, M_{NS} represents the remaining maturity of a netting set and is defined in the same way as M_i in the Basel III standardised CVA risk capital charge (please refer to section 7.3.1).

In general, the reduced BA-CVA uses the same input parameters as the Basel III standardised CVA risk capital charge. To achieve the goal of a more risk sensitive approach,

---

31   If no external rating is available or not recognised within a jurisdiction, banks may map their internal rating to an external rating and assign it to IG or HY (Cf. BCBS 424, page 111, para 14).

the risk weights are calibrated not only to an external rating but also to the sector of a counterparty. Thus, the risk weights provide a more sensitive way to explain the volatility of the credit spreads of a counterparty. Furthermore, to align the BA-CVA capital charge with other initiatives of the Basel Committee, the SA CCR has been introduced within the CVA risk framework.

For banks that hedge the CVA risk arising from their CVA book, the CVA capital charge K_{full} is determined using Equation 7.10, which takes hedging transactions into account, provided the hedges are eligible.

Equation 7.10

$$K_{full} = \beta * K_{reduced} + (1 - \beta) * K_{hedged} \tag{7.10}$$

$K_{reduced}$ is part of the full version of the BA-CVA capital charge and restricts the effectiveness of hedging. The supervisory factor β provides a floor of 25% to the reduced BA-CVA risk capital charge. Therefore, hedging can reduce the CVA capital charge up to 75%. K_{hedged} is defined in Equation 7.11:

Equation 7.11

$$K_{hedged} = \sqrt{\left(\rho \sum_c (SCVA_c - SNH_c) - IH\right)^2 + (1 - \rho^2) \sum_c (SCVA_c - SNH_c)^2 + \sum_c HMA_c} \tag{7.11}$$

As under the Basel III accord, only transactions used to mitigate credit spread risk and managed in a dedicated function are eligible hedges to be included in the CVA risk capital charge. Eligible instruments include single-name and single-name contingent CDS as well as index CDS. In contrast to the Basel III standard, eligible single-name hedges can also reference an entity legally related to the counterparty or reference an entity that belongs to the same sector and region as the counterparty and must not reference the counterparty directly. Therefore, indirect hedges are allowed as well but the impact of indirect hedges on the CVA risk capital charge is limited by a hedging misalignment parameter (HMA_c) as an indirect hedge cannot fully offset movements in the credit spreads of counterparty c. Thus, in presence of indirect hedges HMA_c as well as K_{hedged} cannot be zero.

In Equation 7.11 ρ and $SCVA_c$ are defined in the same way as in the reduced BA-CVA capital charge. SNH_c describes the effect of single-name hedges on the CVA risk capital charge and is determined by calculating the product of the discounted notional amount B_h^{SN},[32] the residual maturity of the affected single name hedge M_h^{SN}, the regulatory risk weight RW_h depending on the affected risk bucket from the perspective

---

32 For single-name contingent CDS, the notional amount equals the current market value of the reference portfolio or instrument.

of the single name hedge as well as the supervisory correlation r_{hc}. r_{hc} represents the correlation between the counterparty credit spread of counterparty c and the credit spread of a single name hedge h of counterparty c . However, the value of r_{hc} varies depending on the type of recognisable single name hedges. Single name hedges, that directly reference counterparty c, are assigned a correlation value of 100%; single name hedges, which establish a so-called "legal relation" with the counterparty in question are assigned a correlation value of 80% and single name hedges, which reference an entity that comes from the same industry and the same region as counterparty c, are assigned a correlation value of 50%.

Accordingly, IH describes the effect of index hedges on the CVA capital charge and is determined by calculating the product of the discounted notional amount B_i^{ind}, the residual maturity of index hedge i M_i^{ind} and the regulatory risk weight RW_i depending on the affected risk bucket from the perspective of the index. The risk weight RW_i is adjusted by the factor 0.7 to account for diversification within the index.

In Figure 7.9, a calculation example for the BA-CVA approach to determine the CVA risk capital charge is outlined. The basis of this example is the same interest rate swap which has already been analysed in the calculation example in section 7.3.1 on the current standardised method under Basel III. In this case, the EAD component will be determined based on the SA CCR method. As an additional input, the sector of the counterparty c – in this case financial – is required. In the first step of the calculation example, the residual maturity will be four years. The resulting CVA risk capital charge

Transaction data:

- Instrument: IR Swap
- Sector of counterparty: Financials
- Notional value: 100,000,000
- Rating: AA
- Maturity: 4 years
- Collateral: not specified
- Market value: 0

SA-CCR	
Market value	0
Multiplier	1
Asset category	Interest Rate
Hedging set	EUR
Maturity bucket	< 5y
Adjusted notional	362,538,494
Regulatory Delta	1
Default factor	1
Effective notional/maturity bucket	362,538,494
Effective notional/hedging set	362,538,494
Supervisory factor	0.50%
AddOn	1,812,692
EAD	**2,537,769**

CVA (Basel IV)	
Disc. EAD	2,300,097
Maturity	4
Alpha	1.4
Risk weight	5%
Capital Charge K	328,585

Figure 7.9: Example calculation B-CVA (1/2)

Transaction data:

- Instrument: IR Swap
- Sector of counterparty: Financials
- Notional value: 100,000,000
- Rating: AA
- Maturity: 10 years
- Collateral: not specified
- Market value: 0

SA-CCR	
Market value	0
Multiplier	1
Asset category	Interest Rate
Hedging set	EUR
Maturity bucket	> 5y
Adjusted notional	786,938,681
Supervisory Delta	1
Maturity factor	1
Effective notional/maturity bucket	786,938,681
Effective notional/hedging set	786,938,681
Supervisory factor	0.50%
AddOn	3,934,693
EAD	**5,508,571**

CVA (NEW)	
Disc. EAD	4,334,907
Maturity	10
Alpha	1,4
Risk weight	5%
Capital Charge K	**1,548,181**

Figure 7.10: Calculation example B-CVA (2/2)

under the premises set forth herein is shown in Figure 7.9. Compared to the calculation example for the current standardised method, it becomes clear that the SA CCR as well as the more risk sensitive risk weights effect the CVA risk capital charge. The risk weights to be applied in the basic CVA calculation are significantly higher than under the old standardised method to determine the CVA.

In the next step, the remaining maturity of the interest rate swap is increased to ten years. The increase of the remaining maturity – as under Basel III – has a significant effect on the CVA risk capital charge in this case. Irrespective of this, several parameters (e.g. the alpha factor or the multiplier) are applied multiplicatively in this constellation, with the result that the value for the EAD component as well as the value for the CVA risk capital charge increases. The results can be observed in Figure 7.10.

7.4 Additional aspects and expected effects

The new approaches to calculate the CVA risk capital charge, suggested by the Basel Committee, provide for a reinforced and more precise contemplation of market risk factor dependencies and hedging measures. As a consequence, the determination of the CVA risk capital charge becomes much more risk sensitive. On the other hand, the expansion of the scope of application of the CVA risk capital charge suggested by the Basel Committee means that the number of transactions to be backed by the CVA risk capital charge increases.

The revision of the CVA framework globally leads to increased efforts. The new approaches of the reviewed CVA framework require new input parameters and calculation procedures. This results in procedural adjustments and increased efforts from the point of view of the affected institutions.

In relation to the **BA-CVA approach**, it can be inferred that capital requirements for the CVA risk will increase depending on the portfolio structure. This is due to the fact that risk weights take into account the sector of the counterparty and not only the external rating as under Basel III. Counterparts that belong to the financial sector are strongly affected as the risk weights will increase significantly. Furthermore, SA CCR is introduced within the CVA risk capital charge. The SA CCR is more sensitive to the residual maturity compared to the current exposure method. Therefore, transactions with a longer term structure in particular will be strongly affected by the new BA-CVA framework.

With reference to the **FRTB-CVA framework**, after IMA-CVA has been removed by the Basel Committee, only SA-CVA will be available in the final version of the standard. Furthermore, after the banking sector reacted in particular to the options to determine exposures for the regulatory CVA (option A: accounting-based/option B: IMM-based) suggested by the Basel Committee and to the requirement of an existing IMM approval in order to be able to apply option A, those details were changed in the final standard. Therefore, the preferred method of determining the CVA based on accounting rules was the only one left and the IMM approval is not obligatory anymore.

The revised CVA Risk Capital Charge framework is expected to enter into force in 2022.

Recommended literature

BCBS128 (2006): International Convergence of Capital Measurement and Capital Standard, A Revised Framework, Comprehensive Version, 2006.

BCBS 189 (2010): A global regulatory framework for more resilient banks and banking systems, 2010.

BCBS 279 (2014): The standardised approach for measuring counterparty credit risk exposures, 2014.

BCBS 325 (2015): Consultative Document. Review of the Credit Valuation Adjustment Risk Framework, 2015.

BCBS 346 (2015): Fundamental Review of the Trading Book – Interim Impact Analysis, 2015.

BCBS 352 (2016): Minimum Capital Requirements for Market Risk, 2016.

BCBS 362 (2016): Consultative Document. Reducing variation in credit risk-weighted assets – constraints on the use of internal model approaches, 2016.

BCBS 424 (2017): Basel III: Finalising post-crisis reforms, 2017.

BCBS 424summary (2017): High-level summary of Basel III reforms, 2017.

BCBS CVA QIS (2016): Instructions: CVA QIS, 2016.

Capital Requirements Regulation; CRR (2013): Regulation (EU) No 575/2013 of the European Parliament and of the Council of 26 June 2013 on prudential requirements for credit institutions and investment firms and amending Regulation (EU) No 646/2012.

Deutsche Bank (2014): Deutsche Bank's response to the Basel Committee on Banking Supervision consultative document on the Fundamental Review of the Trading Book, 2014. Available under: http://www.bipageorg/publ/bcbs265/deutschebank.pdf

European Banking Authority; EBA (2015): Opinion of the European Banking Authority on Credit Valuation Adjustment (CVA); (EBA/Op/2015/02), 2015.

International Accounting Standards Board; IASB (2011): IFRS 13. Bemessung des beizulegenden Zeitwerts, 2011.

Ludwig, Sven/Martin, Marcus R.W./Wehn, Carsten Seite (publisher) (2012): Kontrahentenrisiko. Bewertung, Steuerung, Unterlegung nach Basel III und IFRS [Counterparty risk. Evaluation, management, backing under Basel III and IFRS], first edition, editorial: Schäffer-Poeschel Verlag (Stuttgart), 2012.

Talkenberger, Dirk/Wehn, Carsten Seite (2012): Kontrahentenrisiko im Überblick, in: Ludwig, Sven/Martin, Marcus R.W./Wehn, Carsten Seite (publisher.): Kontrahentenrisiko. Bewertung, Steuerung, Unterlegung nach Basel III und IFRS [Counterparty risk. Evaluation, management, backing under Basel III and IFRS], first edition, editorial: Schäffer-Poeschel Verlag (Stuttgart), 2012, pages 1–19.

8 Operational Risk

Jennifer Pattwell, Peter Büttel and Jan Eichstedt

8.1 Introduction

Banks and supervisory authorities first focused on "operational risk" (also referred to as OpRisk) in the 1990s. The Basel Committee on Banking Supervision explicitly addressed OpRisk from a banking supervision perspective for the purposes of risk management for the first time in 1998 in the form of a consultation paper.[1] The BCBS underscored the increased importance of appropriate OpRisk management, especially within the context of the significant losses financial institutions suffered that decade.

As a result, the BCBS stipulated – for the first time within the scope of the first consultation paper issued in June 1999 to review capital adequacy standards (Basel II) – the implementation of capital requirements for operational risk and the initiation of the development of an adequate capital charge.[2] As things developed, the BCBS specified the requirements for appropriate OpRisk capital adequacy and highlighted the operational risk as the most significant of the other risks.[3]

While the BCBS did not provide an unambiguous and generally accepted definition of OpRisk in the consultation paper of 1998 by referring to it as "any risk not categorised as market or credit risk", over time, the BCBS adopted an operational risk definition from the banking sector. Nowadays, the regulatory definition of OpRisk is the following: "the risk of loss resulting from inadequate or failed internal processes, people and systems or from external events".[4] Figure 8.1 outlines the delimitation of operational risk within the relevant risks for regulatory purposes.

The financial crisis showed that capital requirements for operational risk turned out to be insufficient to cover the related losses incurred by some firms. It also demonstrated the difficulty of using internal models to estimate operational risk capital requirements given the nature of these losses, such as those related to misconduct and inadequate systems and controls.

In December 2017 the Basel Committee (BCBS) published its outstanding Basel III post-crisis regulatory reforms. Based on the points of criticisms of the current approaches used to determine capital requirements for operational risk, the BCBS replaces the existing three approaches with a single risk-sensitive standardised approach (SA) to be used by all firms.

The goal of this chapter is to present the methodology of the Standardised Approach and to describe the most important changes as well as future effects.

---

1   Cf. BIS (1998).
2   Cf. BCBS 50 (1999).
3   Cf. Hofmann (2015).
4   Cf. BCBS 128 (2004).

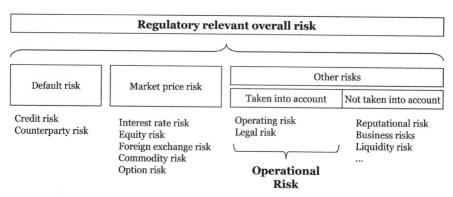

Figure 8.1: Delimitation of operational risk

8.2 Current methods pursuant to Basel II[5]

Under Basel II, banks have three alternatives at their disposal to determine adequate operational risk capital requirements. These are the Basic Indicator Approach (BIA), the Standardised Approach (STA) and the Advanced Measurement Approaches (AMA). The characteristics of increased risk sensitivity on the one hand, and the rising level of requirements in quantitative and qualitative terms, on the other hand, which are inevitable in order to apply the different approaches, has given rise to the idea of a "continuum of approaches" among supervisors.

Figure 8.2 illustrates the different degrees of measurement accuracy and the increasing scope of qualitative requirements.

8.2.1 Basic Indicator Approach and Standardised Approach

According to the provisions of the BCBS, the BIA, as an entry procedure, does not require a special approval on the part of the supervisory authority. However, the "Principles for the Sound Management of Operational Risk"[6] lay out fundamental

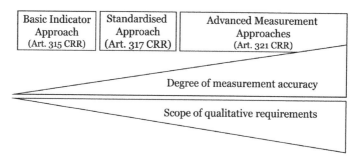

Figure 8.2: Comparison of previous approaches

---

5   Cf. BCBS 128 (2004).
6   Cf. Details on the national implementation: BaFin (2012), MaRisk BTR 4 "Operationelle Risiken" [Operational Risks] and BCBS 292 (2014).

minimum standards to determine and manage OpRisk, with which BIA users must comply.[7] Basically, the BIA can be applied by any bank except by those which operate internationally or are exposed to significant OpRisk (e.g. banks specialising in trans-action consulting).[8] With the aid of the BIA, the operational risk capital requirements are calculated as shown in Equation 8.1.

Equation 8.1: Operational risk capital requirements pursuant to the BIA[9]

$$C_{BIA} = \left[\sum_{i=1}^{n} (GIi \times \alpha) \right] \div n \qquad (8.1)$$

where:

GI = annual gross income (where positive) over the previous three years
n = number of the previous three years for which gross income is positive
α = 15% (which is set by the Committee – establishes the ratio between the required capital and the gross income)

STA is based on a more sophisticated method. A bank applying the STA must comply with the requirements for the use of the STA as well as their practical implementation as part of a notification sent to the respective supervisory/regulatory authority.[10] The higher risk sensitivity of the STA compared to the BIA is due to the fact that the bank's activities are divided into eight business lines[11] and each line is assigned an individual beta factor. Following the underlying logic of the BIA, the calculation formula for the STA to calculate operational risk capital requirements is shown in Equation 8.2.

Equation 8.2: Operational risk capital requirements pursuant to the STA[12]

$$GI_{STA} = \left\{ \sum_{n=1}^{3} max \left[\sum_{i=1}^{8} (GIni \times \beta i), 0 \right] \right\} \div 3 \qquad (8.2)$$

where:

GI_{1-8} = annual gross income for each of the bank's eight business lines
n   = respective year (total of 3 years)
β_{1-8} = fixed percentages set by the Committee (12%, 15% and 18%)

Moreover, the BCBS allows the use of an alternative standardised approach, which nevertheless requires an approval procedure as well as a notification procedure of the bank using this approach by the authority.[13]

---

7   Cf. Neisen (2016).
8   Cf. BCBS 128 (2004).
9   Cf. BCBS 128 (2004), S. 138.
10 Cf. BaFin/Deutsche Bundesbank [German Central Bank] (2007).
11 Cf. Art. 317 CRR: Corporate finance, trading and sales, retail brokerage, commercial banking, retail banking, payment and settlement, agency services as well as asset management.
12 Cf. BCBS 128 (2004).
13 Cf. BaFin/Deutsche Bundesbank [German Central Bank] (2007).

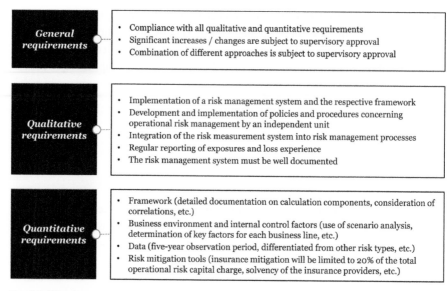

General requirements	• Compliance with all qualitative and quantitative requirements • Significant increases / changes are subject to supervisory approval • Combination of different approaches is subject to supervisory approval
Qualitative requirements	• Implementation of a risk management system and the respective framework • Development and implementation of policies and procedures concerning operational risk management by an independent unit • Integration of the risk measurement system into risk management processes • Regular reporting of exposures and loss experience • The risk management system must be well documented
Quantitative requirements	• Framework (detailed documentation on calculation components, consideration of correlations, etc.) • Business environment and internal control factors (use of scenario analysis, determination of key factors for each business line, etc.) • Data (five-year observation period, differentiated from other risk types, etc.) • Risk mitigation tools (insurance mitigation will be limited to 20% of the total operational risk capital charge, solvency of the insurance providers, etc.)

Figure 8.3: AMA requirements at a glance

8.2.2 Advanced Measurement Approaches[14]

AMA constitutes the most challenging calculation to determine regulatory operational risk capital requirements. Under these approaches, loss events, as well as mitigation measures, are modelled and, as a result, the necessary capital requirement is determined based on the bank's internal business structure.

The use of an individual AMA is subject to approval, preceded by a notification procedure as well as an approval procedure where the applicant bank must confirm in writing compliance with an extensive list of specifications, which contains the STA framework conditions among others. Furthermore, the AMA approval requirements can be divided into three categories: general, qualitative and quantitative requirements (Figure 8.3).

Within the scope of the AMA, internal loss data of a minimum five-year observation period, supplemented with external data such as external loss data or scenario analysis, is used to calculate the operational risk capital requirements. Moreover, the BCBS grants the banks applying the AMA several risk mitigation techniques as, for example, in the form of insurances or inclusion of expected losses in the budgeting.

Under the *partial use,* a bank may use a combination of the AMA and the BIA or the STA.

---

14   Cf. BCBS 128 (2004).

8.2.3 Criticism of the existing approaches[15]

Although the BIA and the STA have their advantages, especially in relation to their comparatively uncomplicated calculation, both methods are subject to growing criticism among supervisors. The BCBS, in particular, highlights the following weaknesses of the BIA and the STA methods in its consultation paper for the purpose of reviewing said approaches:

- The assumption that the bank's operational risk increases linearly in proportion to revenue proved to be false.
- Loss increases due to operational risks indirectly lead to a decrease of operational risk capital requirements.
- The bank's absolute size does not have an impact on the level of the operational risk.

The AMA has also been the subject of criticism, especially because of the inherent complexity and the lack of comparability arising from a wide range of internal modelling practices, which also leads to rising variability in risk-weighted asset calculations.

8.3 Overview: From Basel II to Basel IV

The BCBS partly addressed the criticisms of the BIA and STA calculation models mentioned in the previous chapter with the consultation paper *Operational Risk – Revisions to the simpler approaches* (BCBS 291) published in October 2014. The consultation paper mainly provided for the consolidation of the two current approaches, the BIA and the STA, and, in connection therewith, the review of the identified weaknesses through a newly developed calculation method.

This revision shall satisfy a set of requirements (Figure 8.4) and completely replace the BIA as well as the STA with a new approach: the *Revised Standardised Approach* (SA).

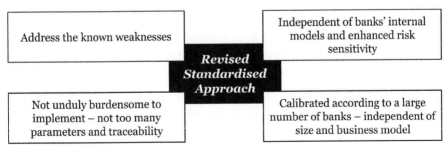

Figure 8.4: Requirements on the revised SA

---

15   Cf. BCBS 291 (2014).

The basic principle is comparable to the mechanics of the BIA; however, a higher risk sensitivity of the parameters of the revised SA can be observed. Within the modelling of the SA, the *Business Indicator* (BI) is of key importance. The BI shall serve as proxy indicator and therefore replace the gross income (GI) used so far to calculate the operational risk capital requirements under the BIA and the STA.

In order to determine the BI, the Committee conducted a comprehensive benchmark study investigating more than 20 potential indicators from the quantitative as well as from the qualitative point of view regarding their suitability to calculate capital requirements. The BCBS is of the opinion that the BI addresses the main weaknesses of the previous indicator GI and consequently constitutes the basis for the revised SA.

An additional significant change in the SA model divides the BI into five *buckets*, which – similar to the previous Basic Indicator and Standard Approach – are assigned a *coefficient* in order to achieve an improved risk sensitivity (Figure 8.6). The revised SA provides for a *coefficient* between 10% and 30%.

Although the elimination of the AMA had already been discussed and announced by the Basel Committee, it only became official with the second consultation paper (BCBS 355). The inherent complexity of the Advanced Measurement Approach and the lack of comparability, limited by a wide range of internal models, results in a loss of confidence in the AMA as a calculation method and, in the end, justified its elimination. As expected, within the scope of BCBS 355 the Basel Committee allows for internal loss data to be used as a relevant indicator to calculate operational risk capital requirements.

8.4 Standardised Approach for operational risk (BCBS 424)

8.4.1 Methodology of the SA

The methodology is based on the basic principle of the Business Indicator (BI) as a new financial-statement-based proxy indicator, which was introduced with the first consultation paper, and the Business Indicator Component (including the classification in "buckets" depending on the level of the Business Indicator). The SA combines said indicator with bank-specific internal loss data (Internal Loss Multiplier). The BCBS 424 states extensive requirements, especially in terms of quality, granularity, time frame and use of internal loss data within risk management.

More specifically the revised SA has an operational risk capital requirement based on the measure of a bank's income (the business indicator component), and on a measure of a bank's historical operational risk related losses (an internal loss multiplier):

- The business indicator component (BIC) incorporates business indicators (BI) relating to various financial reporting (mainly income) measures; and
- The internal loss multiplier (ILM) is based on historical operational loss experience relative to the BIC.

The Business Indicator (BI)

The Business Indicator (BI) is the sum of three components: the interest, leases and dividends component (Figure 8.5); the services component and the financial component, all calculated as averages over a three-year period.

Equation 8.3: Calculation of the Business Indicator under the SMA

$$BI = ILDC_{Avg} + SC_{Avg} + FC_{Avg} \qquad (8.3)$$

where:

Avg   = Average of the individual components over the last 3 years
ILDC = Interest, lease and dividend component
SC   = Services component
FC   = Financial component

The remaining components of the calculation method to determine the BI are, due to their complexity, outlined separately below.

Compared to the first consultation paper, dividend income is taken into account as part of the interest component. This serves the purpose of addressing the criticism concerning the fact that inconsistent treatment of dividend income could result, for example, in arbitrage opportunities within the Business Indicator. An additional point of criticism the BCBS takes into account is the treatment of banks with a high net interest margin. The application of the previously consulted BI resulted in capital requirements that were high in comparison to the operational risk of said banks.

Equation 8.4: Calculation of the interest, lease and dividend component

$$ILDC_{Avg} = Min \left[Abs \left(Interest\ Income_{Avg} - Interest\ Expense_{Avg} \right) ; 0,0225 \right.$$
$$\left. \times\ Interest\ Earning\ Assets_{Avg} \right] + Dividend\ Income_{Avg} \qquad (8.4)$$

The services component underwent the most significant changes in its structure compared to the second consultation paper. In the second consultation paper, the Basel Committee addresses the criticism of the operational risk requirements in the case of banks with a high net interest margin with the aid of the parameter uBI, which

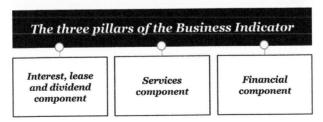

Figure 8.5: Composition of the Business Indicator

was assigned a general factor of 0.5 and consequently reduces capital requirements. In BCBS 424 the potential simplification is not contained anymore.

Equation 8.5: Calculation of the service component

$$SC_{Avg} = Max \left(Other\ Operating\ Income_{Avg}; Other\ Operating\ Expenses_{Avg} \right)$$
$$+ Max \left(Fee\ Income_{Avg}; Fee\ Expenses_{Avg} \right) \tag{8.5}$$

The composition and calculation logic of the financial component did not undergo any changes compared to the second consultation paper. The net profit/loss on the trading book as well as on the banking book are taken into account as an average of the last three years (absolute value).

Equation 8.6: Calculation of the financial component

$$FC_{Avg} = Abs \left(Net\ P\&L\ Trading\ Book_{Avg} \right) + Abs \left(Net\ P\&L\ BankingBook_{Avg} \right) \tag{8.6}$$

The Business Indicator Component (BIC)

To calculate the Business Indicator Component (BIC), the BI is multiplied by the marginal coefficients (αi).

Equation 8.7: Calculation of the BIC

$$BIC = \sum (\alpha i \times BI) \tag{8.7}$$

Similar to the draft in the consultation papers, the BI is split into buckets, which are each assigned a coefficient (αi) in order to calculate the BI component. The marginal coefficients increase with the size of the BI as shown in Figure 8.6.

Compared to the second consultation paper in BCBS 424 the number of BI buckets for the purpose of applying the marginal BI coefficient (α) has been reduced from five to three. The range and level of the marginal BI coefficient (α) has also been reduced from 0.11–0.29 to 0.12–0.18 and eliminating a constant term from the calculation for each bucket.

"Bucket"	Business Indicator	Marginal BI coefficient (ai)
1	≤ € 1bn	0.12
2	> € 1bn ≤ € 30bn	0.15
3	> € 30bn	0.18

Figure 8.6: The BIC under the SA

For example, should a BI = € 35bn, the calculation is as follows:

Bucket 1: €1bn x 12% = € 0.12bn

Bucket 2: €(30-1)bn x 15% = € 4.35bn

Bucket 3: €(35-30)bn x 18% = € 0.9bn

BIC = sum of buckets 1-3 = € 5.37bn

The Internal Loss Multiplier and Loss Component

Introduced in the second consultation paper is the consideration of internal operational loss data the most important change in the methodology. The analyses of the Basel Committee revealed that a bank's business volume is not the only factor that influences operational risk and that, in order to increase risk sensitivity, the consideration of additional indicators is also vital. Based on these analyses, internal loss data were identified as key indicators which banks within the parameters of bucket 2 must consider in their calculation of operational risk capital requirements.

Users of the advanced measurement approaches are currently already recording information on loss data at such granular levels and should, therefore, be in a position to calculate the loss component in the future. Banks applying the SA, are recording operational loss data to fulfil further internal qualitative requirements. The results of the analysis by the Basel Committee show that over 80% of banks with a BI greater than EUR 1 billion do not use the BIA to calculate operational risks, but apply the SA or the AMA[16] instead.

The Internal Loss Multiplier (ILM) is a function of the BIC and the Loss Component (LC), where the latter is equal to 15 times a firm's average historical operational risk losses over the preceding 10 years, shown in Equations 8.8 and 8.9.

Equations 8.8 and 8.9: Calculation of the Internal Loss Multiplier

$$Internal\ Loss\ Multilplier = Ln\left(\exp(1) - 1 + \left(\frac{Loss\ Component}{BI\ Component}\right)0,8\right) \qquad (8.8)$$

where:

$$Loss\ Component = 15 \times Average\ annual\ operational\ risk\ losses \qquad (8.9)$$

Transitional arrangements will allow firms who do not have, in 2022, 10 years of loss data maintained to an appropriate standard, to use a minimum of 5 years of loss data.

The logarithmic function $Ln(\exp(1) - 1) \approx 0{,}541$ is designed in such a way that the Internal Loss Multiplier also increases at increasing losses. As an example, Figure 8.7 outlines the relation between the loss component and the multiplier based on internal losses when the BI component remains constant.

---

16   Cf. BCBS 355 (2016).

Evolution of the Internal Loss Indicator

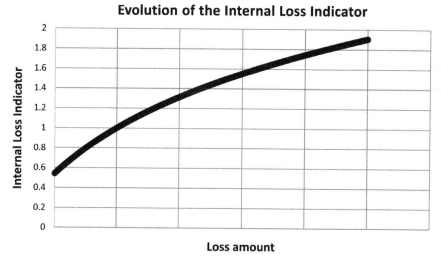

Figure 8.7: Evolution of the Internal Loss Multiplier

The increase of the multiplier positively correlates to increasing losses; nonetheless, the graph shows that the multiplier does not increase in the same relative magnitude. When the indicator surpasses 1, this means in terms of operational risk capital require-ments that the necessary capital under the BI component increases by a factor greater than 1. Consequently, larger banks with several small or with extremely large loss expo-sure contributions will be subject to higher operational risk capital requirements than smaller banks included in bucket 1, for example. In the case of larger banks with fewer losses, the capital requirement under the BI component decreases through an Internal Loss Multiplier smaller than 1. Thus, effective operational risk management also has a direct impact on capital requirements.

The BCBS has calibrated the ILM formula so that where $LC = BIC$, the ILM factor is equal to 1, and it effectively becomes the default ILM level in certain circumstances:

- The ILM is set to 1 for firms with BI levels less than €1bn although national super-visors may choose to apply the full ILM calculation to all firms in their jurisdiction;
- National supervisors may set the ILM to 1 for all firms in their jurisdiction;
- Firms that do not meet operational risk data maintenance standards must have an ILM set to at least 1 but with national supervisory discretion to set higher levels; and
- Under transitional arrangements, firms who do not have 5 years of loss data of ade-quate quality, must set their ILM to 1 although national supervisors may require firms to use their calculated ILM factor where this is greater than 1.

Example for the calculation

Based on the new calculation methods, the individual operational risk capital require-ments will change. According to the currently employed approach, this can result in significant differences for banks.

Expenses (in millions)		Income (in millions)	
Interest expenses	2,000	Interest income	2,500
General administration expenses	1,900	Current income	100
Fee expenses	1,000	Fee income	4,000
Depreciation	400	Income from write-ups	50
Other operating expenses	1,000	Other operating income	500
Expenses trading book	1,500	Income trading book	1,000
Expenses banking book	500	Income banking book	1,000
Lease expenses	150	Dividend income	700
		Lease income	0
Total expenses	8,450	Total income	9,850

Figure 8.8: Fictional P&L statement of the Model Bank

The following simplified example demonstrates the possible effects resulting from the implementation of BCBS 424 in relation to operational risk capital requirements and the differences compared to the previous provisions under the BIA and the first consultation paper of the Basel Committee. Whilst all analysed models target a period of several years; the following example only refers to a one-year time horizon for reasons of clarity and transparency.

The profit and loss statement of a fictional bank (see Figure 8.8) is the basis used to calculate operational risk capital requirements under the BIA and the Standardised Approach (BCBS 424). Internal loss data, identified as an essential influencing factor within the framework of the second consultation paper, will not be taken into account in the following example in order to ensure comparability among indicators.

Based on the assumption that the Model Bank applies the BIA pursuant to Basel II to calculate the operational risk capital requirements, the capital requirement amounts to EUR 608 MM (see Figure 8.9.).

The Interest Earning Assets (IEA) in BCBS 424 is defined as total gross outstanding loans, advances, interest-bearing securities, and lease assets measured at the end of each financial year (balance sheet items). The example in Figure 8.10 shows the estimated IEA as EUR 30,000 MM.

Between the BIA and SA (BCBS 424) and before taking into account internal loss data, the capital requirements increase by EUR 612 MM.

Based on an estimated average total annual loss from operational risk of EUR 50 MM, the total capital requirements for the Model Bank pursuant to BCBS 424 are expressed in Figure 8.11 below:

This simplified example highlights the significant changes and challenges arising from substituting the BIA or the STA by the SA (BCBS 424). The advanced BI and the average

Interest income
= Interest income − interest expenses
= 2,500 − 2,000 = **500**

+ Income received for services provided
= Fee income − Fee expenses + other operating income
= 4,000 − 1,000 + 500 = **3,500**

+ Income trading book
= Net P&L trading book
= 1,000 − 1,500 = **−500**

+ Dividend income
= **700**

+ Lease result (component of other income)
= **−150**

= Gross income = 4,050

➡ Alpha = 15%

= Capital requirement = 4,050 × 15% = 608

Figure 8.9: Capital requirements pursuant to Basel II (BIA)

ILDC
= Min[Abs (interest income − interest expenses); 0.0225 × IEA] + dividend income
= Min[Abs (2,500 − 2,000); 0.0225 × 30,000] + 700 = **1,200**

FC
= Abs(Net P&L trading book) + Abs(Net P&L banking book)
= 500 + 500 = **1,000**

SC
= Max(Other Operating Income; Other Operating Expenses) + Max(Fee Income; Fee Expenses)
= Max(500; 1,000) + Max(4,000; 1,000) = **5,000**

Business Indicator: ILDC + FC + SC = 1,200 + 1,000 + 5,000 = **7,200**

Bucket	BI range (in millions)	BI margin coefficient
1	≤ 1,000	12 %
2	1,000 < BI ≤ 30,000	15 %
3	> 30,000	18 %

= Business Indicator Component (BIC)
= 1,000 × 12% + (7,200 − 1,000) × 15% = 1,020

Figure 8.10: Calculation of the BIC pursuant to BCBS 424

Loss component
= 15 × average total annual loss
= 15 × 50 = **750**

Business Indicator Component
= **1,020**

= **Internal Loss Multiplier (ILM):**
= ln(exp(1) – 1 + (loss component / BI component))
= **0.916**

= **Capital requirement = BI component × ILM**
= 1,020 × 0.916
= **934.3**

Figure 8.11: Total capital requirements (BCBS 424) in millions

increased coefficients in buckets 2 to 3 compared to the BIA, as well as the contemplation of internal losses, tend to lead to higher capital requirements.

8.4.2 Minimum standards for the use of loss data

The goal of the Basel Committee is that, in the future, medium and large banks take into account internal loss data to calculate operational risk capital requirements. Regarding the use of internal loss data, BCBS 424 sets out the requirements and where data does not fulfil said requirements, banks must apply at least 100% of the BI component for operational risk capital requirements. Compared to the second consultation paper the minimum threshold for the inclusion of loss data has increased from €10,000 to €20,000 – and up to €100,000 for larger firms with supervisory approval.

A number of general and specific criteria must be complied with in order to use internal loss data within the scope of the SA. Figure 8.12 shows an extract of the minimum requirements defined within the final framework.

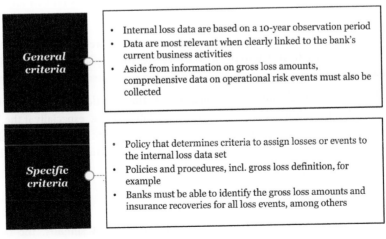

Figure 8.12: Minimum standards for the use of loss data

The SA requires loss data to be identified, collected, treated and maintained to a high standard. This involves appropriate associated systems and controls that are subject to independent review by internal and/or external audit functions. National supervisors will also review the quality of data.

The revised approach also specifies a range of requirements relating to:

- The exact data attributes to be collected, such as the dates the events occurred; were discovered; and accounted for; together with their nature and causes. Losses caused by a common or related operational risk event, but accounted for over several years, should be allocated to the corresponding year in the loss database in line with the accounting treatment. (In the consultation, there was a choice between date of discovery and date of accounting, and common or related losses were to be grouped and recorded as a single loss.)
- The mapping of loss data to the Basel supervisory loss types.
- The exclusion of operational loss events related to credit risk that are reflected in credit risk weighted assets from operational loss data sets and where the loss events are no longer relevant to a bank's risk profile. The BCBS expects these exclusions to be rare and firms will need to demonstrate that the loss events have no relevance to other continuing activities or products.

8.5 Future impact

8.5.1 Capital requirements for OpRisk

Based on the new calculation methods, the individual operational risk capital requirements will change. According to the currently employed approach and the future allocation to the corresponding buckets, this can result in significant differences for banks.

The individual impact on capital requirements for banks depends on two important elements:

1. The current approach (AMA vs SA): In cases where banks are currently using AMA, these banks will have to switch to the mandatory SA. The impact can differ markedly from bank to bank.

2. The BI and thus the classification to bucket 1–3: The consideration of internal loss data can lead to lower capital requirements for operational risk, especially if the bank is currently using one of the standardised approaches. Attention should be paid to national supervisory authorities, who can set up the ILM at national discretion. Therefore the impact strongly depends on the local regulator.

8.5.2 Practical considerations

Whilst considerable steps have been taken to enhance, yet simplify, the overall approach to determining OpRisk capital requirements, there remain a number of questions and practical considerations in terms of the overall application and benefit of applying capital requirements to OpRisk.

For example, it is still questioned if holding more or less capital for OpRisk directly impacts the loss potential for banks. Historical data sets of 5–10 years may be easily skewed by one-off loss events, the impact of which might overly impact a bank's RWA levels, whether negatively or positively, without truly representing its current and future level of OpRisk management. Additionally, the risk landscape for banks continues to evolve with new/increasing areas of OpRisk, such as those related to cyber and technology, which may yet significantly impact banks in terms of loss levels, but should still be factored in for future OpRisk considerations. It is therefore questionable how such a heavy reliance on historical loss data will benefit the detection, control and prevention of future OpRisks. Linked with this evolution of banks' OpRisks is how the comparability of banks will be achieved on a consistent basis as the spectrum of risks evolves and internal definitions of OpRisk across banks differ.

Depending on the approaches currently employed by banks, the impact of the SA is anticipated to be significant, in particular when compared to current BIA levels. However, ultimately, the difference between OpRisk and that of its Credit & Market Risk counterparts, is that it can't be managed in the same way by managing RWAs and subsequent capital implications.

8.5.3 Disclosure

In February 2018 the Basel Committee on Banking Supervision issued a consultation paper (BCBS 432) regarding Pillar 3 disclosure requirements. Most of the proposed requirements are related to BCBS 424 and include revised and new requirements for operational risk.

Based on this consultation paper banks are required to disclose the following information on an annual basis:

1. General qualitative information on a bank's operational risk framework.

2. Historical losses incurred over the past 10 years (table is mandatory only for banks that are in the second or third BI bucket, or those in the first bucket and have received supervisory approval to include internal loss data to calculate the capital requirements).

3. BI and subcomponents of the actual and all prior periods (three years) minimum required operational risk capital.

8.6 Conclusion

Since 1998, when the BCBS focused on this topic for the first time, the determination of adequate operational risk capital requirements as well as appropriate internal operational risk management has continually increased in significance up until the implementation of the Basel II provisions.

With Basel II, three admissible methods to determine operational risk capital require-ments were introduced by the BCBS: the BIA, the STA and the AMA. Especially the BIA and the STA were subject to growing criticism. The linear relation between a bank's income and operational risk and the non-consideration of absolute values of the respective banks are asserted as weaknesses of the BIA and the STA.

With the publication of the first consultation paper BCBS 291, the BCBS addressed the partly fundamental criticism on the methods of both the BIA and the STA. It replaced both approaches with the SA, a newly conceived approach that addressed criticism only to a limited extent and accentuated even more the unequal treatment of different business models. The BI, composed of the *interest component, services component* and *financial component*, is introduced as new proxy indicator to remedy the weaknesses of its predecessor. Using additional general weighting factors, the SA applies gradations in the level of the BI to differentiate operational risk capital requirements by classifying the BI according to its absolute value in *buckets* and weighting them with the respective specific factors. Moreover, this approach did not offer an alternative for AMA users.

The Basel Committee addressed criticism of the SA with the publication of the second consultation paper as well as the finalised revised SA in BCBS 424. The differences in the business models, which could have led to regulatory arbitrage, were reduced, additional components in the Business Indicator and new weighting factors were introduced.Furthermore, with the introduction of the loss indicator, the Basel Committee accounted for actual losses not considered in the operational risk calculation, and consequently tried to create an equivalent to the AMA.

In comparison to the previous requirements pursuant to the BIA and STA, increasing operational risk capital requirements tend to arise from the limited offsetting of income and expenses. The introduction of the loss component not only increases the risk sensitivity of the new calculation method, but also serves as an incentive factor for banks to continue developing their operational risk management. A big challenge arises for banks that have not used the AMA so far, but will be forced in the near future to consider internal loss data as minimum requirement to calculate, analyse and maintain loss data over a time period of up to 10 years. Comprehensive data collection and analyses will be necessary in this regard. An effective operational risk management will have a positive impact on capital requirements for these banks as a consequence of the implementation of the new approach. This will thus compensate the increasing requirements introduced by the new system.

The few banks currently using the Advanced Approach may already partially address these requirements as part of their operational risk management framework required under Basel II and their existing reporting of operational risk losses to national supervisors. But banks will still need to consider enhancing their data collection and maintenance capacity and systems well ahead of January 2022.

The finalised, revised SA includes data standards for the use of loss data with corresponding requirements for related systems and controls. These are set to be subject to supervisory review. There are also internal audit and/or external audit review requirements over those. This may lead to a need to enhance systems and controls including governance arrangements with a related increase in operating costs.

Significant impact on capital requirements is expected to be observed by banks that currently apply the AMA. A significant increase of the capital requirements is expected in this case due to the prescribed standardised determination of the BI.

Recommended Literature

BaFin [Federal Financial Supervisory Authority]/Deutsche Bundesbank [German Central Bank] (2007): Merkblatt zur Anzeige der Anwendung des Standardansatzes für das operationelle Risiko sowie zur Beantragung der Zustimmung zur Nutzung eines alternativen Indikators, 2007. [Instructions on the notification regarding the use of the standardised approach for operational risks as well as on the application for the approval to use an alternative indicator.]

BCBS 128 (2004): International Convergence of Capital Measurement and Capital Standards, 2004.

BCBS 291 (2014): Consultative Document: Operational risk – Revisions to the simpler approaches, 2014.

BCBS 292 (2014): Review of the Principles for the Sound Management of Operational Risk, 2014.

BCBS 355 (2016): Consultative Document: Standardised Measurement Approach for operational risk, 2016.

BCBS 50 (1999): A New Capital Adequacy Framework, 1999.

BIS (1998): Operational Risk Management, 1998.

Bundesanstalt für Finanzdienstleistungsaufsicht [Federal Financial Supervisory Authority]; BaFin (2012): Mindestanforderungen an das Risikomanagement – MaRisk (Rundschreiben 10/2012 (BA)), BTR 4, 2012. [Minimum Requirements for Risk Management]

CRR (Capital Requirements Regulation) (2013): Regulation (EU) No 575/2013 of the European Parliament and of the Council of 26 June 2013 on prudential requirements for credit institutions and investment firms and amending Regulation (EU) No 648/2012.

Hofmann, Gerhard (2015): Basel III, Risikomanagement und neue Bankenaufsicht, Frankfurt School Verlag (Frankfurt am Main), 2015.

Ingves, Stefan (2015): From the Vasa to the Basel framework: The dangers of instability, Speech at Unique Lecture at the 2015 Annual Convention of the Asociación de Mercados Financieros, 2 November 2015, Madrid, Spain, 2015.

Neisen, Martin (2016): Eigenmittelanforderungen für das operationelle Risiko [Operational Risk Capital Requirements], in: Boos/Fischer/Schulte-Mattler (Hrsg.)

[publisher]: KWG, CRR: Kommentar zum Kreditwesengesetz und VO (EU) Nr. 575/2013, 5. Aufl., Verlag C.H. Beck (Frankfurt am Main), 2016. [KWG, CRR: Commentary on the German Banking Act and the Regulation (EU) No 575/2013, 5th edition, Publisher C.H. Beck]

9 Capital Floors

Martin Neisen and Justin Waller

9.1 Introduction

When on the 7 December 2017 the Basel Committee published its final rules on the revision of the calculation of risk weighted assets, the committee was at least one year behind its original schedule. Already, since the Basel Committee meeting on 28 November 2016 in Santiago, all open issues regarding the standardised approach for credit risk (C-SA), internal rating based approach (IRB Approach) and the CVA risk capital charge were agreed. The last open point, and the reason for the delay, was the new capital floor. As the introduction and calibration of the capital floor will have direct and eventually extremely significant effects on the capital requirements for banks, this element of Basel IV is next to the treatment of real estate collateral under the standardised approach and the extent portfolios eligible for IRB-approaches one of the most controversially discussed issues. It took the Basel Committee more than one more year until its members found a compromise. This shows how important this topic is for supervisors and for banks around the globe.

At the end of 2014, the Basel Committee on Banking Supervision (BCBS) published the first consultative paper on the redesign of existing capital floors for minimum capital requirements when applying internal models.[1] Two potential approaches were proposed at that time. One approach was an aggregated output floor which covered all types of risks that are included in the capital requirement calculations of Pillar I. The second approach was designed as a more granular capital floor, which had to be calculated per risk type. The consultation paper even discussed the possibility of even more granular capital floors that are defined based on asset classes, exposure classes or even on a sub-portfolio level. In the end, after long and intensive discussions the Basel Committee decided on a capital floor, which is applied on an aggregated level across all types of Pillar I risks. While there was an intense discussion on the general concept of the future capital floors, the calibration of the floors was a major reason behind the delay in the finalisation of the framework.

The reason for such lengthy discussions was that there were two factions of supervisors in the Basel Committee. Each of them with a different level of trust in internal models.

On the one hand, there were supervisors that promoted the use of internal models. These supervisors have been consistently promoting internal models over the last 20 years and still believe that internal models, which have received supervisory approval, are better than standardised models. They claim that internal models are not

---

[1] The floor regulation is based on a study of the Committee on the balance of risk sensitivity, simplicity and comparability. Cf. BCBS 258 (2013).

only the better basis for the calculation of capital requirements, but also believe that internal Pillar I models support the banks in enhancing their overall risk management processes for market and credit risk. By that time, operational risk was already out of the picture, because it was clear that the internal models for operational risk would be replaced by a new more risk sensitive standardised approach (see Chapter 8). The largest opposition to the output floor has come from European banks, due to their reliance on internal modelling to calculate their risk weights, but also because the exposures of European banks tend to be more heavily concentrated in lower risk weighted areas such as residential mortgage lending and market risk trading positions.

On the other hand, there was a faction of supervisors who, over the years, had been very reluctant to approve internal models for the calculation of Pillar I capital requirements, or even did not give banks the opportunity of using these kinds of models. In comparison with their EU counterparts, US officials like the floor as it limits banks' ability to game the system. The US banks would be less affected than European banks, given the difference in the relative role of banks in credit intermediation and the intensity of risk on the balance sheets of banks.

During the consultation process, it was very quickly agreed that a new capital floor is necessary, but the concept and the calibration were difficult to agree on. It was clear that both cannot be discussed in an isolated manner. While a more granular capital floor was favoured by the pro internal models supervisors, the aggregated floor was more favoured by the supervisors more sceptical with regard to internal models. With regards to the calibration, the conflict was similar. Supervisors in favour of internal models wanted the calibration of the capital floor to be as low as possible. This would still give banks an incentive to use and enhance their internal models. This faction made initial suggestions for calibration of between 50% and 60%, based on the RWA calculated according to the new standardised approaches.[2] The other faction, of course, favoured a high calibration of at least 80% based on the new standardised approaches.

In the end, it was possible to find a compromise with a calibration of the capital floor at 72.5%. This result seems quite high for a compromise but comes along with other reductions of risk weights for the IRB Approach and the standardised approach for credit risk. Another concession was a long phase-in period starting in 2022, and lasting until 2027.

Before we give you a detailed overview of the requirements for the new capital floor in section 9.3, we would like to provide an overview of the Basel Committee's reasons for changing the existing floor calculation in section 9.2. To understand why the capital floor has higher impacts for some banks and countries than for others, it is necessary to look into the requirements for the original Basel I floor, which will be replaced by the

---

2 Only a very small minority took the position that a capital floor limiting the RWA based on standardised approaches was not needed at all. Another small faction wanted to remove internal models from the framework completely.

new rules in 2022. We will do this in section 9.3.2, and will also provide some examples of how the Basel I floor has been implemented in different countries in the past.

The new capital floor will cause many challenges to banks, not only because banks will have to calculate both standardised and internal models in parallel, but also because of the much bigger challenge – the impact on the capital ratios and how the possible additional capital requirements will be considered in the banks' capital allocation and pricing processes. We will use section 9.4 to give you an insight into the challenges for the business models and risk strategies of banks.

9.2 Reasons for the new capital floor

After the use of internal market risk models to determine capital requirements was introduced in 1996, the introduction of Basel II in 2004 allowed banks to measure capital requirements for credit risks and operational risks using internal models as well (IRBA or AMA).[3] To make sure that the resulting capital requirements did not fall below the desired regulatory level, the Basel I capital floor was introduced. This provision ensured that, even when internal models are used, banks had to maintain a level of capital related to the capital requirements pursuant to Basel I, multiplied by a factor determined by the regulatory authority. A more detailed description of the Basel I floor will follow later in this chapter, including some examples of the individual national interpretations and implementations. According to the original Basel II document in 2004, the capital floor should have been abolished by 2010. Now, almost 15 years later, the Basel Committee has decided that there is still the need for a capital floor. But the Basel I capital floor will be replaced by a newly designed capital floor.

The Basel Committee considers that the revision of the existing floor is necessary due to four major reasons.

1. **Out-of-date or no Basel I calculation systems.** The Basel I floor was originally introduced in 2004 for banks moving from Basel I to internal models for credit and operational risk under Basel II. After more than 15 years many banks do not have the IT systems in place anymore that can properly calculate the Basel I capital requirements. Considering mergers, start-up banks that started their business later than the introduction of Basel II, and countries in which Basel I was never implemented, it can no longer be ensured that all banks still have the ability to determine their capital requirements according to Basel I. Additionally, for the banks that still have the old systems in place, the advantage of a Basel I floor does not justify the maintenance costs for the systems.

2. **Individual implementation of Basel I and the Basel I capital floor.** Both Basel I and the Basel I capital floor were implemented on a national level with minor or sometimes significant adjustments. In several jurisdictions that implemented Basel II, Basel I

---

3   Cf. BCBS 128 (2006), page 13, marginal no. 45–47.

was never implemented. Therefore, there is no reliable basis for the floor calculation in these countries. In the EU for example, before the coming into force of the CRR, capital floors were implemented very differently in the member states, i.e. partly as explicitly binding capital requirements and partly for information purposes only. Nevertheless, the CRR version of the Basel I capital floor also diverges significantly from the proposed version of the Basel Committee.

3. **The scope of the Basel I floor.** Since the first application of Basel II and the Basel I capital floor, the requirements on regulatory capital changed, additional capital ratios under Basel III were introduced as well as new capital requirements under Basel II.5 and Basel III. The Basel I capital floor was developed and calibrated without considering these changes and therefore does not lead to the intended effect.

4. **Development of new standardised approaches.** Finally, the Basel I floor does not reflect the latest changes to the standardised approach for credit risk, market risk, counterparty credit risk and operational risk that are discussed in the other chapters of this book. These changes would have actually already made necessary the redevelopment and recalibration of the capital floor.

Besides these points of criticism regarding the current Basel I floor, there were also additional aspects that motivated the Basel Committee to carry on the work on the capital floor. The Basel Committee considers that the capital floor is an important component of the banking supervisory framework for the following reasons.

Empirical research by the Basel Committee based on hypothetical portfolios shows the banks' wide leeway in determining capital requirements based on internal models. As an example, Figure 9.1 shows how strongly risk weights of different banks can vary in a hypothetical sovereign portfolio compared to the average value of all banks considered.

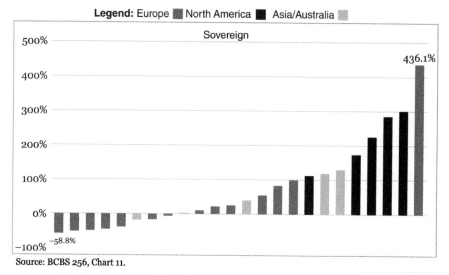

Source: BCBS 256, Chart 11.

Figure 9.1: Risk weight variations under IRBA

The comparability of capital requirements among banks as well as over time is hereby impaired. Moreover, the regulatory goal of ensuring transparency is also affected when investors are not able to conclude from the published information on capital requirements and risk-weighted assets the magnitude of the actual risks incurred. This applies all the more under the so-called partial use granted to IRB banks, when a portion of their exposures is permanently or transitionally allocated to the standardised approach and, thus, they profit from zero-risk-weighted government bonds, for example.

Another important reason for the variations of RWA is the different implementation and interpretation of the rules for internal models. Many requirements in the Basel framework do not provide sufficient details on how exactly banks have to implement certain rules. Therefore, banks need to make their own interpretations while developing and implementing internal models. The same issue also exists for national supervisors that have the goal of providing more details to their supervised banks on certain modelling issues. Even if they provide more details and harmonised interpretations, these interpretations can still be different from the interpretations of other supervisors in different countries. For example, on the EU level there is currently a big harmonisation initiative. First, the Basel framework is now implemented as an EU regulation (Capital requirements regulation – CRR) and therefore directly applicable to all banks without any national implementation needed. Supervisory discretion was reduced in the CRR compared to the prior national regulations. Secondly, many interpretations will be given now and in the future via so-called Regulatory Technical Standards (RTS), developed by the European Banking Authority (EBA). These RTS are also EU regulations and directly applicable to banks.[4]

Also, the approval process for internal models was – and is – very different from country to country. While some countries conducted very detailed approval audits including intensive on-site missions, other countries only asked for the documentation and conducted a high-level desktop review before granting the approval. Internal modelling is a very complicated subject. Therefore it is natural that banks do not always fulfil the expectations of the supervisors or that their interpretations are not the ones intended by the Basel Committee. Only a detailed standardised approval process of national supervisors can ensure a correct and – as much as possible – a harmonised internal model implementation.[5]

Besides differences in the implementation of the Basel II regulation at national level, the reasons for RWA variations may well be due to the fact that banks, when modelling, make conscious use of discretionary powers inherent in internal models in order to

---

4   Additionally there are also FAQs.
5   On EU level for instance, a detailed RTS addressing national supervisors was developed. This RTS sets minimum standards that supervisors must follow if they approve new or changed internal models. For banks that are supervised since 2014 by the European Central Bank (ECB), there is another initiative to harmonise internal models implementation. The ECB started in 2016 their Targeted Review of Internal Models (TRIM). In this initiative the ECB will re-audit most of the internal models, which were previously approved by national supervisors.

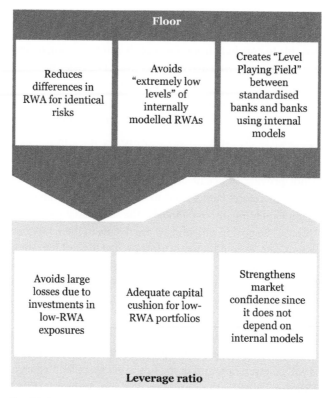

Figure 9.2: Floor and leverage ratio

achieve lower capital requirements. However, with such consciously optimistic modelling decisions, the capital falls below the levels deemed prudent by the regulators.

Ultimately, internal models are, to a certain degree, also subject to model risks. Model
risk is the risk that reality is not adequately modelled, resulting in inadequately high
or low capital requirements.

Similar arguments were already presented by the Basel Committee in relation to
the introduction of the leverage ratio. Yet, the Basel Committee considers that the
capital floor and leverage ratio are not redundant but rather complement each other
(Figure 9.2).[6]

9.3 Basel IV Capital Floor

The BCBS decided on a capital floor based on an aggregate RWA-approach, calculated
by multiplying the total standardised RWA with the floor factor of 72.5%. The
aggregated RWA approach allows for the offsetting of the effects of individual risk

---

6   Cf. BCBS 306 (2014), page 4.

categories. According to the Basel Committee's point of view, an aggregated floor is easier to communicate and to interpret than other approaches, which has been reflected in the final rules.

9.3.1 Capital Floors in Basel I and II

While Basel I introduced the capital requirements for Credit Risk, Basel II went one step ahead and acknowledged other material risks such as the Market and Operational risk. The Basel II framework also introduced a floor for the capital requirements and the floor was calibrated at 80% of the Basel 1 requirements. The implementation of the Basel I floor has been inconsistent across the countries, partly because of the differing interpretations of the requirement and also because it is based on the Basel 1 standards, which many banks and jurisdictions no longer apply.

As shown in Figure 9.3 below, Basel IV has lowered the floor on the capital requirements, starting at 50% in 2022 and increasing to 72.5% by the year 2027. We are already seeing national supervisors adopt different approaches to implementaiton. For example, the Australian Prudential Regulatory Authority (APRA)[7] does not intend to adopt the phase-in arrangements, and expects to implement the floor in line with other proposed changes in risk weights.

To illustrate the differences in the national Basel I implementations, we would like to compare the original Basel I capital floor requirement and the individual implementation of the Basel I floor according to the CRR in the EU.

The EU version of the capital floor requires that the regulatory capital must not fall below the level of 80% of the capital requirements according to Basel I.

Evolution of Capital Floor Requirements	Basel II	Basel IV
General	80% of the Basel I RWA	1 January 2022: 50% 1 January 2023: 55% 1 January 2024: 60% 1 January 2025: 65% 1 January 2026: 70% 1 January 2027: 72.5%
Europe	80% of the Basel I RWA	Not published yet.
Australia	80% of the Basel I RWA has since been removed	1 January 2022: 72.5%
Canada	80% of the Basel I RWA has since been removed	Q2 2018: 70% Q3 2018: 72.5% Q4 2018: 75% Currently under existing capital framework.

Figure 9.3: Evolution of Capital Floor Requirements

---

7   https://www.apra.gov.au/sites/default/files/Revisions%2520to%2520the%2520capital%2520framework%2520 for%2520ADIs.pdf

		Credit risk	- Asset Class A	- Asset Class B	- Asset Class C	Market risk	Operational risk (not modelled)	Total RWA
General	Pre-Floor RWA	40	32	3	5	1.5	8	49.5
	Standardised RWA	60	45	6	9	2	8	70
	Basel II (80% of RWA)[1]	48	36	4.8	7.2	0	0	48
	Basel IV (50% of RWA)[2]	30	22.5	3	4.5	1	8	39
	Basel IV (72.5% of RWA) [3]	43.5	32.6	4.4	6.5	1.5	8	52.95

[1] As of 1st January 2018
[2] As of 1st January 2022
[3] As of 1st January 2027

Figure 9.4: Changes to Capital Requirements between Basel II and IV

Equation 9.1

$$C_i > r_{Basel\ I,i} \times 80\% \times 0.08 \tag{9.1}$$

Where

C_i = Regulatory capital of Bank i
$r_{Basel\ Ii}$ = Capital requirements of Bank I according to Basel I

This is a completely different concept than the original Basel I floor, that requires that the RWA calculated by using IRB and /or AMA must not fall below 80% of the RWA calculated according to Basel I.

Equation 9.2

$$RWA_i > RWA_{Basel\ I,i} \times 80\% \tag{9.2}$$

Where

$RWAi$ = Risk weighted assets of Bank i according to Basel II
$RWA_{Basel\ I}$ = Risk weighted assets of Bank i according to Basel I

The reasoning behind the Basel I framework is in line with the goal of this requirement, which is to ensure that the global level of capital in the financial market should not fall under a certain level. The original Basel I floor ensure that the level of RWA will not fall under a certain level or expressed based on the capital ratios, the capital ratios should not fall under a certain level compared to the capital ratios based on the Basel I framework. The original Basel I floor indirectly ensures the goal of the European Basel I floor as well but is much more transparent on the effect of the new calculation methods of Basel II to the capital ratios or RWA. The following example illustrates the different approaches:

A Bank i has in total capital of 15. The sum of RWA according to Basel I is 170 (Figure 9.5).

RWA Basel I	
Credit risk	160
Market risk	10
Sum	170

Figure 9.5: Example 1: RWA according to Basel I

If the Bank applies the Basel II Framework, the RWA based on internal models for credit risk and for operational risk are 105 (Figure 9.6).

RWA Basel II	
Credit risk	90
Market risk	10
Operational	5
Sum	105

Figure 9.6: Example 2: RWA according to Basel II

If we apply equation (9.1) for the Basel I capital floor according to the EU rules:

Equation 9.3

$$15 > 170 \times 0.08 \times 80\% \tag{9.3}$$

we can see that the capital floor condition is fulfilled and has no implication for the bank.

On the other hand, if we apply equation (9.2) for the original Basel I capital floor:

Equation 9.4

$$105 > 170 \times 80\% \tag{9.4}$$

we can see, that the condition is not fulfilled. The bank has to consider additional RWA of 31 (170 $*$ 80%–105).

This shows that the original Basel I capital floor increases the RWA by 29.5%, while the EU version does not trigger anything. Only if the bank would set not needed regulatory capital free, e.g. by an extra dividend payment, the capital floor might trigger. The impact becomes even clearer if we compare the capital ratios according to Basel I, Basel II and EU version of the Basel I capital floor.

The regulatory capital ratio increased by 61% in the EU scenario and by 25% in the original Basel I capital floor scenario. If we assume a return on regulatory capital of 10% and that the bank can invest c.p. in the same portfolio structure, then the bank

RWA	170.00	105.00	105.00
Floor effect	--	33.00	--
Regulatory capital	15.00	15.00	15.00
Capital ratio	8.82%	10.87%	14.29%

Figure 9.7: Example 3: Overview of results

RWA Basel I		RWA Basel II		RWA Basel IV SA		RWA Basel IV IM	
Credit risk	160	Credit risk	90	Credit risk	150	Credit risk	95
Market risk	10	Market risk	10	Market risk	10	Market risk	10
		Operational	5	Operational	10	Operational	10
Sum	170	Sum	105	Sum	170	Sum	115

Figure 9.8: Example 4: Overview of results incl. Basel IV

can generate additional income in the EU scenario of 3.1, if the bank wants to archive the same regulatory capital ratio as in the original Basel I capital floor scenario.

To illustrate the potential impact of the new Basel IV capital floor compared to the Basel I floor (both EU version and original version), we would like to pick up the example of chapter above (Figure 9.8).

To make the example work, we have to consider now also the RWA according to the new Basel IV standardised approaches and the RWA according to the new Basel IV internal models approaches (new internal models for credit risk and market risk but the new standardised approach for operational risk. The Basel IV capital floor can be described by the following formula:

Equation 9.5

$$RWA_{Basel\ IV,i} > RWA_{Basel\ IV\ SA,i} \times 72.5\% \tag{9.5}$$

The RWA of bank i according to the standardised approaches are 170. Applying the capital floor calibrated at 72.5 without considering transitional rules,

Equation 9.6

$$115 > 170 \times 72.5\% \tag{9.6}$$

shows that the new capital floor will be triggered and leads to an additional RWA of 8.25. Considering the impact on capital ratios shows that banks in the EU face a much higher impact on the capital ratio as bank in jurisdictions that implemented the original Basel I floor (Figure 9.9).

The capital ratio for bank i falls in this example by 2.12% (12.17–14.29%) compared to the Basel II capital ratio in the EU scenario. While for a bank that had to consider the original Basel I can even increase its capital ratio in this example by 1.14% (12.17–11.03%).

Regulatory capital ratio				
	Basel I	Basel II	Basel II EU floor	Basel IV
RWA	170.00	105.00	105.00	115
Floor effect	--	31.00	--	8.25
Regulatory capital	15.00	15.00	15.00	15.00
Capital ratio	8.82%	11.03%	14.29%	12.17%

Figure 9.9: Example 5: Overview of Capital ratios incl. Basel IV

9.3.2 Calculation of the floor

Banks must calculate the risk-weighted assets for determining the capital to be held as the maximum of:

a) The total risk-weighted assets calculated using the approaches that the bank has supervisory approval to use in accordance with the Basel capital framework (including both standardised and internally-modelled approaches); and

b) 72.5% of the total risk weighted assets, calculated using only the standardised approaches listed below.

The following six standardised approaches will be used when calculating the output floor:

1. **Credit risk.** The standardised approach for credit risk. When calculating the degree of credit risk mitigation, banks must use the carrying value when applying the simple approach or the comprehensive approach with standard supervisory haircuts.[8]

2. **Counterparty credit risk.** To calculate the exposure for derivatives, banks must use the standardised approach for measuring counterparty credit risk (SA-CCR). The exposure amounts must then be multiplied by the relevant borrower risk weight using the standardised approach for credit risk to calculate RWA under the standardised approach for credit risk.

3. **Credit valuation adjustment risk.** The standardised approach for CVA (SA-CVA), the Basic Approach (BA-CVA) or 100% of a bank's counterparty credit risk capital requirement (depending on which approach the bank uses for CVA risk).

4. **Securitisation framework.** The external ratings-based approach (SEC_ERBA), the standardised approach (SEC-SA) or a risk-weight of 1,250%.

5. **Market risk.** The standardised approach for market risk. The SEC-ERBA, SEC-SA, or a risk-weight of 1,250% must be used when determining the default risk charge component for securitisations held in the trading book.

6. **Operational risk.** The standardised approach for operational risk.

---

8   This also includes failed trades and non-delivery-versus-payment transactions as set out in Annex 3 of the Basel II framework (June 2006).

Applying the above-described requirements to the calculation of CET1 ratio the general formula is:

Equation 9.7

$$CET1 - Ratio = \cfrac{CET1}{Max\left[RWA_{INT} = [RWA_{int} + RWA_{std}]; RWA_{STD} \times \begin{Bmatrix} 0.5 \\ 0.55 \\ 0.6 \\ 0.65 \\ 0.70 \\ 0.725 \end{Bmatrix} \right]}$$

(9.7)

Where:

RWA_{INT} = Total risk weighted assets for banks using internal models
RWA_{int} = Part of total risk weighted assets calculated by internal models
RWA_{std} = Part of total risk weighted assets calculated by standardised approaches
RWA_{STD} = Total risk weighted assets only calculated by standardised approaches

9.3.3 Transitional Cap Rules

In addition, at national discretion, supervisors may cap the increase in a bank's total RWAs that result from the application of the output floor during its phase-in period. The transitional cap on the increase in RWAs will be set at 25% of a bank's RWAs before the application of the floor. Put differently, if the supervisor uses this discretion, the bank's RWAs will effectively be capped at 1.25 times the internally calculated RWAs during that time. The cap would apply for the duration of the phase-in period of the output floor (i.e. the cap would be removed on 1 January 2027).

More generally, a jurisdiction that does not implement some or all of the internal-modelled approaches but instead only implements the standardised approaches is compliant with the Basel framework. Also, jurisdictions may elect to implement requirements that are more conservative and/or accelerated transitional arrangements, as the Basel framework constitutes minimum standards only.

Figures 9.10 and 9.11 are simple illustrated examples, showing how the floor is calculated for multiple scenarios with different values for Standardised Approach (SA) RWA and Internal Model (IM) RWA.

In Figure 9.10, as the floored RWAs (103) are higher than the pre-floor RWAs (50) in this example, the bank would use the floored RWAs to determine the capital requirements. Since the Transitional Cap Rule limits the increase in the RWA to 25% of its Pre-Floor level, it results in a total capital required of $62.5m compared to the $103m calculated through the 72.5% capital floor. This results in an additional capital requirement of $12.5 m, compared to the $53 m that would be needed with just the capital

Risk-class	Pre-floor RWAs - (a)	Standardised RWAs - (b)	72.5% of Standardised RWAs - (c)	Transitional Cap Rule RWA - (d)	Additional Capital Required - [Min(d,c)-a]
Credit risk	40	130	94.3		
- Asset Class A	32	80	58		
- Asset Class B	3	45	32.6		
- Asset Class C (not modelled)	5	5	3.6		
Market risk	2	4	2.9		
Operational risk (not modelled)	8	8	5.8		
Total RWA	50	142	103	60	10

Figure 9.10: Scenario 1: High SA versus Low IM ('m $)

Risk-class	Pre-floor RWAs - (a)	Standardised RWAs - (b)	72.5% of Standardised RWAs - (c)	Transitional Cap Rule RWA - (d)	Additional Capital Required - [Min(d,c)-a]
Credit risk	40	46	33.4		
- Asset Class A	32	36	26.1		
- Asset Class B	3	5	3.6		
- Asset Class C (not modelled)	5	5	3.6		
Market risk	2	3	2.2		
Operational risk (not modelled)	8	8	5.8		
Total RWA	50	57	41.3	60	0

Figure 9.11: Scenario 2: Low SA versus Low IM ('m $)

floors. Overall, the transactional cap rule exists to lower the additional capital requirements at times when the difference between the RWAs calculated through IM and SA is high.

This example also illustrates how the aggregate RWA floor is more beneficial than at the individual risk class level as banks that don't use internal models across all classes will have the ability to use additional RWA headroom to offset for other classes. For large banks that have approved internal models for all risk types at their disposal, the differences between these two approaches should be less aggravating since the floor is applicable to all risk categories.

In Figure 9.11 the RWA calculated through the SA is lower than that for RWA. In scenarios like this, the transactional cap rule does not yield much benefits since the cap is above the SA RWA anyway.

9.3.4 Choice of which standardised approach

The Basel Committee also considers taking the standardised approach to determine the floor. The following challenges were specifically identified by the Committee.

1. For individual risk categories there is more than just one standardised approach (e.g. in the Basel III framework on operational risk).

2. The implementation of standardised approaches is subject to national discretion.

3. The standardised approaches contain particular elements that require supervisory approval (e.g. within the framework of credit risk mitigation).

In this regard, the Basel Committee arrives at the conclusion that banks should make use of the standardised approach that they have implemented. Even if this causes some variability among banks with regard to the calculated capital requirements, this method seems to make more sense than the alternative of predefining certain standardised approaches and methods to determine the floor. Moreover, the effects of the mentioned points will most likely be moderated once the new standardised approaches come into force within the framework of Basel IV.

9.3.5 Global implementation

As of writing, only a few prudential regulatory bodies have commented on the capital floor. The Canadian and Australian prudential authorities have expedited the phase-in requirements of the capital floor, under the existing capital framework or the revised RWA requirements when they are implemented. No prudential regulatory authority has publically announced that they will delay implementation outside of Basel timeframes, or beneath the BCBS minimum of 72.5%.

The Australian Prudential Regulatory Authority has indicated that they will implement the floor in line with other proposed changes to risk weights, instead of phasing it in as per the BCBS reform. In a similar manner, Office of the Superintendent of Financial Institutions (OSFI) will implement a capital floor based on the existing capital framework, which will be set at 70% in Q2 2018, 72.5% in Q3 2018, and 75% in Q4 2018. OSFI has mentioned that the capital floor is to be updated further as changes are made to OSFI's capital framework as part of the Capital Framework.

Finally, with the implementation of the capital floor, any jurisdiction that does not implement some or all of the internal-modelled approaches, but instead only implements the standardised approaches is compliant with the Basel framework. Consistent with the approach from APRA and OSFI, jurisdictions may elect to implement more conservative requirements and/or accelerated transitional arrangements, as the Basel framework constitutes minimum standards only. We expect that jurisdictions, such as Europe, will not accelerate the implementation.

9.4 Interactions and interdependencies to other Basel IV rules

When the Basel Committee started in 2012 the consultations for the new approaches to calculate the RWA for credit risk, market risk and operational risk, the goal was to finalise the reform of the Basel framework that started after the financial crisis with the first consultation paper on Basel III in December 2009. Published in 2010, the final Basel III framework was only the first step to reform the Basel II framework of 2004. The changes of Basel III mainly focused on:

- the quality of regulatory capital (new definitions of regulatory capital, new capital ratios, the requirements on certain capital instruments, stricter rules on capital deductions and the capital buffers),
- the introduction of the leverage ratio as an additional backstop capital ratio that is not risk sensitive,
- two new liquidity ratios, the liquidity coverage ratio (LCR) and the net stable funding ratio (NSFR), and
- a new capital requirement for the CVA risk.

On the other hand, the changes published in December 2017, and earlier in 2016 and 2015, are the second step in the reform, focusing more on the calculation of RWA. The changes in the second step can be divided into five groups of topics (Figures 9.12–9.16).

Capital floors

- RWA (using internal model approaches) floored by a percentage of RWA as determined through the standardised approaches
- Capital output floor will be applied to total RWA not to each major risk category
- Calibration of the output floor at 72.5%
- Transitional phase-in rules until 2027

Figure 9.12: Overview of Basel IV

Credit risk

- Revised standardised approach including broadly revised risk weights and additional due diligence requirements. Biggest changes can be seen for the exposure classes banks, corporates, equity positions and positions secured by real estate collaterals

- Constraints on the application of internal ratings for some exposure classes, introduction of parameter input floors, new formulas for the calculation of risk mitigation effects and general changes in the qualitative requirements on the IRB Approach

Figure 9.13: Overview of Basel IV

Market risk

- Revised boundary of the trading book and stricter approval of internal models

- Sensitivities-based analysis as new standardised approach, which also serves as a floor for the internal model approach

- Internal model approach with expected shortfall based on stressed calibration as key metric and considering product-specific liquidity horizon

Figure 9.14: Overview of Basel IV

Operational risk

- Replacement of existing approaches by a new standardised approach

- Fundamental assumption that operational risk is related to size

- Use of the "unadjusted business indicator" as a measure of operational risk exposure combined with collection and analysis of historical loss data

Figure 9.15: Overview of Basel IV

Other topics

- Ban on use of internal models-based approach and introduction of a standardised approach for CVA
- Global standard for large exposure with harmonised definition on exposures and groups of connected clients
- Standardised disclosure templates and new disclosure requirement for all new RWA approaches
- New rules for securitisation RWA and STS securitisations
- Pillar II and indirect Pillar I requirements on step in risk
- Phase-in of "old" Basel III rules

Figure 9.16: Overview of Basel IV

9.4.1 Overview of the goals and quantitative impact of the capital floor and other Basel IV changes

The overall goal of these Basel IV changes is to restore trust and credibility in the methods of calculating RWA and therefore also in the Pillar I capital ratios. Basel IV will enhance the robustness and the risk sensitivity of all standardised approaches. This includes credit risk, market risk and operational risk. Combined with enhanced Pillar III disclosure requirements, Basel IV will increase the transparency and comparability of banks' capital ratios on a global level.

While the standardised approaches will become more complex and risk sensitive, the use of internal models will be constrained by placing limits on certain inputs to calculate RWA under the IRB Approach, by removing the possibility to use the Advanced Measurement Approaches (AMA) for operational risk and by redesigning fundamentally the requirements for internal market risk models and the corresponding approval and backtesting process. Apart from the changes to the RWA calculation methods, the Basel Committee also finalised the leverage ratio. There will be a fixed 3% minimum requirement and an additional buffer for global systemically important banks (G-SIBs). Last but not least the capital floor, calibrated at 72.5%, will limit the variation of RWA based on internal models.

The challenge of the Basel Committee while designing the new rules was to archive the above-mentioned goals, while not increasing the total RWA significantly, at least not on an aggregated global level. A significant increase was defined at 10% compared to current RWA levels.

Based on results of the cumulative quantitative impact study (QIS), which was published in December 2017 together with the final Basel IV rules, the Basel Committee considers this goal to be achieved. Nevertheless, it can be stated that the impact of Basel IV can vary significantly depending on the size of the bank, the business model and on the extent to which the bank uses internal models for the calculation of RWA.[9] The results of the above mentioned QIS were strongly criticised by experts from the banking industry, supervisors and also from independent experts. The strongest point of criticism was the data quality of the submissions of banks. Independent observations show that the quality of the submissions varied significantly. Also, the way the figures were presented on a very high aggregated level hide that in certain jurisdictions and banks the impact is much higher than indicated by the QIS. It was further criticised that the figures of the QIS show only the impact of the changes published in December 2017, and not changes that were already finalised and published in 2016 and 2015. This applies especially to the changes in market risk known as the Fundamental Review of the Trading Book (FRTB). But the true impact of Basel IV can only be understood if all changes to the methods of RWA calculation are analysed at the same time.

Based on internal data collected within a large number of detailed test calculations with banks across the globe, the variation of the impact is much higher than indicated by the QIS. Internal results show that the impact varies between a reduction of RWA of more than 10% on the one hand side and an increase in total RWA of more than 50% on the other side. Especially for large banking groups that use internal models for most of their portfolios in credit risk and market risk, the capital floor will be the main driver of a high RWA increase.

When analysing the impact of the capital floor on RWA and therefore on the business models of banks, is very important to do this analysis not only considering the capital floor rules. There are many interactions between the new capital floor and other new rules like the new standardised approaches, the new rules for the partial use of internal market risk models and the new rules for the IRB models.

9.4.2 Impact of the capital floor on the standardised approaches and their implementation

Banks that use internal models for the main part of their business did not pay much attention to the standardised approaches in the past. This will change significantly in the future. There are two major reasons for the increased focus that banks using internal models will have to make on the standardised approaches.

First, internal models banks will have to always calculate risk weighted assets according to both standardised approaches and internal models in parallel. Banks should not underestimate the effort for the implementation of standardised approaches, both from a technical perspective and from an IT perspective.

---

9   On average, minimum required Tier 1 capital at the target level (Tier 1) decreases by 0.5% for Group 1 banks and increases by 3.8% for Group 2 banks (see also Table 1). Average risk-based capital ratios will increase by 0.2 percentage points for Group 1 banks and by 0.1 percentage points for Group 2 banks, relative to the current national implementation of the Basel III framework as agreed up to January 2016 (for details see BCBS d426)

For example, banks that currently use internal market risk models will have to develop and implement expected shortfall models for each trading desk and on an aggregated level for the total trading portfolio. Because backtesting of expected shortfall models is still a big academic challenge, these banks will have to perform their backtesting based on the "old" VaR models. Again, both on trading desk level and on the aggregated level for the total trading portfolio. The supervisory approval for internal market risk models will be granted in the future on a trading desk by desk basis. If certain requirements are not fulfilled for certain trading desks, the bank has to fall back on the standardised approach for market risk for this desk. This means that a bank has to implement the standardised approach for each trading desk. And, of course, banks have to implement the standardised approach on the aggregated level for the capital floor calculation. Altogether banks will have to implement two internal models (VaR and Expected shortfall) and a new standardised approach. Both have to be implemented in a way that allows a daily parallel calculation on the aggregated level and on a desk by desk basis. This is a huge challenge for the IT infrastructure of a bank and will be one of the main drivers for implementation and maintenance costs of internal market risk models. The same challenge also applies to the IRB Approach.

The second major reason for the increasing importance of the standardised approachs in internal models banks is disclosure. The Basel Committee published a first consultation paper in March 2018 on the new disclosure requirements related to the changes published in December 2017. This includes disclosure requirements for the capital floor and its calculation. For details, please refer to Chapter 11. In this consultation paper, the Basel Committee proposes very detailed disclosure requirements not only for the pure calculation of the capital floors, but also very detailed requirements on the parallel disclosure of the standardised RWA estimation approaches, which are used as a basis for the capital floor. This huge increase in transparency will also boost the importance of the standardised approaches. Actually, it will be possible to compare the RWA of all banks on a global level, no matter if they are using internal models or not. There will always be detailed information on the RWA according to the standardised approaches available. It can be expected that analysts will adapt to this and will consider standardised RWA as a major input in the rating assessment of banks.

9.4.3 Optimisation of the standardised approaches

The standardised approach will not only get more into the focus for banks because of the higher implementation and IT effort. The standardised approaches are also becoming more important because they will have much more influence on the total RWA than in the past. As mentioned above, banks that were using internal models for the RWA calculation applied the standardised approaches only for very small parts of their portfolios. This so-called partial use of standardised approaches can have many reasons. The reasons can be, for example:

- the portfolio is a run-off portfolio
- the business is new, and the existing models cannot be applied to this portfolio

- the development of models is not possible due to the lack of own data
- there is no fitting theoretical concept that can be used for this specific portfolio
- to develop a model is too great a burden for the bank compared to the benefit of using an internal model for this portfolio
- the supervisors exclude in general the use of internal models for this kind of portfolio
- the portfolio falls under the scope of an economic development scheme, and the risk weight shall be the same for all banks in this state
- ...

The rules for the partial use, both for market and credit risk are quite different from country to country. But, in general, the part of the portfolio that falls into the partial use is rather small compared to the part that is considered in the internal models. This leads very often to the situation that the effort put into the implementation and optimisation of the standardised approaches is not as big as it could be. For example, banks sometimes do not use risk mitigation techniques in the standardised approach for credit risk, even if the RWA could be reduced by 10–20%. The reason is simply that the implementation costs for using risk mitigation are higher than the RWA savings of a small partial use portfolio.[10]

This will change dramatically with the new capital floor. Banks must not implement the standardised approach in the simplest and least expensive way for the total portfolio anymore. Instead, they will also have to optimise the standardised approaches as much as possible. The RWA calculated using standardised approaches will be the assessment basis for the capital floor and therefore the basis for the future total RWA. The best and most optimised internal models will lose their benefit in terms of RWA calculation, if at the same moment the standardised approaches are not optimised as well.

Figure 9.17 shows the relationship between standardised approach RWA, internal models RWA, the RWA considering capital floors and the optimisation potential.

The effect can be best described using a simplified example. A bank that is affected by the RWA limitation of the capital floor at full extent (internal models RWA is far lower than 72.5%) has RWA according to the standardised approach of 500 billion euros. This is the assessment basis for the calculation of the capital floor. The bank uses internal models for both market risk and credit risk. The RWA according to the internal models including a small partial use portfolio is 300 billion euros (60% RWA compared to the standardised approaches). Without considering the transition rules, the RWA for this bank considering the capital floor calibrated at 72.5 % is 362.5 billion euros. This means that the capital floor results in an incremental RWA increase of 62.5 billion euros. After a detailed analysis of the portfolios and the mechanisms of the standardised approaches, the bank optimises the standardised approaches and realises a reduction in RWA for the standardised approaches of 18% (40 billion euros for market

---

10 If the partial use portfolio accounts for only 10% of the total RWA, and the RWA savings are 15% of that portfolio, the total effect of optimisation would be only 1.5% of the total RWA.

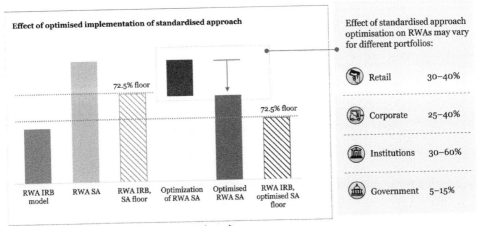

Effect of optimised implementation of standardised approach

72.5% floor

72.5% floor

| RWA IRB model | RWA SA | RWA IRB, SA floor | Optimization of RWA SA | Optimised RWA SA | RWA IRB, optimised SA floor |

Effect of standardised approach optimisation on RWAs may vary for different portfolios:

Retail 30–40%

Corporate 25–40%

Institutions 30–60%

Government 5–15%

Source: PwC analysis, EBA 2016 EU-wide transparency exercise results

Figure 9.17: Optimisation of the standardised approaches

risk, 50 billion euros for credit risk, in total 90 billion euros). The new capital floor after optimisation is 297.25 billion euros, which is even lower than the current RWA according to the internal models (300 billion euros).[11] The optimisation leads therefore to the situation where the bank again can fully benefit from internal models. The total RWA will be 62.5 billion euros lower than before the optimisation.

The optimisation potential for the standardised approaches depends on many variables, such as:

- national discretion for the standardised approaches, e.g. use of external ratings in the standardised approach for credit risk
- data quality
- trading and treasury strategy
- use of collateral
- …

According to several analyses in large international banks, the potential for RWA optimisation in the standardised approach for credit risk can vary from 5% to 15% for sovereign exposures up to 30% to 60% for corporate portfolios. Each bank will have to analyse individually how big the optimisation potential is, and calculate a business case, comparing benefits of reducing RWA and implementation costs.

9.4.4 Impact of the capital floor on pricing models

Capital costs play a very important role in the overall pricing models of banks. Considering the huge potential impact of the capital floor for some banks that are

---

11   In this case the bank will have to optimise the internal models approaches as well.

Total RWA internal:	300
Total capital costs internal:	1.5
Total RWA standadised:	500
Total capital costs standadised:	2.5
Total RWA capital floor:	362.5
Total capital costs capital floor:	1.8125

Figure 9.18: Example 2, Case 1: Overview of RWA, capital costs and capital floor

using internal models, this will also have a significant impact on their pricing. This applies not only to the prices themselves, but also to the pricing models, which will now have to be changed. The pricing models have to change such that they would consider additional constraints from the capital floor.

The consideration of the capital floor in pricing models is not straightforward. There are several difficulties that must be considered here. First, whether the capital floor is a constraint at all. For example, for a bank in which the difference between RWA according to internal models and the RWA according to standardised approaches is below 27.5%, the capital floor is not a constraint. In this case, the capital costs to be considered in the pricing models is the same as if there were no capital floor at all. Second, if there is a difference greater than 27.5% between RWA according to internal models and the RWA according to standardised approaches, what are the individual RWA of a exposure according to the internal models and according to the capital floor? The three following simplified examples show how this can affect total capital costs.

The bank has an individual target CET 1 ratio of 10% and a return on regulatory capital of 5%.

Situation in $t = 0$

As you can see, the RWA considering the capital floor is higher than according to the internal models. Therefore the capital costs the bank has to consider are higher (1.815) than only considering the internal models (1.5).

Case 1:

In $t = 1$ the bank grants a new credit i to one of its customers. The RWA calculated isolated for credit i is as shown in Figure 9.19.

The capital costs to be considered in the pricing models should not be based on the isolated calculation of RWA for credit i, neither considering only internal models (0.25), nor standardised approaches (0.35).

The capital cost must be considered on the portfolio level including the effect of the capital floor.

Hypothetical RWA and capital costs for an additional credit i	
RWA credit i internal:	50
Capital costs credit i internal:	0.25
RWA credit i standardised:	70
Capital costs credit i standardised:	0.35

Figure 9.19: Example 2, Case 1: Hypothetical RWA and capital costs

Total RWA and capital costs for an additional credit i	
Total RWA internal plus credit i	350
Total capital costs plus credit i internal:	1.75
Marginal capital costs internal plus credit i	0.25
Total RWA standardised plus credit i	570
Total capital costs standardised plus credit i	2.85
Marginal capital costs standardised plus credit i	0.35
Total RWA capital floor plus credit i	413.25
Total capital costs capital floor plus credit i:	2.06625
Marginal capital costs capital floor plus credit i	0.25375

Figure 9.20: Example 2, Case 1: Total and marginal capital costs

As Figure 9.20 shows, the capital cost to be considered in the pricing of credit i must be the marginal contribution of credit i to the total capital cost for the portfolio (0.25375) considering the effect of the capital floors.

As mentioned above, there might be cases where the RWA for a credit i according to internal models and standardised approaches are much closer, or the RWA of internal models are even higher than in the standardised approaches. This makes the consideration of the capital floors in the pricing models even more challenging. Please consider Case 2.

Case 2:

The initial RWA in t = 0 is the same as in case 1.

The RWA calculated isolated for credit i is now as shown in Figure 9.21.

In this case, the RWA for credit i according to internal models (80) is higher than according to the standardised approaches (70).

On a portfolio level, the marginal contribution to capital costs according to the capital floor is lower than both standardised approaches (0.35) or internal models (0.4). This seems counterintuitive, but illustrates the compensating effect of the capital floor in certain circumstances when investing in high-risk exposures (Figure 9.22).

This effect can vary depending on how close RWA according to standardised approaches and internal models are for certain exposures.

Hypothetical RWA and capital costs for an additional credit i	
RWA credit i internal:	80
Capital costs credit i internal:	0.4
RWA credit i standardised:	70
Capital costs credit i standardised:	0.35

Figure 9.21: Example 2, Case 2: Hypothetical RWA and capital costs

Total RWA and capital costs for an additional credit i	
Total RWA internal plus credit i	380
Total capital costs plus credit i internal:	1.9
Marginal capital costs internal plus credit i	0.4
Total RWA standardised plus credit i	570
Total capital costs standardised plus credit i	2.85
Marginal capital costs standardised plus credit i	0.35
Total RWA capital floor plus credit i	413.25
Total capital costs capital floor plus credit i:	2.06625
Marginal capital costs capital floor plus credit i	0.25375

Figure 9.22: Example 2, Case 2: Total RWA and capital costs

Please note that, while for credit risk in the banking book (standardised approach for credit risk and IRB Approach), no portfolio effects are taken into account in the calculation of RWA, for market risk both the Sensitivity based approach (SBA) and the Internal models approach (IMA) consider portfolio effects. This has an additional influence on the calculation of capital costs and therefore makes considering the effect of the capital floor even more challenging.

The last example shows the effect of the capital floor to marginal capital costs if RWA according to the standardised approaches and internal models are almost on the same level and a credit i is granted where the RWA according to internal models is much lower for this credit than according to the standardised approach.

Case 3:

The RWA and capital costs in t = 0 are shown in Figure 9.23.

Total RWA internal:	370
Total capital costs internal:	1.85
Total RWA standadised:	500
Total capital costs standadised:	2.5
Total RWA capital floor:	362.5
Total capital costs capital floor:	1.85

Figure 9.23: Example 2, Case 3: Overview of RWA, capital costs and capital floor

Hypothetical RWA and capital costs for an additional credit i	
RWA credit i internal:	10
Capital costs credit i internal:	0.05
RWA credit i standardised:	70
Capital costs credit i standardised:	0.35

Figure 9.24: Example 2, Case 3: Hypothetical RWA and capital costs

Total RWA and capital costs for an additional credit i	
Total RWA internal plus credit i	380
Total capital costs plus credit i internal:	1.9
Marginal capital costs internal plus credit i	0.05
Total RWA standardised plus credit i	570
Total capital costs standardised plus credit i	2.85
Marginal capital costs standardised plus credit i	0.35
Total RWA capital floor plus credit i	413.25
Total capital costs capital floor plus credit i:	2.06625
Marginal capital costs capital floor plus credit i	0.21625

Figure 9.25: Example 2, Case 3: Total and marginal capital costs

The level of RWA according to internal models is slightly higher (370) than according to the capital floor (362.5). Therefore, the capital costs (1.85) are based on the RWA according to the internal models, not based on the RWA considering the capital floor effect.

In $t = 1$ the bank grants a credit i with isolated RWA as shown in Figure 9.24.

The RWA according to the internal models of credit i is much lower than according to the standardised approaches.

Considering the RWA and the capital costs on portfolio level shows that the effect of the capital floor can be very high for low-risk exposures according to the internal models (Figure 9.25). In this case, the factor between the marginal capital costs according to the internal models (0.05) compared to the marginal capital costs according to the capital floors (0.21625) is 4.3. This might lead to the effect that the introduction of the capital floor will significantly increase the pricing for low-risk exposures like sovereign exposures.

9.4.5 Relationship between the capital floor and the scope of application of the IRB Approach

Apart from the introduction of a new capital floor, another important change for banks using the IRB Approach is that the IRB Approach cannot be applied to all exposure classes anymore or that only the foundation IRB can be used for the calculation of RWA. This will also have a significant influence on RWA and the pricing of exposures.

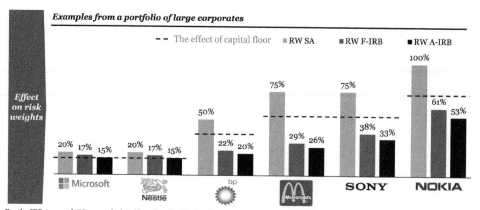

For the IRB Approach PDs are calculated based on the 'shadow bond' modeling approach and benchmark LGDs are used, for the New Standardised Approach base risk weights are obtained from the BCBS look-up table, capital floor is set up at 72.5%

Figure 9.26: Removal of the IRB option and new capital floors

This should always be analysed in combination with the effects of the capital floor. Both effects can mitigate each other or can even build each other up, depending on the combination. Figure 9.26 shows the differences between RWA for large international corporates according to the standardised approach, the foundation IRB, the advanced IRB Approach, and how this relates to the capital floors on a single exposure level. In some cases, the capital floor has no effect on the RWA considering the foundation approach (see Figure 9.24). In other cases, the capital floor is limiting the RWA for both advanced and foundation IRB Approach. These examples ignore, for illustrative purposes, the fact that the capital floor is always applied on a portfolio level.

The examples above are all simplified for illustrative purposes. In real life, many more variables must be considered. Especially the development of portfolios and the severity of the capital floor effect over time must be considered. One example would be whether or not, according to the business plan of the bank, the RWA of internal models and standardised approached will converge or diverge over time. Another example is that it should be considered whether the average risk (and therefore risk weights) of new business will be generally higher or lower.

The capital costs that will be considered in future pricing models must not be considered on a stand-alone basis anymore. Due to the capital floor, the capital costs must always be considered as marginal capital costs depending on the total portfolio and how the portfolio will evolve over time.

9.5 Conclusions

The introduction of the new Basel IV capital floor was the most discussed topic during the consultation and almost resulted in no agreement being reached at all. Considering the potential impact of the capital floor, it is justifiable that the discussions took so long. Even when the requirements of the new capital floor are not very complex, the implications for certain banks can be huge. The range of impact of the capital floor on the RWA of banks can vary depending on whether or not, and to what extent, banks use internal models. The impact might also depend on the business model, the risk strategy or the current market environment. Each of these factors alone makes the capital floor a challenge for banks, but the real challenge lays within the many possible combinations of factors that influence the impact of the capital floor. Currently, there is no full picture of how the capital floors will impact the banks or how this will affect the real economy in the end. This is why it is so important for banks to analyse as soon as possible all effects and interactions of the capital floor on their business and the business of their competitors. The first bank that is fully aware of these effects will have the better market position in the future and will be able to increase its profitability.

Recommended Literature

Basel Committee on Banking Supervision; BCBS 128 (2006): International Convergence of Capital Measurement and Capital Standards: A Revised Framework Comprehensive Version, 2006.

Basel Committee on Banking Supervision; BCBS 157 (2009): Enhancements to the Basel II framework, 2009.

Basel Committee on Banking Supervision; BCBS 256 (2013): Regulatory Consistency Assessment Programme (RCAP) – Analysis of risk-weighted assets for credit risk in the banking book, 2013.

Basel Committee on Banking Supervision; BCBS 258 (2013): Discussion paper. The regulatory framework: balancing risk sensitivity, simplicity and comparability, 2013.

Basel Committee on Banking Supervision; BCBS 298 (2014): Reducing excessive variability in banks' regulatory capital ratios: A report to the G20, 2014.

Basel Committee on Banking Supervision; BCBS 306 (2014): Consultative Document. Capital Floors: the design of a framework based on standardised approaches, 2014.

Commission Delegated Regulation (EU) No 183/2014 of 20 December 2013 supplementing Regulation (EU) No 575/2013 of the European Parliament and of the Council on prudential requirements for credit institutions and investment firms, with regard to regulatory technical standards for specifying the calculation of specific and general credit risk adjustments

Ingves, Stefan (2015): From the Vasa to the Basel framework: The dangers of instability, Speech at Unique Lecture at the 2015 Annual Convention of the Asociación de Mercados Financieros, 2 November 2015, Madrid, Spain, 2015.

10 New Basel Framework for Large Exposures

Christoph Himmelmann and Hortense Huez

On 15 April 2014, as the result of a consultation started in March 2013, the Basel Committee on Banking Supervision (BCBS) published the final Supervisory Framework for Measuring and Controlling Large Exposures (BCBS 283).[1] The BCBS expects the full implementation of the new regulation as of 1 January 2019. Within the EU, the implementation of the new Basel framework will result in significant adjustments to the CRR's large exposures regime, which entered into force in January 2014.

This paper first illustrates the background of the new large exposures framework of the Basel Committee, before expanding on the content of the new framework and the significant changes to the CRR's existing large exposures regime in the following chapters.[2]

10.1 Background

The last time the Basel Committee formulated its general recommendations for a sound monitoring of large exposures[3] was in 1991. The following, well established regulations and procedures of individual national supervisory authorities formed the cornerstones of the Basel paper, but without providing any detailed provisions:

- Comprehensive definition of credit exposure.
- Comprehensive definition of counterparties.
- Establishment of a reporting limit of maximum 10% as well as an upper limit of maximum 25% of the regulatory capital.
- Special attention to receivables from related companies and persons.
- Establishment of appropriate mechanisms for monitoring risks arising from credit concentration in geographic areas or economic sectors.

With the publication of the new and clearly more differentiated framework in 2014, the BCBS once again illustrates the importance of the large exposures regime as a necessary complement to the supervisory requirements for credit risk. The risk-sensitive capital requirements for credit risk implicitly assume that institutions have a sufficiently granular and diversified credit risk portfolio. But it can't be assumed that this will automatically be the case and, it is therefore the aim of the large exposures regulations to ensure, as a "back-stop regime", that an institution's going concern will not be imperilled in case of default of one large exposure to a single client or a group of connected clients.

---

1 Cf. BCBS 283 (2014).
2 The EU large exposure regime is taken as a reference to gauge the impact of the BCBS proposals on EU banks. However, in countries that have not implemented large exposure regulations so far, the impact will naturally be even more pronounced.
3 Cf. BCBS 121 (1991).

The new Basel framework focuses mainly on the concentration risks arising from these large exposures – other concentration risks (for example, geographical or sectoral concentrations) and exposures within the institution's own group are not yet considered in this framework. In addition, the standard also provides guidance in terms of how to proceed with trading book positions, risks from exposures to funds and securitisation structures, as well as commitments related to the settlement of transactions through central counterparties (CCP).

10.2 Scope

The frameworks of the Basel Committee are designed for *international banks or banking groups*. The relevant supervisory authorities then have the possibility of fully or partially extending the scope of the requirements to other banks. The EU for example has so far extended application of the Basel rules to all institutions via the Capital Requirements Regulation (CRR). It can therefore be assumed that the changes considered by the Basel Committee will lead to a modification of the existing large exposure regime under Part 4 of the CRR, and that these will then have to be implemented by all institutions that are subject to the requirements of the CRR.[4]

CRR implementation itself leaves some room for national interpretations. For instance, in the UK, the PRA has given more precise guidance on its expectations in relation to large exposures requirements within the CRR. It covers applications to include undertakings within a core UK group (CRR Article 113(6)) and non-core large exposure group (CRR 400(2)(c)) as well as sovereign large exposures exemptions (CRR Article 400(2)(g or h)) and exposures to trustees. In Germany, competent authorities have also specified the exemptions regarding intra-group exposures which are cross-border and therefore not meeting the strict CRR requirements. Furthermore, the management board of a German institution is required to take an unanimous decision before granting, prolonging or increasing a large exposure which is a purely national regulation beyond BCBS or CRR requirements.

10.3 Large exposure limits

If the sum of all relevant exposures to a single borrower or group of connected clients equals or exceeds the amount of 10% of the bank's eligible capital, it will be considered a large exposure (large exposure definition limit).

As in the CRR's current large exposures regime, a bank's large exposures should never exceed an upper limit of 25% of the institution's eligible capital (large exposure upper

---

4   The European Commission already published a first draft of the amended CRR ("CVRR II") on 23 November 2016 including a partially revised large exposure framework.

limit). In the case of exposures between global systemically important banks (G-SIBs), a reduced upper limit of 15% will apply when the updated Basel framework is implemented.

According to the Basel Committee, this reduced limit could be extended to exposures between domestic systemically important banks (D-SIBs), global systemically important financial institutions (G-SIFIs) or even exposures of smaller institutions against G-SIBs as a next step. Figure 10.1 shows the new prescribed large exposure upper limits as well as the recommendations of the Basel Committee regarding the application of reduced large exposure upper limits for certain exposures within the financial sector.

Any breach of these large exposure upper limits must be reported immediately to the competent supervisory authority and shall remain an exception. The affected exposures shall be reduced under the upper limit as soon as possible.

The current CRR large exposure definition and upper limits has remained unchanged with the exception of the special regulations for G-SIBs. The absolute large exposure upper limit of EUR 150 million for exposures to other institutions, which

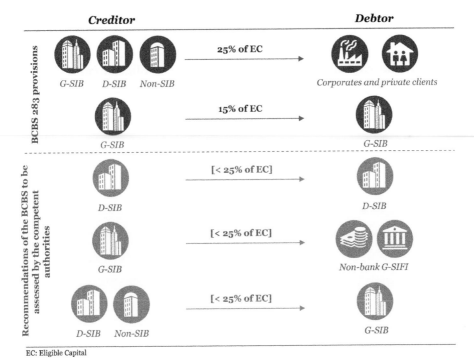

EC: Eligible Capital

Figure 10.1: Large exposure upper limits according to BCBS 283

in the case of smaller institutions with an eligible capital of less than EUR 600 million compares favourably to the 25% upper limit, has not been considered in the Basel paper. This may also be due to the fact that the provisions issued by the Basel Committee were initially directed at large international institutions.

10.4 Eligible capital

Large exposure limits are calculated as a percentage of eligible capital, which is composed of the Core Equity Tier 1 capital and the Additional Tier 1 capital, determined in accordance with the requirements of the Basel III framework. An inclusion of *subordinated capital* components (Tier 2) as part of the eligible capital is not allowed, since these would not be available to cover the losses, in terms of a going-concern approach, in the event of sudden default of a (large) debtor.

With the exclusion of Tier 2 capital from the eligible capital, the Basel Committee stipulates a far-reaching change in the relevant definition of capital compared to the CRR's current large exposures regime, which allows the eligibility of Tier 2 capital up to one third of the Tier 1 capital (Art. 4 (1) (71) CRR). Figure 10.2 shows the changes to eligible capital relevant for large exposure limits in the EU.

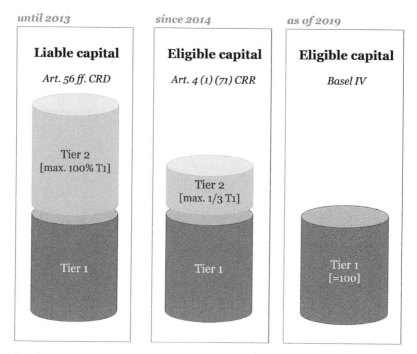

Figure 10.2: Development of eligible capital

10.5 Counterparties and connected counterparties

In principle, the provisions of the Basel framework are fully applicable to all counterparties. Exemptions and special rules apply to central governments, banks, central counterparties, and investment and securitisation vehicles, which we will discuss in more detail later in this chapter.

If control relationships or economic interdependencies exist among individual counterparties, they shall be regarded as a group of connected clients. In this case, the group is regarded as one counterparty and all exposures to the members of the group must be aggregated for large exposure purposes.

Institutions must accordingly examine their clients' existing control relationships and other interdependencies. If a client holds more than 50% of a company's voting rights, they have to be considered as a group in any case. Furthermore, the following aspects must also be considered in the assessment of potential control relationships:

- voting agreements,
- significant influence on the composition of management or the supervisory or administrative body, and
- significant influence on management.

Moreover, the Basel Committee expects banks to take into account the provisions on consolidation requirements or control relationships according to internationally recognised accounting standards.

In exceptional cases, banks have the opportunity to prove to the competent supervisory authorities that even though one of said control criteria is present, no group of connected clients exists.

Institutions must also carry out a deeper analysis of a client's potential economic dependencies when the exposure amount exceeds 5% of the eligible capital. In doing so, relationships between clients should be identified, which indicate that the financial distress or the insolvency of one client is connected with the financial distress or the insolvency of another client.

Table 10.1 shows some examples of significant economic ties between clients.

Obligor A	Obligor B/other third party
Lessor	Tenant who provides 50% or more of the gross annual income of the lessor
Warrantee	Warrantor who would get himself into financial difficulties in the event of a warranty claim
Producer/service provider	Customer who acquires a substantial part of the producer's or service provider's products and services

Table 10.1: Examples of economic dependencies according to BCBS 283

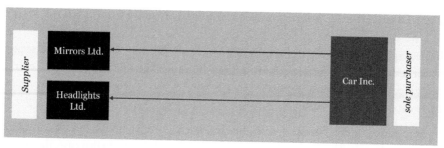

Figure 10.3: Example: Economic dependencies

In addition, an existential economic interdependence is also suspected when two or more clients depend on the same source of funding and no alternative source of funding can be found.

The concept of economic dependencies was implemented in the EU in 2010 with the revision of the Capital Requirements Directive ("CRD II"). European and national implementation guidelines have provided further examples and taken up individual interpretation issues.[5]

Under current administrative practice the example shown in Figure 10.3 would lead to a group of connected clients due to economic dependencies.

Figure 10.3 shows the two legally independent automotive suppliers Mirrors Ltd. and Headlights Ltd. who are clients of the reporting institution. The institution's responsible credit officers have analysed both companies' economic situation and found out that Car Inc. is the sole purchaser of their specialty products. The advisers assume that both suppliers would be in serious economic difficulties if Car Inc. were, for example, to stop or change production. Current estimates do not expect any significant compensating purchasers for their specialty products. Therefore, both suppliers must be regarded as one group of connected clients, because they are exposed to the same economic risk through Car Inc., and as a result could face economic difficulties at the same time. If the institution also has a relevant business relationship with Car Inc. (e.g. acquired shares or bonds in the banking or trading book), then Car Inc. must be included in the group of connected clients together with the two suppliers.

Similar to the assessment of existing control relationships, in the case of potential economic dependencies, an institution may also present evidence to the competent supervisory authority to state that in spite of the identified links, no "contagion" from another obligor should be assumed and therefore the clients should not be regarded as a single connected group.

Generally this is an area where a lot of banks struggle either to properly identify connections and economic dependencies or, in other cases, provide proof of the lack of economic links.

---

5   Cf. CEBS (2009) as well as BaFin (2011).

In the case of central governments and public sector entities, which may be treated as central governments, the formation of groups of connected clients may be omitted. This also applies to central counterparties (CCP) provided that the risk position to the CCP concerns clearing-related transactions.

Overall, the concept of connected obligors outlined in the Basel paper corresponds to the currently applicable provisions on the formation of groups of connected clients contained in the CRR (Art. 4 (1) (39) CRR). The extent to which changes in the detailed specifications and the administrative practice will arise is not foreseeable, since the Basel Committee is scarce on details regarding the criteria for grouping. It is worth noting, however, that the Basel Committee's exemption for central governments is broader than the CRR's so-called "silo approach". Furthermore, it permits a minimum limit for the in-depth analysis in search of economic links of 5% of the eligible capital. In contrast, CRD II and supplementary CEBS guidelines have called for the need of analysis from 2% of capital upwards.[6] In Germany a targeted analysis from an even lower limit of EUR 750,000 upwards was established in view of the minimum limit according to Para. 18 of the German Banking Act (Kreditwesengesetz, KWG).[7]

However, Basel provides for tighter operational requirements regarding the refutation of groups of connected clients on the basis of economic ties. Here the Basel paper stipulates that the institution must provide evidence to the competent supervisory authority if it finds an economic interdependence between two clients, but sees no "contagion" in terms of credit risk in that individual case.

10.6 Definition of exposure

All exposures considered for the purpose of calculating capital requirements are also valid exposures for large exposure provisions. This includes both balance sheet assets and off-balance sheet items in the trading and banking book. In addition, instruments that are subject to counterparty risk (derivatives, securities lending and repo transactions) must be included in the large exposure assessment base.

Items that were deducted during the calculation of regulatory capital may not increase the assessment base. Furthermore, intraday exposures to other banks are also exempted from the large exposure reporting requirement as well as from the large exposure upper limit. The reason for the exemption of short-term interbank claims is that the large exposure limits should not have a negative impact on the implementation of payments and the clearing, settlement or custody of financial instruments. Whether interbank exposures lasting more than one day (i.e. overnight exposures) are subject to the exemption is still to be determined, following the completion of an observation phase by the Basel Committee.

---

6   Cf. CEBS (2009).
7   Cf. BaFin (2011).

Advances from securities and exchange rate transactions as well as overnight exposures related to payments and client-oriented performances of financial instrument clearing, settlement or custody services, which are excluded under the current EU definition of credit set forth in Art. 390 (6) CRR, are not yet excluded according to the Basel paper, at least not explicitly.

10.7 Assessment base

10.7.1 On and off-balance sheet items in the banking book

In the case of non-derivative assets contained in the banking book, the assessment base should be the carrying amount in accordance with applicable accounting standards, net of specific credit risk adjustments and impairments. This corresponds to the currently applicable EU rules according to Art. 389 in conjunction with Art. 111 CRR.

In the future, however, off-balance sheet banking book items are to be converted into credit equivalent amounts by applying the conversion factors from the credit risk stan-dardised approach, with a floor of 10%. Thus, when the new framework applies, the large exposure assessment base will be further aligned with that of the credit risk stan-dardised approach, whereas currently in the EU, the application of conversion factors is explicitly excluded in the large exposure framework.

Currently a number of large exposure-specific exceptions for off-balance sheet items apply. According to Art. 400 CRR, certain low and medium risk off-balance sheet items are completely or partially excluded from the large exposure upper limit. Hence, the foreseen implementation of the conversion factors would, on the one hand, decrease the assessment base relevant to triggering the reporting obligation. On the other hand, a complete exemption from the application of the large exposure upper limit for low risk off-balance sheet transactions, as is currently the case, would no longer be possible due to the stipulated 10% conversion factor floor.

10.7.2 Counterparty risk

In the new framework, the assessment base for derivative positions is to be determined uniformly according to the new standardised approach for measuring counterparty credit risk (SA-CCR).[8] The mark-to-market or current exposure method (MtM resp. CEM) that is currently used by most institutions will therefore be replaced for large exposure purposes. It is also notable that the alternative use of the Internal Model Method (IMM) will no longer be permitted. As a result, considerable increases in derivative assessment bases should be expected, especially for institutions that have approval to use the IMM.

In the case of securities financing transactions (SFTs), the comprehensive approach for financial collateral, which has also been revised, will be implemented and will be

---

8   For details, see Chapter 3 of this book.

limited to the use of supervisory haircuts.[9] Thus, the use of self-estimated haircuts for financial collaterals as well as the determination of the assessment base using IMM will no longer be possible in future, which under certain circumstances could result in substantial increases in large exposure amounts for repo and lending transactions.

10.7.3 Trading book items

Issuer risk items in the trading book are also to be added to the same counterparty's or group of connected clients' banking book items, in order to determine the overall risk position.

The determination of the assessment base will remain unchanged, and continues to be based on the methods for RWA determination for trading book items. In determining the assessment base for trading book items, corresponding long and short positions in the trading book may be offset against each other within the same issue.

Long and short positions from different issues of the same counterparty, however, may only be offset against each other if the short position is subordinated to or has the same seniority as the long position. For these purposes, institutions must assign their trading book items to individual seniority buckets such as equity, subordinated debt and senior debt. If the institution is not able to do so, the netting of trading book items in different issues is not allowed.

Offsetting items across the trading and banking books is not permitted under any circumstances.

Collateralisation of trading book items through credit derivatives may be netted when the underlying position of the associated hedge meets the seniority requirements for long and short positions mentioned above. In addition, the item hedged by the credit derivative must be added to the warrantor's exposure. As long as the warrantor is not a financial company, the counterparty credit risk determined according to SA-CCR is counted towards the large exposure limit instead of the secured amount.

10.8 Recognition of credit risk mitigation

The new Basel requirements continue to allow the use of credit risk mitigation techniques to reduce the amount that is counted towards the large exposure upper limit. This applies to unfunded credit protection such as warranties and credit derivatives as well as financial collateral, whereby the applicable general recognition criteria of the credit risk standardised approach must be met. Other forms of collateralisation, which may be considered under the internal ratings-based approach (IRB), are not permitted. These include in particular mortgages on residential and commercial properties that are eligible under current CRR requirements in the EU.

---

9 For details, see Chapter 1 of this book.

The eligible amount of financial collaterals is calculated with the method used for RWA determination, i.e. either the simple method or the (revised) comprehensive method using supervisory haircuts.

In any case, the secured amount must be added as a substitute for the warrantor's or the issuer of the financial collateral's exposure.[10] Thus, the approach currently known as "substitution approach" (Art. 403 CRR) must be observed when applying the comprehensive method.

Figure 10.4 shows the effects of the "substitution approach" using a simplified example. It also depicts the impact of the obligatory consideration of the substitution effect on the relevant exposure amounts compared to the current application of the comprehensive method in accordance with Art. 401 CRR.

It should also be noted that the Basel Committee formulates that the application of credit risk mitigation techniques will be mandatory, provided that they are used in the RWA calculation. This represents a remarkable departure from the CRR's voluntary nature.

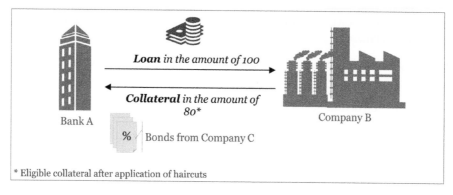

* Eligible collateral after application of haircuts

Large exposures bank A		Direct exposure before CRM	Indirect exposure	Credit risk mitigation	Exposure value after CRM
CRR	Company B	100	0	−80	20
	Company C	0	0	0	0
BCBS 283	Company B	100	0	−80	20
	Company C	0	80	0	80

Figure 10.4: Substitution effect in the weighting of financial collaterals (credit risk mitigation)

---

10   In the case of credit derivatives (CDS), the amount of the counterparty default risk determined in accordance with SA-CCR is to be weighted towards the warrantor's large exposure amount under certain circumstances.

10.9 Exemptions

The CRR's current regulations and the complementary national large exposures regimes allow for a reduction of the exposure value or a complete exemption from being counted towards the large exposure limit for certain low-risk transactions or counterparties. The risk positions shown in Figure 10.5 may currently be completely or partially ignored in the weighting towards the large exposure limit.

In contrast, the new Basel framework's catalogue of exemptions is much smaller and less differentiated. On the one hand, this is due to the fact that according to Basel the assessment base of off-balance sheet transactions shall already be adjusted by applying credit conversion factors, so that no additional reductions of the exposure value are necessary. On the other hand, the treatment of intra-group claims is explicitly not covered by the Basel paper; so further publications are to be expected. At the European level, the CRR covers those, with an intra-group waiver in Art. 400.2(c). Given the CRR leaves a temporary discretion for national supervisors in the implementation of those waivers, the implementation has been more or less restrictive depending on the country. In this context, the European Central Bank has published additional strict criteria, which have overall reduced the number of exemptions for SSM banks. In the UK, the PRA allows banks to apply for waivers to exempt exposures to other group entities that are in the UK and apply more generous limits to non-UK group entities. In Germany, there is on the one hand a partial exemption of 75% for intra-group exposures not meeting the strict CRR requirements. On the other hand, German institutions may apply for exempting intra-group exposures up to 93.75% if they can prove to the competent authority that the exposure is an essential outcome of a centralised liquidity or risk management within the group.

Exemptions in accordance to Art. 400 (1) CRR (excerpt)	Exemptions in accordance to Art. 1 and 2 GroMiKV (German Large Loans Directive) (excerpt)
• Exposures to central governments, central banks, international organisations, multilateral development banks, regional governments or local authorities in the EEA (if SA-RW = 0%)	• Covered bonds
	• 80% of exposures to regional governments or local authorities in the EEA and to other obligors, which are explicitly guaranteed by these entities (if SA-RW = 20%)
• Exposures carrying the explicit guarantee of central governments, central banks, international organisations, multilateral development banks or public sector entities (if SA-RW = 0%)	• Overnight exposures to banks if they don't represent own funds and are not denominated in a major trading currency
• Intra-group exposures, provided that the requirements of Art. 113 (6) CRR are fulfilled (on request)	• Claims on central banks from a minimum reserve requirement as well as claims on central governments to meet statutory liquidity requirements
• Exposures to counterparties of the same institutional protection scheme, provided that the requirements of Art. 113 (7) CRR are fulfilled (on request)	• 50% of certain medium/low risk off-balance sheet transactions
• Exposures that are secured by a cash deposit placed with the lending institution	• Claims on recognised stock exchanges
• Uncommitted, undrawn credit facilities	• Loans explicitly granted for development aid

• Trade exposures to central counterparties and default fund contributions	• Exemptions for intra-group exposures:
	  – Holdings (in full) in subsidiaries, if they do not exceed 25% of the institution's eligible capital
	  – 75% of other intra-group exposures

• Positions in deposit guarantee schemes	• 50% of shares in regional or central banks

Figure 10.5: Overview of currently applicable reductions in capital requirements

Exposures to central governments and public sector entities, which may be treated as central governments, are fully excluded from being counted towards the large exposure upper limit under the new Basel framework. The same applies to items that are explicitly guaranteed by central governments and public sector entities or by financial collateral issued by central governments and public sector entities.

As in current CRR provisions, the Basel framework also includes exemptions with respect to covered bonds. If certain requirements on the pledged assets (the minimum loan-to-value ratio in the case of mortgages on residential and commercial properties as well as the minimum over-collateralisation ratio) are met, a partial reduction of the amount weighted towards the large exposure limit of up to a maximum of 80% of the notional may be granted. However, the zero-weighting of covered bonds currently allowed under Art. 400 CRR is no longer provided for.

Furthermore it is striking, that the new Basel paper contains no explicit exemptions for loans from development banks granted as part of their promotional mandate. At present, these may be completely exempted from being weighted towards the large exposure upper limit.

Exposures to qualified central counterparties (QCCPs) may be completely excluded from being counted towards the large exposure upper limit, pending the outcome of an additional observation period.

In contrast, a more differentiated approach is used for non-qualified central counterparties (non-QCCPs). Institutions must differentiate certain types of exposures to central counterparties. Any non-clearing-related exposure to central counterparties should be handled in accordance with the general large exposures regime and – unless other exemptions apply – be completely counted towards the large exposure upper limit. The weighting approaches and amounts of clearing-related positions can then be derived from the allocation of the single exposure, as shown in Table 10.2.

Category	Weighting towards the large exposure upper limit
Trading risk positions	Complete weighting of the exposure value. The exposure value is determined by applying the methods used for RWA determination (e.g. in the case of SA-CCR derivatives)
Segregated initial margin payments	Complete exemption from being weighted towards the large exposure upper limit (0%-weighting)
Non-segregated initial margin payments	Complete weighting in the amount of the nominal value of the performed margin payments
Deposits to the CCP's default fund	Complete weighting in the amount of the performed payment
Not yet covered contributions to the CCP's default fund	Complete exemption (0%-weighting)
Shares of the CCP's capital	Weighting in the amount of the nominal value (if these were not deducted from the eligible capital)

Table 10.2: Claims on central counterparties

10.10 Look-through of funds and securitisations

In the case of risk positions in funds and securitisations as well as other transactions with underlying credit risks, the Basel framework provides for a look-through and transparency principle which is comparable to the current provisions of the CRR.[11] This principle establishes a "look-through" to the transactions underlying the funds and securitisations, in order to determine the individual indirect obligors and proportionate credit amounts for the purposes of large exposure reporting and monitoring. If the institution has invested in a fund, the investment amount should not be allocated to the fund company or the fund manager, but distributed to the counterparties in which the fund invests. The indirect obligors determined in this manner should be treated as direct obligors of the institution, with regard to large exposure reporting, requirements of upper limits and the grouping with other obligors in one group of connected clients. If the institution cannot determine the individual underlying counterparties, the exposures to all unknown counterparties should be grouped together as one so-called "unknown client", which will also be limited to the large exposure upper limit of 25% of eligible capital. The individual look-through requirements and exemptions are as follows.

- If an institution can prove that the proportional investments in the underlying credit risks do not exceed the amount of 0.25% of the eligible capital, there will be no need for a complete look-through. This requirement is deemed as fulfilled in the case of investments in transactions, which in total do not exceed an amount of 0.25% of the eligible capital.
- In the case of underlying positions whose proportional exposure values exceed the minimum limit of 0.25% of the eligible capital, the institution must identify the corresponding counterparties in such a way that the proportional exposure values can be assigned to this counterparty with respect to any remaining direct and indirect risk positions of the institution.
- If an institution is unable to determine the positions underlying a transaction with look-through obligation, it must assign the total exposure amount to the unknown client. In the case of transactions whose total investment value does not exceed an amount of 0.25%, this can be waived; instead, the individual transaction is to be regarded as an obligor for large exposure purposes.

In any case, institutions must be able to prove that the mentioned materiality thresholds were not used to exploit arbitrage opportunities and that the "immaterial" exposures have not been deliberately invested in several smaller transactions, which ultimately share the same underlying credit risk, for example.

Figure 10.6 shows the various methods of handling transactions with look-through obligations.

---

11 See Art. 390 (7) CRR, in connection with Commission Delegated Regulation (EU) No. 1187/2014.

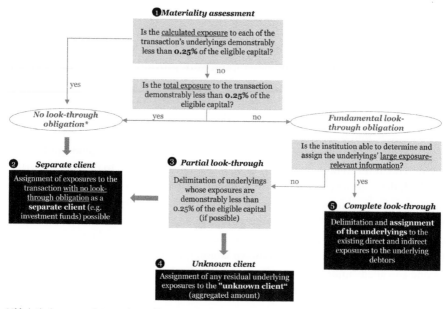

Figure 10.6: Look-through methods

In order to calculate the individual exposure amounts of the underlying obligors, the institution's so-called pro-rata share of the transaction should be multiplied by the value of the underlying positions.

If an institution X holds e.g. 20% of the shares of an investment fund, which has invested in shares of companies A to E in the amount of EUR 10 million each, the respective exposure values to the underlying debtors total EUR 2 million each (Figure 10.7).

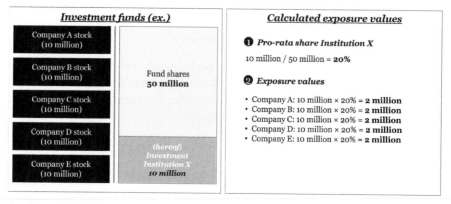

Figure 10.7: Look-through: determination of exposure values (ex. 1)

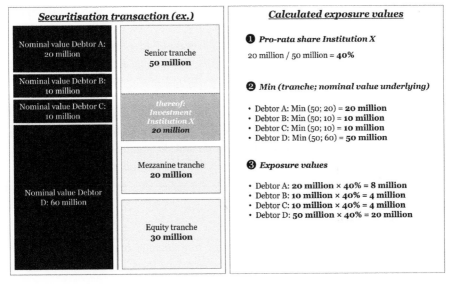

Figure 10.8: Look-through: determination of exposure values (ex. 2)

In the case of transactions where the investors do *not equally* participate in the value of the underlying positions (non pari-passu, e.g. securitisation transactions), the pro-rata share will be represented by the institution's share in the respective tranche. This value has to be multiplied by the lower value of (1) the tranche's total value and (2) the corresponding underlying's nominal value. Figure 10.8 shows the mechanism of the minimum function with regard to the relevant large exposure amounts.

With EUR 20 million, institution X holds 40% of the senior tranche of a securitisation transaction. The underlying loan portfolio consists of debtors A to D. The relevant exposure values are shown in the right-hand column.

The background of the represented calculation method is the assumption that institution X's maximum loss resulting from the default of any single debtor in the loan portfolio will be the lower amount of the total investment in the respective tranche and the underlying exposure values allocated to this debtor. This "worst-case scenario" thus ignores the probability of default of the individual debtor and any risk-mitigating effects of the loss allocation to the equity and mezzanine tranches. This differentiates the large exposures provision significantly from the methods used to determine the capital requirements. In light of the meaning and purpose of the large exposures regime, this may result in the sum of the relevant amounts allocated to the underlying debtors exceeding the total investment value of the institution X (in this example: sum of exposure values in the amount of EUR 36 million with a total investment of EUR 20 million).

As is the case under the current large exposures regime, the Basel framework also stipulates that, in addition to the look-through, institutions must analyse whether additional risks with third parties might arise from the structure of a transaction subject to the look-through requirement. In this context the originator of a securitisation position, the fund manager or potential liquidity or collateral providers are cited as examples. Under certain circumstances, a fund manager may be regarded as a common risk factor for the funds under his management, so that an institution's investments in said funds must be aggregated and limited to the amount of the large exposure upper limit. Generally applicable criteria for the existence of additional risk are not specified. The Basel Committee, however, clearly establishes that this must be a case-by-case assessment in light of the individual structure of a transaction and the applicable legal framework, e.g. the regulatory requirements that are applicable for the fund manager.

10.11 Regulatory reporting

The new Basel framework only specifies some fundamental requirements on future large exposure reporting, which are already covered by the CRR's current reporting obligations. Specifically, the following items are to be reported.

- All large exposures (before and after application of credit risk mitigation techniques, exemptions and reductions in capital requirements).
- The 20 largest exposures regardless of the large exposure definition limit (before and after application of credit risk mitigation techniques).

Further details of future reporting requirements are not provided in the Basel framework. So the described requirements will not lead to a significant expansion of large exposure reporting in comparison to CRR.

10.12 Implementation of the updated framework in the CRR II

At the EU level, the recent CRR II draft broadly reflects the amendments of the new Basel large exposures regime whilst in some key aspects the proposed CRR II still deviates from the requirements laid down in BCBS 283. However, overall the amended CRR may still result in significantly tightened large exposure limits and further operational challenges for many EU institutions.

First and foremost, the large exposure definition and the large exposure limits under CRR II will refer only to the institution's Tier 1 capital. Hence, as foreseen in BCBS 283, it is no longer permitted to include Tier 2 capital in the relevant capital basis as it is currently the case under CRR which is referring to the institution's "eligible capital". Furthermore, derogating from the generally applicable large exposure limit of 25% of an institution's Tier 1 capital, global systemically important institutions (G-SII) shall not incur any exposure to another G-SII which exceeds 15% of their Tier 1 capital.

The general definition of the group of connected clients in the CRR is not going to change in the course of the CRR II implementation. However, EBA published its final

Guidelines 2017/15 on connected clients in November 2017 which are consistent with the BCBS standards, but of course much more detailed and covering further topics, e.g. an alternative approach for sovereign exposures.[12]

To determine the exposure value for derivatives, institutions shall only be allowed to use the new SA-CCR, the simplified SA-CCR or the Original Exposure Method, even when they have the permission to make use of the Internal Model Method (IMM) for RWA purposes. However, whether it will be still allowed to use the IMM for calculating the exposure values for securities financing transactions (SFT) is still under debate.

According to the CRR II draft, institutions shall consistently use credit risk mitigation techniques for large exposure purposes when they use them for RWA purposes as long as the additional requirements can be met. In cases of financial collateral, regardless of the applied method, institutions have to take into account the collateralised part of the exposure when calculating the exposure to the protection provider, i.e. the issuer of the financial collateral. Hence, the mandatory substitution approach will be part of the CRR II as required in BCBS 283. However, contrary to the view of the Basel Committee, immovable properties shall still be permitted as credit risk mitigation for large exposure purposes.

The large exposure reporting for EU institutions will be amended *inter alia* in two major aspects: First, the additional reporting requirement for exposures equal or larger than EUR 300 million will be applicable for every institution that has to comply with CRR's large exposure reporting requirements. Furthermore, institutions will have to report their 10 largest exposures to shadow banking entities, whereas EBA is asked to develop draft technical standards to specify the definition of shadow banking entities. It can be expected that this definition will be aligned to the one laid down in EBA Guidelines 2015/20 on exposures to shadow banking entities.

With respect to the future reporting frequency, the CRR II draft hasn't yet settled. In line with the general proportionality concept of the CRR II, it was first intended that the frequency would depend on the size of the institution, i.e. small institutions shall only report large exposures on an annual basis, whereas all other institutions shall report no less frequently than on a semi-annual basis. However, the latest draft seems to return to the current quarterly reporting for any institution irrespective of its size.

10.13 Summary

The Basel Committee's framework, published in 2014, contains detailed requirements for measuring, controlling and monitoring large exposures. The present article illustrates that these requirements are broadly reflected in the large exposures regime applicable in the EU since the introduction of the CRR, at least with regard to its basic

---

12   Cf. EBA (2017).

features. Nevertheless, it can be assumed that, due to the **complete elimination of tier 2 capital components** in the calculation of eligible capital, many institutions will face significant impacts on their existing credit and trading limits, and consequently also on their business and capital strategy. Thus "Basel IV" also diminishes the importance of tier 2 capital with regard to the calculation of large exposure limits.

Other significant changes arising from the full implementation of the large exposure framework, which is foreseen for 2020 at the earliest, can be expected especially in the **interbank market**. In the future all exposures between G-SIBs should be subject to a severely reduced large exposure upper limit of 15% of the eligible capital. Within this context, it is also suggested that it shall be analysed whether the reduced upper limit should also be applied to exposures between domestic systemically important banks as well as exposures from smaller institutions against global systemically important banks and financial institutions. It is also debatable whether the currently applicable absolute limit of EUR 150 million, which is advantageous for smaller institutions, may still be used.

Also, counterparty credit risks arising from derivative transactions are envisaged to be determined in accordance with the new standardised approach for measuring counterparty credit risks (SA-CCR). In the case of repo/lending transactions, supervisory haircuts will have to be applied for financial collateral. Thus, the application of the internal model method (IMM) or the consideration of internally estimated haircuts will no longer be permissible for derivative and repo/lending transactions. According to current estimates it can be assumed that this will lead to a significant increase in the exposure values for counterparty credit risks.

The proposed elimination of the full exemption of covered bonds from the application of the large exposure upper limit may significantly increase the exposure values resulting from exposures to mortgage banks. Moreover, it has not yet been finally established whether the currently applicable privileges for short-term interbank claims (overnight) will remain valid under the Basel requirements.

Figure 10.9 outlines the potential cumulative effect the interaction of the individual tightening of interbank claims could have on the maximum credit and trading limits in relation to institutions.

Overall, it should be noted that there will be considerable changes affecting the utilisation of large exposure limits, in particular for **larger institutions**. Firstly, this can be traced back to increasing exposure values for derivatives and repo/lending transactions, more restrictive trading book netting rules (long and short positions may only be offset against each other if they are part of the same issuance or if it can be proven that the short position is subordinated to or has the same seniority as the long position) and the reduction of eligible collateral values due to the use of supervisory haircuts. Secondly, stricter large exposure upper limits may be implemented for systemically important banks.

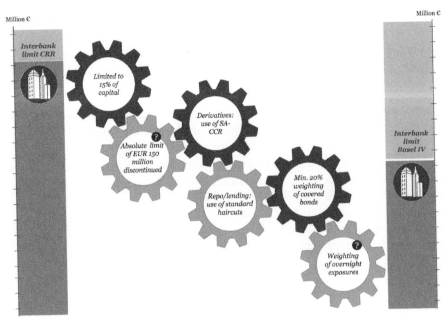

Figure 10.9: Potential tightening of large exposure provisions for interbank claims (outline)

But there are also other remarkable changes that should affect all institutions. With the introduction of an obligation to implement credit risk mitigation techniques in the large exposure framework, the institutions will face increased operating costs, with further tightening affecting the large exposure upper limit and the operative processes in reporting. On the one hand, in future the catalogue of eligible collaterals will be restricted to warranties and credit derivatives as well as financial collaterals. Mortgages on residential and commercial properties may therefore no longer be used to reduce the amount that is subject to the large exposure upper limit. On the other hand, the implementation of credit risk mitigation techniques in the large exposure framework is envisaged to be mandatory, if they are used for calculating RWA and capital requirements. Hence, this requires even more synchronised provisions and procedures which are currently not common in most institutions. In determining the collateralisation effect, eligible financial collaterals are to be calculated either using the simple or the (revised) comprehensive method using supervisory standard haircuts. In any case the secured amount must be added to the large exposure value of the issuer of the financial collateral ("substitution"). While the implementation of the current substitution method in accordance with Art. 403 CRR is usually an exception in most institutions due to operational reasons, it will have to become the standard procedure for recognising financial collaterals.

In addition, other changes could lead to increased standards regarding the determination, monitoring and reporting of large exposures. This includes in particular the general obligation of institutions to provide evidence for the **formation of groups of**

connected clients. If the institution has identified evidence of control relationships or economic dependencies, but does not assume that there is an increased risk of contagion, in the future it will have to be able to present corresponding proof, pertaining to that particular case, to the competent supervisory authority and thus will have to meet significantly increased documentation requirements.

Together with other significant initiatives with regard to credit reporting in the EU, like AnaCredit,[13] and the regulation of exposures to shadow banks,[14] the Basel large exposure framework emphasises the need for a granular database of quantitative and qualitative information as well as sound governance for measuring, monitoring and limiting concentration risks. Due to the closer links between the large exposures regime and the standard procedures for RWA calculation and the restrictive use of credit risk mitigation options, the new Basel rules highlight more than ever the use of the large exposures regime as a "back-stop regime" complementing the risk-sensitive capital adequacy methods. Along with the relevant and well-known capital and liquidity measures, large exposure limits also become increasingly significant in strategic and operational bank management.

Recommended Literature

Basel Committee on Banking Supervision; BCBS 121 (1991): Measuring and Controlling Large Credit Exposures, 1991.

Basel Committee on Banking Supervision; BCBS 283 (2014): Standards. Supervisory framework for measuring and controlling large exposures, 2014.

Bundesanstalt für Finanzdienstleistungsaufsicht; BaFin (2011) Rundschreiben 8/2011 (BA) – Umsetzung der CEBS-Großkreditleitlinie vom 11.12.2009 sowie weitere Auslegungsentscheidungen zu Großkreditvorschriften, 2011 [Circular 8/2011 (BA) – Implementation of the CEBS large exposures guideline from 11/12/2009 and other interpretation decisions on large exposures provisions, 2011].

Capital Requirements Regulation; CRR (2013): Regulation (EU) No 575/2013 of the European Parliament and of the Council of June 26, 2013 on prudential requirements for credit institutions and investment firms and amending Regulation (EU) No 646/2012.

Committee of European Banking Supervisors; CEBS (2009): Guidelines on the implementation of the revised large exposures regime, 2009.

Commission Delegated Regulation (EU) No 1187/2014 of October 2, 2014, supplementing Regulation (EU) No 575/2013 of the European Parliament and of the Council as regards regulatory technical standards for determining the overall exposure to a client or a group of connected clients in respect of transactions with underlying assets.

---

13   For further details regarding AnaCredit: EZB (2014).
14   For details regarding the regulation of claims on shadow banks: EBA (2015).

European Central Bank, ECB (2014) DECISION OF THE EUROPEAN CENTRAL BANK of 24 February 2014, on the organisation of preparatory measures for the collection of granular data on loans by the European System of Central Banks (ECB/2014/6).

European Banking Authority; EBA (2017): Guidelines on connected clients under Article 4(1) (39) of Regulation (EU) No 575/2013 (EBA/GL/2017/15), 2017.

European Banking Authority; EBA (2015): Limits on exposures to shadow banking entities which carry out banking activities outside a regulated framework (EBA/GL/2015/20), 2015.

Prudential Regulation Authority (UK) Supervisory Statement 16/13 'Large Exposures'.

Prudential Regulation Authority (UK) Consultation Paper 20/17 'Changes to the PRA's large exposures framework'.

11 Disclosure

David Brewin, Natasa Grabez, Hana Musai and Gabriela Tsekova

11.1 Introduction

The Basel Committee on Banking Supervision (BCBS) has repeatedly criticised banks' regulatory disclosure practices since their incorporation in the framework of Basel II in 2004. The lack of consistency and comparability of disclosed information were particularly emphasised. Further, the financial crisis (2007–2009) has shown that the existing Pillar 3 framework failed to enable the identification of material risks or to inform market participants in a sufficient manner. Subsequently, proposals to further develop disclosure requirements were outlined. Basel IV fundamentally changes the disclosure requirements. Due to the scope of the planned changes, the work was divided into three phases (Figure 11.1).

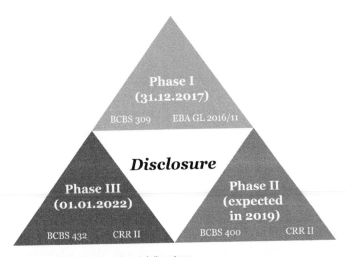

Figure 11.1: Pillar 3 disclosure requirements in three phases

The BCBS 309 – Revised Pillar 3 disclosure requirements (Phase I) was published in January 2015 and provides a comprehensive revision of disclosure requirements.[1] In March 2017 the BCBS published a consecutive standard BCBS 400 – Pillar 3 disclosure requirements – consolidated and enhanced framework (Phase II) that comprises changes to existing (BCBS 309) as well as new disclosure requirements and modifications of the frequency and implementation dates of the revised Pillar 3 framework and represents a consolidation of all existing and prospective BCBS disclosure

---

1   Cf. BCBS 309 (2015).

requirements into the Pillar 3 framework.[2] BCBS 432 – Pillar 3 disclosure requirements – updated framework (Phase III), which is not yet finalised at the editorial
deadline, is related to the finalisation of the Basel III Framework, respectively Basel
IV initiatives.[3] The phases of revision are shown in Figure 11.2.

Phase 1	Phase 2	Phase 3

• Establishment of five principles for the disclosure in the following areas
  – Credit risk
  – Counterparty credit risk
  – Securitisation
  – Market risk
  – Holdings
• Establishing standardised table formats, independent Pillar 3 report, disclosure frequency and timing, adopted from 31/12/2016
	• Harmonisation of disclosure requirements including the unrevised parts of phase I and new areas
	  – **previous BCBS papers which were not included in phase I:** IRRBB, LR, G-SIB, LCR, NSFR, Countercyclical Buffer, Capital, Remuneration
	  – **New areas included in phase II:** TLAC, regulatory ratios, prudent valuation and changes to market risk
	• Implementation dates will come into force at different times 31/12/2017 until 31/12/2019
		• Harmonisation of disclosure requirements arising from the finalisation of the Basel III Framework:
		  – Credit risk (incl. prudential treatment of problem assets)
		  – Operational risk
		  – Leverage ratio
		  – CVA risk
		  – Standardised approach RWA to benchmark IM capital requirements
		  – Asset encumbrance
		  – Capital distribution constraints
		  – Composition of regulatory capital

Figure 11.2: Pillar 3 phases of revision

A key goal of Basel IV disclosure requirements is to ensure consistency and comparability of disclosed information both among banks and over time by establishing
a single, coherent package of disclosure requirements with standardised formats of
tables and templates. To this end, harmonised templates are introduced. A more flexible approach is used to convey additional (quantitative and qualitative) information
which reflects bank-specific characteristics.

11.2 Disclosure guidelines

BCBS 309 contains a complete revision of the existing disclosure requirements of
the Basel framework regarding risk management and RWA, while those disclosure
obligations that were newly introduced or reviewed within the course of Basel III
as, for example, those on capital adequacy and leverage ratio, remained unaffected
(Figure 11.3). According to the Basel Committee, disclosure practices following BCBS
309 guidelines were implemented for the first time at the end of the financial year 2016.
In addition, in December 2016 the European Banking Authority (EBA) published its
Final Report regarding the EU implementation of BCBS 309 disclosure requirements
(EBA/GL/2016/11) which required the banks to comply with the requirements for the
first time at the end of financial year 2017 (G-SIBS had to disclose selected content
already at the end of financial year 2016).[4]

---

2   Cf. BCBS 400 (2017).
3   Cf. BCBS 432 (2018).
4   Cf. EBA 2016.

Tables and templates	Format		Reporting frequency			Content	
	Fixed	Flexible	Quarterly	Semi-annually	Annually	Quantitative	Qualitative
Risk management and RWA	1	1	1		1	1	1
Linkages between financial statements and regulatory exposures		3			3	2	1
Credit risk	8	7	1	8	6	10	5
Counterparty credit risk	6	3	1	7	1	8	1
Securitisation	2	3		4	1	4	1
Market risk	3	3	1	3	2	4	2
Total (11 tables & 29 templates)	20	20	4	22	14	29	11

Figure 11.3: Reporting frequency and formats of Phase I

As a result of a number of interpretation questions related to BCBS 309, the Basel Committee has published BCBS 376 (FAQs on the revised Pillar 3 disclosure requirements)[5] to help ensure consistent global implementation of the requirements. This document provides answers along with interpretative guidance in the fields of overview of risk management and RWA, linkages between financial statements and regulatory exposures, credit risk, counterparty credit risk, securitisation and market risk.

In March of 2017 the BCBS issued the final document BCBS 400 as a second step of the Pillar 3 review. In this standard the Basel Committee consolidates and complements the existing requirements for disclosure (Figure 11.4). The Committee proposes

Tables and templates	Format		Reporting frequency			Content	
	Fixed	Flexible	Quarterly	Semi-annually	Annually	Quantitative	Qualitative
Linkages between financial statements and regulatory exposures	1	3			4	3	1
Credit risk	8	7	1	8	6	10	5
Counterparty credit risk	6	3	1	7	1	8	1
Securitisation	2	3		4	1	4	1
Risk management, Key Metrics & RWA	3	1	3		1	3	1
Market risk	3	4	1	4	2	4	3
Capital and TLAC	4	2		6		5	1
Macroprudential Measures	1	1		1	1	2	
Leverage Ratio	2		2			2	
Liquidity	2	1	1	1	1	2	1
Interest Rate Risk in the banking book	1	1			2	1	1
Remuneration		4			4	3	1
Total (63)	33	30	9	31	23	47	16

Figure 11.4: Phase I and Phase II reporting frequency and format of disclosure

---

5   Cf. BCBS 376 (2016).

three general enhancements to the revised Pillar 3 framework with regard to the disclosure of key metrics (new templates KM1 and KM2), disclosure of hypothetical risk-weighted assets (new templates HYP1 and HYP2) and the disclosure requirements for prudent valuation adjustments (new template PV1). Further additions, like disclosure requirements for the TLAC regime for G-SIBs[6] and revised disclosure requirements for market risk[7] reflect the reforms to the Basel III regulatory framework.

In February 2018 the BCBS issued the consultative document BCBS 432 as a final step of the Pillar 3 review (Figure 11.5). BCBS 432 comprises revisions (revised disclosure requirements for credit risk, operational risk, leverage ratio, CVA and overview templates on risk management, RWA and key prudential metrics) and additions (disclosure requirements to benchmark the internal model RWA according to standardised approaches) as a result of the finalisation of the Basel IV initiatives, new disclosure requirements on asset encumbrance (Template ENC) and capital distribution (Template CDC) as well as amendments to the scope of application of disclosure on the composition of regulatory capital (Template CC1 – reproduced from BCBS 400).

Tables and templates	Format		Reporting frequency			Content	
	Fixed	Flexible	Quarterly	Semi-annually	Annually	Quantitative	Qualitative
Credit risk	2	2		3	1	3	1
Operational risk	3	1			4	3	1
Leverage ratio	2		2			2	
Credit valuation adjustments	4	2	1	3	2	4	2
Benchmarking	2		1	1		2	
Overview of risk management, key prudential metrics and RWA	2		2			2	
Asset encumbrance	1			1		1	
Capital distribution constraints		1			1	1	
Composition of capital and TLAC	1			1		1	
Total (23)	17	6	6	9	8	19	4

Figure 11.5: Phase III reporting frequency and format of disclosure

In March 2018 the Basel Committee opened a consultation on technical amendments to the Pillar 3 disclosure requirements – regulatory treatment of accounting provisions.[8] The consultation is related to additional disclosure requirements for those jurisdictions implementing an expected credit loss (ECL) accounting model as well as for those adopting transitional arrangements for the regulatory treatment of accounting provisions. The amendments are meant to ensure that the disclosed information fully reflects any transitional effects of ECL accounting on regulatory capital. Furthermore, the additional disclosures are required to get an overview of the

---

6   Cf. BCBS 387 (2016).
7   Cf. BCBS 352 (2016).
8   Cf. BCBS 435 (2018).

allocation of general and specific provisions during the transitional period. Technical amendments made additional requirements to the template CR1 (Credit quality of assets), template KM2 (Key metrics – TLAC requirements (at resolution group level)) and table CRB (Additional disclosure related to the credit quality of assets). The additional amendments to the Pillar 3 standard are applicable from 1 January 2019.

The review of the disclosure requirements by the Basel Committee is based on the five guiding principles shown in Figure 11.6. Adherence to these principles shall be ensured by means of new provisions regarding governance of disclosure, among others. That means that, for example, the quality of disclosed information and the internal control procedures used in the disclosure report shall be in line with financial reporting (annual, semi-annual and quarterly financial reports). Banks must establish a board-approved disclosure policy, internal controls and procedures for information subject to disclosure and publish them. Management must take measures to ensure the quality of the information disclosed, which must be signed by at least one senior officer.

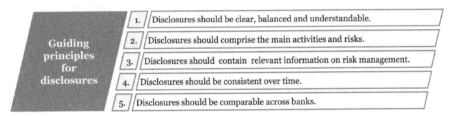

Figure 11.6: Guiding principles for disclosures

In future, the disclosure frequency will vary between annual, semi-annual and quarterly disclosures; the disclosure time frame has been completely redefined compared to the applicable CRR guidelines. Henceforth, banks will no longer determine the frequency of disclosure based on their own indicators.[9]

Instead, the reporting frequency will depend on each disclosure requirement. Consequently, all banks will be required to submit quarterly disclosures, adapt the respective processes and automate them adequately in order to comply with increased disclosure frequency.

As to the presentation of disclosed information, there is a distinction between:

1. templates with a fixed format for quantitative data;
2. tables with a flexible format for qualitative data.

Fixed templates are used to disclose quantitative information; however, a certain degree of flexibility is granted as to the form (e.g., when linked to the financial statement layout; see section 11.4). Tables are used to disclose qualitative information, accordingly they are described as flexible; however, the information provided must be presented at a similar level of granularity as set forth in the standard.

---

9 Cf. EBA (2014c) as well as BaFin (2015).

Templates with a fixed format may exceptionally be altered by adding or eliminating fields in order to ensure that the disclosed information is meaningful. As a result, the materiality criterion became a relevant component of the Pillar 3 revision. Should changes be made, the reason for doing so must be explained comprehensively. Moreover, compliance with the five disclosure principles must be ensured.

In future, the disclosure report shall be submitted as a separate document. The purpose hereof is to eliminate the possibility of integrating or "hiding" information within other sets of figures. However, exceptions may apply where:

- the other source is clearly referenced;
- a comparable degree of reliability is given; and
- the outsourced content is clearly specified.

When fixed-format information is disclosed in a separate document, additional requirements must be fulfilled (e.g., the content must refer to the same scope of consolidation).

Furthermore, quantitative and qualitative information will be expected to be supplemented with additional narrative commentary. Said commentary shall be subject to the five principles. Disclosure of additional figures shall be accompanied by a qualitative discussion. As a general rule, banks must explain in any case the significant changes that took place during the reporting period.

11.3 Risk management, key prudential metrics and risk-weighted assets (RWA)

The overview section of a bank's Pillar 3 Report shall provide a snapshot of the bank's risk profile and risk management. In Phase I, this section contained Table OVA and Template OV1, with a set of qualitative and quantitative information in order to provide the users with a clear understanding of the bank's risk tolerance and risk appetite, bank's main activities and significant risks. During Phase II, two templates (KM1 and KM2) containing key regulatory ratios were added, with the aim of facilitating the comparison of banks' performances over time. With BCBS 432, templates KM1 and OV1 were updated to include additional information to be disclosed.

Table 11.1 shows the disclosure requirements on risk management, key prudential metrics and RWA.

Name	Designation	Type	Format	Frequency
KM1	Key metrics (at consolidated group level)	Quantitative	Fixed	Quarterly
KM2	Key metrics – TLAC requirements (at resolution group level)	Quantitative	Fixed	Quarterly
OVA	Risk management approach	Qualitative	Flexible	Annually
OV1	Overview of RWA	Quantitative	Fixed	Quarterly

Table 11.1: Overview of risk management, key prudential metrics and RWA

Template KM1

This template was introduced during Phase II and further specified in Phase III (BCBS 432). The aim of the template is to provide users with the information on a bank's key prudential ratios at a consolidated group level related to risk-based capital ratios, leverage ratio and liquidity standards. Banks are required to disclose the information on available amounts of capital, RWA and Basel III leverage ratio exposure as well as capital and Basel III leverage ratios supplemented with values for fully loaded expected credit loss (ECL), in case of an ECL-based accounting model. According to the Basel publication on the regulatory treatment of accounting provisions,[10] it is expected that banks disclose whether they are applying a transitional arrangement for the impact of expected credit loss accounting on regulatory capital. The template will thus enable comparison between the values under transitional arrangements (if they exist) and fully-loaded values. The template further requires information on capital buffers, LCR and NSFR. All information is to be presented over the last five quarters.

Additional information to be disclosed introduced with BCBS 432 refers to the measures of total RWA and capital ratios that exclude the output floor in the computation of RWA as well as leverage ratios including and excluding the impact of any applicable temporary exemption of central bank reserves. Figure 11.7 presents Template KM1.

Template KM2

Template KM2 was also introduced in Phase II, without further changes in BCBS 432. It represents a quarterly report of key metrics related to institution's total loss absorbing capacity (TLAC) available at a G-SIB's resolution group level. It is used for resolution group level under the single point of entry (SPE) and multiple point of entry (MPE). In the latter case, the template is disclosed for each resolution group. Information in addition to TLAC available to be disclosed include total RWA at the level of the resolution group, TLAC as a percentage of RWA, leverage ratio at the resolution group level, TLAC as a percentage of leverage ratio exposure and additional information.

Template KM2 was amended with BCBS 435 in order to provide further disclosure of the "fully loaded" impact of ECL transitional arrangement used in TLAC key metrics. These changes are reflected in Figure 11.8.

Furthermore, on a European level, the EBA published guidelines on uniform disclosure formats for institutions' disclosures required under Article 473a CRR II draft as regards the transitional period for mitigating the impact of the introduction of IFRS 9 on own funds.[11] Template IFRS 9–FL provides a comparison of the banks' own funds, capital and leverage ratios with and without application of transitional arrangements for IFRS 9 or similar ECLs.

---

10   Cf. BCBS 401 (2017).
11   Cf. EBA (2018a).

		a T	b T-1	c T-2	d T-3	e T-4
	Available capital (amounts)					
1	Common Equity Tier 1 (CET1)					
1a	Fully loaded ECL accounting model					
2	Tier 1					
2a	Fully loaded ECL accounting model Tier 1					
3	Total capital					
3a	Fully loaded ECL accounting model total capital					
	Risk-weighted assets (amounts)					
4	Total risk-weighted assets (RWA)					
4a	Total risk-weighted assets (pre-floor)					
	Risk-based capital ratios as a percentage of RWA					
5	CET1 ratio (%)					
5a	Fully loaded ECL accounting model CET1 (%)					
5b	CET1 ratio (%) (pre-floor ratio)					
6	Tier 1 ratio (%)					
6a	Fully loaded ECL accounting model Tier 1 ratio (%)					
6b	Tier 1 ratio (%) (pre-floor ratio)					
7	Total capital ratio (%)					
7a	Fully loaded ECL accounting model total capital ratio (%)					
7b	Total capital ratio (%) (pre-floor ratio)					
	Additional CET1 buffer requirements as a percentage of RWA					
8	Capital conservation buffer requirement (2.5% from 2019)					
9	Countercyclical buffer requirement (%)					
10	Bank G-SIB and/or D-SIB additional requirements (%)					
11	Total of bank CET1 specific buffer requirements (%) (row 8 + row 9 + row 10)					
12	CET1 available after meeting the bank's minimum capital requirements (%)					
	Basel III leverage ratio					
13	Total Basel III leverage ratio exposure measure					
14	Basel III leverage ratio (%) (including the impact of any applicable temporary exemption of central bank reserves)					
14a	Fully loaded ECL accounting model Basel III leverage ratio (including the impact of any applicable temporary exemption of central bank reserves) (%)					
14b	Basel III leverage ratio (%) (excluding the impact of any applicable temporary exemption of central bank reserves)					

Figure 11.7: KM1 template

		a T	b T-1	c T-2	d T-3	e T-4
	Resolution group 1					
1	Total Loss Absorbing Capacity (TLAC) available					
1a	Fully loaded ECL accounting model TLAC available					
2	Total RWA at the level of the resolution group					
3	TLAC as a percentage of RWA (row1/row2) (%)					
3a	Fully loaded ECL accounting model TLAC as a percentage of fully loaded ECL accounting model RWA (%)					
4	Leverage exposure measure at the level of the resolution group					
5	TLAC as a percentage of leverage exposure measure (row1/row4) (%)					
5a	Fully loaded ECL accounting model TLAC as a percentage of fully loaded ECL accounting model Leverage exposure measure (%)					
6a	Does the subordination exemption in the antepenultimate paragraph of Section 11 of te FSB TLAC Term Sheet apply?					
6b	Does the subordination exemption in the penultimate paragraph of Section 11 of the FSB TLAC Term Sheet apply?					
6c	If the capped subordination exemption applies, the amount of funding issued that ranks pari passu with Excluded Liabilities and that is recognised as external TLAC, divided by funding issued that ranks pari passu with Excluded Liabilities and that would be recognised as external TLAC if no cap was applied (%)					

Figure 11.8: KM2 template BCBS 435

Table OVA

Table OVA was introduced by BCBS 309, without further amendments in BCBS 400 and BCBS 432. It provides for the qualitative disclosure of risk management objectives and policies. This includes, among others, information on the business model and risk strategy, risk governance, risk reporting and risk mitigation as well as stress testing.

What particularly stands out compared to the corresponding CRR provisions is that neither a statement signed by the Board concerning the adequacy of risk management (cf. Article 435 (1) (e) CRR) nor very detailed provisions in relation to the committee structure (number of mandates, diversity, cf. Article 435 (2) CRR) are required. These requirements remain limited to EU institutions, with no corresponding Basel requirement, being implemented in the CRR and EBA/GL/2016/11 respectively. On the other hand, the requirements regarding risk culture and the role of stress testing go beyond the scope of current CRR provisions.

Although a higher degree of detail is partly requested, banks can complete this table to a large extent based on existing information. Only small content-related adjustments are required compared to the current provisions in force in the EU.

Template OV1

Template OV1 was introduced by BCBS 309, with further enhancements in BCBS 400 and BCBS 432. The template provides a detailed overview on risk-weighted assets and capital requirements under Pillar 1 for each reporting period. These are itemised according to the individual risk types (credit risk, market risk, operational risk, etc.) and to the different approaches applied. Several Basel IV approaches, such as the SA-CCR, the new securitisation regulation and disclosures related to capital floors, were already covered in Phase I. Phase II increases the granularity of the RWA subcategories to be disclosed individually.

Enhancements to the template coming from BCBS 432 relate to the disclosure of the level of the aggregate capital floor applied by the bank and the resulting floor adjustment (before and after the application of the transitional cap). Thus, the template is largely consistent with the disclosure requirements pursuant to Article 438 CRR.

The disclosure of Basel IV requirements is predominantly not possible before their coming into force. Hence, banks should adjust the template in order to ensure consistent disclosure of all capital requirements under Pillar 1.

11.4 Linkages between financial statements and regulatory exposures

BCBS 309 introduced three templates intended to provide information on linkages between financial statement assets and liabilities and amounts used in the regulatory capital framework. In addition, BCBS 400 introduced a prudential valuation adjustment template which is due to apply from end-2018. The other templates have been applicable since end-2016. Table 11.2 summarises these disclosure requirements.

Name	Designation	Type	Format	Frequency
LIA	Differences between accounting and supervisory law	Quantitative	Flexible	Annually
LI1	Divergent scopes of consolidation and mapping of balance sheet to regulatory risk categories	Quantitative	Flexible	Annually
LI2	Differences between carrying values and exposures	Quantitative	Flexible	Annually
PV1	Prudent valuation adjustments (PVA)	Quantitative	Fixed	Annually

Table 11.2: Disclosure of the linkage between accounting and regulatory law

Template LIA: Explanation of differences between accounting and regulatory exposure amounts

Table LIA provides qualitative explanations and descriptions relating to the quantitative disclosures in templates LI1 and LI2. These include:

- significant differences identified in LI1 arising from the scope of consolidation between the carrying values of assets and liabilities in banks' published financial statements and the regulatory scope of consolidation;
- items that are included in more than one risk category in LI1;
- the types of difference identified in the LI2 reconciliation; and
- PVA related prudent valuation systems and controls including valuation methodologies, the independent price verification process and procedures for valuation adjustments.

Template LI1: Differences in the scope of consolidation and mapping of financial statement categories in relation to regulatory risk categories

The purpose of template LI1 disclosure is to:

- identify differences arising from the scope of consolidation between the carrying values of assets and liabilities in banks' published financial statements and the regulatory scope of consolidation by listing them side-by-side; and
- show which parts of the capital requirements framework these assets and liabilities are subject to by analysing the carrying amounts across corresponding regulatory risk categories.

This template has a flexible format but requires banks to align asset, liabilities and shareholders' equity line items in the template to their published financial statements. The regulatory risk categories comprise: credit risk, counterparty credit risk, securitisation and market risk. There is an additional category to record items not subject to capital requirements or which are deducted from regulatory capital.

BCBS acknowledges that some items may be subject to regulatory capital charges relating to more than one risk category and so should be included in more than one risk category in the template. Banks are expected to provide an accompanying explanatory narrative (see also Table LIA).

Template LI2: Main sources of differences between regulatory exposure amounts and carrying values in financial statements

The purpose of template LI2 is to provide quantitative information on the nature of the differences between the carrying values, analysed by regulatory risk category identified in LI1, and the regulatory exposure amounts used as the starting point in RWA calculations. The template takes the form of a reconciliation, by regulatory risk category, between regulatory carrying values (net of related liabilities) and regulatory exposure amounts.

BCBS provides illustrative types of reconciliation differences but expects banks to adapt them to provide the most meaningful descriptions of differences as appropriate. The types of differences include:

- off-balance sheet amounts,
- valuations,
- other netting/offset, and
- prudential filters.

Banks are expected to provide an accompanying explanatory narrative (see Table LIA).

Template PV1: Prudent valuation adjustments (PVA)

Template PV1 requires banks to provide details of the prudential valuation adjustment for assets held at fair value analysed by nature and risk type. Disclosure of the aggregate PVA is already disclosed in the composition of regulatory capital template CC1. Banks are expected to explain the types of financial instruments that give rise to the highest PVAs and provide additional detail where adjustments occur outside the categories specified in the table. The format of this disclosure is shown in Figure 11.9.

		a	b	c	d	e	f	g	h
		Equity	Interest rates	FX	Credit	Commodities	Total	Of which: In the trading book	Of which: In the banking book
1	Closeout uncertainty, of which:								
2	Mid-market value								
3	Closeout cost								
4	Concentration								
5	Early termination								
6	Model risk								
7	Operational risk								
8	Investing and funding costs								
9	Unearned credit spreads								
10	Future administrative costs								
11	Other								
12	total adjustment								

Figure 11.9: Prudent valuation adjustments template – PVA

11.5 Composition of capital and TLAC

BCBS originally set out its composition of capital disclosure requirements in BCBS 221 in 2012. But in BCBS 400, these disclosures were reformatted to align them with the revised Pillar 3 framework. BCBS 400 also introduced new disclosure requirements incorporating the total loss absorbing capacity regime (TLAC) applicable to G-SIBs arising from FSB's November 2015 TLAC principles and term sheet and BCBS 387 in October 2016. The regulatory capital templates (CC templates) are due to apply from end-2018. The TLAC templates are due to apply from 1 January 2019, aligning with the commencement of implementation of the TLAC regime. BCBS 432 proposes expanding the scope of composition of capital disclosure to include resolution groups. Table 11.3 summarises these disclosure requirements.

Name	Designation	Type	Format	Frequency
CC1	Composition of regulatory capital	Quantitative	Fixed	Semi-annually
CC2	Reconciliation of regulatory capital to balance sheet	Quantitative	Flexible	Semi-annually
CCA	Main features of regulatory capital instruments and of other TLAC-eligible instruments	Quantitative and Qualitative	Flexible	Semi-annually
TLAC1	TLAC composition for G-SIBs (at resolution group level)	Quantitative	Fixed	Semi-annually
TLAC2	Material subgroup entity – creditor ranking at legal entity level	Quantitative	Fixed	Semi-annually
TLAC3	Resolution entity – creditor ranking at legal entity level	Quantitative	Fixed	Semi-annually

Table 11.3: Disclosure of composition of capital and TLAC

Template CC1: Composition of regulatory capital

Template CC1 requires a detailed breakdown of the composition of capital and includes 85 line items. It includes analyses of:

- deductions and adjustments to CET1, AT1 and T2 components of regulatory capital;
- capital instruments subject to phase-out arrangements;
- T2 capital subject to caps arising from limits on levels of T2 in relation T1 capital;
- amounts below thresholds for deductions; and
- national regulatory capital minima if different from BCBS minima.

The format of the disclosure is illustrated by the CET1 component of the CC1 template set out in Figure 11.10.

In Phase III, BCBS 432 proposes expanding the scope of template CC1, composition of regulatory capital, to cover not only the regulatory consolidated group level but

		a	b
		Amounts	Source based on reference numbers/ letters of the balance sheet under the regulatory scope of consolidation
	Common Equity Tier 1 capital: instruments and reserves		
1	Directly issued qualifying common share (and equivalent for non-joint stock companies) capital plus related stock surplus		(h)
2	Retained earnings		
3	Accumulated other comprehensive income (and other reserves)		
4	*Directly issued capital subject to phase-out from CET1 (only applicable to non-joint stock companies)*		
5	Common share capital issued by subsidiaries and held by third parties (amount allowed in group CET1)		
6	**Common Equity Tier 1 capital before regulatory adjustments**		
	Common Equity Tier 1 capital: regulatory adjustments		
7	Prudent valuation adjustments		
8	Goodwill (net of related tax liability)		(a) minus (d)
9	Other intangibles other than mortgage servicing rights (net of related tax liability)		(b) minus (e)
10	Deferred tax assets that rely on future profitability, excluding those arising from temporary differences (net of related tax liability)		
11	Cash flow hedge reserve		
12	Shortfall of provisions to expected losses		
13	Securitisation gain on sale (as set out in paragraph 36 of Basel III securitisation framework)		
14	Gains and losses due to changes in own credit risk on fair valued liabilities		
15	Defined benefit pension fund net assets		
16	Investments in own shares (if not already subtracted from paid-in capital on reported balance sheet)		
17	Reciprocal cross-holdings in common equity		
18	Investments in the capital of banking, financial and insurance entities that are outside the scope of regulatory consolidation, where the bank does not own more than 10% of the issued share capital (amount above 10% threshold)		
19	Significant investments in the common stock of banking, financial and insurance entities that are outside the scope of regulatory consolidation (amount above 10% threshold)		
20	Mortgage servicing rights (amount above 10% threshold)		(c) minus (f) minus 10% threshold

Figure 11.10: Composition of regulatory capital template – CC1 extract CET 1 component

also each resolution group level. Under BCBS 400, resolution groups must provide information on the composition of their TLAC, but not on the full composition of regulatory capital.

Template CC2: Reconciliation of regulatory capital to balance sheet

The purpose of Template CC2 is to:

- show the link between a bank's balance sheet in its published financial statements and line items in the composition of capital template CC1; and
- enable users to identify differences on a line-by-line basis in the scope of accounting consolidation and the scope of regulatory consolidation.

This template has a flexible format but requires banks to align asset, liabilities and shareholders' equity line items to their published financial statements. Banks are also required to expand line items in CC2 as appropriate to enable cross-referencing of all amounts disclosed in template CC1 to its location in template CC2.

Where the accounting and regulatory scopes of consolidation differ, banks must list the legal entities excluded from either scope. Entities included within both scopes but where the method of consolidation differs, must also be listed. For all entities listed, details of their total assets, equity and a description of their principle activities must also be disclosed.

Table CCA: Main features of regulatory capital instruments and of other TLAC-eligible instruments

Table CCA requires banks to disclose a minimum level of specified information for each instrument in issue. It applies to all banks in respect of regulatory capital instruments and to G-SIBs for TLAC-eligible instruments. National authorities are encouraged to add additional information requirements if there are additional features that are important to disclose in the context of the banks they supervise. Banks are also required to make available on their websites the full terms and conditions of all instruments included in regulatory capital and of all TLAC-eligible instruments.

Template TLAC1: TLAC composition for G-SIBs (at resolution group level)

Template TLAC1 provides details of the TLAC positions of G-SIBs at each resolution group level. Banks should consider including details of its resolution strategy, including the approach (single point of entry or multiple point of entry) and structure, to which the resolution measures are applied.

Template TLAC2: Material subgroup entity – creditor ranking at legal entity level

Template TLAC2 provides creditors with information regarding their ranking in the liabilities structure of a material subgroup entity (i.e. an entity that is part of a material subgroup) which has issued internal TLAC to a G-SIB resolution entity. It provides information on the amount and residual maturity of TLAC and on other instruments that rank equally or are junior to the TLAC instruments, identifying separately where the creditor is a resolution entity.

Disclosure is required in respect of every material subgroup entity within each resolution group of a G-SIB. Banks should provide a description of each creditor ranking.

Template TLAC3: Resolution entity – creditor ranking at legal entity level

Template TLAC3 is similar to TLAC 2 but disclosure is in respect of every resolution entity within the G-SIB.

11.6 Macroprudential supervisory measures

BCBS 400 introduced two additional templates covering the indicators used to determine the designation of banks as G-SIBs and on the countercyclical buffer. The countercyclical buffer template has been applicable since end-2017. The G-SIB indicator template is due to apply from end-2018. Table 11.4 summarises these disclosure requirements.

Name	Designation	Type	Format	Frequency
GSIB1	Disclosure of G-SIB indicators	Quantitative	Flexible	Annually
CCyB1	Geographical distribution of credit exposures used in the countercyclical buffer	Quantitative	Flexible	Semi-annually

Table 11.4: Disclosure of macroprudential supervisory measures

Template GSIB1: Disclosure of G-SIB indicators

Template GSIB1 is applicable by all banks that are G-SIBs, that have a leverage ratio exposure measure > €200bn or the bank was included in the assessment sample by the relevant national authority based on supervisory judgement. Its purpose is to provide an overview of the indicators that BCBS uses for assessing the systemic importance of banks. The methodology it uses is set out in BCBS 255 respectively BCBS 424.[12] Banks are required to disclose these indicators and they cover five categories: cross-jurisdictional activity, size, interconnectedness within the financial system, substitutability/financial institution infrastructure and complexity. These are further broken down into twelve individual indicators. National authorities have discretion to require disclosure of a more detailed breakdown of these indicators.

Template CCyB1: Geographical distribution of credit exposures used in the countercyclical buffer

Template CCyB1 requires disclosure of a geographical breakdown of the applicable country-specific countercyclical buffer (CCyB) rate, exposure values and RWA as well as the overall bank-specific CCyB rate and amount. Banks should disclose their geographical asset allocation methodology. Banks should, where possible, allocate exposures on the basis of the geographical location of the 'ultimate risk'. The format of this disclosure is shown in Figure 11.11.

Geographical breakdown	a Countercyclical capital buffer rate	b Exposure values and/or risk-weighted assets used in the computation of the countercyclical capital buffer		c	d Bank-specific countercyclical capital buffer rate	e Countercyclical buffer amount
		Exposure values	Risk-weighted assets			
(Home) Country 1						
Country 2						
Country 3						
⋮						
Country N						
Sum						
Total						

Figure 11.11: Geographical distribution of credit exposures used in the countercyclical capital buffer template – CCyB1

12 Cf. BCBS 424 (2017).

11.7 Leverage Ratio

The Basel Committee on Banking Supervision set out the leverage ratio disclosure standards in BCBS 270 in January 2014. BCBS 400 consolidated these disclosures into the Pillar 3 framework and comprises two templates. They apply from end-2017. BCBS 432 proposes updates to these templates which are due to apply from 1 January 2022. Table 11.5 summarises these disclosure requirements.

Name	Designation	Type	Format	Frequency
LR1	Summary comparison of accounting assets vs leverage exposure measure	Quantitative	Fixed	Quarterly
LR2	Leverage ratio common disclosure template	Quantitative	Fixed	Quarterly

Table 11.5: Disclosure of the leverage ratio

Template LR1: Summary comparison of accounting assets vs leverage exposure measure

Template LR1 requires a reconciliation of the total assets published in banks' financial statements and their leverage ratio exposure measure. Banks should disclose the basis of calculation for their disclosures (e.g. quarter-end, daily averaging or monthly averaging),

Template LR2: Leverage ratio common disclosure template

Template LR2 includes a detailed breakdown of the components of the leverage ratio exposure measure, the denominator component of the ratio. The four components comprise the following exposures: on-balance sheet, derivatives, securities financing transactions and other off-balance sheet. The current format of this disclosure is shown in Figure 11.12.

BCBS 432: proposed changes

BCBS 432 proposes to update the LR templates to take account of changes introduced by BCBS 424. These concern the leverage ratio buffer regime that is to apply to G-SIBs and refinements of the exposure measure. This results in additional line items in the LR1 reconciliation and LR2 leverage ratio component analysis.

BCBS indicates that it continues to review incentives that banks have to "window dress" their balance sheets at period ends by making changes to their balance sheets that enhance their ratios. It indicates that the outcome of that review could lead to additional changes to these disclosure requirements.

		a	b
		T	T-1
On-balance sheet exposures			
1	On-balance sheet exposures (excluding derivatives and securities financing transactions (SFTs), but including collateral)		
2	(Asset amounts deducted in determining Basel III Tier 1 capital)		
3	**Total on-balance sheet exposures** (excluding derivatives and SFTs) (sum of rows 1 and 2)		
Derivative exposures			
4	Replacement cost associated with all derivatives transactions (where applicable net of eligible cash variation margin and/or with bilateral netting)		
5	Add-on amounts for PFE associated with all derivatives transactions		
6	Gross-up for derivatives collateral provided where deducted from the balance sheet assets pursuant to the operative accounting framework		
7	(Deductions of receivables assets for cash variation margin provided in derivatives transactions)		
8	(Exempted CCP leg of client-cleared trade exposures)		
9	Adjusted effective notional amount of written credit derivatives		
10	(Adjusted effective notional offsets and add-on deductions for written credit derivatives)		
11	**Total derivative exposures (sum of rows 4 to 10)**		
Securities financing transaction exposures			
12	Gross SFT assets (with no recognition of netting), after adjusting for sale accounting transactions		
13	(Netted amounts of cash payables and cash receivables of gross SFT assets)		
14	CCR exposure for SFT assets		
15	Agent transaction exposures		
16	**Total securities financing transaction exposures (sum of rows 12 to 15)**		
Other off-balance sheet exposures			
17	Off-balance sheet exposure at gross notional amount		
18	(Adjustments for conversion to credit equivalent amounts)		
19	**Off-balance sheet items (sum of rows 17 and 18)**		
Capital and total exposures			
20	**Tier 1 capital**		
21	**Total exposures (sum of rows 3, 11, 16 and 19)**		
Leverage ratio			
22	**Basel III leverage ratio**		

Figure 11.12: Leverage ratio common disclosure template – LR2

11.8 Disclosures related to liquidity

In addition to the review of the existing disclosure requirements established by BCBS 309, the Basel Committee also published new disclosure guidelines focused on liquidity rules. First, Basel III introduced internationally standardised liquidity requirements,[13] which are now supplemented with the respective provisions regarding disclosure. These provisions refer to the Liquidity Coverage Ratio (LCR)[14] and the Net Stable Funding Ratio (NSFR)[15] as well as additional quantitative and qualitative disclosure requirements.

BCBS 400 made a coherent system of disclosure requirements related to liquidity by bringing the disclosure requirements of LCR and NSFR together in one section and adding a table with general information on liquidity risk management. Apart from that, no changes to the LCR and NSFR templates occurred within Phase II or

---

13   Cf. BCBS 283238 (2013) and BCBS 295 (2014), respectively.
14   Cf. BCBS 272 (2014).
15   Cf. BCBS 324 (2015).

Phase III. The set of formats related to liquidity disclosure requirements are presented in the following table.

To ensure greater consistency and comparability, Template LIQ1 is to be published quarterly, beginning with the financial year-end 2017, Template LIQ2 is to be published semi-annually, with a bank's first semi-annual report in 2018 and LIQA to be published annually.

Within the EU, the CRR does not currently impose an obligation in terms of LCR and NSFR disclosures. The EBA, however, published guidelines regarding LCR disclosure in 2016.[16] These guidelines will have to be transposed into national legislation by the individual EU member states.

Name	Designation	Type	Format	Frequency
LIQA	Liquidity risk management	Qualitative / Quantitative	Flexible	Annually
LIQ1	Liquidity Coverage Ratio (LCR)	Quantitative	Fixed	Quarterly
LIQ2	Net Stable Funding ratio (NSFR)	Quantitative	Fixed	Semiannual

Table 11.6: Disclosure requirements related to liquidity

The disclosure requirements related to LCR and NSFR as well as additional specifications regarding the disclosure of quantitative and qualitative information are discussed below. An overview of the information to be disclosed is included in Figure 11.13.

Disclosure requirements for LCR
- Market discipline through insight into the banks' liquidity situation
- Disclosure of quantitative information ("common disclosure template") and qualitative descriptions
- Became effective as of 1 January 2015
- Disclosures included in published financial reports
- Disclosure of average of daily observations

Disclosure requirements for NSFR
- Market discipline through insight into the banks' liquidity situation
- Disclosure of quantitative information ("common disclosure template") and qualitative descriptions
- Became effective as of 1 January 2018
- Disclosures included in published financial reports
- Disclosure of end of quarter figures

Liquidity risk

Additional quantitative disclosure
- Additional Monitoring Metrics (AMM)
- Balance-sheet structure
- Cash-flow projections
- Concentration by collateral types and funding sources
- Information on subsidiaries and branches
- Liquidity Maturity Ladder

Additional qualitative disclosure
- Governance structures: involvement of the board, risk appetite, responsibilities, risk reporting ...
- Funding strategy: diversification (sources, maturities ...)
- Liquidity risk hedging
- Use of stress tests
- Contingency Funding Plans

Figure 11.13: Overview of disclosures related to liquidity indicators

---

16   Cf. EBA (2016).

Table LIQA – Liquidity risk management

The Basel Committee is aware of the fact that information pertaining to the LCR and NSFR represents only a part of a bank's liquidity situation and therefore added additional Table LIQA. This table is intended to provide the users with information on bank's liquidity risk management framework and liquidity position. The table consists of qualitative and quantitative parts. These additional pieces of information are based on reports such as Additional Liquidity Monitoring Metrics (ALMM)[17] and the Internal Liquidity Adequacy Assessment Process (ILAAP).[18]

The former part encompasses disclosures on the governance of liquidity management in terms of structure and responsibilities within a bank, internal systems for measurement and reporting, funding strategy (diversification of funding, funding strategy), liquidity risk mitigation techniques, stress testing and description of contingency funding plans.

The latter part consists of internal tools or metrics that assess the structure of a bank's balance sheet, make projections of cash flows and liquidity positions, concentration of funding, liquidity gap, liquidity exposures and funding needs at the individual entity level and operational limitations on the transferability of liquidity.

Template LIQ1: Disclosure requirements for the Liquidity Coverage Ratio (LCR)

The Basel Committee requests that the disclosure requirements for the LCR be complied with using the common disclosure template. This template is equivalent to those of BCBS 309 (disclosure of quantitative information in a fixed format). It is aligned with the Basel guidelines on LCR, which is why it is expected that the EBA will make adjustments to its pending recommendation with regard to the implementation of LCR within the EU.

Moreover, Basel requires that the LCR be presented as averages of daily observations and that the number of data points used in calculating the average figures be provided. This implies that it would be necessary to calculate the LCR on a daily basis. In practice, this could be challenging since many banks still rely on manual processing steps, which are not performed daily, when calculating the LCR. Sometimes, only the automatically generated portion of the LCR is made available and controlled daily and the necessary manual processing takes place solely on the monthly reporting deadlines. In order to cope with this problem, the Basel Committee pointed out that it would be acceptable to publish the average monthly values during a transition phase until beginning of 2017.

A separate disclosure of LCR in foreign currency is not required.

---

17 Cf. BCBS 238 (2013) as well as EBA (2014a).
18 Cf. EBA (2014b).

Figure 11.14 shows the common disclosure template of LCR with the information to be disclosed.

LCR common disclosure template

(in local currency)	Total Unweighted Value (average)	Total weighted Value (average)
High-Quality Liquid Assets		
1 Total high-quality liquid assets (HQLA)		
Cash Outflows		
2 Retail deposits and deposits from small business customers; of which:		
3 Stable deposits		
4 Less stable deposits		
5 Unsecured sholesale funding, of which:		
6 Operational deposits (all counterparties) and deposits in networks of cooperative banks		
7 Non-operational deposits (all counterparties)		
8 Unsecured debt		
9 Secured wholesale funding		
10 Additional requirements, of which:		
11 Outflows related to derivative exposures and other collateral requirements		
12 Outflows related to loss of funding on debt products		
13 Credit and liquidity facilities		
14 Other contractual funding obligations		
15 Other contingent funding obligations		
16 Total Cash Outflows		
Cash Inflows		
17 Secured lending (eg reverse repo)		
18 Inflows from fully performing exposures		
19 Other cash inflows		
20 Total Cash Inflows		

		Total Adjusted Value
21 Total HQLA		
22 Total Net Cash Outflows		
23 Liquidity Coverage Ratio (%)		

Figure 11.14: LCR common disclosure template

On top of the quantitative requirements regarding the minimum liquidity ratio, banks shall also make available qualitative data to determine the Liquidity Coverage Ratio. The Basel Committee suggests that the following information be provided for this purpose.

- main drivers that significantly influenced the LCR evolution as well as its evolution over time;
- intra-period changes of the LCR;
- composition of HQLA (High Quality Liquid Assets);
- concentration of funding sources;
- derivate exposures and potential collateral calls;

- currency mismatches;
- description of significant inflows and outflows that are not captured in the common disclosure template.

Template LIQ2: The Net Stable Funding Ratio (NSFR)

The Basel Committee requests that the disclosure requirements for the NSFR shall also be complied with by using a common disclosure template. Provided the implementation in the EU takes place in the near future, adjustments will most likely be made hereto. Compared to the LCR, no disclosure based on daily values is requested. Instead, data must be presented as quarter-end figures. For banks disclosing on a semi-annual basis, the values of each of the two preceding quarters, or for all four preceding quarters in the case of annual disclosure, must be reported.

The common disclosure template provides for the disclosure of the information shown in Figure 11.15, i.e. available stable funding (ASF) and required stable funding (RSF)

ASF Item	
1	Capital:
2	Regulatory Capital
3	Other capital instruments
4	Retail deposits and deposits from small business customers:
5	Stable deposits
6	Less stable deposits
7	Wholesale funding:
8	Operational deposits
9	Other wholesale funding
10	Liabilities with matching interdependent assets
11	Other liabilities:
12	NSFR derivative liabilities
13	All other liabilities and equity not included in the above categories
14	Total ASF

RSF Item	
15	Total NSFR high-quality liquid assets (HQLA)
16	Deposits held at other financial institutions for operational purposes
17	Performing loans and securities:
18	Performing loans to financial institutions secured by Level 1 HQLA
19	Performing loans to financial institutions secured by non-Level 1 HQLA and unsecured performing loans to financial institutions

20	Performing loans to non-financial corporate clients, loans to retail and small business customers and loans to sovereigns, central banks and PSEs, of which:
21	With a risk weight of less than or equal to 35% under the Basel II Standardised Approach for credit risk
22	Performing residential mortgages, of which:
23	With a risk weight of less than or equal to 35% under the Basel II Standardised Approach for credit risk
24	Securities that are not in default and do not qualify as HQLA, including exchange-traded equities
25	Assets with matching interdependent liabilities
26	Other assets:
27	Physical traded commodities, including gold
28	Assets posted as initial margin for derivative contracts and contributions to default funds of CCPs
29	NSFR derivative assets
30	NSFR derivative liabilities before deduction of variation margin posted
31	All other assets not included in the above categories
32	Off-balance sheet items
33	Total RSF
34	Net Stable Funding Ratio (%)

Figure 11.15: NSFR common disclosure template

for the time buckets less than six months, from six months to one year, and greater than one year, and exposures without maturity for non-weighted assets as well as the disclosure of weighted assets.

In addition to the quantitative data on liquidity contained in the template, banks should also provide qualitative information related to the NSFR structure. This facilitates the understanding of the quantitative results as well as the accompanying data. The reasons for significant intra-period changes as well as changes over time, for example, could be subject to further discussion. The composition of interdependent assets and liabilities and to what extent these transactions are interrelated, is listed as an additional aspect in the standard.

In summary, the challenges for banks regarding the disclosure requirements for liquidity indicators are the calculation of **averages based on daily observations** as well as the analysis of related changes.

Moreover, the disclosure of indicators (LCR, NSFR and ALMM) of the reporting system is linked to information obtained from the **internal risk management**, which represents a challenge for all institutions that do not use the same database for external reporting and internal risk management. The consequence for said institutions is that comprehensive adjustments and transitions regarding information consistency will have to be performed.

Furthermore, with respect to the disclosure requirements regarding liquidity, it should be noted that the European Banking Authority (EBA) will have to carry out changes to the suggestions of the Basel Committee when implementing said provisions in **European law**. This is due to the fact that the reporting forms on the liquidity indicator "LCR" are different (Basel versus CRR, delegated act) and that the disclosure scheme must, in consequence, be adjusted.

11.9 Credit risk

In order to achieve its primary goal and enhance the comparability and consistency of disclosures, BCBS 309 introduced harmonised templates and a "hierarchy" of disclosures. It combines prescriptive fixed form templates used for quantitative information deemed to be essential for the market participants and templates with a more flexible format for information considered to be meaningful but not fundamental for the analysis of a bank's regulatory capital adequacy. As a consequence, several new pieces of information had to be identified in the banks' systems and disclosed.

Whereas there were no amendments to the disclosure templates for credit risk during Phase II (BCBS 400), BCBS 432 (Phase III) suggested some revisions and additions to the Pillar 3 framework arising from the finalisation of Basel IV. Furthermore, the technical amendments in BCBS 435 made additional disclosure requirements related to the

ECL accounting model. The purpose of the revisions to the standardised approach (SA) is to increase the risk sensitivity and granularity and, at the same time, to reduce the reliance on credit ratings. The revisions to the internal ratings-based approach (IRB) result, on the one hand, in the introduction of floored values for IRB parameters (i.e. probability of default (PD) as well as loss-given-default (LGD) and exposure-at-default (EAD) for the advanced IRB Approach) and, on the other hand, in the prohibition of the use of the advanced IRB Approach for certain asset classes, which are inherently difficult to model. The significant changes are discussed in detail below.

The disclosure of credit risks merely comprises the credit risk in the narrower sense, i.e. counterparty credit risk (see section 11.10) as well as securitisations (see section 11.11) are not included herein.

A differentiation between qualitative and quantitative data to be disclosed must also be made in terms of credit risk. Separate disclosure requirements are in force for banks that use an internal ratings-based approach approved by the regulatory authorities to determine capital requirements for credit risks (IRB). Table 11.7 provides an overview of the individual disclosure tables and templates.

Name	Designation	Type	Format	Frequency
CRA	General qualitative information about credit risk	Qualitative	Flexible	Annually
CR1	Credit quality of assets	Quantitative	Fixed	Semi-annually
CR2	Changes in stock of defaulted loans and debt securities	Quantitative	Fixed	Semi-annually
CRB	Additional disclosure related to the credit quality of assets	Qualitative	Flexible	Annually
CRB-A	Additional disclosure related to prudential treatment of problem assets	Qualitative	Flexible	Annually
CRC	Qualitative disclosure requirements related to credit risk mitigation techniques	Qualitative	Flexible	Annually
CR3	Credit risk mitigation techniques – overview	Quantitative	Fixed	Semi-annually
CRD	Qualitative disclosures on banks' use of external credit ratings under the standardised approach for credit risk	Qualitative	Flexible	Annually
CR4	Standardised approach – credit risk exposure and Credit Risk Mitigation (CRM) effects	Quantitative	Fixed	Semi-annually
CR5	Standardised approach – exposures by asset classes and risk weights	Quantitative	Fixed	Semi-annually
CRE	Qualitative disclosures related to IRB models	Qualitative	Flexible	Annually
CR6	IRBA – credit risk exposure by portfolio and PD range	Quantitative	Fixed	Semi-annually
CR7	IRBA – Effect on RWA of credit derivatives used as CRM techniques	Quantitative	Fixed	Semi-annually
CR8	IRBA – RWA flow statements of credit risk exposures under IRB	Quantitative	Fixed	Quarterly
CR9	IRBA – Backtesting of probability of default (PD) per portfolio	Quantitative	Flexible	Annually
CR10	IRBA – equities under simple risk weight method (Phase I) and specialised lending under the slotting approach	Quantitative	Flexible	Semi-annually

Table 11.7: Disclosure requirements related to credit risks

11.9.1 General information on credit risk

General information on credit risk comprises qualitative data on credit risk management (Table CRA) and credit quality (Table CRB) in addition to quantitative data on credit quality, i.e. the value of defaulted exposures (CR1) and risk provisions (CR2). In addition to the above-mentioned tables and templates introduced with BCBS 309 during Phase I, a new table (CRB-A) has been proposed by BCBS 432 to reflect the new disclosure requirements resulting from the guideline on prudential treatment of problem assets. However, it is only relevant for banks when required by their national supervisor.

After the revisions of the disclosure framework in Phase 3, additional technical amendments to Template CR1 and Table CRB were made within BCBS 435. These changes include information on allocation of accounting provisions for jurisdictions implementing ECL accounting models and transitional arrangements. Bearing in mind that the distinction between general and specific provisions in the SA does not directly correspond to the way the provisions are measured under the ECL accounting standards, the additional disclosures are required to get an overview of the allocation of provisions during the transitional period.

Table CRA: General qualitative information on credit risk

Table CRA encompasses general qualitative information on credit risk management objectives and instruments. The following requirements are differ from the respective provisions contained in Article 435 (1) CRR.

- approach used to determine the credit risk strategy and management including the setting of credit risk limits;
- relationship between credit risk management on the one hand and risk control and compliance functions as well as internal audit functions on the other.

The information needed should already be at hand in banks' internal documents (strategy, policies or instructions).

Templates CR1 and CR2: Credit quality and stock of defaulted exposures

Template CR1 contains quantitative information about the credit quality of on-balance sheet assets (loans, debt securities) and off-balance sheet items. The following must be stated:

- gross carrying values of defaulted exposures;
- gross carrying values of non-defaulted exposures;
- allowances and impairments; and
- net values.

It must be taken into account that, in terms of carrying values, banks must resort to financial statement values, which must then be reconciled with the regulatory scope of consolidation. However, the default definition to be applied is the regulatory definition (see Article 178 CRR). The quantitative information to be disclosed is contained in Figure 11.16.

		a	b	c	d
		Gross carrying values of		Allowances/ impairments	Net values (a+b-c)
		Defaulted exposures	Non-defaulted exposures		
1	Loans				
2	Debt Securities				
3	Off-balance sheet exposures				
4	Total				

Figure 11.16: CR1 Template BCBS 309

The template CR1 was amended with the BCBS 435 in order to provide further disclosure of allowances and impairments separated to the SA and IRB level. Further on, the allowances in SA have to be distinct in specific and general regulatory accounting provisions, due to the fact that the regulatory distinction between general and specific provisions in SA does not correspond directly to the measurement of provisions used in the ECL accounting standards. These changes are reflected in Figure 11.17.

		a	b	c	d	e	f	g
		Gross carrying values of		Allowances/ impairments	Of which accounting provisions on SA exposures		Of which accounting provisions on IRB exposures	Net values (a+b-c)
		Defaulted exposures	Non-defaulted exposures		Allocated in regulatory category of Specific	Allocated in regulatory category of General		
1	Loans							
2	Debt Securities							
3	Off-balance sheet exposures							
4	Total							

Figure 11.17: CR1 Template BCBS 435

Similarly to CR1, CR2 also requests that carrying values at the level of the regulatory scope of consolidation be indicated. The stock of defaulted exposures (loans and debt securities) of the previous reporting period must be reconciled with the stock of the last reporting period. New defaults, positions returned to non-defaulted status, amounts written off and other changes must also be specified.

Additionally, the main drivers of change must be elucidated and the default definition applied must be explained.

As with the disclosure of linkages between accounting and regulatory law, the challenges of combining accounting and regulatory definitions and delimitations and, if necessary, reconciling these with the regulatory scope of consolidation, remain also in relation to credit quality.

The corresponding provisions pursuant to Article 442 CRR can broadly be complied with based on the regulatory reporting systems database, since only regulatory definitions (exposure, credit risk adjustment, among others) are applied here. In the past, the German supervisory authority allowed banks to present accounting data about credit quality based on the scope of consolidation under commercial law if this was unveiled accordingly. However, this solution is no longer compatible with the revised Pillar 3 disclosure requirements.

Table CRB: Additional disclosure related to the credit quality of assets

Table CRB supplements quantitative data of the CR1 and CR2 templates with information on credit quality. Beyond the current provisions of Article 442 CCR (definitions for accounting purposes of "past due" and "impaired", as well as a description of the approaches and methods adopted for determining specific and general credit risk adjustment), the following information should be disclosed:

- exposures that have been past due for more than 90 days that are not considered to be impaired and the reasons for this;
- definition of a restructured exposure;
- past-due exposures broken down by the amount of time in past-due status; as well as
- restructured exposures broken down between impaired and non impaired exposures.

In addition to above, the BCBS 435 requires the banks to explain the reasons for categorisation of accounting provisions under SA in general and specific categories as a supplement for Template CR1.

Table CRB-A: Additional disclosure related to prudential treatment of problem assets

Table CRB-A presents additional information related to non-performing exposures and forbearance. It is intended to supplement the quantitative templates and includes, among others, following disclosures:

- either bank's own definition of non-performing exposures (NPEs) and forborne exposures or the definitions provided in the guidelines on prudential treatment of problem assets issued by the Committee;

- gross carrying value of total performing and non-performing exposures as well as accumulated provisions for NPEs broken down by debt securities, loans and off-balance sheet exposures.

The quantitative information that should be disclosed in the Table CRB-A is based on carrying values, which correspond to the accounting values reported in financial statements but according to the regulatory scope of consolidation. As a matter of fact, this is the biggest challenge banks face when filling in the table.

11.9.2 Credit risk mitigation

In order to make use of credit risk mitigation techniques, qualitative (Table CRC) as well as quantitative information (Template CR3) must be provided.

Table CRC: Qualitative disclosure requirements related to credit risk mitigation techniques

The qualitative information on credit risk mitigation according to Table CRC is entirely embodied in the requirements currently in force according to Article 453 CRR and is therefore not set out in detail in the following.

Template CR3: Credit risk mitigation techniques – overview

Template CR3 stipulates that the following information for loans and debt securities shall be disclosed. However, defaulted exposures shall be disclosed separately.

- Net carrying amount of unsecured exposures;
- net carrying amount of secured exposures;
- net carrying amount of the secured amount of the secured exposure;
- net carrying amount of exposures secured by financial guarantees;
- net carrying amount of the secured amount of exposures secured by financial guarantees;
- net carrying amount of exposures secured by credit derivatives; and
- net carrying amount of the secured amount of exposures secured by credit derivatives.

Here again it is challenging to harmonise carrying amounts (book values) with regulatory provisions (presence of collateral recognised as credit risk mitigation). Moreover, under the IRB Approach, the consideration of collateral does not always take place by differentiating the secured from the unsecured part of an exposure, but rather by means of the Loss Given Default (LGD). In these cases, determining the secured part of an exposure can be challenging since the secured part was not required so far to determine risk-weighted assets.

11.9.3 Credit risk under the standardised approach

Qualitative (CRD) and quantitative information (CR4, CR5) must be disclosed for exposures for which capital requirements are calculated based on the credit risk standardised approach.

Table CRD: Qualitative disclosure on the use of external credit ratings under the standardised approach

The information to be completed in Table CRD must currently be disclosed according to Article 444 CRR and is therefore not discussed in detail in the following.

Templates CR4 and CR5: Credit risk mitigation and risk weights under the credit risk standardised approach

Templates CR4 and CR5 were introduced during the Phase I (BCBS 309) and demand the disclosure of the assessment basis and the exposure values of exposures under the credit risk standardised approach. Compared to the disclosure requirements presented so far (CR1 to CR3), only the regulatory amounts need to be recorded here. No linkage takes place between the accounting values or categories.

Both templates have been amended in Phase III (BCBS 432) due to the revisions to the SA under the finalised Basel III framework. The adjustments are necessary due to the introduction of new asset classes (e.g. covered bonds) and updated risk weights.

In Template CR4, the following information must be disclosed for each exposure class under the standardised approach:

- assessment basis before credit conversion factor (CCF) and credit risk mitigation (CRM);
- assessment basis post credit conversion factor (CCF) and credit risk mitigation (CRM); and
- risk-weighted assets (RWA) and average risk weights (RWA density).

In template CR5, the assessment basis post credit conversion factor (CCF) and credit risk mitigation (CRM), broken down by predefined risk weights, must be recorded for each exposure class. For the sake of consistency with the existing disclosure requirements regarding the IRB Approach (Template CR6), BCBS 432 proposes more granular disclosure of credit conversion factors under the standardised approach in Template CR5.

EU banks should be able to derive the necessary data largely from existing databases currently in use to complete the COREP disclosure forms.

11.9.4 Credit risk under the IRB Approach

Disclosure under the IRB encompasses qualitative information (Table CRE) as well as quantitative data (Templates CR6 to CR10), which were introduced in Phase I. As a consequence of revisions to the SA and IRB frameworks, the disclosure requirements related to IRB had to be updated as well. With BCBS 432, Template CR10 was changed to remove the treatment of equity positions under the IRB's simple risk-weight approach, as these exposures are moved to the SA under the revised frameworks.

Data requirements should either partially match information that is already subject to disclosure or be ascertainable from existing databases. This applies to the following templates, among others:

- template CR6: Exposure, average PD, average LGD and RWA for each credit risk exposure class and predefined PD scales;
- template CR9: Backtesting of PD indicating the number of obligors, defaulted obligors per credit risk exposure class and PD scale; and
- template CR10: Information on specialised lending and equity positions.

Thus, the templates are not discussed in detail in the following.

Table CRE: Qualitative disclosures related to IRB models

The qualitative disclosure requirements of Table CRE are largely consistent with the existing requirements pursuant to Article 452 CRR in the EU. However, additional information must be disclosed in the following areas:

- all the relevant data on the development and changes of internal models, including relevant functions;
- the scope and main content of the reporting related to credit risk models;
- the part of EAD for each portfolio, covered by the F-IRB or AIRB Approach as well as the part covered by IRB roll-out plans; and
- the number of models used with respect to each portfolio as well as a short description of the main differences among the models used for each portfolio.

Template CR7: IRB – Effect of credit derivatives used as credit risk mitigation techniques

Template CR7 requires the disclosure of RWA by each exposure class under the F-IRB and AIRB Approach before and after the use of credit derivatives as credit risk mitigation technique.

Template CR8: Quarterly variation in RWA

Template CR8 requires the disclosure of RWA changes when using the IRB Approach. As to content, the variations of the RWA in the elapsed quarter shall be disclosed based on different influencing factors (e.g. asset size and quality, model updates, methodology and procedure adjustments, acquisitions and disposals of assets, foreign exchange movements). Banks are expected to supplement the template with a narrative commentary on the main changes over the previous reporting period including the key drivers of such changes.

This requirement will present a big challenge for several banks. Only the total RWA for the current and the previous reporting period can for example be taken from the COREP disclosure forms. All other pieces of information must be calculated, which could come hand in hand with additional complexities and interdependencies, for instance due to multiple simultaneous effects (e.g. deterioration in the creditworthiness of a borrower on top of model adjustment in the period).

11.10 Counterparty credit risk

The disclosure requirements for Counterparty Credit Risks (CCR) were extensively expanded within BCBS 309. The focus here was placed particularly on the new capital requirements introduced by Basel III such as the CVA Risk Capital Charge and the treatment of exposures to central counterparties (CCP), as well as on the requirements reviewed in the course of Basel IV to determine the assessment basis by means of the new standardised approach for counterparty credit risk (SA-CCR, see Chapter 3). The disclosure requirements basically affect all exposures subject to counterparty credit risk, regardless of whether they are assigned to the banking or the trading book.

Following the revised framework for CVA, a broad spectrum of new disclosure requirements relating to CVA risk was introduced with BCBS 432; these are discussed in detail further below.

In relation to counterparty credit risk, a difference must be made between qualitative and quantitative information to be disclosed. Separate disclosure requirements are in place for banks that make use of an internal model approved by the regulatory authority to determine the assessment basis for counterparty credit risks (Internal Model Method – IMM, compare Article 283 and following of the CRR). Table 11.8 provides a summary of the individual disclosure tables and templates.

The qualitative disclosure requirements (CCRA) as well as the disclosure of credit derivatives (CCR6) match extensively the existing requirements pursuant to Article 439 (a) to (d) as well as (g) and (h) of the CRR and are therefore not discussed in detail.

Name	Designation	Type	Format	Frequency
CCRA	Qualitative disclosure related to counterparty credit risk	Qualitative	Flexible	Annually
CCR1	Counterparty credit risk by approach	Quantitative	Fixed	Semi-annually
CCR2	CVA Risk Capital Charge	Quantitative	Fixed	Semi-annually
CCR3	Counterparty credit risk by exposure class and risk weight (standardised approach)	Quantitative	Fixed	Semi-annually
CCR4	Counterparty credit risk by exposure class and PD scale (IRBA)	Quantitative	Fixed	Semi-annually
CCR5	Collaterals for counterparty credit risk	Quantitative	Flexible	Semi-annually
CCR6	Credit derivatives	Quantitative	Flexible	Semi-annually
CCR7	RWA changes	Quantitative	Fixed	Quarterly
CCR8	Exposures to central counterparties	Quantitative	Fixed	Semi-annually

Table 11.8: Disclosure of counterparty credit risks

Template CCR1: Counterparty credit risk by approach

Template CCR1 requires the disclosure of exposures subject to counterparty credit risk for derivatives and Securities Financing Transactions (SFTs) according to the approaches used to determine the assessment base:

- derivatives: SA-CCR and IMM; and
- SFTs: simple and comprehensive approach, VaR approach and IMM.

In both cases, the exposure amount after applying credit risk mitigation techniques as well as the risk-weighted assets must be disclosed. In relation to derivatives, individual components of the assessment base must be provided separately (e.g. replacement costs and potential future exposure under the SA-CCR, expected effective positive exposure as well as the alpha factor used within the IMM).

Information on the use of the SA-CCR represents a new requirement, since the SA-CCR will be implemented in the EU as part of the CRR II package. Within the course of the implementation the corresponding disclosure requirements will have to be taken into account.

Template CCR2: CVA Risk Capital Charge

A separate obligation to disclose information on CVA Risk Capital Charge is introduced with Template CCR2. In fact, this was already implemented with Basel III; however, an explicit disclosure requirement did not exist so far, even though several banks already voluntarily reveal CVA Risk Capital Charge as part of the provisions pursuant to Article 438 CRR in order to achieve reconcilability between capital requirements and capital ratios.

Under Template CCR2, information on exposure values must be disclosed after credit risk mitigation and risk-weighted assets for all exposures that are considered either using the advanced approach (Article 383 CRR) or the standardised approach (Article 384 CRR) to determine the CVA Risk Capital Charge. In the case of the advanced CVA Risk Capital Charge, a breakdown by VaR and sVaR components must also be performed. Figure 11.18 offers an overview of the information to be disclosed.

		a	b
		EAD post CRM	RWA
	Total portfolios subject to the Advanced CVA capital charge		
1	(i) VaR component (including the 3×multiplier)		
2	(ii) Stressed component (including the 3×multiplier)		
3	All portfolios subject to the Standardised CVA capital charge		
4	Total subject to the CVA capital charge		

Figure 11.18: CCR2 template

The vast majority of banks that currently apply the standardised method to determine the CVA Risk Capital Charge will therefore only have to complete two lines of the template. The revisions of the CVA framework in BCBS 424 make new sets of disclosure requirements for CVA risk necessary. CCR2 Template thus becomes obsolete with the implementation of new CVA templates (see below). These new templates are however not applicable for banks deciding to set their CVA capital requirement equal to 100% of capital requirements for counterparty credit risk.

Templates CCR3 and CCR4: Counterparty credit risk under the standardised approach and the IRB

Template CCR3 (standardised approach) and CCR4 (IRB) provide an overview of exposure amounts subject to counterparty credit risk according to the standardised approach or the foundation and advanced IRB respectively. The exposure value must be broken down by exposure class and risk weights (according to the standardised approach) or by PD scale (according to the IRB). Moreover, according to the IRB, the following information must also be completed for each exposure class and PD scale:

- EAD-weighted, average PD;
- Number of obligors;
- EAD-weighted, average LGD;
- EAD-weighted, average maturity;
- Risk-weighted assets;
- RWA density (average risk weight).

A challenge arises mainly with respect to the mapping of PD scales which are predefined by the Basel Committee and do not necessarily match the PD scales to be applied within the frame of COREP solvency reporting in the EU.

Template CCR5 (collaterals for counterparty credit risk)

Template CCR5 calls for an overview of all collateral posted to reduce counterparty credit risk. To this end, the carrying values of collateral, used in derivative transactions or securities financing transactions, are accounted for. Transactions with central counterparties must be included. Figure 11.19 shows an overview of the breakdown.

	a	b	c	d	e	f
	Collateral used in derivative transactions				Collateral is SFTs	
	Fair value of collateral received		Fair value of posted collateral		Fair value of collateral received	Fair value of posted collateral
	Segregated	Unsegregated	Segregated	Unsegregated		
Cash – domestic currency						
Cash – other currencies						
Domestic sovereign debt						
Other sovereign debt						
Government agency debt						
Corporate bonds						
Equity securities						
Other collateral						
Total						

Figure 11.19: CCR5 template

Completing the template will most likely represent a big challenge for most banks since the requested information is not available in the systems with the necessary granularity. This affects the difference between segregated and non-segregated collateral in particular. In future it should, however, be possible to link part of the information with, for example, the implementation of the SACCR.

Template CCR7: RWA changes under IMM

Template CCR7 shows the RWA changes determined based on the Internal Model Method compared to the previous quarter. This template is therefore equivalent to template CR8 for the IRB and MR2 for market risk. Just like these templates, it also requires that RWA changes be assigned to different influencing factors (Figure 11.20).

		a
		Amounts
1	RWA as at end of previous reporting period	
2	Asset size	
3	Credit quality of counterparties	
4	Model updates (IMM only)	
5	Methodology and policy (IMM only)	
6	Acquisitions and disposals	
7	Foreign exchange movements	
8	Other	
9	RWA as at end of current reporting period	

Figure 11.20: CCR7 template

This goes hand in hand with big implementation challenges since the necessary information does not have to be determined up to this point, and many influencing factors may have a simultaneous effect which would make an accurate allocation extremely difficult. At the same time, it will herewith be disclosed to what extent a reduction of capital requirements can be achieved, not only by reducing the volume or risk, but also, for instance, by changing models.

Template CCR8: Exposures to CCPs

Template CCR8 contains an overview of exposures to central counterparties and the corresponding risk-weighted assets. A distinction is made among the following three main categories:

- transaction types (OTC derivatives, exchange-traded derivatives, securities financing transactions, cross-product netting sets);
- initial margin (segregated and non-segregated); and
- contributions made to the default fund of the central counterparty (pre-funded or unfunded contributions).

In addition, a distinction is made between qualified and non-qualified central counterparties.

Similarly to CCR5, breaking collateral down into segregated and non-segregated collateral is probably challenging provided that banks operate with both of these types of collateral and are therefore not able to disregard one type beforehand.

11.11 Securitisation

In connection with securitisations, qualitative as well as quantitative disclosure requirements, which apply partially to all securitisation exposures (SECA, SEC1, SEC2) and partially only comprise banking book securitisation positions with significant risk transfer (SEC3, SEC4), must be complied with. Securitisation positions in the trading book are subject to the respective market risk disclosure requirements. Table 11.9 provides an overview of the individual disclosure templates and tables.

Name	Designation	Type	Format	Frequency
SECA	Qualitative disclosure requirements related to securitisation	Qualitative	Flexible	Annually
SEC1	Securitisation exposures in the banking book	Quantitative	Flexible	Semi-annually
SEC2	Securitisation exposures in the trading book	Quantitative	Flexible	Semi-annually
SEC3	Originator and sponsor positions	Quantitative	Fixed	Semi-annually
SEC4	Investor positions	Quantitative	Fixed	Semi-annually

Table 11.9: Disclosures related to securitisation

Compared to the current EU disclosure requirements pursuant to Article 449 CRR, it can be observed that the requirements issued by the Basel Committee partially lag behind those of the CRR. Especially in relation to the qualitative disclosure requirements, the CRR contains several additional obligations. To a large extent, the quantitative requirements are similar to the current disclosure forms. In view of the above, a detailed portrayal of the individual disclosure forms is not provided.

11.12 Market risk

Disclosure requirements for market risk were subject to extensive changes throughout Phase I and Phase II of the disclosure framework review. In order to increase the availability of information for external users of institutions' data and the comparability between institutions, a set of qualitative requirements regarding general information on market risk and risk management of banks using the Internal Model Approach (IMA), as well as a number of templates containing quantitative information on capital requirements for market risk were introduced with BCBS 309. With the revision of the market risk framework (see Chapter 6 of this book) in January 2016, the disclosure requirements for market risk were updated to reflect these changes, first with Consultation paper BCBS 356 in March 2016, and then in the final document of Phase II, BCBS 400, when some of the provisions were streamlined and compacted compared to the Consultation paper (such as granularity of quantitative information in MR1 Template, see below). The revised market risk disclosures are expected to be implemented simultaneously with the FRTB, and will then replace the disclosure requirements published in Phase I. In this regard, the disclosure requirements from both phases will be discussed, bearing in mind the implementation date for each of the formats given in Table 11.10.

The guidelines regarding the disclosure of a bank's market risk comprise the capital requirements calculated for the trading book and those banking book exposures that are subject to market risk capital charges (interest rate, equity risk, foreign exchange risk and commodity risk). This also includes capital requirements for securitisation exposures in the trading book. In contrast, the capital charge for these exposures which arises from counterparty credit risk is to be reported in the counterparty credit risk templates. Concerning market risk, qualitative as well as quantitative information must be disclosed. At this point a distinction must be made among banks that have an internal model approved to measure market risks and banks that apply the standardised approaches. Table 11.10 gives an overview of the templates and tables.

Table MRA: General qualitative information on market risk

Table MRA includes qualitative information on risk management of market risk. Institutions are obliged to disclose information on their strategic objectives in

Name	Designation	Type	Format	Frequency	Implementation Date
MRA	General qualitative disclosures related to market risk	Qualitative	Flexible	Annually	Phase I: end-2016 Phase II: with FRTB
MR1	Market risk under the standardised approach	Quantitative	Fixed	Semi-annually	Phase I: end- 2016 Phase II: with FRTB
MRB	Qualitative disclosures for banks using IMA	Qualitative	Flexible	Annually	Phase I: end- 2016 Phase II: with FRTB
MRC	The structure of desks for banks using the IMA	Quantitative	Fixed	Semi-annually	with FRTB
MR2	RWA flow statements of market risk exposures under IMA (Phase I only) Market risk IMA per risk type (Phase II only)	Quantitative	Fixed	Quarterly (Phase I) Semi-annually (Phase II)	Phase I: end- 2016 Phase II: with FRTB
MR3	IMA values for trading portfolios (Phase I only) RWA flow statements of market risk exposures under IMA (Phase II only)	Quantitative	Fixed	Semi-annually (Phase I) Quarterly (Phase II)	Phase I: end- 2016 Phase II: with FRTB
MR4	Comparison of VaR estimates with gains/losses (Phase I only)	Quantitative	Flexible	Semi-annually	Phase I: end- 2016

Table 11.10: Disclosure related to market risk

undertaking trading activities, as well as a description of processes for risk identification, measurement, management and control (including hedging policies) of market risks. Further on, the information on governance structure and organisation of the market risk function should be provided, which should include communication mechanisms between different parties in market risk management. A description of measurement and reporting systems is also required. These requirements were set in Phase I and are also valid for Phase II.

The additional qualitative requirements arising from the revised market risk framework which are expected to be introduced with Phase II relate to descriptions of the desk structure, as defined in the market risk framework and types of instruments included in the desks/desk categories not covered by Table MRC (see below). Institutions are to describe their policies for the designation of positions in trading category (including definition and management of stale positions), exemptions to the general rules in the assignment of positions to banking or trading book (disclosing gross fair value of those cases) and cases of positions moving from one book to another since the previous period, providing the rationale for those movement as well as the information on gross fair value of moved positions.

Table MRB: Qualitative disclosures for banks using IMA

Table MRB contains exhaustive list of qualitative information to be disclosed by institutions using internal models. In Phase I the disclosure requirements refer to details regarding the models used for VaR (Value at Risk), sVaR (stressed Value at Risk), IRC (Incremental Risk Charge, additional migration and default risk) and CRM (Comprehensive Risk Measure for the Correlation Trading Portfolio). General information such as the models used at a group-wide level, the risks covered by the models, as well as the differences between the models which are used for regulatory purposes and internally used models have to be reported.

Figure 11.21 provides an overview of the information to be disclosed.

VaR	sVaR	IRC	CRM
Data updating frequency, length of data period and weighting scheme used	Method to determine the predefined 10-day holding period (one-day scale up or 10-day modelling)	General description of the applied methodology (spread-based or transition matrix, among others)	General description of the applied methodology (spread-based or transition matrix, among other)
Method to determine the predefined 10-day holding period (one-day scale up or 10-day modelling)	Stress period chosen and the rationale behind this choice	Information on the calibration of the transition matrix as well as on the applied correlation assumptions	Information used to determine LGD of tranches (constant or stochastic)
Description of method for aggregating specific and general risks	Valuation approach (full revaluation or use of approximations)	Approach used to determine liquidity horizons	Approach used to determine liquidity horizons
Valuation approach (full revaluation or use of approximations)	Description of stress testing applied to the modelling parameters	Description of the methodology used to achieve a capital assessment consistent with the required soundness standard	Description of the methodology used to achieve a capital assessment consistent with the required soundness standard
Use of absolute or relative returns or a mixed approach when simulating potential changes in prices	Disclosure of the approach used for validation and backtesting of the internal models and modelling processes	Description of the approach used in the validation of the model	Description of the approach used in the validation of the model

Figure 11.21: Disclosure related to internal market risk models

The disclosure obligations following Table MRB clearly go beyond the current EU requirements pursuant to Article 455 (a) CRR. The current guidelines also request information on internal models, but not at the same level of granularity as asked for by Basel.

Following the introduction of the FRTB, qualitative information on details on expected shortfall (ES), default risk charge (DRC) and information on stressed capital add-on for non modellable risk factors (NMRFs) is to be provided. Institutions are to describe

the main characteristics of the models used at the group-wide level (scope of regulatory consolidation) and supplement the table with the information on percentage of
coverage for each of the regulatory models used.

For ES, information to be disclosed contains the following.

- activities and risks covered by the ES models, as well as description of data not
  included in the regulatory ES due to lack of historical data or model constraints;
- soundness criteria on which internal capital adequacy is based (forward-looking
  stress testing);
- general description of ES models (i.e. historical simulation, Monte Carlo simulation,
  other appropriate analytical methods, observation period, weighting methods);
- data updating frequency;
- description of stress testing applied to main modelled portfolios; and
- a general description of the methodology: information about the characteristics
  and scope of the VaR and whether different models are used for different exposure
  classes.

For DRC, information to be disclosed contains the following.

- information on the scope and characteristics of VaR and models used for different
  exposure classes;
- methodology used to achieve a capital assessment that is consistent with both
  the required soundness standard and requirement to have separate internal
  model for default risk, as required in new market risk framework (para 186 of
  BCBS 352);
- the approaches used in the validation of the models and modelling processes,
  describing general approaches used (e.g. stress tests, sensitivity analysis, scenario
  analysis), and the types of assumptions and benchmarks on which they rely.

For NMRFs, banks should disclose the methodology used to achieve a capital assessment which is consistent with the required soundness standard.

Table MRC: The structure of desks for banks using the IMA

This Table has been introduced during Phase II, as a consequence of the revised market risk framework. It includes qualitative disclosure on the structure of banks' trading
desks. Banks have to disclose individually all desks deemed representative for their
trading book under IMA (at least five with the highest aggregate standalone capital charge) and to explain the reasoning behind the selection of representative desks.
Banks have to additionally disclose information on the number of desks not separately
disclosed and on the main risks and products traded by these desks not included in
the overview. To make the disclosed information comparable, the overview is included

where banks are expected to fill in categories of risks for each desk (GIIR, equity, commodities, FX, credit spread and other) as well as products applicable per desk (cash, forwards, futures, plain vanilla options, complex options, ABS, MBS, IR swaps, FX swaps, CDS). Additional narrative is expected on different types of risks covered and especially for the category "other" risks.

Template MR1: Market risk under the standardised approach

Template MR1 presents information on capital requirements for market risk under the standardised approach. The structure of the template from BCBS 309 corresponds to the current approach for calculating market risk according to the standardised approach, as prescribed under the current Basel framework and CRR, showing the calculation of RWA divided into three sub-segments: outright products (interest rate risk, equity risk, foreign exchange risk and commodity risk), options (simplified approach, delta-plus method and scenario approach) and securitisations.

Following the introduction of the revised market risk framework, changes to Template MR1 have been included in BCBS 356, encompassing detailed information on the calculation of market risk according to the revised standardised approach. The disclosure of capital charges according to the standardised approach is presented for each of the seven risk classes (interest rate risk, equity risk, foreign exchange risk, commodity risk, credit spread risk for non-securitisations, credit spread risk for securitisations and credit spread risk for correlation trading portfolio) as well as for the default risk charge and residual risk add-on. BCBS 356 initially suggested disclosing information on capital charges for linear risks "delta" and "vega", and the non-linear "curvature" risk for each of the seven risk classes. With BCBS 400, Template MR1 has been simplified to require only the aggregate capital charge per risk class to be reported, as presented in Figure 11.22.

		Capital charge in SA
1	General interest rate risk	
2	Equity risk	
3	Commodity risk	
4	Foreign exchange risk	
5	Credit spread risk – non-securitisations	
6	Credit spread risk – securitisations (non-correlation trading portfolio)	
7	Credit spread risk – securitisation (correlation trading portfolio)	
8	Default risk – non-securitisations	
9	Default risk – securitisations (non-correlation trading portfolio)	
10	Default risk – securitisations (correlation trading portfolio)	
11	Residual risk add-on	
12	**Total**	

Figure 11.22: MR1 Template (Phase II)

Template MR2: Market risk IMA per risk type (Phase II only)

Template MR2 showing market risk capital charges according to IMA by risk type has been included in Phase II. Template MR2 from Phase I showing RWA flow under internal models is renamed MR3 in Phase II and will further be discussed as MR3 (see below).

During the discussion process of Phase II, the disclosure of market risk IMA per desk as well as per risk type was foreseen in two separate templates, requesting desk-level disclosure relating to capital requirements, expected shortfall and backtesting exceptions. In the finalisation of Phase II, these two templates were combined into one and simplified, abandoning the request for disclosure of information on a desk-level.

In template MR2, banks should report the amount of unconstrained expected shortfall, ES for regulatory classes, constrained ES, capital charge for non-modellable risk factors, default risk charge, as well as standardised approach capital for the entire trading book, as depicted in Figure 11.23.

			a	b	c	d	e
			Most recent	Average	High	Low	99.0%
			Risk measure: for previous 60 days / 12 weeks:				Number of backtesting exceptions
1		Unconstrained expected shortfall					
2	ES for the regulatory risk classes	General interest rate risk					
3		Equity risk					
4		Commodity risk					
5		Foreign exchange risk					
6		Credit spread risk					
7		Constrained expected shortfall (IMCC) (Rho*Unconstrained ES+(1-Rho)*aggregated risk class ES)					
8		Capital charge for non-modellable risk factors					
9		Default risk charge					
10		Subtotal: a=7+8+9, b=multiplier*7+8+9					
11		Total capital charge					
12		Standardised approach capital charge for the entire trading book (ie all trading desks, including those subject to IMA)					

Figure 11.23: Market risk IMA per risk type

Banks have to report the components of their total capital charge for both the previous 60 days and 12 weeks. Banks must also provide a comparison of VaR estimates with actual gains/losses experienced by the bank, with an analysis of important "outliers" in the backtesting results.

Template MR3: RWA flow statements of market risk exposures under IMA (Phase II only)

Template MR3 shows changes in RWA compared to the previous quarter calculated using internal models (Template MR2 under Phase I). This template is therefore in line with Templates CR8 for the IRB and CCR7 for counterparty credit risk. Just like the latter two, this template also requests that RWA changes be allocated to different influencing factors.

In Phase I, the fixed rows were foreseen to enable explanation of RWA changes between two periods (Figure 11.24).

		a	b	c	d	e	f
		VaR	Stressed VaR	ICR	CRM	Other	Total RWA
1	RWA at previous quarter end						
2	Movement in risk levels						
3	Model updates/changes						
4	Methodology and policy						
5	Acquisitions and disposals						
6	Foreign exchange movements						
7	Other						
8	RWA at end of reporting period						

Figure 11.24: RWA flow (Phase I)

By disclosing the causes for RWA changes, the regulatory authorities aim at improving the often criticised lack of transparency of capital requirements computed by internal models. This represents an increased disclosure effort for banks in order to identify and link all the necessary information. As a general rule, the department in charge of the internal model will most likely have to provide the requested information.

In Phase II, the template is simplified in terms of fixed rows to be reported: information on RWA at the beginning and the end of current and previous period and regulatory adjustments (Figure 11.25). In addition to fixed rows, banks can use additional rows, where information on RWA change is available: movement in risk levels, model changes, regulatory changes, acquisitions and disposals, foreign exchange and others.

		ES	NMRF	DRC	Total RWA
1	RWA at previous quarter-end				
2	Regulatory adjustment				
3	RWA at end of day previous quarter				
4	RWA at end of day previous current quarter				
5	Regulatory adjustment				
6	RWA at end of reporting period				

Figure 11.25: RWA flow (Phase II)

Templates on IMA values for trading portfolio and Comparison of VaR estimates with gains/losses are valid for Phase I only and are briefly illustrated below.

Template MR3: IMA values for trading portfolios (Phase I only)

The information to be disclosed in Template IMA values for trading portfolios encompasses minimum, maximum, average and period-end values for regulatory VaR and sVaR (10 days horizon, 99% confidence level), IRC (99.9% confidence level) and Comprehensive risk capital charge (99.9%). The numbers for comprehensive risk capital charge are unfloored, so an additional column has been inserted to calculate floor values (8% of the capital charge for specific risk according to the standardised measurement method). The template should also contain explanations of any significant changes over the reporting period and the key drivers of such changes.

Template MR4: Comparison of VaR estimates with actual and hypothetical gains and losses (Phase I only)

For the purposes of disclosure, Template MR4 provides a general idea of the model accuracy of the internal models used by comparing the projected Value at Risk estimates with the actual value changes of exposures (backtesting). As a result hereof, so-called outliers, for which the actual change in value was higher than the losses predicted by the VaR model, become transparent. Based on the chosen confidence level within the scope of the VaR model, said outliers are expected; however, the disclosure report specifies their frequency as well as the date within the analysed reporting period.

Compared to the almost identical EU disclosure requirements pursuant to Article 455 (g) CRR, Template MR4 requires a comparison to determine not only actual gains and losses, but also hypothetical gains and losses which would have occurred if no changes had taken place within the portfolio on the given day. The predefined tables bring about further improvements as to transparency since banks had several possibilities in the past to creatively hide model weaknesses.

In addition to the quantitative representation, the following explanations must be included.

- description of the models used; portion of the total capital requirement for market risks calculated with the internal model;
- analysis of backtesting exceptions within the specified time frame as well as of the key drivers that brought about these exceptions;
- description of how valuation reserves are handled as well as if commissions and fees are included in the backtesting.

Figure 11.26 shows an example of disclosure of backtesting results pursuant to Article 455 CRR.

Clean P&L backtesting results

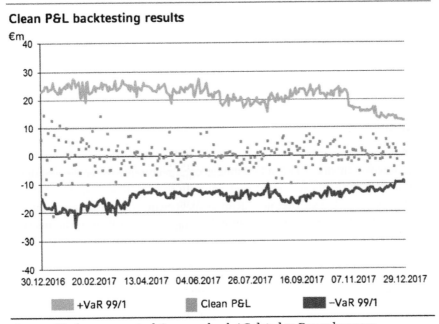

Source: Disclosure report of Commerzbank AG dated 31 December 2017

Figure 11.26: Clean P&L backtesting results

11.13 Interest rate risk in the banking book

Disclosure requirements related to interest rate risk in the banking book were originally part of Pillar III in Basel II, and as such were not subject to change during Phase I.
These requirements related to general qualitative description of risk management and
policies (strategies, policies and procedures for management and hedging of IRRBB,
as well as measurement and reporting systems), assumptions regarding loan prepay-
ments and non-maturity depositors' behaviour, and quantitative requirements related
to disclosure of changes in earnings and capital arising from upward and downward
interest rate shocks.

With the revisions of the standards for IRRBB in April 2016 (see Chapter 12 of this
book), it became necessary to revise the disclosure framework for IRRBB as well. This
was done in Phase II, by including enhanced disclosure requirements in the measurement and management of IRRBB in the overall disclosure framework.

Implementation of the revised IRRBB standards and its disclosure requirements is
required starting from 2018, based on the financials as of 31 December 2017. Disclosure requirements for IRRBB are presented in the Table 11.11.

Name	Designation	Type	Format	Frequency
IRRBBA	IRRBB risk management and objective and policies	Qualitative / Quantitative	Flexible	Annually
IRRBB1	Quantitative information on IRRBB	Quantitative	Fixed	Annually

Table 11.11: Disclosures related to IRRBB

Table IRRBBA

This Table comprises of two parts, a qualitative and quantitative one. The qualitative disclosure requirements go beyond existing general requirements for the description of risk management, measurement and control. They include with more details, a description of a bank's overall IRRBB management and mitigation strategies, description of techniques used to measure the sensitivity of IRRBB (including stress scenarios description), as well as the frequency of IRRBB measure calculation, hedging techniques and accounting treatment. Further on, significant divergences in modelling assumptions used in internal measurement system (arising for example from the calculations of economic value of equity (EVE) used for ICAAP purposes) compared to the calculation in Template IRRBB1 should be explained, and a description of modelling assumptions for the calculation of changes in EVE and changes in net interest income (NII) should be provided. The quantitative part of disclosure requirements relates to information on the average and the longest repricing maturity assigned to non-maturity deposits (NMDs).

Template IRRBB1

The quantitative disclosures to IRRBB relate to the change in EVE and NII for each of the given interest rate shock scenarios in the reporting period, as well as in the previous period. The novelty within the quantitative disclosures of IRRBB compared to the current Basel framework is that banks are disclosing the information based on a set of scenarios provided by the supervisors which should enhance the comparability of disclosed information between institutions. The prescribed scenarios for movements in interest rates are: parallel up, parallel down (impact on EVE and NII), steepener, flattener, short rate up and short rate down (impact on EVE).

11.14 Remuneration

One of the FSB Principles to be incorporated in Pillar 2, in an attempt to strengthen the risk management practices after the financial crisis, was the one related to sound compensation practices. Upon recognition that information on compensation practices diverges across jurisdictions, standardised requirements related to remuneration were incorporated in Pillar III. Being sensitive by nature, the disclosure requirements related to remuneration were carefully crafted in a separate paper, issued in July 2011, with the aim of achieving sufficient granularity of disclosed information, but not disclosing confidential information.[19] With the consolidation of all existing BCBS disclosure requirements within Phase II in BCBS 400, the part relating to remuneration was also consolidated and revised. Table 11.12 contains a list of disclosure formats related to remuneration.

Name	Designation	Type	Format	Frequency
REMA	Remuneration policy	Qualitative /	Flexible	Annually
REM1	Remuneration awarded during the financial year	Qualitative /	Flexible	Annually
REM2	Special payments	Qualitative /	Flexible	Annually
REM3	Deferred remuneration	Qualitative /	Flexible	Annually

Table 11.12: Disclosures related to remuneration

Table REMA

The Table provides users of Pillar III data with a description of institutions' remuneration policy, including governance, processes, models, risks and controls. In particular, banks should describe composition and mandates of bodies that oversee remuneration, types of employees considered to be material risk-takers and senior managers.

Disclosures relating to the structure of the remuneration process include a description of the remuneration policy and changes to the policy within the period. Further on, banks should describe how they ensure independent remuneration of risk and compliance employees.

Banks should also describe an overview of key current and future risks relating to remuneration and how they are taken into account in the remuneration processes.

With regard to the relation between performance and the level of remuneration, banks should disclose their main performance metrics, for business lines as well as for individuals, how individual remuneration is linked to bank-wide and individual performance, and how the banks determine "weak" performance metrics.

Banks should describe the way longer-term performance is taken into account in remuneration, including a description of policy on deferral and vesting of variable remuneration, including factors that influence differences in the fraction of variable remuneration across employees, if any. Different forms of variable remuneration used should be described.

Templates REM1, REM2 and REM3

Template REM1 discloses remuneration amounts for senior management and other material risk takers. Disclosures are made separately for fixed and variable

---

19   Cf. BCBS 197 (2011).

remuneration. For both, the amount of cash, share-based compensation and any other form of compensation are to be disclosed separately, also including the deferred amount in each of the categories. Template REM2 discloses the amount of special payments (guaranteed bonuses, sign-on fees and severance payments) by number of employees and total amounts, making distinction between senior management and other material risk takers. Template REM3 discloses information on deferred remuneration (outstanding amounts, reductions and amounts paid out) by remuneration instrument (e.g. cash, shares) for senior management and other material risk takers.

The disclosure requirements should be published annually, with the first disclosures due in a bank's Pillar 3 report at its financial year-end 2017. In the cases when the release of a bank's remuneration information is not done at the same time with the publication of its annual report, disclosures related to remuneration should be made as soon as possible thereafter.

11.15 Benchmarking

The Output floor introduced by BCBS 424 published in December 2017 requires banks to disclose two sets of capital adequacy ratios – one that includes the capital floor in the calculation of RWA and the other without the capital floor.

BCBS 432 introduces two new templates to specify the disclosure of more granular information related to the calculation of RWA under the internally modelled and standardised approaches. BCBS proposes that these new templates apply from 1 January 2022, aligning the disclosure with the introduction of the phasing-in of the output floor. Table 11.13 summarises the disclosure requirements.

Name	Designation	Type	Format	Frequency
BEN1	Benchmarking RWA calculated according to the standardised approaches and internally modelled approaches	Quantitative	Fixed	Quarterly
BEN2	Benchmarking RWA calculated according to standardised approaches for credit risk (excluding counterparty credit risk) at asset class level	Quantitative	Fixed	Semi-annually

Table 11.13: Disclosure of benchmarking

Template BEN1: Benchmarking RWA calculated according to the standardised approaches and internally modelled approaches

Template BEN1 applies to all banks using internal models and provides users with a comparison between modelled and standardised RWA. BCBS provides an illustrative example and this is set out in Figure 11.27. This shows total RWA of 80 (column (a))

		a	b	c	d
				RWA	
		Actual RWA calculated under internal models-based approaches	Corresponding standardised approach RWA for column (a)	Actual RWA calculated under standardised approaches	RWA under full standardised approach for benchmarking
1	Credit risk (excluding counterparty credit risk)	50	100	10	110
2	Counterparty credit risk	10	15	0	15
3	Credit valuation adjustment			5	5
4	Securitisation exposures in the banking book	5	8	5	13
5	Market risk	15	30	25	55
6	Operational risk			30	30
7	Residual risk			10	10
8	Total	80 (a)	153 (b)	85 (c)	238 (d) = (b) + (c)

Figure 11.27: Proposed benchmarking template illustrative example – BEN1

for a bank's exposures subject to internally modelled approaches which if calculated using the corresponding standardised approaches would result in RWA of 153 (column (b)). The bank also has RWA of 85 (column (c)) for other exposures that are already subject to standardised approaches. This gives a benchmarking RWA of 238 (85+153) – the full standardised RWA amount to which the output floor is applied (column (d)).

Where the standardised approaches allows for different treatments/methodologies, banks should explain, with further quantitative disclosure where appropriate and the extent to which they are used in the calculation. For example, the approach for securitisations allows an external ratings based approach, a standardised approach or a risk weighting of 1,250%.

Template BEN2: Benchmarking RWA calculated according to standardised approaches for credit risk (excluding counterparty credit risk) at asset class level

Template BEN2 has the same format as BEN1 but it provides further analysis by asset class and sub-asset class of the credit risk row (excluding counterparty credit risk) of BEN1. Banks are encouraged to add further rows where this explains sources of significant differences.

11.16 Operational risk

BCBS 356 proposed operational risk disclosures based on the March 2016 draft operational risk capital requirement proposals of BCBS 355. BCBS 400 deferred issuing these revised disclosure requirements pending the finalisation of the revised operational risk framework. This finalisation occurred through the issue of BCBS 424 in December

2017 and the consultation of BCBS 432 in March 2018 that includes the corresponding revised operational risk disclosures. The original disclosure requirements set out in the 2004 Pillar 3 framework[20] remain applicable until the implementation of the revised operational risk framework in January 2022. Table 11.14 summarises the new disclosure requirements set out in BCBS 432.

Name	Designation	Type	Format	Frequency
ORA	General qualitative information on a bank's operational risk framework	Qualitative	Flexible	Annually
OR1	Historical losses	Quantitative	Fixed	Annually
OR2	Business indicator and subcomponents	Quantitative	Fixed	Annually
OR3	Minimum required operational risk capital	Quantitative	Fixed	Annually

Table 11.14: Disclosure of operational risk

Table ORA: General qualitative information on a bank's operational risk framework

Table ORA requires qualitative disclosure of the characteristics and elements of banks' operational risk management frameworks including:

- policies, frameworks and guidelines;
- risk measurement systems; and
- risk mitigation and risk transfer used in the management of risk.

Template OR1: Historical losses

Template OR1 requires disclosure of aggregate operational risk losses incurred over the past ten years based on their accounting recognition date. It applies to banks with a Business indicator (BI) amount > EUR 1bn. This includes those banks in jurisdictions whose national authority has set the internal loss multiplier (ILM) to one for all its banks. It also applies to banks with a BI < EUR 1bn who are permitted by their national authority to use internal loss data in their operational risk capital requirement calculation. The operational risk standard provides that the minimum threshold for including a loss event in data collection and the calculation of average annual losses is EUR 20,000. At national authority discretion, this may be increased to EUR 100,000. But disclosure is required on the basis of both thresholds. The format of this disclosure provides transparency relating to exclusions (e.g. divested activities) and is set out in Figure 11.28.

---

20   Cf. BCBS 107 (2004) and BCBS 128 (2006).

	a	b	c	d	e	f	g	h	i	j	K
	T	T-1	T-2	T-3	T-4	T-5	T-6	T-7	T-8	T-9	Ten-year average
Using €20,000 threshold											
1	Total amount of operational losses net of recoveries (no exclusions)										
2	Total amount of excluded operational risk losses										
3	Total number of operational risk losses										
4	Total amount of operational losses net of recoveries and net of excluded losses										
Using €100,000 threshold											
5	Total amount of operational losses net of recoveries (no exclusions)										
6	Total amount of excluded operational risk losses										
7	Total number of operational risk losses										
8	Total amount of operational losses net of recoveries and net of excluded losses										
Details of operational risk capital calculation											
9	Are losses used to calculate the ILM (yes/no)?										
10	If "no" in row 9, is the exclusion of internal loss data due to non-compliance with the minimum loss data standards (yes/no)?										
11	Loss event threshold: €20,000 or €100,000 for the operational risk capital calculation if applicable										

Figure 11.28: Proposed operational risk historical losses template – OR1

Transitional arrangements allow for the use of a minimum of five year loss data for calculation purposes. Disclosure must align with the number of years of loss data banks' national authority permits banks to use in their calculation. Banks must disclose if internal loss data has been excluded due to non-compliance with data collection standards. The required disclosures are net of recoveries but banks are expected to make additional disclosures where recoveries are material. Banks should also explain the rationale for any new exclusions and provide details of recent large losses.

Template OR2: Business indicator (BI) and subcomponents

Template OR2 requires an analysis of the three BI components and corresponding ten sub-components over the past three years. The effect on BI of the exclusion of divested activities is also required. Banks are expected to provide explanatory narrative where they have received national authority approval to exclude divested activities from the calculation of BI.

Template OR3: Minimum required operational risk capital

Template OR3 requires summary information on the operational risk capital computation: BI component, ILM, operational risk capital requirement and corresponding risk weighted asset equivalent. Banks must disclose if an ILM has been set by the national authority due to non-compliance with data collection standards together with an accompanying narrative.

11.17 Credit valuation adjustments

BCBS 432 introduces two new tables and four new templates to reflect the new capital requirements for CVA risk included in BCBS 424 published in December 2017. BCBS indicates that, other than table CVA-A, these disclosures do not apply to banks that have chosen, with national authority approval, to set their CVA capital requirement equal to 100% of their capital requirement for counterparty credit risk. BCBS 424 indicates this is available to banks whose aggregate notional amount of non-centrally cleared derivatives is ≤ EUR 100bn.

BCBS 432 proposes these new disclosures apply from 1 January 2022, aligned with the implementation of the new capital requirements for CVA risk. Until then, template CCR2 remains applicable – see counterparty credit risk section 11.10. Table 11.15 summarises the proposed disclosure requirements.

Name	Designation	Type	Format	Frequency
CVA-A	General qualitative disclosure requirements related to CVA	Qualitative	Flexible	Annually
CVA-B	Qualitative disclosures for banks using the standardised approach for CVA (SA-CVA)	Qualitative	Flexible	Annually
CVA1	The reduced basic approach for CVA (BA-CVA)	Quantitative	Fixed	Semi-annually
CVA2	The full basic approach for CVA (BA-CVA)	Quantitative	Fixed	Semi-annually
CVA3	The standardised approach for CVA (SA-CVA)	Quantitative	Fixed	Semi-annually
CVA4	RWA flow statements of CVA risk exposures under SA-CVA	Quantitative	Fixed	Quarterly

Table 11.15: Disclosure of credit valuation adjustments

Table CVA-A: General qualitative disclosure requirements related to CVA

Table CVA-A is applicable to all banks and requires them to provide a description of its risk management objectives and policies for CVA risk. This includes, processes implemented to identify, measure, monitor and control CVA risk, incorporating where appropriate, policies and procedures for hedging CVA risk and ensuring its ongoing effectiveness. Banks that have set their CVA capital requirement equal to 100% of their capital requirement for counterparty credit risk need to disclose only this table.

Table CVA-B: Qualitative disclosures for banks using the standardised approach for CVA (SA-CVA)

Table CVA-B is applicable to banks using the SA-CVA approach for CVA risk and requires banks to disclose information regarding the scope, main characteristics and modelling choices used for the sensitivity computation of CVA risks, the components of the capital charge under the SA-CVA approach and flow statements explaining variations in capital requirements for CVA risk determined under this approach. Banks should also make disclosures concerning the related risk management framework and governance, including the extent of senior management involvement.

Template CVA1: The reduced basic approach for CVA (BA-CVA)

Template CVA1 applies to banks using the reduced basic approach for CVA risk, using only the amounts obtained from the netting sets applicable to the reduced BA-CVA. It requires banks to disclose quantitatively, the components of the capital requirement under this approach. Banks must also describe the types of hedges they use even if they are not taken account of under this approach.

Template CVA2: The full basic approach for CVA (BA-CVA)

Template CVA2 applies to banks using the full basic approach for CVA risk, using only the amounts obtained from the netting sets applicable to the full BA-CVA. It requires banks to disclose quantitatively, the components of the capital requirement, including hedging components. Banks must also describe the types of hedges they use. The format of this disclosure is shown in Figure 11.29.

		a	b
		Components	Capital charge in BA-CVA
1	Aggregation of systematic components of unhedged CVA risk		
2	Aggregation of idiosyncratic components of unhedged CVA risk		
3	K Reduced		
4	Aggregation of systematic components of hedged CVA risk – bank's counterparties and single name hedges		
5	Aggregation of index hedges		
6	Aggregation of idiosyncratic components of hedged CVA risk		
7	Aggregation of misaligned components of indirect hedges		
8	K Hedged		
9	**Total**		

Figure 11.29: Proposed full basic approach for CVA risk (BA-CVA) template – CVA 2

Template CVA3 and CVA4: The standardised approach for CVA (SA-CVA) and RWA flow statements under SA-CVA

Template CVA3 applies to banks using the SA-CVA approach for CVA risk. It requires banks to disclose the components of capital requirement analysed by risk source e.g. interest rate, foreign exchange or commodity. Banks must also describe the types of hedges they use. Template CVA4 requires the disclosure of the capital requirement at quarter ends including an explanation of significant changes over the reporting period.

11.18 Asset encumbrance

The Basel Committee on Banking Supervision considers disclosure of information on encumbered and unencumbered assets provides users with an overview of the extent to which a bank's assets remain available to creditors in the event of insolvency. As a result, in BCBS 432, BCBS proposes introducing an asset encumbrance template. BCBS indicates implementation from year end-2019.

Name	Designation	Type	Format	Frequency
ENC	Asset encumbrance	Quantitative	Fixed	Semi- annually

Table 11.16: Disclosure of asset encumbrance

Table ENC: Asset encumbrance

Table ENC requires disclosure of an analysis of the balance sheet broken down between encumbered and unencumbered assets. Whilst BCBS 432 describes this as fixed format template, there is flexibility as to the breakdown of the balance sheet and of encumbered and unencumbered assets. BCBS suggests that encumbered and unencumbered assets should be further analysed by transaction type but that national authorities should specify this and where appropriate provide guidance on the classification of assets as encumbered or unencumbered. The format of the disclosure is shown in Figure 11.30.

	a	b	c	d	[Optional]	e	f	g	h	i
	Encumbered assets					**Unencumbered assets**				**Total**
	Transaction Type 1 [e.g. covered bonds]	Transaction Type 2 [e.g. securitisations]	Transaction Type 3 [e.g. other]	Total	Central bank facilities	Category 1 [e.g. readily available for encumbrance]	Category 2 [e.g. other assets that are capable of being encumbered]	Category 3 [e.g. cannot be encumbered]	Total	
The assets on the balance sheet would be disaggregated; there can be as much disaggregation as desired										

Figure 11.30: Proposed asset encumbrance template – ENC

BCBS is aware that disclosure of encumbered assets due to banks' transactions with central banks could be sensitive due to the visibility it may give in respect of central banks' monetary operations or the provision of liquidity to banks. The template includes an optional separate column for central bank facilities but it is for national authorities to specify. Where there is separate disclosure of central bank facilities, banks should describe the types of assets and facilities included.

11.19 European implementation

11.19.1 European implementation of phase I

In order to ensure the consistent implementation of the Pillar 3 requirements of BCBS 309 throughout the European Union, the European Banking Authority (EBA)

published in December 2016 the final guideline "Guidelines on disclosure requirements under Part Eight of Regulation (EU) No 575/2013" (EBA Guideline 2016/11).

The Basel guidelines were adopted on the European level without major differences.
Nevertheless, the Basel provisions differ to some extent from the European provisions.
Noteworthy deviations have been made to the timing and the scope of application. The
new disclosure requirements of the EBA Guideline 2016/11 have applied since end of
2017 (G-SIBS had to disclose selected content already at the end of financial year 2016).
In comparison to BCBS 309, these guidelines are applicable to all systemically important institutions (G-SIIs and O-SIIs) that are subject to the disclosure requirements
under Part 8 CRR, including partial implementation by significant banks (e.g. SSM
banks) and significant subsidiaries. Supervisory authorities are able to oblige further
banks to comply with the requirements. Banks that are not in scope of EBA Guideline
2016/11 have to adopt only the requirements with respect to Part 8 CRR. In addition,
as opposed to BCBS 309, securitisation disclosures are not part of the EBA Guideline
2016/11.

EBA Guideline 2016/11 provides specific guidance to the disclosure requirements in
accordance with Part 8 of the CRR. The guideline concretise the already existing disclosure requirements of the CRR through specifying mandatory tables and templates.

The EBA Guideline on materiality, proprietary and confidentiality and on disclosure
frequency[21] was supplemented and extended with regard to the requirements that
should be disclosed more frequently for the institutions covered by the new EBA
Guideline 2016/11. While provisions with respect to information to be disclosed quarterly or semi-annually are already in force today, these are now linked to materiality
thresholds (balance sheet total, total exposure measure of the Leverage Ratio). With
Basel, on the contrary, the disclosure frequency depends on the type of information,
regardless of the institution's size. The disclosure requirements according to EBA
Guideline 2016/11 and changes to BCBS 309 are shown in Figure 11.31.

Topic	Number of tables	Disclosure frequency			Changes to BCBS 309	
		Quarterly	Semi-annually	Yearly	New	Changed
Risk Management and Governance	4	–	–	4	–	3
Group structure and scope of application	4	–	–	4	1	2
Own funds	See Delegated Regulation 1423/2013					
Capital requirements	3	1	2	-	1	2
Macroprudential measures	See Delegated Regulation 2015/1555 and Delegated Regulation 2014/1030					
Credit risk – general	14	–	8	6	9	4
Credit risk – SA approach	3	–	2	1	–	3
Credit risk – IRB Approach	5	1	2	2	–	4
Counterparty credit risk	9	1	8	–	2	7
Unencumbered assets	See EBA RTS 2017/03					
Market risk	6	1	4	1	1	2
Remuneration	See EBA GL 2015/22					
Leverage Ratio	See Delegated Regulation 2016/200					
Sum	48	4	26	18	14	27

Figure 11.31: Phase I in European level– EBA GL 2016/11 disclosure requirements

---

21   Cf. EBA GL 2014/14 (2014).

11.19.2 European implementation of phase II

On 23 November 2016 the EU commission launched its drafts for amendments to the CRR and CRD that will implement large parts of the Basel IV provisions on the EU level. Through various global and European initiatives, the CRR II proposals in the areas of disclosure are significant. The CRR II draft contains references to all new disclosure requirements contained in the Basel Phase I and II documents but also strengthens the principle of proportionality by distinguishing between institutions' size and capital market orientation.

In particular, with respect to the size and complexity of institutions there are provisions to the scope and frequency of disclosure. In the future, institutions will be classified into three categories based on their size (large institutions, small institutions and other institutions), with a further distinction to listed and unlisted institutions. Listed large institutions will be required to disclose annually all the information required under Part Eight of the CRR, plus disclosures of selected information on a semi-annual and quarterly basis. Small non listed institutions will be required to disclose selected information on governance, remuneration, risk management and the key metrics table on an annual basis (Figure 11.32).

	Listed Institutions			Non listed Institutions	
	Annual	Semi-annual	Quarterly	Annual	Semi-annual
Large Institutions	●	◕	◑	●	◔
Other Institutions	●	◔		◕	◔
Small Institutions	◕	◔		◑	

● Full disclosure according to part 8 of CRR

◕ Disclosure of selected information, which cover main requirements of part 8 CRR

◑ Disclosure of selected information, which cover partly requirements of part 8 CRR

◔ Solely disclosure of key metrics template

Figure 11.32: Phase II in European level – CRR II consideration of proportionality

These proposals will be subject to further discussions within the European Parliament and Council.

11.20 Conclusions and expected effects

With the new Basel papers on Pillar III, the disclosure requirements for banks become significantly more formalised than to date. With these publications, evident conclusions are drawn from the banks' disclosure practices which have been criticised as deficient time and again. From the Basel Committee's point of view, only with the aid of predefined disclosure templates and tables will a **direct comparability** of information disclosed by different institutes be ensured. This evolution is not unexpected since it was already blatantly obvious in the previous provisions on disclosure of capital requirements, leverage ratio and liquidity coverage ratio.

The new disclosure requirements demand **a high degree of data granularity and volume**. These will require institutions to disclose more and more information and ensure the reconcilability of information from different data sources. The use of different systems and models make it difficult to gather the required information. Besides the impacts mentioned, the disclosed information needs to be published more frequently. This requires that historical data is available at a granular level which increases the storage requirements. The boxes shown in Figure 11.33 represent only a small selection of challenging data requirements regarding the new disclosure requirements.

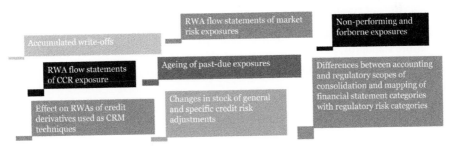

Figure 11.33: Challenging data requirements regarding the implementation of Phase I

The biggest challenge in practice is, however, the **reconciliation with accounting**. The required transferability of carrying values between the scope of consolidation under commercial law and the regulatory scope of regulation as well as the regulatory exposure definitions forces banks to establish data availability and transferability on a single item basis that has not been necessary so far for accounting purposes. The interface to similar Basel provisions for aggregation of risk data (keyword BCBS 239) becomes apparent at this point. Another challenge is the required reconciliation of the development of RWA during the reporting period. Even though disclosure traditionally played the role of the neglected stepchild within banking supervision, it becomes clear now that the implementation of the new provisions goes hand in hand with higher requirements regarding resources and data and that it is not isolated from other projects to achieve a standardised data-household in a bank's financial and risk departments.

It remains to be seen whether the banking supervisory objective of safeguarding the stability of financial markets through the market discipline of Pillar 3 will be achieved better than has been the case up to now.

Recommended Literature

Basel Committee on Banking Supervision; BCBS 107 (2004): International Convergence of Capital Measurement and Capital Standards, 2004.

Basel Committee on Banking Supervision; BCBS 128 (2006): International Convergence of Capital Measurement and Capital Standards – comprehensive version, 2006.

Basel Committee on Banking Supervision; BCBS 197 (2011): Pillar 3 disclosure requirements for remuneration, 2011.

Basel Committee on Banking Supervision; BCBS 221 (2012): Composition of capital disclosure requirements, 2012.

Basel Committee on Banking Supervision; BCBS 238 (2013): Basel III: The Liquidity Coverage Ratio and liquidity risk monitoring tools, 2013.

Basel Committee on Banking Supervision; BCBS 255 (2013): Globally systemically important banks: updated assessment methodology and the higher loss absorbency requirement, 2013.

Basel Committee on Banking Supervision; BCBS 270 (2014): Basel III Leverage Ratio Framework and Disclosure Requirements, 2014.

Basel Committee on Banking Supervision; BCBS 272 (2014): Liquidity coverage ratio disclosure standards, 2014.

Basel Committee on Banking Supervision; BCBS 295 (2014): Basel III: the net stable funding ratio, 2014.

Basel Committee on Banking Supervision; BCBS 309 (2015): Revised Pillar 3 Disclosure Requirements, 2015.

Basel Committee on Banking Supervision; BCBS 324 (2015): Net Stable Funding Ratio disclosure standards, 2015.

Basel Committee on Banking Supervision; BCBS 352 (2016): Minimum capital requirements for market risk, 2016.

Basel Committee on Banking Supervision; BCBS 356 (2016): Pillar 3 disclosure requirements – consolidated and enhanced framework (Consultative Document), 2016.

Basel Committee on Banking Supervision; BCBS 376 (2016): Frequently asked questions on the revised Pillar 3 disclosure requirements, 2016.

Basel Committee on Banking Supervision; BCBS 387 (2016): TLAC holdings, 2016.

Basel Committee on Banking Supervision; BCBS 400 (2017): Pillar 3 disclosure requirements – consolidated and enhanced framework, 2017.

Basel Committee on Banking Supervision; BCBS 401 (2017): Regulatory treatment of accounting provisions – interim approach and transitional arrangements, 2017.

Basel Committee on Banking Supervision; BCBS 424 (2017): Basel III: Finalising post-crisis reforms, 2017.

Basel Committee on Banking Supervision; BCBS 432 (2018): Pillar 3 disclosure requirements – updated framework (Consultative Document), 2018.

Basel Committee on Banking Supervision; BCBS 435 (2018): Pillar 3 disclosure requirements – regulatory treatment of accounting provisions

Bundesanstalt für Finanzdienstleistungsaufsicht [Federal Financial Supervisory Authority]; BaFin (2015): Rundschreiben 05/2015 (BA) – Umsetzung der EBA-Leitlinien zur Offenlegung, 2015. [Implementation of EBA guidelines regarding disclosure]

Capital Requirements Regulation; CRR (2013): Regulation (EU) No 575/2013 of the European Parliament and of the Council of 26 June 2013 on prudential requirements for credit institutions and investment firms and amending Regulation (EU) No 646/2012.

Commerzbank (2015): Offenlegungsbericht gemäß Capital Requirements Regulation zum 31. Dezember 2014. [Disclosure report pursuant to Capital Requirements Regulation as of 31 December 2014]

European Banking Authority; EBA (2014a): EBA final draft implementing technical standards on additional liquidity monitoring metrics under Article 415 (3) (b) CRR (ITS 2013/11, revised 24/07/2014).

European Banking Authority; EBA (2014b): Guidelines on common procedures and methodologies for the supervisory review and evaluation process (SREP) (GL 2014/13).

European Banking Authority; EBA (2014c): Guidelines on materiality, proprietary and confidentiality and on disclosure frequency under Articles 432 (1), 432 (2) and 433 of CRR (GL 2014/14), 2014.

European Banking Authority; EBA (2016): The EBA 2016 Annual Work Programme (Revised), 2016.

European Banking Authority; EBA (2016b): Guidelines on disclosure requirements under Part Eight of CRR (EBA/GL/2016/11), 2016.

European Banking Authority; EBA (2016c): Draft Guidelines on LCR disclosure to complement the disclosure of Liquidity Management under Article 435 of Regulation (EU) No. 575/2013(EBA/CP/2016/06), 2016.

European Banking Authority; EBA (2018a): Guidelines on uniform disclosure under Article 473a of Regulation (EU) No. 575/2013 as regards the transitional period for mitigating the impact of the introduction of IFRS 9 on own funds (EBA/GL/2018/01), 2018.

12 Interest Rate Risk in the Banking Book (IRRBB)

Matthias Eisert, Martina Bäthe-Guski and Nicole Geysel

12.1 Introduction

The interest rate risk in the banking book (IRRBB) describes the risk that impacts equity capital and arises from changing interest rates on interest-bearing items in the banking book. Interest rate risk has two forms: the volatility of economic value and the volatility of earnings. These forms are complementary: Fixed interest rate cash flows over a long time horizon will enable a bank to reduce its exposure to the volatility of net interest income (NII) but will expose the bank to the volatility of the economic value (EV). This is complemented by so-called floating interest rate payments that are regularly adjusted to the current market level of interest rates and reduce the volatility of EV but enlarge the volatility of NII.

In 2015 the Basel Committee presented the consultation paper BCBS 319 which suggested a standardised framework for IRRBB under Pillar I and an extended approach under Pillar II. However, after intensive consultation with the banking industry, which criticised the lack of consideration of the complexity and heterogeneity of various business models, the Basel Committee understood the need for developing internal models to identify, measure, monitor and control IRRBB and therefore refrained from introducing a standardised framework under Pillar I.

On 21 April 2016, the Basel Committee on Banking Supervision published the final paper BCBS 368 for interest rate risk in the banking book. The aim of the reviewed principles is to ensure the banks' capital adequacy with respect to interest rate risks in the banking book within the framework of the ICAAP.[1] So the final document gives principles on sound practices for measuring, managing, monitoring and controlling interest rate risk in the banking book. The former standardised framework for Pillar I has been significantly modified for the final paper and henceforth serves as a default model; supervisors can mandate banks to follow this standardised framework for Pillar II or banks may choose to adopt it on their own.

Even when a standardised approach for IRRBB is no longer required, the objective of comparability between the different banks still exists. BCBS 368 achieves this aim by presenting principles for disclosure to promote greater consistency, transparency and comparability in the measurement and management of IRRBB.

The principles described in BCBS 368 must be implemented from 2018 on.

The remainder of this chapter is outlined in the following. The focus lies on describing the principles on management and supervision of interest rate risks in the banking

---

1 Guidelines on ICAAP and ILAAP information collected for SREP purposes (EBA Guideline 2016/10).

book of BCBS 368 within the framework of Pillar 2. In this context, the Guidelines on IRRBB[2] published by the European Banking Authority (EBA) are also presented. Overlaps and contradictions between the two publications are explained. To conclude, the standardised framework will be briefly reviewed.

12.2 Principles for treatment within the framework of Pillar 2

12.2.1 Definitions

In BCBS 368 the Basel Committee defines the following three types of sub-risk as the main components of interest rate risk in the banking book:

- Gap risk: risk due to parallel and non-parallel changes of yield curves.
- Basis risk: effects of relative changes in interest rates on financial instruments with similar maturities, which are measured using different yield curves.
- Option risk: risk arising from option derivative positions or optional elements embedded in assets, liabilities and/or off-balance sheet items, where the bank or its customer can change the amount and timing of its cash flows; further subdivision into automatic option risk and behavioural option risk.

All three sub-risk types affect the value and timing of future cash flows. These have an impact on the value of assets, liabilities and off-balance sheet items.

In addition to the three sub-types of IRRBB, the Basel Committee classifies credit spread risk in the banking book (CSRBB) as a risk to be monitored and evaluated in the context of interest rate risk management. To this end, CSRBB designates all types of asset/liability spread risks of credit risk instruments which cannot be explained by IRRBB and the expected credit/jump-to-default risk.

The amount of the measured IRRBB depends essentially on the modeling of future cash flows. Since their timing and height are uncertain in many cases especially due to termination rights and deposits with no fixed maturity, their modeling is based to a large extent on the individual assumptions of the banks. Therefore, these assumptions are of great importance for the measurement of IRRBB.

12.2.2 The twelve Principles for the management of IRRBB

The current principles from Basel on the treatment of interest rate risk in the banking book within Pillar II do not contain any specifications for calculation methods as known from Pillar I (see section 12.3), but so-called Principles for banks (1–9) and for competent authorities (10–12). The contents of the principles are outlined below.

---

2   Cf. EBA (2015).

Principles for banks

1. IRRBB is an important risk for all banks that must be specifically identified, measured, monitored and controlled. In addition, banks should monitor and assess CSRBB.

2. Governing body is responsible for the supervision of IRRBB management framework and determination of the risk appetite for IRRBB. Management needs awareness of the effects of IRRBB strategy and links to other risk types as well as sufficient expertise of individual members. A delegation of IRRBB's monitoring and controlling to experts or committees and regular review and analysis of the system's effectiveness is possible.

3. Determination of risk appetite with regard to both EV and NII. Banks must implement policy limits that target maintaining IRRBB exposures consistent with their risk appetite.

4. Measurement of IRRBB based on results of both EV and earnings-based measures using a range of shock and stress scenarios.

5. In measuring IRRBB, key behavioural and modelling assumptions should be fully understood, conceptually sound and documented. Such assumptions should be rigorously tested and aligned with the bank's business strategy.

6. Complete and correct data basis for evaluation systems and models. Adequate documentation and tests as well as stable internal and independent validation processes for the models.

7. Regular internal reporting on valuation results for IRRBB and hedging strategies at various consolidation levels and currencies.

8. Regular disclosure on IRRBB exposure and the procedures for measuring and controlling interest rate risk to competent authorities and the general public.

9. Appropriate allocation of internal capital for IRRBB in line with risk appetite as part of the ICAAP.

Principles for competent authorities

10. Obtain standardised information on a regular basis for monitoring trends in exposure, assessing the reliability of IRRBB's management and identifying (and advising appropriate measures for) outlier banks.

11. Regular assessment of banks' IRRBB and the effectiveness of approaches for identification, evaluation, monitoring and management of IRRBB, the involvement of experts, information exchange between competent authorities in terms of supervising IRRBB risk positions.

12. Publication of supervisors' criteria for identifying outlier banks, obligation to advise mitigation actions and/or additional capital requirements in the event of inadequate management or excessive risk relative to the banks' capital, earnings, or general risk profile.

The requirements for IRRBB are not entirely new; however, the revised principles emphasise certain issues. For example, in the **first principle**, the identification of all interest-dependent positions is required. While it is obvious that a fixed income bond is interest rate dependent, it is not always clear that non-interest-bearing deposits or even pension liabilities might be part of the interest rate risk in the banking book.

The **second principle** clarifies that the primary responsibility for the bank's risk appetite for IRRBB lies with the governing body. The governing body is allowed to delegate some of the tasks of managing and monitoring the risk but is still required to understand the implications of the bank's IRRBB strategies and to challenge the reports made to the governing body. If the governing body delegates some of the tasks, it has to ensure that the bank's organisational structure enables the delegates to carry out their responsibilities.

The **third principle** asks for the implementation of appropriate limits and sublimits to ensure that the exposures at risk are consistent with the risk appetite. This applies to both EV risk and NII risk. As EV risk and NII risk are complementary, it is impossible to stabilise both forms of risks at the same time. Therefore, the bank has to decide for one of the risks as the major risk, the managing process will focus on. However, this does not release the bank from the task of ongoing monitoring the other form of risk. The requirement to consider both EV risk and NII risk was the most challenging requirement for most of the banks. The majority of banks had implemented in the past either an EV approach or an NII approach and now have to integrate the other approach in their risk management.

The measurement of both forms of risk is also subject of the **fourth principle**. The principle gives detailed guidelines on the design of the interest rate shocks and stress scenarios to monitor and manage the IRRBB (see section 12.2.3).

The **fifth principle** is on modelling assumptions. When financial instruments as loans are subject to prepayment risk, BCBS 368 distinguishes between the different behaviour of corporates and retail customers. Embedded options in corporate loans/deposits can be reliably valuated with a common option pricing model as corporates normally will behave rationally (so-called automatic options). Exercising the option depends solely on the financial interest of the option holder and not on factors such as depositor behaviour. The behaviour of retail customers will be impacted by other drivers, so an option pricing model will not be appropriate. Instead, time series with data on the behaviour of retail consumers are required to develop assumptions on prepayment/early redemption risk. With the actual long period of steadily decreasing interest rates, the main challenge for banks is to develop assumptions of behaviour in times of increasing interest rates. The modelling assumptions have to be regularly validated.

The subjects of the **sixth principle** are measurement systems, data integrity and the model governance process. The principle requires retrieving accurate IRRBB information in a timely manner, which means that input data has to be accurate and the data process has to be automated as much as possible. For Germany, these are not significant innovations, since the "Principles for effective risk data aggregation and risk reporting" (BCBS 239) are already included in the MaRisk (2017). The principle demands model risk management and validation of the IRRBB models independent from development which is challenging for smaller banks with only a few risk controllers. In such a case a validation unit independent from risk controlling is commonly not feasible; for this case, at least, development and validation should be done by different persons within the risk controlling function. If a bank purchases the IRRBB models from third-party vendors, it should have enough information on the implemented assumptions to determine if those are reasonable for their business and characteristics. This forces vendors to give more insights into their models as they are volunteering.

The **seventh principle** requires regular reporting and gives detailed instructions on the contents of the reporting that has to be provided. The term "regularly" is not defined by BCBS 368; while some of the reporting requirements as summaries of the IRRBB exposures have to be reported more frequently – dependent on the business model of the bank – summaries of the reviews of the policies are normally reported annually.

The **eighth principle** requests comprehensive disclosure of the level of IRRBB exposure to the public. While Principles 1–7 emphasise the necessity of individually tailored models and assumptions appropriate for the banks business strategy, this principle aims at improvement of comparability between banks. In this principle, e.g. the following topics are explained in order to achieve an identical approach for them: treatment of own equity in the EV risk, the meaning of the "constant balance sheet approach" for NII and the way the interest rate for discounting purposes has to be derived. In addition, transparency on the extent of the risks is to be established by giving a template for the disclosure of the assumptions and the resulting risk.

The **ninth principle** demands consideration of IRRBB in the ICAAP. In a first step, the capital adequacy of IRRBB has to be assessed by several points as size and tenor of limits, circumstances by which the risk might crystallise, sensitivity to key model assumptions and so on. Again it is emphasised that a bank has to develop its own models based on its own risk appetite and that it is not sufficient to rely of supervisory assessment of capital adequacy.

In **principles 10–12** the supervisors are asked to collect sufficient information on banks and to assess the effectiveness of the management and measurement approach regularly. Based on the six prescribed interest rate shock scenarios in Annex 2 the supervisor shall implement outlier/materiality tests of the Banks' EV risk when comparing the bank's maximum EV risk with the 15% of its Tier 1 capital. When a supervisor determines, that a bank's internal measurement system is deficient, it might require the bank to use the standardised framework.

12.2.3 Interest rate shock scenario design

In developing interest rate shock scenarios, the Basel Committee pursues the aim of simulating a stressful interest rate environment that reflects the current interest rate

environment in all affected jurisdictions respective currencies and avoids national discretions and leeway. The specified six interest rate shock scenarios are as follows.

1. Parallel shock up.

2. Parallel shock down.

3. Short rates down and long rates up.

4. Short rates up and long rates down.

5. Short rates shock up.

6. Short rates shock down.

The starting point for each given situation is the risk-free interest rate for each time
bucket and currency. The shock takes place by means of a given interest rate change,
which is defined in each case for the three scenarios (parallel, short, long). The given
interest rate shocks are defined by the Basel Committee for a total of 21 different currencies, based on a time series covering the last 16 years. These shocks are used as inputs
for scenario-specific formulas to calculate the stressed interest rate per currency.

The interest rate shock calibration is set to a six-month holding period. According to
the Basel Committee, this is based on the fact that banks should be able to adjust their
interest rate risk to a shock within six months. Under ordinary circumstances this could
be achieved in a much shorter period of time; but, for a stress period, a conservative
six-month time frame is deemed adequate.

In order to avoid unrealistically high or low results, floors (change of the risk-free interest rate as a result of the shock) and caps are introduced for the level of the shocks.
Moreover, the shocked risk-free interest rate is capped at 0%, i.e. no negative interest
rates can result from the interest rate shock. The Basel Committee reserves the right
to adjust the level of the shocks as well as the caps and floors in case this should be
necessary for the future based on the interest rate development.

The list of the six supervisory interest rate shock scenarios is not exhaustive; further
stress scenarios have to be applied. This involves not only simulating different yield
curve developments but also taking into account effects from changing customer
behaviour depending on the curve development (e.g. volume of deposits will decrease
when interest rates increase). These so-called dynamic scenarios represent an essential
part of the IRRBB measurement.

12.2.4 The EBA guidelines on the management of interest rate risk arising from non-trading book activities

At European level, the EBA published the "Guidelines on the management of interest
rate risk arising from non-trading activities" in 2015 with effect from 1 January 2016.
These guidelines replace the CEBS Guidelines on "Technical aspects of the management of interest rate risk arising from non-trading activities under the supervisory

review process" of October 2006 and contain five High-Level Guidelines supplemented by so-called Detailed Guidelines. The content of the High-Level Guidelines has changed only slightly in comparison to the previously valid CEBS Guidelines and covers the following topics:

1. Demonstration of adequate economic capital in relation to interest rate risk, taking into account the impact of interest rate changes on available capital and future earnings as well as the availability of capital at the various consolidation and group levels.

2. Determination of risk exposure as a change in EV and NII.

3. Ongoing evaluation of EV's and NII's sensitivity in various scenarios for the change of the yield curve (parallel shift, rotation etc.).

4. Establishment of stable internal governance and existence of documentation (instruction system) to address all aspects of IRRBB.

5. Report of standard interest rate shock to competent authorities in accordance with Art. 98 CRD IV.

The supplementary Detailed Guidelines describe in detail the requirements for scenarios and stress tests to be used, as well as assumptions and methods for measuring interest rate risk. In addition, the EBA specifies its expectations regarding the control of interest rate risk and the determination, calculation and allocation of capital.

The EBA does not set out any guidelines for competent authorities; those have been incorporated into the SREP Guidelines. The requirements are not fundamentally new and already existed to a large extent.

In October 2017 a Consultation paper for "Draft guidelines on the management of interest rate risk arising from non-trading book activities" was published by the EBA. The updated guideline introduces changes to the structure of the guideline. There are no longer separate High-level Guidelines and Detailed Guidelines but combined guidelines that are structured as follows:

1. Definitions

2. General provisions

3. Capital identification, calculation and allocation

4. Governance

5. Measurement

6. Supervisory outlier test.

12.2.5 Similarities and differences between the BCBS Principles and the EBA Guidelines

Both the BCBS Principles and the EBA Guidelines cover the treatment of interest rate risks from the banking book and non-trading activities such as their integration in

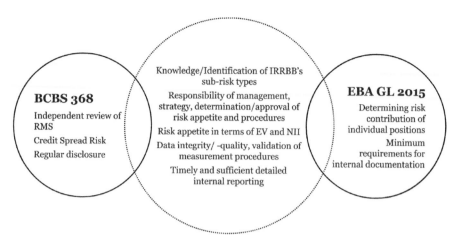

BCBS 368

Independent review of RMS
Credit Spread Risk
Regular disclosure

Knowledge/Identification of IRRBB's sub-risk types
Responsibility of management, strategy, determination/approval of risk appetite and procedures
Risk appetite in terms of EV and NII
Data integrity/ -quality, validation of measurement procedures
Timely and sufficient detailed internal reporting

EBA GL 2015

Determining risk contribution of individual positions
Minimum requirements for internal documentation

Figure 12.1: BCBS 368 vs EBA Guidelines 2015

internal management of internal capital. In the EBA Guidelines, the importance of measuring interest rate risk in the banking book is emphasised and the comparability for supervisory purposes is pursued. With the standardised framework in Pillar I, the BCBS paper also provides competent authorities with a comparison tool for IRRBB measurements across institutions. However, the paper's focus is the internal measurement of interest rate risk under Pillar II.

The overlap between the BCBS Principles and the EBA Guidelines on interest rate risk in the banking book is wide and covers the main process components of interest rate risk management, e.g. identification of the risk or sub-risk types, the definition of responsibilities to methods for determining risk and appropriate reporting of the results. The differences of the papers relate to details of the aforementioned topics, independence requirements, documentation contents and regular disclosure. In the following, the overlaps and contradictions (with regard to Pillar II) between both papers are briefly discussed.

One of the main differences between BCBS 368 and the current EBA Guidelines is the treatment of Credit Spread Risk. While Credit Spread Risk is in BCBS 368's scope of IRRBB, it is so far explicitly excluded from IRRBB by EBA. But the EBA Consultation Paper overcomes this difference. The Consultation Paper now extends the scope of application on Credit Spread Risk.

There is a broad agreement between the Basel Committee and EBA on the design of interest rate scenarios. Besides the six supervisory interest rate scenarios, both institutions demand additional scenarios such as those used in ICAAP, as well as scenarios based on historical and hypothetical time series developments. The BCBS paper also considers the modelling of highly concentrated markets (negative effect on the possibility to liquidate positions) and the effect of changes in interest rate volatility (relevant for embedded options such as floors) for banks with significant option risk. Additionally, BCBS 368, as well as EBA Guideline 2015/08, ask for the implementation of scenarios that consider changes in the business model, changes in the competitive environment or the profile of the bank etc. Also, competent authorities may advise the implementation of further interest rate shock scenarios. The Basel Committee requires the annual publication of the six supervisory scenario results, and the EBA expects scenario analyses to be carried out at least on a quarterly basis, and even more frequently in periods of high-interest rate volatility or a significant ratio of risk level to business activity.

The EBA and the Basel Committee also formulate similar requirements with regard to the data used and its integrity, although they set different priorities in this respect. For example, the Basel Committee calls for main data sources to be appropriately documented and for data input to be as automated as possible in order to minimise administrative errors. Controls must be implemented, and data mapping must be reviewed on a regular basis. Further, the EBA supplements its requirement for ensuring the reliability of market and internal data by reviews of external information sources used to set up a database for historical interest rates and the frequency with which the database is updated. In addition, appropriate procedures for data processing must be implemented and ensured, such as procedures for handling discrepancies and irregularities in the context of data processing. In particular, the consistency of data used for measuring IRRBB and for corporate planning is emphasised.

While both actual papers require the validation of the models used for the IRRBB calculation, the Basel Committee formulated the components of an effective and continuous validation framework more specifically than the EBA and included requirements on the appropriate management of model risk. This difference between the two papers is now overcome by the EBA Consultation Paper. There are requirements on management of model risk included in the EBA Consultation Paper. The former missing requirement on the independent review of the Risk Management System is part of the EBA Guideline.

In summary, it can be stated that the two papers set out different priorities in the requirements. But the Principles and Guidelines have clearly converged with the EBA Consultation Paper.

12.3 The Standardised Framework

12.3.1 Introduction

The aim pursued by the Basel Committee with the standardised framework for interest rate risks in the banking book is to ascertain consistency, transparency and comparability in terms of interest rate risks incurred by banks. These overarching goals should be reached together with the other approaches submitted to consultation within the scope of Basel IV. Moreover, it shall also be ensured that the consideration given to interest rate risks is not distorted by regulatory requirements such as the distinction between trading and banking books or by accounting specifications such as the differentiation between the valuation at amortised cost or at fair value.

Within the standardised framework, the interest rate risk in the banking book comprises exclusively the risk arising from changes of risk-free interest rates. The Framework does not encompass credit spread risks. Although this had been discussed in detail by the TFIR and the respective information was retrieved from the banks in the first Quantitative Impact Study in 2014, credit spread risks in the banking book (CSRBB) only play a role within the scope of the Pillar 2 approach.

12.3.2 Assigning positions to time buckets

The starting point in determining interest rate risks in the banking book is the allocation of all interest-bearing items on the asset and the liability side as well as off-balance sheet items to time buckets. Non-interest bearing items such as holdings or fixed assets are an exception to this, as they are items which must be deducted when determining regulatory capital such as own funds instruments of companies in the financial sector, which are subject to deduction.[3]

Basically, cash flows resulting from interest-bearing items must be classified into time buckets. Fixed interest rate items are assigned according to the repricing maturities of cash flows. Variable interest rate positions are either assigned to the time bucket for which one of the parties is entitled to unilaterally change the interest rate or to one for which the interest rate is adjusted automatically in response to a change in the reference interest rate.

Figure 12.2 outlines the regulatory time buckets.

Furthermore, a distinction is also made if a position's cash flows can be modelled following standardised procedures.

1. Amenable positions: comprise all positions that are not subject to uncertainties regarding the timing of cash flows.

Short term	O/N	O/N–1M	1–3M	3–6M	6–9M	9M–1Y	1–1.5Y	1.5–2Y
Medium term	2–3Y	3–4Y	4–5Y	5–6Y	6–7Y			
Long term	7–8Y	8–9Y	9–10Y	10–15Y	15–20Y	> 20Y		

Figure 12.2: Time buckets

---

3   Cf. Section 63 CRR.

2. Less amenable positions: include all products where uncertainty regarding the timing of cash flows is present, but that can, however, be projected within the scope of standardised proceedings ("automatic interest rate options").

3. Not amenable positions: cover all positions for which uncertainties cannot be determined based on standardised proceedings ("behavioural interest rate options").

Amenable positions are slotted by means of the above-described procedure based on the timing of cash flows or the occurrence of an interest rate change.

Less amenable positions are products subject to uncertainties as to the cash flow amount and timing due to embedded or explicit optionalities. Compared to not amenable positions, automatic optionality must be taken into account here. Exercising the option depends solely on the financial interest of the option holder and not on factors such as depositor behaviour. Typical examples of these products are embedded interest rate options such as caps and floors.

Because of this optionality, the effects of interest rate shocks cannot be estimated by delta-equivalent approximations. Instead, a complete re-evaluation based on the interest rate shock scenario and the assumption of increased volatility must be performed. The resulting fair value change of the options is then added to the change in the economic value of equity caused by the amenable and not-amenable positions.

In the case of **not amenable positions,** the product optionality depends on the behaviour of the depositor or the borrower. Examples given by the Basel Committee include non-maturity deposits (current accounts, call deposit accounts), mortgages subject to prepayment risk as well as fixed rate loan commitments. For these positions, explicit modelling assumptions are provided by BCBS 368.

The treatment of not amenable positions is explained below, taking non-maturity deposits (NMDs) as an example. The borrower is free to withdraw these deposits at any time; however, in practice, said deposits are relatively insensitive to interest rate changes. The challenge, therefore, is to differentiate between stable and less stable deposits and to slot them accordingly to the different time buckets. Compared to the LCR, no stress scenario is assumed here.[4] Hence, no conservative outflow assumptions apply as they would not be appropriate in the case of the IRRBB. The basic procedure for slotting NMDs is illustrated in Figure 12.3.

Deposits must first be segmented into "retail" (i.e. deposits made by individual persons and deposits made by legal entities of up to a total amount of EUR 1 million) and "wholesale" (i.e. deposits made by legal persons, partnerships, etc.). Retail deposits must further be classified into transactional accounts, e.g. when the depositor uses a current account for rent and salary payments, which is an indication of the stability of the deposit.

---

4   Cf. DVO 2015/61, Art. 24 f.

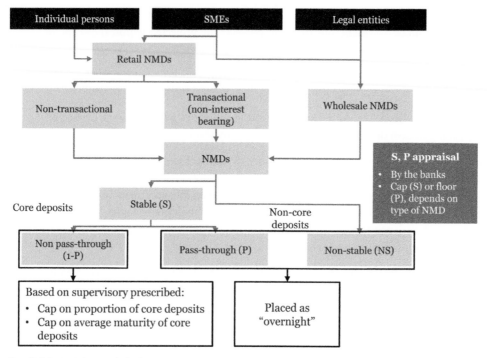

The next step is to distinguish between stable and non-stable deposits based on historic data. In contrast to BCBS 319, no caps are provided for the proportion of deposits that may be classified as stable.

Within stable deposits, a further distinction must be drawn between core and non-core deposits. It is assumed that banks pass through interest rate changes proportionally and not entirely. Core deposits are the proportion of stable deposits not subject to interest rate changes due to the pass through. Depending on the deposit's classification, regulatory provisions may apply. Up to 90% of stable retail/transactional deposits, but only 50% of stable wholesale deposits, may be classified as core deposits.

Non-core deposits are completely assigned to time bucket 1 ("overnight"). Core deposits are slotted into time buckets between 5y (Retail/transactional) and 4y (Wholesale).

12.3.3 Estimating the impact on EVE

As mentioned in the Introduction, the impact of interest rate risks on the EVE must be determined in four steps:

1. The cash flows per time bucket and currency are netted.

2. The net cash flow per time bucket is weighted with a risk-free interest rate discount factor.

$$\text{Standardised EVE risk measure} = \max_{i \in \{1,2,\dots,6\}} \left\{ \max \left(0; \underbrace{\sum_{C:\,\Delta EVE_{i,c}>0} \Delta EVE_{i,c}}_{\text{loss in currency } c} \right) \right\}$$

Figure 12.4: Calculation of minimum capital requirements

3. The risk-weighted net positions per time bucket are added to determine the EVE under each scenario and currency.

4. The impact on the economic value of equity by currency and scenario is determined by subtracting the value of step 3 from the initial economic value of equity plus the amount for automatic interest rate option risks.

It must be taken into account that by means of the described procedure no hidden reserves or liabilities derived from past changes in interest rates are realised since only the effects of the prescribed interest rate shock on future cash flows are measured. The economic value of equity is, however, not compared to the book value of the items. The Basel Committee decided against this in order to reduce the complexity of the procedure.

12.3.4 Calculation of minimum capital requirements

Capital requirements for interest rate risks in the banking book arise from a combination of effects of the interest rate shock scenarios on the economic value of equity.

As part of capital requirement calculations, an assumption must be made as to how the impact of the interest rate shock can be aggregated in different currencies. According to the Basel Committee, it cannot be assumed that an interest rate shock occurs simultaneously in all affected currencies. For this reason, the provisions regulate how partial offsetting shall be effected in different currencies. Ultimately, the complexity is reduced by establishing that only those currencies in which more than 5 percent of the assets or liabilities are held must be taken into account.

The aggregation of the EVE changes in all currencies and scenarios is displayed in Figure 12.4 below.

12.4 Conclusion and outlook

At the end of 2016, new drafts of the Capital Requirements Directive (CRD V) and the Capital Requirements Regulation (CRR II) were put up for consultation, which include the topic IRRBB. For the European area, the EBA recently submitted a new draft of its IRRBB guidelines for consultation in October 2017. The German supervisor is also currently pushing ahead with a revision of its Circular Letter 11/2011, which requires credit institutions to deal with the supervisory interest rate shock of +/− 200bp.

The aim pursued by the competent authorities in their most recent publications is to synchronise the numerous guidelines and proposals for controlling IRRBB. This is also the greatest challenge for institutions, which have to meet a multitude of innovations in terms of conceptual and technical implementation. A vigilant look at the ongoing discussions and future developments on IRRBB is therefore a basic requisite for ensuring compliance when the new requirements come into force.

Recommended literature

BCBS 108 (2004): Principles for the Management and Supervision of Interest Rate Risk, 2004.

CEBS (2006): Technical aspects of the management of interest rate risk arising from non-trading activities under the supervisory review process

BCBS 319 (2015): Consultative Document. Interest rate risk in the banking book, 2015.

BCBS 368 (2016): Interest rate risk in the banking book, 2016.

Bundesanstalt für Finanzdienstleistungsaufsicht [Federal Financial Supervisory Authority]; BaFin (2011): Zinsänderungsrisiken im Anlagebuch; Ermittlung der Auswirkungen einer plötzlichen und unerwarteten Zinsänderung (Rundschreiben 11/2011 (BA)), 2011. [Interest rate risks in the banking book; Impact calculation of sudden and unexpected interest rate changes]

Bundesanstalt für Finanzdienstleistungsaufsicht [Federal Financial Supervisory Authority]; BaFin (2012): Mindestanforderungen an das Risikomanagement – MaRisk (Rundschreiben 10/2012 (BA)), BTR 2.3, 2012. [Minimum Requirements for Risk Management]

Bundesanstalt für Finanzdienstleistungsaufsicht [Federal Financial Supervisory Authority]; BaFin (2017): Zinsänderungsrisiken im Anlagebuch (Konsultation 13/2017 (BA)), 2017. [Interest rate risks in the banking book]

Bundesanstalt für Finanzdienstleistungsaufsicht [Federal Financial Supervisory Authority]; BaFin (2017): Mindestanforderungen an das Risikomanagement – MaRisk (Rundschreiben 09/2017 (BA)), BTR 2.3, 2017. [Minimum Requirements for Risk Management]

Capital Requirements Regulation; CRR (2013): Regulation (EU) No 575/2013 of the European Parliament and of the Council of 26 June 2013 on prudential requirements for credit institutions and investment firms and amending Regulation (EU) No 646/2012.

Commission Delegated Regulation (EU) 2015/61 of 10 October 2014 to supplement Regulation (EU) No 575/2013 of the European Parliament and the Council with regard to liquidity coverage requirement for Credit Institutions.

European Banking Authority; EBA (2015): Guidelines on the management of interest rate risk arising from non-trading activities (EBA Guideline 2015/08), 2015.

European Banking Authority; EBA (2016): Guidelines on ICAAP and ILAAP information collected for SREP purposes (EBA Guideline 2016 10), 2016.

European Banking Authority; EBA (2017): Draft Guidelines on the management of interest rate risk arising from non-trading activities (EBA CP 2017/19), 2017.

13 TLAC and MREL – The Extension of the Regulatory Capital Definition and the Scope of Supervision

Stefanie Dreke and Martin Wollinsky

13.1 Background

During the financial crisis it could be observed that credit institutions in severe difficulties received support from the state, in part with enormous sums, due to a potential contagion effect within the financial services industry and the negative impact on the real economy. Since then, this phenomenon has been highly criticised, being referred to as "too big to fail".

Stricter capital requirements, specific liquidity regulations and the leverage ratio introduced by Basel III aimed at increasing banks' resilience in general. The same goal is pursued by the initiatives currently launched by the Basel Committee (and presented in the previous chapters), which focus on the revision of risk measurement.

Hence, the premises for maintaining the operations of a bank ("going concern") were improved. However, if a bank faces an unsolvable crisis and, as a consequence, has to be resolved ("gone concern"), the previously existing regulatory framework reaches its limits. Against this backdrop, the banking supervisory law is complemented by regulations introducing specific measures regarding the resolution of banks. These measures or tools comprise arrangements for a so-called "bail-in". The bail-in tool follows the objective to make use of shareholder and creditor capital for covering losses instead of relying on governmental bailout measures. The resolution framework applies once the "point of non-viability" is reached and serves as a substitution for regular insolvency proceedings.[1] It is based on the assumption that the resolution of certain critical functions and core business lines of the institution is neither "feasible" nor "credible" due to their importance for the financial sector or the real economy. An additional goal is to minimise losses – including those suffered by creditors – using a procedure specially tailored to the situation of (large) credit institutions. The superior principle when carrying out a resolution is that no creditor shall be worse off than in the case of insolvency ("no creditor worse off" – NCWO). Figure 13.1 outlines the bail-in ranking.

The "TLAC" initiative of the Financial Stability Board and the Basel Committee on Banking Supervision (BCBS) as well as the "MREL" initiative (the counterpart at EU level), were developed in this context. TLAC stands for "Total Loss Absorbing Capacity" and is designed to ensure that, on top of the regulatory capital, banks have sufficient long term debt for a bail-in in the case of resolution.[2] MREL stands for "Minimum Requirements for Own Funds and Eligible Liabilities" and pursues the same goal.[3]

---

1 Cf. FSB (2014) and Guideline 2014/59/EU (BRRD).
2 Cf. FSB (2015).
3 Cf. EBA (2015a).

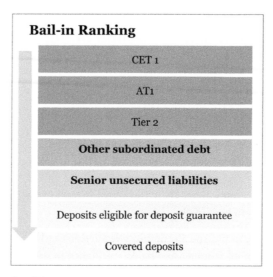

Figure 13.1: Bail-in ranking

The main content-related differences between both initiatives are as follows:

- TLAC applies to Globally Systemically Important Banks (G-SIB); MREL, on the contrary, applies to all institutions within the scope of the BRRD;[4]
- TLAC is designed as a standardised Pillar I minimum requirement, MREL is a firm-specific requirement and set by the responsible resolution authority.

Irrespective hereof, both initiatives are based on the same basic principles, pursue the same goals and have the "same DNA".[5]

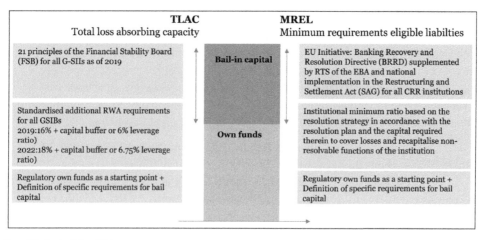

Figure 13.2: Overview TLAC and MREL

---

4   Cf. Directive 2014/59/EU (BRRD).
5   Cf. Gracie (2015).

This chapter is divided into two parts. The first part describes the international TLAC requirement addressed to all G-SII. Within the second part, the details on the specific EU-implementation – relevant for all EU-institutions – are explained.

13.2 TLAC

13.2.1 TLAC implementation

The TLAC publications by the FSB are international standards that need to be implemented nationally in order to become binding standards. The texts serve as the main guideline and need to be detailed by the relevant legislators. The following chapter provides an overview on the FSB TLAC standards.

13.2.2 TLAC calibration

The FSB proposal requires that the minimum TLAC for G-SIBs must be at least 16% of the resolution group's RWAs plus capital buffers as from 2019. From 2022 the ratio will increase to 18%. The FSB proposal includes a paragraph which allows resolution authorities to set a firm-specific requirement above the minimum ratio for individual institutions. A capital requirement of at least 6% (2019) and 6.75% (2022) of the leverage ratio exposures serves as floor.[6]

Where does the ratio come from? The overarching assumption for the new regime is that large banks can hardly be resolved, as critical functions need to be maintained in order to avoid disruptions of the entire financial market. The TLAC requirement roughly equals twice the Pillar I minimum requirements plus a buffer. This implicitly assumes that the minimum Pillar 1 requirement of at least 8% will be consumed for the absorption of incurred losses and the same amount is needed to restore the capital ratios.

13.2.3 TLAC eligible instruments

The TLAC ratio can be met with regulatory capital as a starting point. In addition, a new instrument category – TLAC eligible instruments – is defined. 33% of TLAC requirements must be met with (long-term) debt issuance that complies with certain conditions.

Relevant instruments are determined in two steps. First, specific categories of liabilities are excluded. Second, the remaining instruments are included if they meet certain operative criteria. Table 13.1 summarises these requirements:[7]

---

6   Cf. FSB (2015), Section 4.
7   Cf. FSB (2015), Sections 7–13.

Excluded instruments	General requirements on TLAC instruments
1. Insured deposits	1. Be paid in
2. Short-term deposits with original maturity < 1 year	2. Be unsecured
3. Liabilities arising from derivatives	3. Not be subject to set off or netting rights that would undermine their loss absorbing capacity in resolution
4. Liabilities with derivative-linked features (structured notes)	4. Minimum remaining maturity of at least 1 year
5. Liabilities arising other than through a contract (e.g. taxes)	5. Not be redeemable by the holder (except if the 1-year remaining maturity condition is fulfilled)
6. Liabilities that are preferred under the relevant insolvency law (secured liabilities)	6. Not be funded directly or indirectly
	7. Instruments issued directly by the resolution authority (exception: equity instruments)
7. Deposits that cannot be converted without giving rise to material risk of successful legal challenge or valid compensation claim under national insolvency law	8. Instruments must be subordinated to excluded liabilities via contractual, structural or legal subordination

Table 13.1: TLAC instruments

As mentioned before, a significant component for complying with the TLAC minimum requirements are regulatory own funds.

The FSB has already drafted additional requirements for the recognition of capital instruments as listed in Table 13.2.[8]

---

a) CET1 used to meet minimum TLAC must not be used to also meet regulatory capital buffers

b) Non-CET1 regulatory capital instruments must be subject to equivalent resolution mechanism or contain a contractual recognition of bail-in tools – if issued in another jurisdiction

c) Non-CET1 issuances by subsidiaries located in another jurisdiction must, with agreement of the relevant home and host authorities, be able to be converted without entry of the subsidiary into resolution proceedings

d) Regulatory capital instruments used to meet minimum TLAC must not be funded by a party related to the resolution

e) Regulatory capital instruments issued from entities forming part of a material sub-group may count towards minimum TLAC under certain conditions and with the approval of the authority

f) As from 2022: must be directly issued by the resolution entity except: CET1 from subsidiaries that are consolidated at resolution group level as well as specific instruments issued by cooperative banks

---

Table 13.2: Requirements for own funds instruments

13.2.4 Resolution entities and internal TLAC

In addition to a prescription of minimum requirements, the final TLAC Term Sheet specifies the distribution of bail-in instruments within group structures, especially in the case of cross-border resolution strategies.[9]

---

8   Cf. FSB (2015), Section 6.
9   Cf. FSB (2015). Section 16–18.

The requirements for TLAC must be complied with at the "resolution entities" level (Figure 13.3). Resolution entities are defined as separate resolution units within the G-SIB group in the resolution strategy. Hence, it is possible that several resolution units with different TLAC requirements exist within one G-SIB group. Additional emphasis lies on "material subgroups". Subgroups are defined for subsidiaries and entities operating in another state than the resolution entity. Sub-groups do not form an individual resolution entity and are not subject to a different TLAC requirement; however, they must comply with a – slightly adjusted – internal TLAC requirement. This is to increase the feasibility of a cross-border resolution strategy.

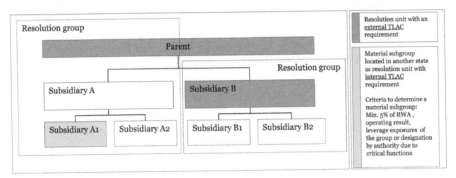

Figure 13.3: TLAC requirements within a group

Depending on the size and the importance of the material sub-group, they must maintain an internal TLAC of 75– 90% based on the TLAC requirement of the resolution entity. The same requirements apply to internal TLAC instruments as to external TLAC instruments. Moreover, collateralised guarantees of the resolution entity are eligible with respect to the material subgroup under specific circumstances.

In December 2016, the FSB published a first consultation detailing specific additional requirements for internal TLAC.[10] In December 2017, the final standard was released. The FSB defines 20 principles specifying the minimum requirements on internal TLAC instruments, as shown in Figure 13.4.[11]

13.2.5 TLAC holdings

Similar to the determination of capital requirements within the framework of Pillar I, the question arises whether specific balance-sheet or off-balance sheet items must be deducted from existing eligible capital or liabilities (deductible items) to determine TLAC. Particularly relevant in this regard are investments in instruments of other institutions that could be subject to a bail-in. Since one of the goals of resolution regulation is to avoid contagion, these interdependences within the financial sector are of great importance also in the context of TLAC.

---

10   Cf. FSB (2016).
11   Cf. FSB (2017).

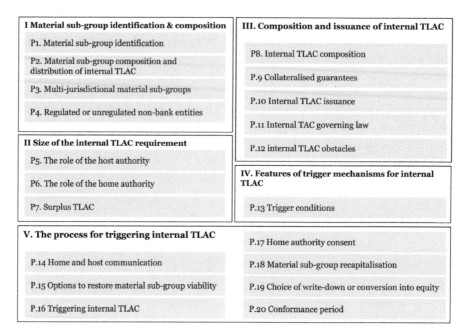

I Material sub-group identification & composition	III. Composition and issuance of internal TLAC
P1. Material sub-group identification	P8. Internal TLAC composition
P2. Material sub-group composition and distribution of internal TLAC	P.9 Collateralised guarantees
P3. Multi-jurisdictional material sub-groups	P.10 Internal TLAC issuance
P4. Regulated or unregulated non-bank entities	P.11 Internal TAC governing law
II Size of the internal TLAC requirement	P.12 internal TLAC obstacles
P5. The role of the host authority	**IV. Features of trigger mechanisms for internal TLAC**
P6. The role of the home authority	
P7. Surplus TLAC	P.13 Trigger conditions
V. The process for triggering internal TLAC	P.17 Home authority consent
P.14 Home and host communication	P.18 Material sub-group recapitalisation
P.15 Options to restore material sub-group viability	P.19 Choice of write-down or conversion into equity
P.16 Triggering internal TLAC	P.20 Conformance period

Figure 13.4: Principles on internal TLAC

The TLAC publication expressly prescribes that G-SIBs must deduct eligible external TLAC instruments and liabilities issued by other G-SIBs from their own TLAC – similarly to the existing provisions for regulatory capital under Basel III. The Basel Committee was assigned to further specify this provision, including the handling of those positions held by non-G-SIBs.

In November 2015, the Basel Committee published the consultation paper "TLAC Holdings" based on this assignment.[12] The paper was finalised in October 2016.[13] The Committee proposes that both – G-SIBs and non-G-SIBs – are required to deduct their net TLAC positions towards other G-SIBs from their own Tier 2 capital. This is explained in part by the fact that since non-G-SIBs are not subject to the TLAC regime they may not have sufficient TLAC resources. In order to obtain a harmonised approach, the deduction of Tier 2 capital instead of a corresponding deduction is favoured. Furthermore, as the cost of Tier 2 capital can be expected to exceed the cost of TLAC, this approach provides an incentive not to invest in these positions. The BCBS considered a CET1 deduction, an increased risk weight and a limitation on (special) large exposure regulations as alternatives, but discarded these options for various reasons.

The Basel Committee clearly refers to the provisions of Basel III on the treatment of equity instruments to calculate TLAC holdings (Figure 13.5).[14]

---

12 Cf. BCBS 387 (2016).
13 Cf. BCBS 400 (2016).
14 Cf. BCBS 342 (2015387 (2016), Annex I; BCBS 189 (2010), no. 77 et seq.

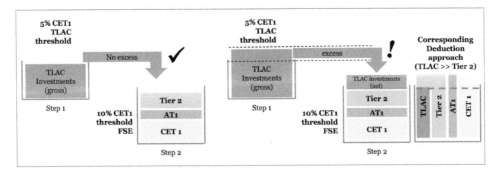

Figure 13.5: Treatment of TLAC holdings

This means that besides direct investments, positions that are indirect (e.g. funds) or synthetic (e.g. resulting from derivative transactions) must be taken into account. In this case, the net position can be calculated; that is, the long position net of short positions in the same underlying exposure. As long as the TLAC investor holds an immaterial investment in the issuer's capital, the regulations on the threshold deduction apply (10% of the bank's CET1).[15] Since this threshold is applied consistently for CET1, AT1 and Tier 2 investments, an additional consideration of TLAC investments could also lead to or increase CET1 and AT1 deductions. In addition to the 10% threshold for capital instruments and TLAC holdings, the final standard on TLAC holdings introduced an additional 5% threshold that can exclusively be used for TLAC holdings in the trading book that are held for not more than 30 days and are considered on a gross basis.[16] For non-G-SIIs no concrete requirements are made for the use of the additional threshold.

With this approach, the existing complex regulations on investment deductions for equity instruments are expanded to senior bonds and similar non-subordinated instruments. Irrespective of specific requirements set by the respective resolution authority, this is also relevant for non-G-SIBs insofar as they are invested in TLAC instruments of G-SIBs.

For investments in own TLAC instruments, the Basel Committee suggests in the consultation paper "TLAC Holdings" that the corresponding deduction approach, similar to equity instruments, is to be used: investments in own TLAC directly reduce the amount of TLAC eligible instruments, without any materiality thresholds. As non-G-SIIs do not have a TLAC requirement, the deduction is only relevant for G-SIIs.

13.2.6 TLAC-Reporting

The FSB Templates do not mention specific requirements for the reporting of the current and forecasted volume of TLAC eligible instruments. It can be expected that,

---

15   Cf. BCBS 189 (2010), no. 80.
16   Cf. BCBS 387 (2016), no. 80a, b.

within the national implementations, reporting requirements will be further detailed. In addition, G-SIIs will have an intrinsic motivation to install calculation processes in order to monitor and ensure compliance with the minimum ratios.

13.2.7 TLAC disclosure

The BCBS included TLAC in its current initiative on enhanced disclosure requirements (see also Chapter 11).[17] Different information on eligible liabilities and the TLAC ratio are to be disclosed in six different templates, summarised in Figure 13.6.

Template		Content	Frequency	Application
KM2	Key metrics	Current TLC ratio plus **forecast** for coming four quarters	**quarterly**	01.01.2019
CC1	**Composition of regulatory capital**	Enhancement of existing template by **TLAC holdings**	Semi-annual	End 2018
CCA	**Main features**	**Uptodate list** of every single TLAC eligible instrument + 40 additional attributes	uptodate	End 2018
TLAC1	**TLAC composition for G-SIIs**	**Detailed breakdown** of TLAC eligible instruments (comparable to composition of regulatory capital)	Semi-annual	01.01.2019
TLAC2/ TLAC3	**Creditor ranking at legal entity and resolution group level**	Amount of TLAC eligible and excluded liabilities in every **insolvency ranking class,** incl. breakdown on maturities	Semi-annual	01.01.2019

Figure 13.6: Overview on TLAC disclosure

TLAC, as a new Pillar I minimum requirement, is identified as a new key metric (template KM2). The overall TLAC ratio is to be disclosed on a quarterly basis. In addition to the current TLAC ratio in reference to RWA and Leverage Ratio, a forecast for the following four quarters needs to be calculated.

The existing disclosure template on the composition of regulatory capital (template CC1) is amended in order to display investments in TLAC-eligible instruments of other institutions (TLAC-holdings). In case the defined materiality thresholds (see also section 13.2.5) are breached, TLAC holdings can have an impact on the capital ratios.

For own funds, institutions need to disclose the main quantitative and qualitative features (e.g. interest rate, applicable law, amount included in own funds) of each instrument on a semi-annual basis. The Basel Committee enhances this requirement: TLAC eligible instruments need to be disclosed in the same way (template CCA). As the number of instruments can be expected to be significantly higher, the disclosure requirements increase to the same extent.

17   Cf. BSBS 400 (2017).

A new and individual disclosure sheet is introduced in order to create transparency on the composition of TLAC eligible instruments and in order to have a basis for the calculation of the current individual TLAC ratio (TLAC1).

All material subgroups and resolution entities need to disclose their liability sheet and the ranking of creditors in insolvency (TLAC2/TLAC3). Detailed information on the insolvency class, the overall volume, excluded liabilities, eligible liabilities and their respective maturity buckets need to be available. For material subgroups, specific information on whether the resolution entity has provided internal TLAC, needs to be provided.

Overall, the new disclosure templates come with completely new and granular data requirements. In addition, the quarterly forecast requirement requires the installation of an internal forecast process. The disclosure of the main features of TLAC eligible instruments on an instrument-by-instrument basis, with the side condition of a constant update, can have a high operational impact.

13.3 MREL

13.3.1 MREL implementation at EU level

Introduction of the SBR

Due to Regulation (EU) No 806/2014 of the European Parliament and of the Council of 15 July 2014 – establishing uniform rules and a uniform procedure for the resolution of credit institutions and certain investment firms in the framework of a Single Resolution Mechanism and a Single Resolution Fund and amending Regulation (EU) No 1093/2010 (SRM Regulation) – a single resolution mechanism (SRM) was introduced, effective as of 1 January 2016. The responsibility for the resolution of specific institutions and groups falls under the remit of the Single Resolution Board (SRB) pursuant to Art. 1 (42) SRM Regulation.

This competence of the SRB can be compared to the concept of supervision within the framework of the SSM pursuant to Council Regulation (EU) No 1024/2013 of 15 October 2013 conferring specific tasks on the European Central Bank concerning policies relating to the prudential supervision of credit institutions (SSM Regulation). Pursuant to Art. 7(2) SRM Regulation, the SRB is responsible for:

- all entities referred to in Art. 2 SRM Regulation that are not part of a group;
- for groups, which are considered as significant in accordance with Art. 6 (4) of Regulation (EU) No 1024/2013, or in relation to which the ECB has decided in accordance with Art. 6 (5)(b) of Regulation (EU) No 1024/2013 to execute directly all of the relevant powers; and
- other cross-border groups.

In summary, this means that institutions or groups that are supervised by the ECB are also subject to the SRM. Moreover, groups with group-associated entities established in more than one SRM member state are also subject to the SRM. The respective national resolution authority is responsible for all other groups and individual institutions (Figure 13.7).

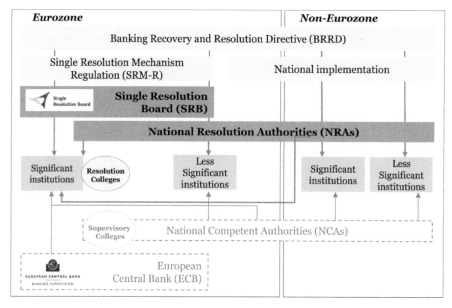

Figure 13.7: Supervisory and resolution authorities in the EU

The determination of MREL minimum requirements according to Art. 12 (8) SRM Regulation includes the requirements for institutions on an individual basis and parent undertakings on a consolidated basis. Subsidiaries established in a non-participating member state or outside of the EU shall be taken into account at consolidated level.

Pursuant to Art. 12 (9) SRM Regulation, minimum requirements for own funds and eligible liabilities shall be applied to the group's subsidiaries on an individual basis. The restriction of Art. 2 SRM Regulation regarding entities established in a partici-pating member state subject to the SRM has to be considered. For entities outside the SRM, the SRB is not competent. Thus, for subsidiaries established in an EU member state not subject to the SRM, the SRB must examine the possibilities for an EU-wide coordination pursuant to Art. 8 (11) (b) SRM Regulation, Art. 45 par. 9 BRRD. For subsidiaries in third countries, the resolution authority responsible for the group must identify appropriate arrangements for cooperation and coordination with the relevant authorities of those third countries pursuant to Art. 12 (1) (c) BRRD and Art. 8 (11) (d) SRM Regulation.

BRRD and CRR II package

As a part of the CRR II package, the BRRD has been modified as well. The eligibility criteria have been moved to the CRR and aligned with own funds and TLAC criteria. The new BRRD rules contain principles for the calibration of individual MREL requirements and details on the required level of subordinated instruments; in the latest drafts, this also includes a minimum requirement for so called top tier banks. The powers of the resolution authority are enhanced by the possibility to declare a moratorium with respect to the resolution entity's contractual obligations, and in the latest drafts by the possibility to restrict distributions to a MREL-based maximum distribution amount (M-MDA). Finally, BRRD II introduces MREL reporting and disclosure requirements.

Figure 13.8 provides an overview of the different MREL relevant provisions in CRR II, CRD V and BRRD II.[18]

The new legal set-up		
CRR	**BRRD**	**CRD**
– TLAC minimum requirement for G-SIIs in the EU – Eligibility criteria for TLAC and MREL – Deduction rules for investments in TLAC instruments for G-SIIs (TLAC-holdings) – TLAC reporting & disclosure	– MREL minimum requirement for all resolution entities and subsidiaries – MREL reporting and disclosure	– Buffer requirements – MREL and TLAC are relevant for the determination of the maximum distributable amount (MDA)

Figure 13.8: Overview CRR, CRD, BRRD

13.3.2 MREL calibration

Own funds plus

With MREL, a new regulatory "capital" ratio has been introduced in addition to the (Core) Tier I ratio and the total own funds ratio. While the latter ensure that a sufficiently large capital buffer for the compensation of losses is available for the ongoing business, MREL aims at ensuring sufficient coverage in case of a bail-in. Hence, the focus of MREL goes beyond equity and lays on the total liabilities of institutes as well. Liabilities shall be assessed according to specific criteria regarding their expected eligibility for a bail-in (bail-in capacity). Furthermore, additional – more operational – criteria have to be met in order to determine the eligibility for MREL. These criteria display strong parallels to requirements for own fund instruments.

Level of MREL requirements

In general, the MREL minimum ratio has to be determined by the responsible resolution authority for each institution on an individual basis within the resolution plan. The

---

18   Cf. EU-COM (2016a), (2016b), (2016c), (2016d).

new BRRD rules require that the MREL requirements are based on two components:[19] a loss absorption and a recapitalisation amount. The loss absorption amount equals the minimum own funds and leverage ratio requirements and is assumed to be consumed for the absorption of incurred losses. The recapitalisation amount is the amount that allows the resolution group to restore compliance with its total capital ratio and leverage ratio requirements at consolidated resolution group level after the implementation of resolution actions and thus equals the requirements that have to be met with respect to the RWA and leverage ratio exposure that remain after the resolution actions that are contained in the resolution plan have been carried out. Where, according to the resolution plan, an entity would be wound-up through national insolvency procedures, the MREL requirement might be limited to the loss absorption amount.

The recapitalisation amount may be complemented by a market confidence buffer that is, in general, set equal to the combined buffer requirement except the countercyclical buffer. Both the market confidence buffer and the Pillar II requirement included in the recapitalisation amount may be adjusted downward if the resolution is deemed to be feasible and credible at a lower amount or upward if deemed necessary. The BRRD II draft provided by the EU commission contains the power to require an additional loss absorption guidance that would be comparable to and limited to the level of the Pillar 2 Guidance. This additional guidance seems to have been dropped in the recent discussions. In any case, the combined buffer has to be complied with on top of the overall MREL requirement (i.e. loss absorption amount, recapitalisation amount, and market confidence buffer). This would lead to a MREL calibration that is broadly in line with the calibration requirements in Delegated Regulation (EU) 2016/1450.[20]

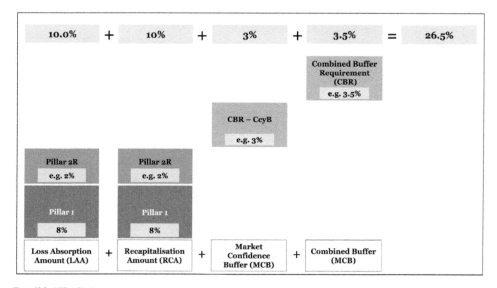

Figure 13.9: MREL calibration

---

19   EU-COM (2016c).
20   EU-COM (2016f).

These requirements are set as a Pillar II measure. For G-SIIs, this is complemented by the Pillar I TLAC requirement of 18% (RWA) and 6.75% (leverage ratio exposure, LRE) that has to be met with subordinated liabilities or own funds. For non-G-SIIs with total assets higher than EUR 100 billion ("top tier banks"), a similar standardised requirement of 13.5% RWA and 5% LRE is discussed. According to the transitional rules provided, this requirement would not become applicable before 2022.

In addition, resolution authorities may require that the MREL requirements are met with own funds and subordinated liabilities up to the lower of 8% of total own funds and liabilities ("TLOF") and 20% RWA. These are the thresholds for access to the resolution fund. The resolution fund may only be used, if 8% of the total liabilities or, under additional conditions, 20% of RWA have been contributed to the resolution via a bail-in. The utilisation of the resolution fund is limited to the case in which bail-in eligible liabilities are excluded from the bail-in for operational reasons (Art. 44 (4) BRRD). The resolution fund may cover the losses not absorbed by these liabilities. Based on the individual resolution plan it is defined if, and to what extent, such a compensation is likely to take place.

Eligible liabilities

For the identification of eligible liabilities, certain liability categories are *per se* excluded from bail-in and therefore not MREL-eligible. In addition, the non-excluded instruments must comply with certain criteria – defined in the CRR II – regarding their terms and conditions (Figure 13.10).

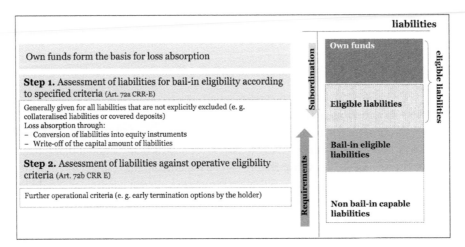

Figure 13.10: Eligible liabilities

(1) Bail-in eligibility

The bail-in tool may be applied to all liabilities of an institution in accordance with Art. 44 (1) BRRD. However, certain liabilities are excluded from the bail-in by definition (see Art. 44 (2) BRRD) and are therefore protected from a bail-in. As part of the CRR II package, the definition of eligible liabilities is harmonised between MREL and TLAC. Art. 45b BRRD II defines the minimum standards via cross reference to Art. 72a CRR II so that for the calculation of MREL – eligible instruments, the categories shown in Table 13.3 need to be excluded.

---

1. Covered deposits

2. Deposits org. maturity < 1 year

3. Deposits eligible for deposit guarantee

4. Secured liabilities

5. Liabilities stemming from insolvency protected client assets/moneys

6. Fiduciary liabilities

7. Institution liabilities with original maturity < 7 days

8. System operator liabilities w. remaining maturity < 7 days

9. Tax liabilities

10. Employee liabilities

11. Critical service liabilities

12. Liabilities to deposit guarantee schemes

13. Liabilities from derivatives

14. Structured liabilities

Table 13.3: Excluded instruments acc. to Art. 72a CRR II

The exclusion of derivatives (13) is due to their potential volatility and difficult valuation. Where TLAC explicitly excludes structured liabilities, the MREL implementation applies a differentiated treatment. Acc. to Art. 45b (2) CRR II any amount that is fixed and not affected by the derivative feature can be included in the eligible instruments. Based on that, instruments that only have a structured interest component, could be considered eligible.[21]

---

21   Cf. FSB (2015), Section 10, letter d.

In exceptional circumstances, the resolution authority may exclude certain liabilities from bail-in. The main reasons are shown in Table 13.4.

1. It is not possible to bail-in that liability within a reasonable time.

2. The exclusion is strictly necessary and appropriate to achieve the continuity of critical functions and core business lines.

3. Exclusion is strictly necessary and proportionate to avoid giving rise to widespread contagion.

4. The application of the bail-in tool would cause a destruction in value such that the losses borne by other creditors would be higher.

Table 13.4: Reasons for exceptional exclusions

(2) MREL-eligibility

In order to assess the operative availability of instruments in a bail-in scenario, the additional criteria shown in Table 13.5 need to be fulfilled by eligible instruments.

1. Instruments fully paid-up

2. Not purchased by resolution entity/group/related entity

3. Purchase not financed by resolution entity

4. Subordinated

5. Not guaranteed or secured by group member

6. Not subject to set-off/netting rights

7. No incentives for early redemption

8. No early redemption clause for investor

9. Call option only for issuer and subject to supervisory approval

10. Repayment cannot be accelerated

11. Interest independent from credit standing

12. Point-of-non-viability clause (PONV)

Table 13.5: Eligible instrument acc. to Art. 72b CRR II

In general, these criteria are very similar to the criteria for regulatory capital instruments pursuant to Art. 28, 52 and 63 CRR. In the current update on CRR it can also be seen that the requirements for own funds are revised and partly enhanced (e.g. requirement on a contractual bail-in clause) in order to ensure a harmonised implementation of own funds and MREL requirements.

One aspect with specific relevance in practice is the topic of market making and possible reductions of eligible instruments prior to maturity. The existing process for the reduction of own funds acc. to Art. 78 CRR is revised and enhanced by rules for eligible instruments. In general, the reduction of own funds and eligible liabilities is first subject to equivalent replacement and second, to supervisory approval.

As the overall volume of eligible instruments and the respective market making activities are significantly higher than in the relatively stable class of capital instruments, a lean approval process would be required in order not to restrict market activities. Art. 78 CRR II mentions a general prior permission that could be obtained by the resolution authority.

(3) Contractual recognition of bail-in

For MREL purposes, eligible liabilities that are subordinated (or "**non-preferred**") play an important role. Therefore, BRRD II introduces a new class of "non-preferred" senior debt instruments that ranks higher than Tier 2 instruments, but lower than regular senior unsecured debt. In order to be classified as a non-preferred senior debt, instruments need to fulfil the following conditions:

- no derivative features, so that there is no risk of complex valuations processes;
- a minimum maturity > 1 year, so that the existence is ensured; and
- an explicit contractual subordination clause. Accepting this contractual term, the creditor acknowledges that the liability might become subject to a full or partial write-down or conversion in the event of the institution's resolution.[22]

This new class shall enable institutions to carry out distinctive issuance activities, by having the option to increase MREL eligible instruments by the issuance of non-preferred senior debt in contrast to instruments used for liquidity management and funding at a lower pricing. In case countries had already implemented a deviating legal basis for the creation of non-preferred senior, the ECB recommends clarifying that this legacy stock would rank *pari passu* with the liabilities issued under the new definition.[23]

EU legislators assume the enforceability of a bail-in for liabilities subject to the law of an EU member state since all member states have to implement the BRRD and must therefore create a legal framework for bail-in effectiveness. This cannot be presumed for **third countries**. For this reason, the resolution authority may require proof of the effectiveness of a possible bail-in. The relevant governing law and contractual recognition of bail-in tools must be taken into account for this purpose. Besides providing proof for MREL purposes, institutions have a general obligation to ensure bail-in effectiveness of all third country liabilities.

Pursuant to Art. 55 (1) (1) BRRD, institutions are required to include a contractual term ("bail-in clause") for certain liabilities subject to the regulations of a third country.

---

22   Cf. EU-COM (2016h).
23   Cf. EZB (2017).

Eligible deposits from natural persons and SMEs in accordance with Art. 108 (6) BRRD are excluded from the requirement of including a contractual recognition of bail-in tools. Protected liabilities that are not subject to bail-in pursuant to the provisions set forth in Art. 44 (2) BRRD are also excluded. For liabilities created before 1 January 2015 grandfathering rules apply so that the existing contractual recognition of bail-in tools is not required. Art. 55(2) BRRD II specifies, that the resolution authority can waive the requirement for instruments where it is operationally, economically or legally not possible or impractical to include a bail-in clause. These instruments cannot be treated as MREL-eligible instruments.

13.3.3 Resolution entities and internal MREL

When determining MREL requirements, a distinction between the relevant levels at which MREL requirements should be complied with is necessary.

Currently, institutions shall comply with the minimum capital requirements for eligible liabilities on an individual basis (Art. 45 (7) BRRD). In addition, the EU parent undertaking has to comply with the minimum requirements on a consolidated basis (Art. 45 (8) BRRD). By means of the BRRD II, the requirement on an individual basis is dropped for resolution entities.[24] For subsidiaries that are not themselves resolution entities the minimum requirement for eligible liabilities applies on an individual basis. The level of MREL has to be determined in the group resolution plan based on a joint decision of the group resolution authority and the resolution authority responsible for the subsidiary.

The national resolution authority of a subsidiary may fully waive the application of minimum requirements for eligible liabilities (Art. 45 (12) BRRD/Art. 45g (5), (5a) BRRD II). The direct reference to the waiver acc. to Art. 7 (1) CRR will probably be cancelled in BRRD II; instead, the MREL waiver will be subject to conditions that are comparable to Art. 7 (1) CRR, especially the inclusion in a resolution group.

For subsidiaries, BRRD II introduces some clarifications regarding the eligible instruments. Basically, MREL-requirements have to be met with internal instruments, i.e. own funds or eligible liabilities that are held by other members of the resolution group, or with own funds instruments that are issued to external entities (i.e. not included in the resolution group), as long as a write down or conversion of these instruments does not affect the control of the resolution entities over the subsidiary. In recent drafts, the latter is extended to eligible liabilities issued to existing shareholders, if the control by the resolution entity is not affected. On a group level, such external instruments would only be eligible to the extent they are needed to cover the subsidiary's MREL.

The internal MREL on a subsidiary level may, with the consent of the subsidiary's resolution authority, be met with a collateralised guarantee by the resolution entity.

---

24 EU-COM (2016c), whereas (13).

13.3.4 MREL holdings

For holdings in MREL, there is currently no final decision made. The EBA wants to assess whether to follow a similar approach as TLAC, so that MREL holdings would be deducted from own MREL instruments. Another method could be the definition of specific large exposure limits for investments in MREL.[25] The current BRRD update does not consider the aspect of MREL holdings.

13.3.5 MREL reporting

Resolution authorities need a detailed insight in the institutions' potential bail-in-ability. Based on Art. 11(4) BRRD, the EBA has developed a set of templates that shall serve as a minimum standard for reporting from institutions to the authorities (Figure 13.11). In June 2016, the templates were implemented by the European commission via Delegated Regulation.[26] The templates comprise information on critical functions, roles and responsibilities in the institution as well as information on the available volume of bail-in eligible liabilities.

Based on these minimum templates, the SRB developed specific MREL reporting templates in 2015 and started detailed data collection processes in 2016. Since then, institutions under SRB remit need to provide comprehensive data on eligible liabilities on an annual basis. The reporting deadline is gradually reduced (2017: 15.05.2017, 2018: 30.4.2018, 2019: 31.03.2019).[27]

In the past, the regulators were focused on assessing risks taken by institutions, so that a very deep understanding of the asset side was required. With MREL, this focus is significantly extended. For the first time, liabilities need to be analysed in detail in order to assess their eligibility for a bail-in.

The data collection consists of ten reporting sheets.[28] The "Template Liability Structure" (T01.00) forms the core sheet in which the entire liability side needs to be displayed. A breakdown of products, counterparties and maturities is required.

One requirement is to show carrying amounts to be reconciled with FINREP as well as outstanding amounts. The outstanding amount is defined as the amount the investor would claim in case of an insolvency, in general notional plus accrued interest payments.

As the calibration of the MREL ratio is also based on existing minimum capital ratios, T02.00 provides an overview of the phase-in and fully-phased-in RWA and capital ratios and buffers. Most of the information can be derived from the COREP Own Funds reporting.

---

25 Cf. EBA (2016a).
26 Cf. EU-COM (2016e).
27 Cf. SRB (2017a).
28 Cf. SRB (2017b).

The SRB puts specific emphasis on intragroup relations. Therefore, three specific sheets (T03.01–T03.03) require information on intragroup liabilities as well as intragroup guarantees provided and received. In this context, transactions that are only internal with regard to the accounting scope of consolidation are to be treated as internal as well.

In sheet T04.00 Securities all tradeable instruments need to be listed. T04.00 requires the highest number of additional attributes. This seems intuitive, as it can be expected that most of the MREL-eligible instruments will belong to this class.

For Deposits (T05.00), a granular reporting is only required for non-covered and non-preferred deposits with a maturity longer than one year. The consideration of these deposits as eligible instruments for the MREL ratio is still under discussion.

Derivative liabilities have to be shown in a separate template (T07.00). Contractual netting sets (in case transactions take place within master agreements) or single contracts need to be shown. The market values prior to and after collateral are requested. In addition, the estimated close out amount needs to be calculated; so far, this position is not mandatory. Template T01.00 also requires a counterparty breakdown of derivatives in the balance sheet as well as a calculation of derivative liabilities applying the leverage ratio methods. The purpose of the different breakdowns is not yet described.

An additional template focusses on secured finance transactions (T08.00), especially repos, for which it is also necessary to derive the amounts prior and after collaterals.

All other financial liabilities that are not covered by any of the previous sheets, have to be reported in Template T06.00. Based on the single data sheet, a detailed drilldown into every aggregated position in the liability data report template is possible.

T00.01 - Identification of the report (A)	Basis information on the reporting institution	complexity
T01.00 - Liability Structure (A)	Central reporting sheet "Liability structure" including a detailed breakdown on liabilities excluded and non-excluded from bail-in, by product types, counterparties, residual maturities; starting point for the assessment of potential MREL volume	
T02.00 - Own Funds (A)	Pillar 1 und 2 requirements plus additional capital buffer	
T03.01 – Intragroup Liabilities (S)	All liabilities withjn the group + 18 additional information	
T03.02 – Intragroup Guarantees-Received (S)	All guarantees received withjn the group + 9 additional information	
T03.03 – Intragroup Guarantees-Provided (S)	Alle guarantees provided withjn the group + 9 additional information	
T04.00 - Securities (S)	Alle securities + 31 additional information	
T05.00 - Deposits (S)	All deposits (non-covered, non-prefered) with a remaining maturity > 1year + 13 additional information	
T06.00 - Financial Liabilities (S)	All other liabilities + 21 additional information	
T07.00 - Derivatives (S)	All nettingsets + 14 additional information	
T08.00 - SFA (S)	All repo-transactions + 10 additional information	

Aggregated data (A)/ Single Contracts (S)

Figure 13.11: Overview MREL reporting

MREL is the most detailed reporting on liabilities the regulator has requested so far. The transformation from short-term project-driven data collections into operating standardised MREL reporting processes will be a challenge for institutions in the upcoming years. A target data base needs to be defined. Data on single contract level need to be stored and to be complemented by attributes that are often not available in the financial data warehouse. Therefore, additional information has to be provided by the treasury (e.g. exchanges listed on, specific interest features) or by the legal department (e.g. insolvency ranking). For subsidiaries, which are often not integrated in central IT landscapes, a solution needs to be found.

In October 2017 the EBA published an update on the minimum standards for reporting for resolution.[29] The new templates are partly comparable to the SRB templates, but not completely identical. Both SRB and EBA declare that the reporting templates will be transferred in a standardised technical format (XBRL). It is not clear whether for SRB banks the EBA templates need to be reported in addition to the SRB templates.

Overall, the future regular reporting format and frequency is still under discussion. Art. 45i BRRD II of the Commission refers to an at least annual reporting requirement for MREL, while later drafts require at least a semi-annual reporting. The outcome of the Trilogue negotiations will give a clear indication.

13.3.6 MREL disclosure

The BRRD II introduces new disclosure requirements for MREL.[30] The amount of own funds and eligible instruments and their composition have to be disclosed, including their maturity profile and ranking in normal insolvency proceedings. In addition, a disclosure of the MREL requirement on RWA and LRE basis is required. No detailed disclosure formats are provided yet, but a disclosure in line with the respective TLAC tables would make sense.

13.4 Outlook and summary

The ongoing work of the FSB and the EBA, as well as the creation, establishment and increasing relevance of the SRB underline the importance that TLAC and MREL gain in the regulatory environment. Both ratios will become more and more management relevant, require a long-term plan and have a significant impact on balance sheet structure and funding costs. This will be intensified by a supervisor with increasing experience that is expected to put more and more focus on detailed data analyses, on site-inspections and ad-hoc exercises. The overarching goal of the resolution authorities is to be prepared for a potential resolution. This is not limited to defined

---

29   Cf. EBA (2017).
30   Art. 45i BRRD II.

Table	#	Name	Format	#	Classification	Volatility	Importance for Resolution	Criticality
T03.01	1	Line	List of values	c020	Master Data			
T03.01	2	Insolvency Ranking	List of values	c030	Master Data			
T03.01	3	Internal identifier	String	c040	Master Data			
T03.01	4	LEI/MFI/Internal Identifier of Lending Entity	String	c050	Master Data			
T03.01	5	Governing Law	List of values	c060	Master Data			
T03.01	6	If Third Country, Contractual Recognition	List of values	c070	Master Data			
T03.01	7	Outstanding Principal Amount	0,00	c080	Transaction Data			
T03.01	8	Accrued Interest	0,00	c090	Transaction Data			
T03.01	9	Currency	List of values	c100	Master Data			
T03.01	10	Issuance Date	YYYY-MM-DD	c110	Master Data			
T03.01	11	Earliest Redemption Date	YYYY-MM-DD	c120	Master Data			
T03.01	12	Legal Maturity	YYYY-MM-DD	c130	Master Data			
T03.01	13	Secured/Unsecured	List of values	c140	Master Data			
T03.01	14	Amount of pledge, lien or collateral	0,00	c150	Transaction Data			
T03.01	15	Guarantor if applicable	String	c160	Master Data			
T03.01	16	Structured or other Non-Standard Terms	List of values	c170	Master Data			
T03.01	17	Qualifying as Own Funds	List of values	c180	Master Data			
T03.01	18	Amount Included in Own Funds, taking into account phase-out as applicable	0,00	c190	Transaction Data			
T03.02 - T03.03	19	Insolvency Ranking	List of values	c020	Master Data			
T03.02 - T03.03	20	Internal Identifier	String	c030	Master Data			
T03.02 - T03.03	21	LEI/MFI/Internal Identifier of Guaranteeing Entity	String	c040	Master Data			
T03.02 - T03.03	22	Governing Law	List of values	c050	Master Data			
T03.02 - T03.03	23	Guarantee Type	List of values	c060	Master Data			

Figure 13.12: Example for a data field assessment for ad-hoc reporting purposes

reporting dates, but could happen at any time, which is why the SRB expresses its clear expectation that, in the medium term, institutions must be able to provide data on an ad-hoc basis.[31] This has to be addressed in the TLAC and MREL implementation plans and requires a clear view on processes, roles and responsibilities, a high data quality level and an increased automation within the MREL calculation that goes far beyond the requirements of a (semi-) annual reporting. When preparing for such an ad-hoc reporting, as a first step banks should assess the volatility and criticality of the relevant data (see Figure 13.12).

In addition, the simulation of a so called resolution weekend would also emphasise valuation challenges that are to be faced in a bail-in situation. In that regard, the BRRD obliges member states to make sure authorities have the power to require a resolution entity to maintain detailed records of financial contracts (Art. 10 (8) BRRD). Although the resolution authorities do not seem to make use of this power on a broad basis yet, EBA has developed a RTS[32] that requires on a very detailed level and with a scope that goes clearly beyond the MREL reporting requirements. In addition to the process-wise and IT aspects, maintaining an appropriate level of TLAC/MREL eligible liabilities requires a prudent management. On one hand, regulatory requirements have to be met, including a sufficient management buffer. On the other hand, too many MREL eligible liabilities might have a negative impact on the profitability of a bank: The Basel Committee estimates that the additional cost of eligible liabilities between 5 and 15 basis points.[33] In other words: TLAC and MREL will continue to bring along new challenges for institutions.

Recommended Literature

Basel Committee on Banking Supervision; BCBS (2015): Assessing the economic costs and benefits of TLAC implementation, 2015.

Basel Committee on Banking Supervision; BCBS 189 (2010): Basel III: A global regulatory framework for more resilient banks and banking systems, 2010.

Basel Committee on Banking Supervision; BCBS 342 (2015): Consultative Document. TLAC Holdings, d342, 2015.

Basel Committee on Banking Supervision; BCBS 387 (2016): Standard. TLAC holdings: Amendments to the Basel III standard on the definition of capital, 2016

Basel Committee on Banking Supervision; BCBS 400 (2017): Standard. Pillar 3 disclosure requirements – consolidated and enhanced framework, 2017

BRRD: Directive 2014/59/EU of the European Parliament and of the Council of 15 May 2014 establishing a framework for the recovery and resolution of credit institutions and investment firms and amending Council Directive 82/891/EEC,

31 Cf. SRB (2017c) and SRB (2017d).
32 EU-COM (2016g).
33 Cf. BCBS (2015).

and Directives 2001/24/EC, 2002/47/EC, 2004/25/EC, 2005/56/EC, 2007/36/EC, 2011/35/EU, 2012/30/EU and 2013/36/EU, and Regulations (EU) No 1093/2010 and (EU) No 648/2012, of the European Parliament and of the Council

European Banking Authority; EBA (2015a): FINAL Draft Regulatory Technical Standards on criteria for determining the minimum requirement for own funds and eligible liabilities under Directive 2014/59/EU (EBA/RTS/2015/05), 2015.

European Banking Authority; EBA (2015b): FINAL Draft Regulatory Technical Standards on the contractual recognition of write-down and conversion powers under Article 55(3) of Directive 2014/59/EU (EBA/RTS/2015/06), 2015.

European Banking Authority; EBA (2016): Final Report on MREL, Report on implementation and design of the MREL framework, EBA-Op-2016-21, 14 December 2016.

European Banking Authority; EBA (2017): Consultation Paper, Draft Implementing Standards, on the provision of information for the purpose of resolution plans under Article 11(3) of Directive 2014/59/EU (EBA/CP/2017/15), 11 October 2017.

European Commission, EU-COM (2016a): Proposal for a Regulation of the European Parliament and of the Council amending Regulation (EU) No 575/2013 as regards the leverage ratio, the net stable funding ratio, requirements for own funds and eligible liabilities, counterparty credit risk, market risk, exposures to central counterparties, exposures to collective investment undertakings, large exposures, reporting and disclosure requirements and amending Regulation (EU) No 648/2012, 23 November 2016.

European Commission, EU-COM (2016b): Proposal for a Directive of the European Parliament and of the Council amending Directive 2013/36/EU as regards exempted entities, financial holding companies, mixed financial holding companies, remuneration, supervisory measures and powers and capital conservation measures, 2016.

European Commission, EU-COM (2016c): Proposal for a Directive of the European Parliament and of the Council amending Directive 2014/59/EU on loss-absorbing and recapitalisation capacity of credit institutions and investment firms and amending Directive 98/26/EC, Directive 2002/47/EC, Directive 2012/30/EU, Directive 2011/35/EU, Directive 2005/56/EC, Directive 2004/25/EC and Directive 2007/36/EC, 2016.

European Commission, EU-COM (2016d): Proposal for a Directive of the European Parliament and of the Council amending Directive 2014/59/EU of the European Parliament and of the Council as regards the ranking of unsecured debt instruments in insolvency hierarchy, 2016.

European Commission, EU-COM (2016e): Commission Implementing Regulation (EU) 2016/1066 of 17 June 2016 laying down implementing technical standards with regard to procedures, standard forms and templates for the provision of information for the purpose of resolution plans for credit institutions and investment firms pursuant to Directive 2014/59/EU of the European Parliament and of the Council, 2016.

European Commission, EU-COM (2016f): Commission Delegated Regulation (EU) 2016/1450 of 23 May 2016 supplementing Directive 2014/59/EU of the European Parliament and of the Council with regard to regulatory technical standards specifying the criteria relating to the methodology for setting the minimum requirement for own funds and eligible liabilities

European Commission, EU-COM (2016g): Commission Delegated Regulation (EU) 2016/1712 of 7 June 2016 supplementing Directive 2014/59/EU of the European Parliament and of the Council establishing a framework for the recovery and resolution of credit institutions and investment firms with regard to regulatory technical standards specifying a minimum set of the information on financial contracts that should be contained in the detailed records and the circumstances in which the requirement should be imposed

European Commission, EU-COM (2016h): Directive 2017/2399 of the European Parliament and of the Council of 12 December 2017 amending Directive 2014/59/EU as regards the ranking of unsecured debt instruments in insolvency hierarchy

European Central Bank; ECB (2017): Opinion of the European Central Bank of 8 March 2017 on a proposal for a directive of the European Parliament and of the Council on amending Directive 2014/59/EU as regards the ranking of unsecured debt instruments in insolvency hierarchy (CON/2017/6), 2017

Financial Stability Board; FSB (2014): Key Attributes of Effective Resolution Regimes for Financial Institutions, 2014

Financial Stability Board; FSB (2015): Principles on Loss-absorbing and Recapitalisation Capacity of G-SIBs in Resolution (TLAC Termsheet), November 2015

Financial Stability Board; FSB (2016): Guiding Principles on the Internal Total Loss-absorbing Capacity of G-SIBs ('Internal TLAC'), Consultative Document, December 2016

Financial Stability Board; FSB (2017): Guiding Principles on the Internal Total Loss-absorbing Capacity of G-SIBs ('Internal TLAC'), Consultative Document, July 2017

Gracie, Andrew (2015): TLAC and MREL – From Design to Implementation, speech at the BBA Loss Absorbing Capacity Forum on 23 July 2015 in London. Available under: http://www.bis.org/review/r150724c.pdf

Single Resolution Board; SRB (2017a): 2018 Guidance on the Liability data report – final – tracked changes, available under: https://srb.europa.eu/en/content/liability-data-report.

Single Resolution Board; SRB (2017b): Liability Data Reporting template 2018 v1.5 available under: https://srb.europa.eu/en/content/liability-data-report.

Single Resolution Board; SRB (2017c): Fifth Industry Dialogue – Liability Data Reporting: Lessons Learned from the 2016 data collection process and changes for the 2017 LDT template and collection process on 31 January 2016 available under https://srb.europa.eu/sites/srbsite/files/fifth_id_-_ldt_final.pdf

Single Resolution Board, SRB (2017d): Sixth Industry Dialogue 2017 MREL Policy on 21. November 2016 available under: https://srb.europa.eu/sites/srbsite/files/20171120_6th_industry_dialogue_item_2_mrel_dominique_laboureix.pdf

14 Strategic Implications

Dr. Philipp Wackerbeck, Jeroen Crijns, Dr. Christel Karsten, Dr. Benedikt Bruognolo and Thom Piethaan

14.1 Introduction

In December 2017 the Basel Committee on Banking Supervision presented the final version of a set of reforms, intended to revise how banks measure and quantify the different types of risk they face. The committee calls these reforms a "recalibration" of the well-known Basel III framework, but among bankers, they are commonly referred to as "Basel IV". The overall goals of these reforms are to limit variation in risk-weighted assets (RWA) and improve comparability across banks, strengthen the sensitivity of Basel III's standardised approach to risk, and ensure the adequacy of banks' internal models for assessing their risk.

Most senior bankers are aware of the existence of the Basel IV proposals, but they have yet to deal with the potential consequences. Bankers may not fully understand the individual elements of the reform package, or they may not combine the results of the studies they conduct on individual types of risk into a holistic view.

With the aim of clarifying the impact of the proposed regulations, we analysed the implication of these reforms for more than 130 European banks that have been part of the 2017 EU-wide transparency exercise of the European Banking Authority.[1] From this detailed study of the European market, banks across the globe can gain a perspective on how the current proposals will affect the industry. Moreover, we outline possible strategic responses on how to soften the potential impact and suggest key areas that banks should focus on when preparing for the implementation of Basel IV.

14.2 The capital squeeze

14.2.1 RWA impact

In total, Basel IV will increase the RWA of European banks[2] by 15–25%, or as much as €2.5 trillion (US$3.1 trillion) in aggregated RWA for all the banks we studied. Figure 14.1 breaks down the overall impact on RWA by the different risk types banks face. The impact is primarily driven by increases in credit risk RWA. Other risks included are operational risk, market risk, and credit-value adjustment (CVA) risk – the risk banks face given potential changes in the creditworthiness of their trading counterparties.

---

1   As a consequence, all calculations and data shown below are as of the first half of 2017; for further details on the analysis see "Fourth time around? European banks confront 'Basel IV'", *Strategy&*, November 2016
2   Due to data availability we focus in this chapter primarily on the impact on the large European banks. Our global analysis shows that the impact can vary significantly from country to country, business model, the use of internal models so far and other reasons. In any case, it can be expected, that large globally active banks will face a similar impact to the large European banks.

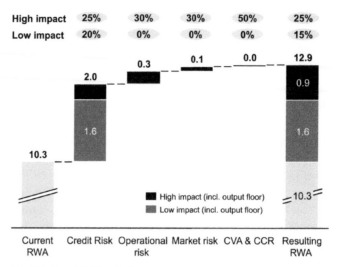

Figure 14.1: Aggregated RWA impact in €tn

The sharp increase in credit risk RWA is due to a combination of the large share of credit in banks' portfolios and the stringency of the new rules for credit risk. The size of the impact for credit risk depends on the composition of the credit portfolio across asset classes (corporate loans, mortgages, etc.) and the extent to which banks currently use internal models to calculate RWA for these asset classes.

Banks using internal models to assess RWA typically have lower current risk weights for their credit exposures than they would have under a standardised approach. Under Basel IV, these banks will face strict restrictions on the inputs for their internal models for some asset classes and will be forced to use standardised approaches for others. If the resulting RWA is still low, a floor may be applied based on the estimated amount of RWA from a standardised approach. Combined, these restrictions, reclassifications, and floors most severely impact RWA for exposures to specialised lending, mortgages, and large corporate loans (see Figure 14.2).

In terms of bank types, the largest institutions are most likely to experience a high impact, because larger banks tend to rely more on internal models to assess RWA. The restrictions on these models and the transition to standardised approaches will likely increase RWA more for these institutions than for banks that currently use standardised approaches and therefore already face higher risk weights.

Basel IV also restricts the use of internal models for operational risk and market risk – and again, the impact for these risk types is expected to be highest for banks that have been relying on internal models. For operational risk, a standardised approach is prescribed in which RWA increases with bank size and with the bank's historical incidence of operational losses. As such, banks that faced substantial operational

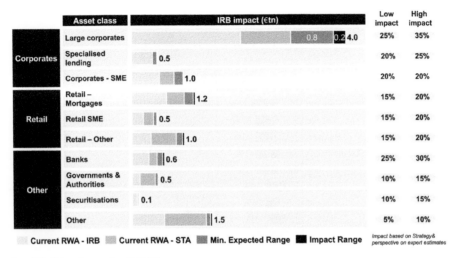

Figure 14.2: Estimated increases in credit risk RWA

losses in the past – due to rogue trading, for example – would expect to see their required capital for operational risk increase.

Finally, RWA for CVA risk is likely to increase significantly above current levels, driven by the mandatory application of the standardised approach, even though the absolute impact on capital required for CVA risk will be moderate for most banks. Still, it may have strategic implications for banks' trading operations.

More importantly, it's not distributed evenly across Europe (see Figure 14.3). Our simulation shows that banks in Northern and Central Europe are far more affected than their Southern European peers. It is particularly the Scandinavian, Dutch and also German and Belgian banks that will feel the heat and could see double-digit RWA increases that go well above 20% or 25%. This is driven by a combination of the extensive use of internal models and the relatively low-risk weights in the current situation.

The increase in risk weights in these countries will result in either a pricing increase for clients or a fall in bank financing for certain asset classes. This drop in bank financing may spur a development of corporate capital markets in these countries

14.2.2 Impact on capital

While banks are contemplating the impact of the proposed reforms, the Basel III capital requirements are still being phased in, leading to even higher minimum capital ratios. We expect the average capital requirement for Single Supervisory Mechanism (SSM) banks – which are subject to supervision by the European Central Bank (ECB) – to increase from the current 11.5% to approximately 12.3% once the Basel III requirements are fully implemented.

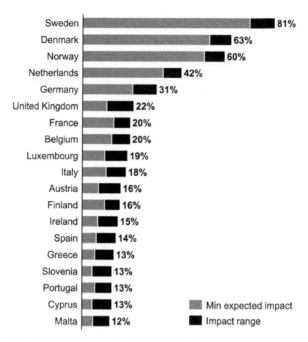

Figure 14.3: Estimated increases in credit risk RWA in different European countries

This parallel development of increasing RWA under Basel IV and rising capital thresholds under Basel III will have a significant compounding effect on the required capital for European banks (see Figure 14.4).

As a result, the banks included in our study will need to increase their capital to an aggregated €1.6 trillion under Basel IV, up from the current required amount of €1.1 trillion (see Figure 14.5). Thus, the amount of capital required by regulation approximately doubles, and far exceeds the industry's available levels of excess capital. More than half of the analysed banks would face capital shortfalls, with an aggregate shortfall of €400 billion to €500 billion.

The results of our study vary significantly from the results of the Quantitative Impact Study published by the Basel Committee in December 2017 together with the final Basel IV rules. It can be stated that the impact of Basel IV can vary significantly depending on the size of the bank, the business model and on the extent to which the bank uses internal models for the calculation of RWA.[3] The results of the above mentioned QIS were strongly criticised by experts from the banking industry, supervisors and also from independent experts. The strongest point of criticism was the data quality of the submissions of banks. Independent observations show that

---

3   On average, minimum required Tier 1 capital at the target level (Tier 1) decreases by 0.5% for Group 1 banks and increases by 3.8% for Group 2 banks. Average risk-based capital ratios will increase by 0.2% for Group 1 banks and by 0.1% for Group 2 banks, relative to the current national implementation of the Basel III framework as agreed up to January 2016 (for details see BCBS d426).

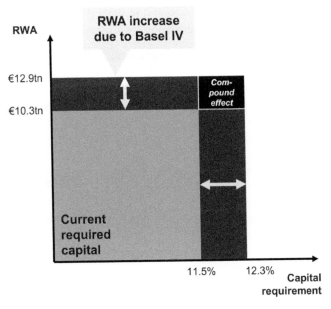

Figure 14.4: Compound effect on required capital

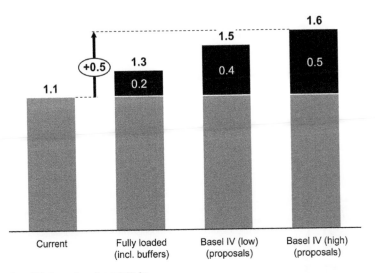

Figure 14.5: Increase in required capital in €tn

the quality of the submissions varied significantly. Also, the way the figures were presented on a very high aggregated level hide that in certain jurisdictions and banks the impact is much higher than indicated by the QIS. It was further criticised that the figures of the QIS show only the impact of the changes published in December 2017, and not changes that were already finalised and published in 2016 and 2015. This applies especially to the changes in market risk known as the Fundamental Review of the Trading Book (FRTB). But the true impact of Basel IV can only be understood if all changes to the methods of RWA calculation are analysed at the same time.

Based on internal data collected within a large number of detailed test calculations with banks across the globe, the variation of the impact is much higher than indicated by the QIS. Internal results show that the impact varies between a reduction of RWA of more than 10% on the one hand and an increase in total RWA of more than 50% on the other. Especially for large banking groups that use internal models for most of their portfolios in credit risk and market risk, the capital floor will be the main driver of a high RWA increase.

When analysing the impact of the capital floor on RWA and therefore on the business models of banks, is very important to do more than consider the capital floor rules during this analysis. There are many interactions between the new capital floor and other new rules like the new standardised approaches, the new rules for the partial use of internal market risk models and the new rules for the IRB models.

14.3 How to cope with Basel IV – Strategic implications

With the final terms of the Basel IV proposal in place, many European banks will need to increase capital levels. The sharp increase in capital requirements implies a capital shortfall for more than half of the 130 banks in the sample. In addition, raising more capital will worsen the already poor profitability of European banks.

To mitigate the impact of the new requirements on their institutions, senior bankers in Europe must take the proposals into account now. Capital markets are expecting

- An increase of the RWA by 15–25% is expected as a result of Basel IV. This will impact banks' capital management practices due to increased capital consumption and re-allocation of capital. During the long phase-in period for a number of elements, it will be key for banks to identify their capital management challenges early on and start phasing in changes in this area.

- There will be disproportionate capital impact for assets with lower underlying risk, due to the input and output floor concepts, and restrictions in the application of internal models. The challenge for banks is to optimise the portfolio composition to reduce the increase in capital requirements, through limitation of certain products affected and repositioning of portfolios with limited impacts.

- Proposed standardised approaches in combination with capital floors are typically geared towards only one specific risk driver. The challenge for banks is finding the right balance between responding to the output floor which is based on the standardised approach requirements, and focusing on reducing risks under the IRB Approaches that remain in place.

- Overall, there will be additional capital impacts across institutions relying more heavily on local subsidiaries with individual capitalisation requirements. Optimising the legal entities structure is a challenge banks will face in trying to respond strategically to the impact of Basel IV.

Figure 14.6: Strategic implication dimensions

banks to develop a plausible and workable strategy for complying with the new capital requirements while delivering appropriate returns to shareholders.

In our experience, many bankers tend to focus on the technical aspects of Basel IV, rather than taking a step back and developing a truly strategic perspective on the proposals. They should assess the strategic impact of the proposals along four key areas – capital management, portfolio composition, product structure, and operational adjustments – and fashion this assessment into a holistic strategic response.

14.3.1 Capital management

Given the expected impact, an update of the capital plan is required looking at raising capital and reducing RWA (see Figure 14.7). According to our simulations, more than half of the banks will have to raise capital or retain a sufficient volume of their earnings to maintain their current asset portfolio. This will pose other challenges to banks as many of them already operate with a negative economic spread. The economic spread describes the difference between the return on equity and the cost of equity. As most banks show a negative economic spread, it will be challenging to convince equity investors to help in raising capital. Since 2008, only around € 200bn in equity has been raised by European banks in the aftermath of the financial crisis, so it's not likely that investors will be willing to contribute enough to close the gap. Especially as the overall performance of many European banks continues to be weak and return on equity gets further under pressure from Basel IV. In general, one can assume

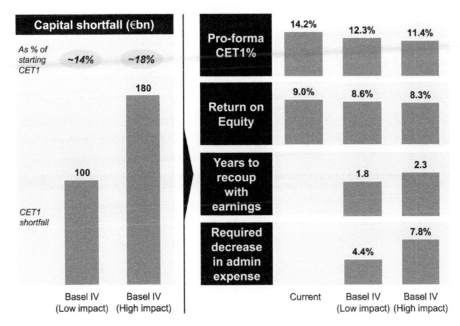

Figure 14.7: Levers to align capital with RWA

that chances are obviously better for stronger, more profitable banks rather than for the ones that struggle with their performance. Building up the required capital internally and maintaining the current business model is not realistic as banks would need to retain their earnings entirely for around two years or cut their admin expenses by an additional 4–8%. This does not sound much, but compared to the limited progress many banks have made over the past years in significantly reducing their expenses, it would be dangerous to bet on this expense reduction to close the capital gap.

Banks, alternatively, will have to deleverage their balance sheets to align available capital with required capital for the asset portfolio. To cope with decreasing income, deleveraging the balance sheet should be accompanied by right-sizing operational costs. However, banks need to find new, innovative ways in smartly deleveraging their balance sheets. Ideally, the top line impact is lower than the positive effect of the capital relief. To achieve this, banks need to develop a smarter deleveraging strategy than securitisation or selling assets/portfolios. They need to convert interest income into fee income, e.g. by establishing direct lending partnerships through club deals with institutional investors or by setting up debt funds or similar vehicles.

In addition to these wider strategic implications on the way balance sheet constraints are handled going forward, there are also potential changes to the way capital management and performance measurement are conducted going forward. While at many banks this is currently done based on RWA, this will most likely have to change given that the flooring on total RWA under Basel IV Regulatory Capital is becoming less suited for capital management and performance measurement due to unintuitive compensation effects.

14.3.2 Portfolio composition

Another quite remarkable consequence of the Basel IV changes will be that some banks are incentivised to take higher risks. Banks will focus their portfolios on higher risk, higher return clients and reduce their exposure to lower risk clients (see Figure 14.8).

Under Basel IV, RWAs are less risk sensitive due to the RWA output floors, risk parameter input floors for IRB models, and mandatory use of the standardised or F-IRB

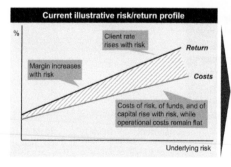
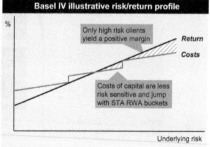

Figure 14.8: Illustrative impact on the risk-return profile

Approaches for specific asset classes. Banks will shift their portfolio focus towards higher risk, higher return clients or products, as these sub-portfolios still yield a positive margin. For those (sub-) portfolios which are no longer profitable, but where the bank has strong expertise or network, an originate-to-distribute model could be introduced to (partially) retain business volume, e.g. through a strategic partnership with insurance companies or pension fund. It may be expected that European banks, in line with US peers, will reduce in asset size and carry higher risk weights.

Banks should aim to replace balance sheet intense interest income with fee income to maintain or improve margins (see Figure 14.9). Banks traditionally offer their book to match depositors and borrowers with net interest margin as a key source of income for banks. Cost of capital can be contained by internal risk models and close risk management. Low-interest rate environment and increased capital requirements are challenging this business model. Banks can reduce their RWA by distributing originated loans. Banks replace their traditional net interest income with fee income through services or transactions for the distributed loans. This allows banks to have a similar level of business volume with lower capital requirements implying a higher return on capital.

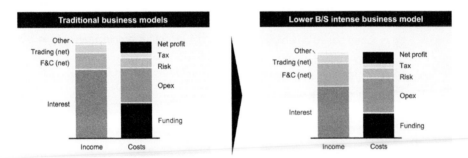

Figure 14.9: Income and costs across bank business models

Basel IV induces banks to review their trading activities and foster the division between flow and specialist players.

Higher capital charges are driven by reduced capital arbitrage possibilities, capturing of tail risk and increased risk sensitivity (especially foreign exchange and interest rate risk). Higher capital charges will fuel the development of "liquid" FICC instruments towards trading on venues (as induced by other regulation, e.g. MiFID II/MiFIR) reducing balance sheet utilisation (i.e. OTC) in order to mitigate the impact, banks need to have differentiating capabilities in asset classes where balance sheet is utilised – banks without differentiation are likely to stop trading respective asset classes. Examples of such potential asset classes are illiquid FICC instruments (including derivatives) and (exotic) equity derivatives. Altogether, the industry is expected to experience further rightsising and an ever stronger division between global flow players (mainly acting as agents) and asset specialist.

14.3.3 Product structure

Banks should adapt their product and pricing structures to reflect the reduced set of risk drivers for RWA calculation. Currently, banks incorporate a wide set of risk drivers in their internal models to determine RWA. Under Basel IV, only a small subset of these risk drivers are incorporated in the estimation. Banks should adapt their product structure and pricing mechanisms to this restricted scheme. Product structures should include pricing adjustments in line with changes to cost-drivers (e.g. collateral value), such that cost of capital is properly reflected in pricing.

For example, mortgage loans should be structured to reflect collateral valuation rather than borrower income (see Figure 14.10). A person-centric product structure is typically applied in most European countries (e.g. Netherlands, France) while a property-centric approach more applied in common law countries (e.g. US, UK). With the implementation of Basel IV, imposed input floors are based on LTV. As capital requirements fluctuate with collateral value, banks should consider redesigning their mortgage products to match this. And as a further consequence, banks could shift towards a more property-centric approach for mortgages.

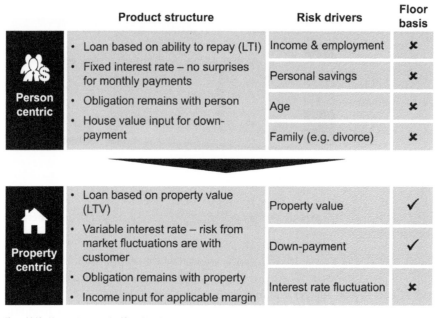

Figure 14.10: Mortgage loan example of Basel IV product structure

14.3.4 Operations

Next to additional capital requirements, Basel IV also imposes additional operational requirements for banks which can be categorised into four buckets:

1. Modelling requirements:

- Introduce Standardised approach calculations for all assets as input for the output floor
- Include parameter input floors for internal models
- Integrate additional constraints on parameter estimations
- Realise relevant asset class split
- Incorporate relevant risk drivers for revised standardised approaches

2. Due Diligence requirements:

- Comply with due diligence requirements under Pillar 1 for assessing the credit-worthiness of counterparties to enhance the requirements surrounding the use of external ratings
- Adjust risk weight upward based on due diligence
- Demonstrate to supervisors that due diligence analyses are appropriate

3. Internal model approvals:

- Comply with additional Basel IV requirements for internal model approval
- Get desk-by-desk approval based on Basel IV criteria to use internal models for regulatory capital determination for market risk
- Adjust internal models for credit risk to reflect additional Basel IV constraints and gain approval for updated models

4. Data and reporting requirements:

- Ensure additional data requirements for constrained internal model and revised standardised approaches are met
- Comply with revised Pillar 3 disclosure requirements including standardised templates to improve comparability of banks disclosures

14.4 Conclusion

In addition to understanding the technical regulatory details of the Basel IV reforms, senior bankers are well advised to step back and develop a perspective on their strategic impact. Especially in Northern and Central European countries that have been hit hard by the new regulations, bank profitability remains very low. Once implemented, Basel IV will make it even more difficult for many banks to produce healthy returns on equity and ultimately move back to a positive economic spread (with return on equity higher than cost of capital). For some banks, this means they will have to fundamentally rethink the way they do business, to ensure long-term viability.

Banks can take a number of steps to cope with the impact of Basel IV going beyond traditional measures such as raising additional capital or cost cutting. A shift in the degree to which banks are using their balance sheets to conduct business will be required, and that will likely force them to create a very different balance sheet structure and devise a fundamentally different way to make money. The sooner banks embark on this complex transition, the greater the strategic advantage they will gain over their slower peers.

Printed and bound by CPI Group (UK) Ltd, Croydon, CR0 4YY